WITH ALL OUR
HEART AND MIND

WITH ALL OUR HEART AND MIND

*The Spiritual Works of Mercy
in a Psychological Age*

Sidney Callahan

Crossroad • New York

1989

The Crossroad Publishing Company
370 Lexington Avenue, New York, N.Y. 10017

Copyright © 1988 by Sidney Callahan

Printed in the United States of America

Library of Congress Cataloging-in-Publication Data

Callahan, Sidney Cornelia.
  With all our heart and mind : the spiritual works of mercy in a
psychological age / Sidney Callahan.
    p. cm.
  ISBN 0-8245-0843-2
  ISBN 0-8245-0971-4 (pbk)
    1. Spiritual works of mercy.   2. Spiritual life—Catholic authors.
I. Title.
BV4647.M4C34   1988
241—dc19   87-34574
                                                                      CIP

*I gratefully dedicate this book
to my aunt, Olive Sharrett de Shazo,
whose love and spiritual witness has deeply affected my life.*

Contents

INTRODUCTION

WHY RECONSIDER THE SPIRITUAL WORKS OF MERCY?

The corporal and spiritual works of mercy have long been enumerated in Church tradition in sets of seven each. The corporal works of mercy are:

> To feed the hungry
> To give drink to the thirsty
> To clothe the naked
> To visit those in prison
> To shelter the homeless
> To bury the dead.

The spiritual works of mercy are:

> To admonish the sinner
> To instruct the ignorant
> To counsel the doubtful
> To comfort the sorrowful
> To bear wrongs patiently
> To forgive all injuries
> To pray for the living and the dead.

When asked to recall these lists, individuals can remember some of the first, but fail to remember the second. I think the selective forgetting of the spiritual works of mercy has an explanation. For centuries the corporal works of mercy have remained much the same, but the spiritual works of mercy must be reinterpreted and reappropriated as a culture changes. Since there has been no recent attention given to renewing our understanding of the spiritual works of mercy, they have faded from the collective consciousness. By contrast, the physical needs of human beings remain constant. Whatever the time or place, the human body does not change its requirements for food, drink, shelter, nursing, succor, and a final resting place. We can see a clear need, and we know what the Christian response should be, whether in a Calcutta slum, an Ethiopian refugee camp, or on the Upper East Side of Manhattan.

Our vision is less clear, however, when we confront "spiritual" needs requiring "spiritual action." With changes in our psychological, social, and theological understanding of human persons, neither the need nor the appropriate response is obvious. How exactly in the present context of my life do I go about admonishing sinners or counseling the doubtful? And surely it is necessary to reinterpret the meaning of bearing wrongs patiently in the light of liberation theology, assertiveness training, and the ongoing struggles for human rights. Our thought patterns and spiritual needs in late-twentieth-century America do not differ totally from those of earlier Christians (else the spiritual classics would not endure), but our spiritual concerns are different enough to warrant a serious reconsideration of the place of the spiritual works of mercy in our common Christian life.

I can remember my frustration when as a young enthusiast I would devour one traditional spiritual classic or saint's biography after another, only to remain unsatisfied in my search for the perfect model for my spiritual life. Like Augustine, I took and read the book, and the next book, and the next, without finding a solution to my problem. In every work I would find wonderful insights, but no ready-made pattern of life to follow. It took years before the truth finally broke through: Sidney, you are not going to find your perfect model because no one before you has lived with the changing cultural conditions you are experiencing. Face it: American Christians have to be creative to cope with this chaotic time of medical, technological, and social revolution.

With hindsight, I can see that the blueprints for the spiritual life inherited from the past were unsuitable for those of us living with new American class structures, gender roles, sexual expectations, and educational opportunities. Even in the secular domain, women were bereft of role models. Like many other middle-class educated women married to professional men, I aspired to have children and a career. Since I wanted six children I was prepared to wait a decade or so before leaving the house, but I would still study and write at home. Our generation was merging social roles previously kept separate: while thoroughly engrossed in the psychological and physical demands of family life, without servants or social support, we were also immersed in professional work. The secular pluralistic society in which we moved was indifferent, if not downright hostile, to family and spiritual concerns, and the Church was not much more understanding of the dilemmas faced by the educated laity.

Certainly, Christians in past eras managed to live spiritual lives in intensely worldly settings (as in the court of Louis XIV, for example), but never before had individuals faced so many different levels of complicated demands with so little leisure or social support. In one day I might be washing diapers and cleaning the bathroom, struggling through a philosophy text for a writing assignment, rushing to a child's school function, and from there home to prepare a dinner party for my husband's colleagues. During the unceasing night-and-day duty of the early childbearing years, even the Trappists' routine seemed comparatively self-indulgent. When children have grown up, family demands recede somewhat, but professional and volunteer commitments increase. Most traditional spiritual writers probably would not have been able to comprehend American lives crammed with work, study, and activity, lives that at the same time are filled to the brim with marriage, childbearing, child rearing, and the perpetual roller coaster (or should I say continuing soap opera?) of family life in turbulent times.

Unfortunately, much of today's writing on living the spiritual life seems equally unsatisfying. Some books seem too woolly with high-flown rhetoric, others too concrete and simplistic. Alas, it may also be the case that some of today's spiritual writers are writing for people who are much more advanced than the majority of us, who still struggle on the bottom rung of the spiritual ladder. But perhaps the most serious problem is the failure to achieve a synthesis of psychological knowledge with spiritual truths. Today we live in a culture so suffused with psychology that we need psychologically astute pathfinders through the therapeutic thickets of spiritual and psychological literature. A new in-depth integration is needed: too often the psychological self-help books scant spirituality while many spiritual works are not psychologically sophisticated enough. Even the spiritual writers who attempt to incorporate psychology often founder. It will not do for Christians to baptize popular psychology (aptly termed *psychobabble*), nor should they canonize one or another psychological theorist (such as Jung.) As I attempt to reconsider the spiritual works of mercy, I shall employ all the psychological astuteness I can muster as both psychologist and Christian.

I can note at once that today the Church probably would not choose to divide the works of mercy into separate corporal and spiritual compartments. This division reflects a gnostic view of the human being in which the spirit is like a ghost in the machine of the body. Advances in both our theological thinking and vast psychological and medical evidence now convince us that the mind and body are fused in a unitary whole. Illness can affect the mind; thinking and emotions can affect the body. The interaction is two-way and immensely complex. Psychosomatic medicine has been vindicated, and is now reborn as behavioral medicine and health psychology. We are our bodies, our bodies are our selves.

But at the same time we are also more than our bodies. As a person I can view the aging or illness of that aspect of me that is my body, and see "it" as separate from some essence of "me." An adult human being exists with a hierarchy of operations: my mind, emotions, and will are in some sense more important to me than my body's function. Who does not fear psychosis, Alzheimer's Disease, or other destroyers of the self far more than blindness or some physical handicap? We also know that our bodies can enjoy the best of health and be exercised into perfect fitness, and yet we are still miserable or in despair. The young, the healthy, the beautiful, the well-nourished, and the affluent regularly kill themselves. They throw their perfectly maintained bodies out of high windows. It is not enough to have corporal needs fulfilled.

The traditional division of corporal and spiritual works of mercy makes sense when it is seen rather as a difference in the focus of attention and emphasis. Physician and psychologist are different if overlapping professions. We must always take into account the spirit and dignity of the unique person when we perform the corporal works of mercy. But it is also the case that spiritual needs may exist in those who do not require physical care; at most one might offer cups of tea, or meals, or walks, or busying tasks, or comfortable seats before the fire, or even physical affection, along with comfort, counsel, or confrontation. In such cases the spiritual need and our spiritual response are the important thing.

WHAT COUNTS AS "SPIRIT" OR "SPIRITUAL?"

How are we going to use the word *spirit*, as in a spiritual work or spiritual need? Confusion arises over these terms because we have not yet found a new Christian synthesis integrating the modern psychologies and theological understandings of the human person. Ever since the admirable Thomistic system fell into disuse, Christians (along with everyone else) have had no compelling theory of personality. Today the fields of psychiatry and psychology study the mind and the emotions, but our psychology of personality still exists at a very primitive level, far below the developed consensus of other scientific disciplines. There is no dominant theory or paradigm to which all investigators give assent. Behaviorists, sociobiologists, neo-Freudians, developmentalists, cognitive psychologists, humanistic existentialists, and various others are still battling over the territory. No theory has decisively triumphed and most contain enough truth to be supported by some concrete evidence. At the same time within theology there exist new questions about the definitions and interrelationships of person, body, self, mind, soul, spirit, and Holy Spirit. Pulling together a synthesis of two bodies of thought in turbulent transition is not an easy task. Therefore when I offer my tentative definition of spirit within a Christian theory of personality, it is offered as a first step toward the new synthesis we badly need, even to order our practical everyday actions.

I interpret the spirit of a person to mean the personal conscious activity that emerges beyond bodily functioning and beyond unconscious determining forces of the past and present environment. Since theologically we know that grace works through nature, the human spirit can be seen as that same activating force of reason, emotion, will, and dispositions which some psychologists and philosophers call the self or person. The more traditional concept of the soul includes the self or spirit but is more inclusive. In order to avoid the many theological controversies over the nature of the soul, I think the soul can best be thought of as referring to the whole existing human being's life as known to God. The individual human spirit or person or self seems the dimension of the soul psychologically knowable to ourselves and others. Thus the *spirit* involved in the needs and works of the spiritual works of mercy is that active, unique, self-conscious capacity for personal consciousness in human persons. A spiritual need is a need of a unique individual person, and a spiritual work is a personal conscious act of an individual self. These spiritual phenomena are person-to-person interactions from one self-conscious self to another.

My definition of *spirit* is that part of the human personality accessible to conscious awareness or available to self-consciousness. But to identify the human spirit with the conscious self does not deny the existence of other dimensions or systems within the complex human organism. I think that the human spirit or conscious self emerges from and interrelates constantly with the functioning of the body, with the functioning of the unconscious and preconscious dimensions of the personality, and, most mysteriously of all, with the operations of the indwelling divine presence. Thus, many things going on within us exist beyond conscious awareness. The brain regulates the body in miraculous feats of order, growth, healing, and homeostasis.

Clearly, the mind functions in part unconsciously (as when we are unconscious, asleep, or amnesiac), but the functions and limits of the unconscious mind are a matter of dispute among psychologists. The status of dreams, for example, is questioned. Sleep researchers tell us that sleep and dreams come in different stages and varieties, so all claims about dreams have some validity. Some dreams may be, as Freud and Jung insisted, meaningful messages from the unconscious; other dreams, as some psychologists have recently proposed, may simply result from the mind discharging the residue of mental computer programs. Dreams in other states of sleep may be intrusions of bits of everyday reality. Whatever their exact status, these functions of the human person are not the self-conscious, aware, awake acts of what I am calling the self or spirit involved in spiritual works.

Between fully aware self-consciousness and completely opaque unconscious operations there are other graduated degrees of consciousness, some right on the edge of full awareness and others almost merged with the unconsciousness of sleep. These in-between modes of human activity, such as occur in daydreaming and under hypnosis, are intensely fascinating and present puzzling questions: Can we control these states? Are we responsible for them? Are these aspects of the self or spirit? It seems clear that these preconscious, or not-quite-conscious human operations include much of the personal temperament, conceptual style, and habits that constitute personality. As human beings we possess personal characteristics that are unique, individual, automatic, habitual, and mostly outside of our full personal awareness. Other people can see these things in us, but we habitually fail to see them in ourselves (just as we rarely confront the way our body looks from behind).

Important preconscious dimensions of personality seem stored in an individual's long-term memory. Like habits and conditioned responses, our memories are only partly under conscious control. Psychologists are studying how personal memories get encoded and stored, how memories are retrieved, and how memory influences perception and thinking. It now seems evident that there is an ongoing preconscious filtering or selection process that accounts for the perceptions and thoughts that we experience as effortlessly 'coming to mind.' But who or what selects and with what criteria? Some fascinating new theories even posit a 'hidden observer' within, monitoring information flow beyond self-consciousness. With conscious efforts we can bring things to mind or at least start searching in memory for something we sense we know. If we start trying to remember and fail, sometime later what we were looking for may suddenly come to us. All these are mysterious operations somewhere between full voluntary conscious activity and unconsciousness.

It also seems clear that some information we might easily notice, know, or remember, is curiously forgotten, ignored, or overlooked. These selective omissions and distortions seem to serve defensive purposes of different sorts. Psychoanalysis has found that human beings avoid pain or seek pleasure through such preconscious selective maneuvers of the mind. Should these almost-out-of-awareness activities count as actions of the self or spirit? They are surely part of the personality but while they remain out of consciousness I don't think they should be included as activities of the self or spirit. Only when something that has been automatic, preconscious, or unconscious comes into awareness and becomes accessible to and is appropriated by the conscious self, does it truly become personal, truly part of my self.

Although I am identifiably the same individual when I am drugged or dreaming or in a state of shock, I cannot be said to be fully my self. My dreams or preconscious defenses may be mainly automatic products of my personality, just as my physical symptoms may be products of my body's unconscious regulating system. But while some things are out of my direct control, I can still be indirectly responsible for much of my automatic personal functioning. If I know that alcohol intoxicates me and makes me not my self, I am responsible if I drink too much. If I am suffering from a disease such as epilepsy or diabetes that can be controlled by taking my medication and I don't do it, I am indirectly responsible for my state when I become impaired. We are also responsible for many of our emotional states, as we shall see in future chapters. The old strategy of avoiding sin by avoiding the occasions of sin is quite pertinent here.

The experience of being a self or spirit only partially in control of one's person is a universal one and has been a perennial intellectual problem for reflective thinkers. Aristotle spoke of *akrasia*, or "weakness of will" and Saint Paul voiced the common human condition when he cried out "that which I would do, I do not; and that which I would not, I do." Paul's description of the spirit warring against the flesh may also refer to one's conscious self in relation to one's recalcitrant, more unconsciously determined personality characteristics. The Gospel's references to transformation, sanctification, liberation, and "putting on the new man," can be interpreted as referring to the process by which the conscious self or spirit becomes more and more the owner and self-regulator of the whole person. The ultimate hope seems to be that this process of transformation can extend to the human body resurrected after death. Christians have always believed this liberation and transformation of the human being can only be accomplished through the redemptive power of Christ living and acting within the person. The process depends upon the self or spirit's voluntary opening to God's power through faith, hope, and love, through prayer, worship, and good works. The promise of the Gospel is that God will be found within the human being, as well as without.

THE SPIRIT AND THE HOLY SPIRIT

The final challenge in attempts to define the spirit, or self, is relating the human spirit to the indwelling Trinity promised by Christ. We believe that God is immanent in Creation as well as transcendently beyond it. But we don't know exactly how the Creator has separated an independent creation and human creatures while at the same time grounding their existence in divine love and power. It is a mystery of simultaneous transcendence and immanence that we can only dimly understand and experience. The belief of Christians has been that God, Christ, and the Holy Spirit reside within us and in them we move and live and have our being. But at the same time, the divine Spirit is separate from the individual human spirit and self; we experience ourselves as free, with independent responses.

We are aware that our movements to open ourselves to God come from some prior divine invitation and initiative of love, but as free spirits we are able to respond in different ways. I can accept, ignore, or refuse the invitation. The mystery is that when I act in a good way I am somehow completely free and yet moved and strengthened by God's loving power. It's like riding on a passenger conveyer at an airport: you can either stand still and be carried, or walk along on the miraculously flowing path. God's grace is similar: you can move ahead through your own individually willed actions but the conveyor so propels you onward that you feel you are truly flying forward to your destination in a cooperative venture. It's also appropriate to the analogy to remember that persons who are too burdened with luggage can rest a while and still be carried along. And yes, there are travelers who scorn the conveyor and choose the unassisted hard way; these people are still better off than the perverse souls who insist on fighting their way backward against the flow of assistance.

Once a person has experienced the divine assistance within, it is possible to repeatedly seek the Spirit's aid. The ordinary operation of human conscience is an example of an inner dialogue that is assisted by the Holy Spirit within the personality. Conscience has even been identified as the light of the Holy Spirit within each person. The image of the light within or inner light has been used to describe these experiences of divine immanence. Other examples of turning one's self over to God's grace and power are also practiced in and out of Christianity. I think that many of the self-help movements, such as Alcoholics Anonymous, are examples of the self's opening the personality to the indwelling Spirit's influence. (We shall discuss this in more detail in later chapters.) Just as one can indirectly open oneself to intoxicating or evil influences so one can open oneself to the work of the Holy Spirit within. The self or spirit is gradually changed by repeated acts of attention and focused energies, whether to good or evil. God's good work of inner psychological transformation has been called by various names: grace, the infusion of virtues, sanctification. We may not completely understand it, but we do experience it.

HOW DOES THE HUMAN SPIRIT DEVELOP?

While the human spirit or self is a separate and individual consciousness, no individual human being can come into existence or come to God alone. Perhaps archangels are truly self-sufficient spirits but human beings are firmly embedded in a collective existence. The wonderfully unique individual self that we possess is a gift of our genetic inheritance and social experience. There is no self-made man or woman. The birth of the self is a gradual process built up from genetic predispositions and capacities interacting with the interpersonal experiences of infancy. Full self-consciousness emerges from many prior experiences of infancy and childhood. Each of us was already a unique personality at our first birthday party but we do not start being the continuous conscious selves we are as adults until much later. God may call us into being at the moment of conception and knows us from our mother's womb, but we do not self-consciously know ourselves until much later.

The social creation of the conscious self grows out of the dialogue of the infant with the world and other persons. The emotional dialogue of sense and feeling may be the most basic way we interact with others in our first experiences. The perceptual interchange of smell, touch, sound, gaze, warmth, feeding, and bathing produces the bonding and attachment from which a conscious self emerges. The mutual gaze of infant and caretaker is particularly significant and provides the model for romantic love and the image of the blissful beatific vision. Being looked at, attended to, cared for, played with, and talked to creates the self that is born from the mutual human exchange. The infant is genetically programmed for this participation with caretakers. Without it an infant will waste away or die. The infant is selectively attuned to faces and emotional exchanges and, most important, is innately prepared to learn language. Whatever language group the infant is born into, he or she will rhythmically respond to it and begin to absorb its rules, rhythms, and vocabulary long before being able to speak.

With the coming of the word and the gradual mastery of language, the self takes a gigantic leap into humanhood. The rush into language is nearly miraculous; the mind's abilities to process experience then increases geometrically, along with the growth of self-consciousness. When a small child first speaks the words *me* and *I*, the personality has given birth to the self-conscious self. The continuity of our innate inner emotional experiences combined with the human dialogue creates the spirit and self that can reflect upon itself as an "I." Descartes should have said, "I think, I feel, I know others, therefore I am." The human spirit is a gift we receive from the care and communication of our caretakers. Human caretakers treat the baby as though it were a self, through play and talk and care, and through this expectant interchange they create the self in response. When we affirm that God first loved us and called us into the life of grace, we are describing a process similar to the initial human attention and attachments which create the self. Each human person is partially created through the spiritual and corporal works of mercy of their parents and other members of their community.

The human motivation engendering the process of bringing a self into existence is natural, innate love. Defining love in its purely natural sense of attachment, bonding, and attentive care is not difficult. Emotions have now been rehabilitated and newly recognized in social science. Psychologists now theorize that the human species has survived because of its capacities for emotions that facilitate adaptation and survival. The innate primary emotional building blocks of the human species are found everywhere and in every culture; they are listed as interest-excitement, joy-ecstasy, sorrow-sadness, anger-rage, shame-humiliation, contempt-disgust, and remorse-guilt. Love is a primary fusion of interest and joy which produces bonding attachment. The emotions motivate human survival and the creation of culture, and the positive emotion of love produces the bonds that keep the nurturing family and community cohesively cooperating. Through evolutionary selection human beings come into the world innately prepared to love and be loved; adults in their turn are predisposed to love and care for infants. The older pessimistic psychoanalytic views describing human nature as selfish and aggressive have been complemented with discoveries of innate tendencies toward empathy, sympathy, altruism, and love.

Christian definitions of love, or *agape*, or charity are firmly based upon natural human predispositions selected by evolutionary forces. But innate good traits are not the whole inheritance. Aggression, selfishness, even self-deception are also innately a part of human nature. (In terms of old theological disputes, the best psychological estimate of our human nature seems to be that we are wounded but not depraved.)

WHAT IS THE PLACE OF THE SPIRITUAL WORKS OF MERCY IN OUR LIFE TOGETHER?

We belong to a social species whose members depend upon human bonds and attachments to survive and flourish. Humans must love and care for each other but are imperfectly prepared to do so. Because human weaknesses and sin are always present, and because of the disordered world in which we find ourselves, every human being needs others. Christians affirm that our human response to life should be to love God with our whole heart and mind, and our neighbor as our self. Theologians now make it clear that love of God and love of neighbor are essentially one and the same, for God is in each of His creatures as well as transcendently beyond all imagining. In Scripture Christ tells us that what we do for the least of our fellow human beings we do for him. From these Gospel injunctions to love and work toward God's kingdom, the Church articulated the traditional teachings on the works of mercy.

The works of mercy are a Christian's response to God's love; they are love in action. In grateful imitation of God's love and mercy to us, Christians attempt to "be merciful as your Father in heaven is merciful." Of course there is a vast difference in what humans can do compared to God's love and power, but we are still called to do what we can. As wounded imperfect persons we do not do works of mercy as though we possess all good things in abundance and dispense them at will. A Lady Bountiful distributing turkeys, baskets of cheer, and instruction is the wrong image. A spiritual or personal psychological work of mercy is not simply a matter of giving things that we have to those without. It must be a very different process. Central to understanding this process is a grasp of the idea that thoughts, prayers, emotions, speech, or goodwill are not really "things" but are essentially personal actions. Acts directed to other self-conscious persons are enacted in a dynamic interrelationship that affects us as we act. In consciousness-to-consciousness communication we change as we reach out to one another. Understanding this mutuality I can quite humbly undertake things that would be inappropriate and arrogant if viewed as a one-way directive or gift from a superior to an inferior.

Fortunately, modern psychologists have come up with an old but new-sounding concept of "the wounded healer." Who can better understand and help another person than one who has suffered the same weakness or can empathetically experience it. In modern forms of personal mediation, those who have recovered from an addiction, those who have been in prison, and those who have been through other crises are acknowledged as those most able to help the similarly afflicted: "I can understand you, I have been there." The incarnational principle that those who have lived through a situation can best help others justifies the Christian efforts to offer help. Every Christian conscious of sin, personal suffering, and the need to be healed can try to meet another's need.

The spiritual or psychological works of mercy are necessary because we have all experienced suffering and the brokenness of life to a certain degree. Who has not sinned, doubted, been ignorant, or hurt? We have all been there, and can respond in love to our fellow beings when they suffer or lose their way. As wounded healers we can reach out to others with humility whatever our stage of spiritual development. Fortunately, we do not have to have reached the illuminated way, or have experienced mystical heights to engage in these ordinary enterprises of daily life among ordinary people. All of us can reconsider and reflect on what these spiritual or self-giving efforts will mean today. And of course there will be different times in our lives when certain works of mercy or ways of loving are more appropriate than others.

Life as we lead it, whether stumbling along or purposefully marching to meet goals, has a way of presenting us with unexpected challenges. Fervent youth may champ at the bit seeking heroic challenge and sacrifices. Older pilgrims know that what turns up will be hard enough. The great Saint Teresa had youthful visions of herself going off to martyrdom among the Moors, but she found dealing with the pettiness and inertia of the people at home enough of a challenge. My own observation has been that everyone, regardless of vocation or goals, eventually experiences a well-rounded spiritual curriculum. Nuns or married women, priests or fathers of families, professionals or peasants, every temperament and intellect seems to need and to receive specifically tailored tutoring to learn to love God and neighbor. These varied experiences cannot all happen at the same time, of course, so persons look as though they are on much more distinct ventures than may really be the case. When we see someone whose life seems spiritually easy, so smoothly flowing, so untroubled by temptation or struggle, I think that we should remember that every life is lived in stages over time. We do not know what has already been struggled with or what may yet come, and our outsider's perspective is very different from a person's inner experience. The same can also be true of lives that outwardly seem unbearably crushed by misfortune, although we should not for this reason feel indifferent or apathetic toward the suffering of others.

God is definitely a God of surprises. New experiences and challenges, both joyful and excruciating, can occur in even the most routine life. In my experience, those who seek God are never bored or becalmed for long. Most of us will never reach those spiritual depths where the saints suffered extended dark nights of the soul. But the testimony seems to be that, even for them, periods of dryness finally pass and give way to new times of growth. Periods of jogging along uneventfully seem relatively brief. Just as we think we have mastered some stage or challenge in life, it changes. Unexpected joys may suddenly come: C. S. Lewis entitled his autobiography *Surprised by Joy*, and he was wise to do so; long after he wrote his book he found new love and a late marriage with a woman named Joy. But it is also true that we can be caught off guard by some particular suffering we could not imagine ever having to confront. After his unexpected idyllic marriage, C. S. Lewis had to suffer the early death of his wife, with all the agonies he could hardly have foreseen in his days as a self-sufficient Oxford don

Like Lewis and everyone else, I too have experienced more joyful things in life than I could ever have dreamed were coming. And like others, I have also experienced suffering and traumas that were total shocks from out of the blue: the sudden death of a parent, a child, an emergency operation, a devastating betrayal of love. In the human condition a person can be catapulted from a totally joyful condition in which all is happiness to the deepest grief, sorrow, and anxiety. In my life unexpected sufferings and crises produced a complete reliance upon God and responsive spiritual acts of mercy on the part of my friends. God rescues us out of the depths of misery and friends offer support. Spiritual assistance is less dramatic but still present in the more slowly developing problems of life that produce chronic suffering: the alienation of a child, problems with alcoholism or disease, struggles with work, or financial problems.

While joys and grace abound, life is also hard. We all need to help and be helped as we struggle on. The great novelist Henry James has his characters ask their friends in moments of stress, "Will you see me through?"—through illness, betrayal, or the task of overcoming evil. So, too, all of us who attempt to lead a Christian life need others to see us through. The spiritual works of mercy are ways that we do this for one another. All such psychological efforts require energy. God makes such expenditures of energy possible, and occasionally even easy to do, but often we have to work against our natural inertia and laziness. It is so much easier not to get involved; the slang expression "Who needs it?" sums up our natural resistance to becoming enmeshed with others when we would just as soon retreat.

Listening to the Church's demand for love and works of mercy spurs us on. Within the tradition of the Church the range of the corporal and spiritual works of mercy serves as a corrective to our penchant for designing a narrower Christian life. Just as the unexpected joys, opportunities, and sufferings that come our way push us in undreamed-of directions, so the breadth of the works of mercy challenges us to expand and expend ourselves. All of these different ways of expressing charity will challenge us at different times and in different situations. Naturally, some actions will be more difficult for us than others; the great struggle in the self's interaction with others is getting things into balance and proportion.

In fact, if one type of action is too easy for us we might be suspicious of our motivation. Am I always, for example, too eager to admonish the sinner, or too ready to weep with the bereaved? Or is it always easier for me to bear wrongs patiently than risk conflict by admonishing the sinner? In God, justice and mercy are joined, but we find it difficult to discern ways to practice both. None of the spiritual acts of mercy come with ready-made patterns to follow.

HOW THIS BOOK IS ORGANIZED

This book contains seven chapters, one for each of the traditional spiritual works of mercy. The traditional order in which they are given reveals to my mind an ascending scale of spiritual and psychological difficulty. It is much easier to admonish sinners or instruct the ignorant than to forgive injuries or pray for others. Is this an intentional ordering of the list, or one of those ways in which Church communal tradition embodies implicit truths that have never been articulated? Piaget, the great developmental psychologist, recognizes a law of human development that applies as well to the Church's development over the centuries of its life. Piaget observed that children can actually perform intelligent problem solving before they are able to articulate what they are doing. In fact their verbal descriptions of what they are doing is couched in the immature inaccurate language they are about to outgrow. They can do it, they just can't fully articulate what they know. Becoming psychologically self-conscious, or growing in spirit and truth, takes time, whether the development is taking place in a person or the Church. Christians are gradually coming to understand what has been done for us in the Creation and The Redemption, and slowly growing in the ability to articulate our communal response. Reflecting upon our traditions and present experience is one way we progress in understanding.

I will treat each of the traditional spiritual works of mercy and reflect upon them in different ways. But the major focus of my attention will not be on the past, but on what these psychological actions of the self or spirit mean for us as persons living today in our pluralistic, complicated world.

Intellectually, our time is a period of ferment, rightly labeled I think, as the beginning of the postmodern world. Many secular idols are crashing down around us. In the past Christians have flourished when an old order gave way. The barbarians at the gates never meant the end, but only a new opportunity. I think this is also a propitious time for the development of Christianity and the forging of a new intellectual syntheses more open to the Spirit of Truth. My modest effort is to rethink the spiritual works of mercy from a psychological perspective.

1

TO ADMONISH THE SINNER

If your brother does something wrong, go and have it out with him alone, between your two selves. If he listens to you, you have won back your brother. (Matthew 18:15)

In wisdom made perfect, instruct and admonish one another. (Colossians 3:16)

A spiritual work of mercy in these psychologically knowledgeable times can be thought of as a conscious effort to enact God's love and imitate God's mercy in the inner life of thought and feeling. Like all mercy it is a form of love in action, a way of meeting human need. The spiritual works of mercy are psychological acts which arise from our innermost personal selves and are directed to another's innermost personal needs of heart and mind. They are unique person-to-person transactions—demanding full attention, mindfulness of self, and consciousness of others as unique selves.

ADMONISHING THE SINNER

What does psychologically supportive love and mercy have to do with "admonishing the sinner"? To admonish the sinner is given first place in the traditional list of the seven spiritual works of mercy, but to our modern ears it is repellent, inducing images of Savonarola thundering damnation, or fundamentalist preachers hurling invective and threats of hellfire. In the present age of tolerance, we can't help but wonder whether we have the right to judge or admonish another.

Those committed to Christian charity wonder whether admonishing sinners is compatible with love: we are told to refrain from judging others. The concept of sin also presents some difficulty for us. Am I even sure that there really *are* sinners out there? And if there are, how do I know who they are, or go about admonishing them?

On reflection perhaps the question of whether sinners exist or not, is the easiest question to settle. Are there sinners? Yes. After all, I know of at least one sinner, namely, myself. Even though I try not to, I sin. This rather compelling firsthand evidence of personal sin leads to the obvious generalization: I am not alone in my sinning. Unfortunately it is clear that I sin, you sin, he, she, and we sin. While it is doubtful that many of us engage in serious mortal sins, we do sin often.

THE FACT OF SIN

The kind of sins most of us commit seem not to be of the dread mortal kind; they are not fully premeditated, completely calculated, free and final rejections of God's goodness and truth in a serious matter. If we are to believe the more optimistic theologians, there may be relatively few mortal sinners among us. From a psychological perspective, many of the gruesome acts we read about in the newspapers can hardly be considered freely committed mortal sins. These crimes seem much too crazy, too much like mental illness, brain seizures, or poisoned toxic states in which persons lose all voluntary control. Perhaps individuals are responsible for getting into such out-of-control states by not seeking help, not taking medication, not abstaining from drugs, not resisting selfish habits of immediate gratification; but once people have become possessed, drugged, or crazed, they can hardly be free enough to consciously and voluntarily sin with full knowledge of what they are doing. They perpetuate evil, commit crimes, and cause untold harm, but they do not seem to be committing mortal sins.

More normal people may also rarely commit mortal sins. It seems sensible to hold that only at the moment of death when one confronts God directly, *for sure,* only at that moment of clarity could one ever understand enough, or be free enough, to irrevocably reject God's grace. In everyday life, many persons may never operate freely enough to be as reprehensible as they appear. The newest psychological research on the mind seems to confirm the existence of powerful unconscious and preconscious automatic determinants of our thought and behavior. So much filtering goes on outside awareness in our ordinary processing of information, that our freedom seems rather more limited than classical theories of freedom have supposed.

Yes, we *can* make free conscious choices, but our personality characteristics interacting with our inherited neurochemistry gradually take on a life of their own. As many before and after Saint Paul have testified, we do evil things we have not consciously willed to do. On the other hand it is also the case that our automatic reactive personalities can be habitually virtuous, so that some persons find it almost impossible to do wrong. For most of us, unfortunately, our inertia more often produces automatic evil acts and strong resistances to changes for the better. Habitual weaknesses can produce a blindness to self and lack of self-control, which, like the psychotic's craziness, may keep many from having enough freedom to truly commit mortal sins. In a sense it is true that only highly controlled, integrated characters can be strong enough for great sins. The anxiety that saints display over their sins may reflect the accurate perception that they are more capable of more serious sins than the rest of us. Greater self-discipline, an achieved self-mastery combined with a greater knowledge of good and evil than most, puts a person at greater risk of freely sinning.

Usually, sin enters ordinary lives through a passive consent to self-deception and other defensive mental moves meant to avoid the voice of conscience. Sin seems only partially premeditated, and so remains in the venial category. When faced with a temptation, we give in by quickly brushing aside or suppressing conscious misgivings; by these moves we allow ourselves to do what we want to do, when we want to do it. I rush to give my destructive bit of gossip, or to deliver my scathing sarcasm to an opponent. We also become quite adept at quickly resisting demands for love or justice which move us; after a disturbed minute or two, we manage to resubmerge ourselves in comfort, and inert laziness. I turn away and harden my heart against the appeal for my time, or money, or action. Our predisposition to avoid pain and seek pleasure and ease helps us to avoid penetrating self-confrontation; we collude with ourselves in bursts of bad faith and don't want to attend to what we're really doing—or really feeling. Camus said that the good person is the one who has the fewest lapses of attention. Letting our attention selectively lapse is the essence of self-deception.

THE SINFUL SELF

At times, we become more actively ensnared in overt sin and nurse anger, bitterness, and envy; we cleverly and subtly seek revenge or another's harm, or try to mar another's happiness or advancement. Once we give in to sin, sin quickly escalates by way of the defensive efforts we must take to suppress guilt, remorse, or repentance. We start to lie and to blame others rather than face the shame of our own wrongdoing. Well-intentioned, fairly normal people can get caught in obsessions or addictions or illusions they absolutely refuse to give up, despite their recognition that what they are doing is both morally wrong and self-destructive. Guilt, shame, and fear fuse with self-loathing, goading individuals on to further sin; they must continue in order to resist the pressure to concede the immorality of their actions. Out of pride they refuse fully to admit their fault.

Like Lucifer, humans can also cry, *"Non serviam"* (I "will not serve," or give in to God, love, truth, or reality). I *will* keep on with my eyes cast down, my gaze averted from everything that might deter me from my fevered course. Consumed by this narrowed obsessive part of myself, I won't listen to what the whole person in me knows to be true. I stubbornly persevere.

Pride engenders all the poisoned fruits of sin that ripen in the disintegrating personality: lies, false accusations, self-pity, angry attacks on the innocent, icy sarcasm, mean cruelties. A person may indulge in "silent tantrums," cutting off and rejecting others through obdurate silence. As sin produces more inner chaos and the person seeks to confuse others, he or she will totally disregard truth and reality, and say anything or do anything to protect the self and its sin. Self-disgusted, but still self-indulgent, one begins to see others as false and weak; cynicism about oneself produces distrust and arrogance toward others. If everyone is corrupt, who could ask anything more of me? To ensure my moral security system, I gradually begin to avoid my more virtuous friends and find myself gravitating toward those I can look down upon, if not despise.

The clinical psychological literature on the way a person defends the self from painful reality is heartily confirmed by our common human experience of sin. The worse the moral state, the more fragile, defensive, and stubborn we become. How often we catch ourselves in the self-protective process of self-deception, yet go on to harden our heart and blind our eyes to the truth. The operation of personal conscience may be mostly a matter of decisions made in fleeting moments. Are we going to recognize reality and focus on our failure, or are we going to choose denial and self-deception by rushing to sweep away what troubles us. The scriptural description of how sinners hate the light and cling to the darkness is an apt depiction of the psychological strategies we use to avoid the light of self-awareness.

RECOGNIZING SIN

After we have had experiences of sin, recognized our self-ensnarement, and repented, we can note the same insidious processes of sin in others. Since we judge ourselves, we cannot help evaluating the failures of others. Knowledge of good and evil and personal experience inevitably propels us into critical moral evaluations. A capacity to evaluate self and others by standards of goodness or excellence emerges in every child during the second or third year—along with the universal emotions of guilt, contempt, and shame. The human animal is innately equipped with something no other species possesses, the ability to acquire and apply standards of morality or achievement in judgments of self and others. Self-evaluation emerges in all children.

This programmed appearance of guilt, shame, and contempt, combined with a loving attachment to caretakers, makes the moral socialization of human beings possible. The child's emerging evaluative abilities make possible instruction in the particular norms, ideals, and taboos of family and community. When a beloved mother is upset and censures a child's attack on a baby sister, the child is inwardly ready to agree, to feel fear of abandonment and guilt over the wrongdoing. After years of being properly brought up, we know moral failure when we see it in ourselves and others.

We become particularly adept at judging the inner motivation of those whom we know well. Unfortunately, this means that we can be most aware of the sins of those we are closest to—the very sins that will pain us most deeply. Persons whom we consistently observe at close range, with whom we have established empathetic connections, are the very ones we can most clearly see sinning. Knowing what their own standards are and what they hold to be wrong, we can see them turn away from the demands of conscience; we watch them give in to pride, selfish desire, or lying defenses, although we know they know better. Our very closeness to them gives us a penetrating view of the way they are morally failing. In the case of more distant acquaintances the evaluation might be more tentative, since their inner life may be more obscure.

When we love a person, the sorrow of seeing them sin, even if it is not wronging us, can be most upsetting. Sometimes, we can't face the fact, and we end up colluding with them in order to deny what is really happening. Here the psychological observation that in many cases there exists an "enabler" who continually contributes to another's weakness, is an accurate one. Good nurturing persons do enable others to continue to drink, or lie, or abuse the innocent, or shirk responsibilities and the painful consequences of their actions. By acquiescing and covering up, by smoothing over and perpetually picking up the pieces, good people can enable their loved ones to continue sinning in ways they would not tolerate in others. With those we dislike, our eyes are unforgivingly clear and our anger easily aroused.

Our innate predisposition to be moral comes with an equally natural bent for moral indignation. A child's first protest comes early; "But it isn't fair!" (often our last deathbed cry as well). And a child's protests are never limited simply to selfish concerns. A human being possesses innately programmed empathy from the beginning; small children are unhappy when others are hurt or sad. Natural empathy, developing into sympathy, urges us to try to right wrongs and help our fellow creatures. Altruism—the tendency to act unselfishly for the good of another—is as much an inherited predisposition from the selective evolution of the species, as our less attractive human tendencies to selfishness, aggression and self-deceit. People seem programmed to leap into altruistic acts without a moment's thought. This altruistic bent to relieve and rescue our fellows develops into a powerful natural wish that righteousness prevail. The need to see the good victorious and wrongdoers vanquished has from time immemorial fueled folktales, myths, epics, and ritual dramas. From childhood on, we are ready (all too ready) to demolish the sinner. Admonishing the sinner may take a great deal more restraint.

ADMONISHING: DISTINCTIONS AND CONSIDERATIONS

Distinctions have to be made when considering what admonishing the sinner involves. What are the limits and boundaries of admonishing? What should the motivation be and what emotional costs are involved? Only after these questions are addressed can the complexities of practical ways and means of admonishment be considered. Of course no blueprints can be drawn for what must be a unique personal encounter, but some rough guidelines may be formulated.

If we begin with our tendency toward moral indignation and the temptation to destroy the wicked, we have to ask how admonishing the sinner differs from an attack or from judgmental condemnation? And at the opposite end of the spectrum of human feeling, the question arises as to how admonishing differs from parental nagging? To admonish, according to the dictionary, means "to remind, to warn of a fault, to reprove gently or kindly, but seriously; to exhort, also to put one in mind of something forgotten by way of warning or exhortation." So defined, admonishing another, cannot be the same as attacking, condemning, or harshly judging. Such hostile acts are not gentle or kind reminders.

Condemnations and judgments decisively end an interpersonal transaction; there is nothing more to be done or said after a denunciation of past misbehavior. Hostile reactions directed to what has been done already, are neither future-oriented nor hopeful. A warning or exhortation should involve an evaluation of present behavior; it should be directed to the future and positive change. And the future envisioned is a shared one, otherwise we would not take the trouble to warn; we would just condemn, shake the dust from our feet, and move on. When we exhort or remind we are not making final judgments, separating ourselves from the sinner as the sheep are separated from the goats or as Lazarus in Abraham's bosom is separated from the rich man in hell.

Admonishing resembles nagging, but there is a difference. Admonishments of sin are more serious, therefore less frequently given. They aim at reminding someone of what he or she prefers to forget and are not specifically aimed at controlling another's behavior. By contrast, in nagging a specific behavior is spelled out and reiterated—again and again and again. Of course I am nagging you for your own good, but my need to have you conform to my will for your own good can gradually become stronger than my desire for your well-being. In contrast, when I admonish you I bring a serious matter involving your conscience to your attention. As I confront, remind, exhort, and warn you, I can only appeal to your inner heart and mind to freely choose another course. Since a sin is, by definition, a matter of your free personal will and exercise of conscience, I have to leave you with your own moral responsibility for your future action. Merely submitting to my control or conforming to my blueprint for your behavior won't work.

Reflecting upon the complexity of this, it seems clear that I should not admonish another until I have searched my own heart. Admonishing should not be a way of manipulating another and exerting external controls. I also have to be sure that I am not up to the old trick of projecting my flaws on you, of seeing the mote in your eye while ignoring the beam in my own. We all have a tendency to notice in others those flaws that we are either tempted toward or are already indulging ourselves. If our vigilant conscience is bent on self-correction, it is also sensitized to those personal weaknesses we have *not* eradicated, and thus our attention is drawn like a magnet to those same failings in others. If I relish the thought of admonishing you, finally controlling you, something may be amiss. I need to stop and examine my motives and goals.

LOVE IS THE MOTIVE FOR ADMONISHING

Ultimately love is the only acceptable motive and goal for acts of admonishment. Love not only comforts, but also discomfits in its commitment to truth and reality. In the end we admonish one another in love because God, Jesus, and the saints and prophets have given us their example of admonishing love. If I care about you and your ultimate good, I will tell you what you would rather not hear, even at the risk of pain, trouble, and your rejection of me. I warn you, remind you, and exhort you for your own sake and for the common good of the community we share.

If I believe that sin leads us away from the love of God and neighbor, I can only be saddened to see you moving away from love and truth—and happiness as well. Sin not only does grievous harm to others; it also makes the sinner miserable. Contrary to popular misconception, and with only rare exceptions, there are few serene and joyful sinners. Sin withers and stunts the spirit. Thrashing about in its snare, lying and blaming to defend and protect one's sin, a person not mentally ill enters upon a preview of purgatory and hell. Hell can begin here and now, as one rejects truth and love and separates one's self from God. The great Teresa of Avila correctly said that all the way to heaven is heaven; and the obverse is also true: all the way to hell is hell. We are daily constructing our future: either we choose life or we choose death and gloom.

ATTACHMENT AND SUFFERING

If I love you I want you to be happy, to flourish, to be moving and enspirited. I can't stand to see you falling apart and spiraling downward to spiritual destruction and death-in-life. Thus I admonish you, urging you to turn again and live. When I care about you, I am emotionally involved in our common future. Here Christianity parts company with other more stoic forms of spirituality that emphasize psychological detachment. Yes, one can control one's personal suffering by resolutely pursuing detachment from desire and human bonds, as the ancient wisdom asserts. Some modern self-help strategies are modeled on ancient blueprints for gaining psychological peace through detachment and a rational mastery of the self.

True, you can change no one's life but your own, and, yes, we ultimately die alone. Assuredly, no person can make another person happy. Marcus Aurelius was correct when he said, "to live happily is an inward power of the soul." The person or soul who turns inward through stoic discipline and self-mastery can become invulnerable to reversals of fortune, disease, death, losses, or human betrayal. But this does not seem the Christian way, which insists that love and desires for mutual happiness with others must be fulfilled in communal bonds. The Kingdom of God must come for us all. Christians can never give each other up. If being involved in others' failures through love and caring brings us personal suffering, so be it. We follow a crucified God, who truly suffered for love rather than retreat to the power of unmoved self-sufficiency and detachment.

For Christians, suffering in this world is not illusory because the individual selves that suffer are not illusory. Our human emotions of love, desire, and sorrow are reflections of the divine persons of the Trinity, not traps to be overcome on the way to Nirvana or to the ultimate unity of all with all. Concern and sorrow over the sins and failings of those we love arise from our deep emotional involvement with them. Efforts must be made to bring them to the communal feast; we must admonish sinners if we love them.

MODES OF ADMONISHMENT

To admonish sinners we have to be as wise as a serpent and as innocent as a dove. It is important to discriminate among the different relationships we have with others. Public persons and those in institutional roles may need to be admonished in special ways. From ancient times there has been a tradition of prophets who admonish leaders and their people. What is different today is the conscious development of effective strategies to be used in collective nonviolent resistance movements. Gandhi and Martin Luther King, Jr., were masters of seizing the right moment and devising appropriate actions. What is effective at one historical moment for Solidarity members in Poland, may or may not be appropriate in the Philippine struggle against oppressive authorities. Our American efforts to exhort and admonish sinners will be shaped by our traditions of freedom and civil liberties—whether within or outside of the Church. Unfortunately, a closer look at such political movements is beyond the scope of our present discussion of individual behavior.

Complex discriminations are called for in our immediate circles. Employers, professional colleagues, pastors, fellow parishioners, community leaders, and local acquaintances present challenges different from those of our family, close colleagues, and friends. Relevant variables seem to be the intimacy, commitment, and power involved in a relationship. Power comes into the picture in two ways. The more power a person has over me, the more difficult, but therefore the more necessary, it is for me to have the courage to admonish them. Those above me in any particular power structure will need me to warn them, for others may cravenly acquiesce or accommodate the boss, the chairman, the rich donor, the pastor, the bishop, or whatever. When private, tactful wise-as-serpents strategies don't get through, one has to meditate on John the Baptist and courageously wade into deeper, riskier waters.

When power runs the other way and I must admonish those with less power than myself, other standards should be applied. Even if my role involves admonishing, I should be slow to do so to those under my authority. God is slow to anger and full of heartfelt mercy and gracious kindness, and so should we be. One swallow does not make a summer, and one lapse would not need admonishment; warnings are only appropriate for repeated, ongoing sins. If a person has repented, he or she by definition no longer needs admonitions or exhortations to remind them of the sin. Did the prodigal son's father deliver dire warnings about future dangers to be avoided, or does the shepherd beat the lost sheep after finding it? Persons who repent need joyful acceptance that conveys the sense of trust that the future will be different. Anxious advice about avoiding sin is a form of debilitating nagging and implies that a person can't cope or change.

Another important discrimination to be made in admonishments is how intimate I am, and how fully I share commitments, with the erring person. Christ admonished his own more freely, as did Paul and other Christians throughout history. If we are all climbing the same mountain, roped together for support, I am much more concerned and obliged to point out your false footing or your dangerous move toward the edge of the ravine. I need your strength more and I care more intensely because if you fall we all go down. Since so much is at stake in our common journey, it is even harder for me to avoid anger when I must admonish you. As family life, civil wars, and all close communities demonstrate, love and hate are more closely related than love and indifference. Caring so much and on so many different levels, I have to be more reflective and self-testing before I speak.

MEANS OF ADMONISHING

Sometimes, of course, we can admonish without speaking. We are able to communicate through deeds and nonverbal channels—in a glance, touch, gesture, pose, or facial expression. Christ's gaze at Peter after his betrayal was a powerful admonishment. So, too, in another way was Christ's washing of his disciples' feet. Gestures along with silence can also speak, as when Christ silently bent down to write in the dirt while a mob raged to stone the woman taken in adultery. In a sense, one's whole life with all its deeds gives more of a message than any word of direct exhortation. This is why the innocent and good are routinely hated by the evil. They are perceived as admonishing others by their example, even when they do not intend to. On the other hand, if one's own deeds contradict an admonishment given others, the hypocrisy cancels the effect of speaking. Again, before acting one must look to one's self.

Once one decides to speak in admonishment, all the workshops or self-help books on communication can be put to good use. These "human relations skills" are justly judged to be superficial, in that they cannot tell you what to say, but they can help in effectively getting a message across. They rightly emphasize choosing a favorable time and place, being aware of one's tone of voice, eye contact, posture, as well as clear wording. Obviously, you can never communicate with others unless you first have their attention. Then, of course, you have to put your message in comprehensible language that will not immediately alienate your listeners. As Paul attests, to the Greeks you must be as a Greek, fitting your words "to the needs of each one." After all, in the Incarnation God reaches out to us humans in a way that we can grasp, so an emphasis upon the medium as the message cannot be all wrong. How we say something, whether gently, kindly, or considerately, delivers a large part of the message. Human beings operate and communicate on many levels, and the emotional exchange in any encounter is as important as the linguistic meanings.

An indirect approach through a teaching story is also a powerful means of communication. Stories are effective because they combine emotionally engrossing narratives with meanings given on different levels at once. The hearer must discover the message through personal emotional response. The prophet Nathan tells King David a story and gets his admonishment across. David responds to the injustice detailed and recognizes his own sinful behavior in a sudden insight. Christ constantly uses parables to warn and admonish—the man building his house upon the sand, the burying of talents, the foolish virgins, and so on. In imaginative sensitive listeners, the use of imagery in a story awakens heart and mind. Defensive obduracy is outwitted: I become engaged in the story and before I can harden my mind and heart to the message that is coming, the moral challenge hooks me. Such great teaching stories exist in many different religious traditions and their powerful images refuse to fade away. Similarly, a story told by a reformed sinner is a powerful method of admonishment. It works wonders in Alcoholics Anonymous and other self-help groups because it gives hope for future happiness through the amendment of one's life.

When, however, admonishment invokes anxiety and fear, the results are likely to be negative. Crime-prevention programs that take juvenile delinquents on tours of prisons have been found to be counterproductive. Fear and anxiety can lead to despair that makes one give up in powerless hopelessness. Lurid sermons on hell and the damnation of sinners were surely equally wrongheaded, wronghearted, and may have led to many sins. Anxiety brings about the feared thing, but love casts out fear and encourages hope. Admonishments will be most effective when love and imagination are used to enlarge the heart and hold up the hope for a more abundant life. Getting to a better and more joyful future with God is what admonishment is all about. Admonishing the sinner is an effort to liberate another through Christ's saving power of love.

AFTERMATHS

If an admonishment has been done in love and done wisely, it will have intrinsic value whether or not it has practical effects for the sinner's behavior. One who admonishes bears witness to community and caring for a unique person, as well as to the importance of religious and moral values. To admonish you I must observe you and take your conscience seriously. Even if I must suffer for what I see as a spiritual response to a need, I have not wasted my pain in a trivial cause. Besides, a momentary or temporary rejection may not be the end of the story. Sometimes a saddening break leads to much more solid relations in the future.

It really does happen sometimes, that a worried-over admonition has an almost miraculous effect. I know a man, a faithful member of Alcoholics Anonymous, who feared he would lose his job by confronting and admonishing his employer with the diagnosis of early-stage alcoholism that was bringing harm to himself, his family, and his business. The employer responded with instant assent and that day stopped drinking. His inner struggles and troubled conscience were triggered into repentance and reform by the tactful, loving admonition of his friend and employee. The extra pressure of an outsider can sometimes be the deciding factor in an inner battle. Such instant feedback for one's effort to reach out to another is rare.

In any event, our charge is to love and respond to a need, even if we cannot guarantee the success of our actions. I must do my part as wisely and as well as I can, and leave the outcome to God.

CONCLUSION

To admonish the sinner is to remind a person, who needs to be reminded, of what he or she already knows in conscience. One calls a person back to a better self, to a whole self with its need for integrity and honor, its need to be true to past aspirations and present standards of conscience. To admonish is to call a person to attention, to serve as a loving witness for the better future with Christ that is presently being negated. One is not really intruding, condescending, or condemning but rather helping another, as one in turn needs to be helped.

When I become mired in self-imposed blindness and inertia I can all too easily avoid recognizing that I am clinging to my sins, despite the harm they bring to me and those around me. When you graciously confront me face to face, I must face the reality of my failure. I need your witness and support. Only through the truth can I become truly free. If we don't care enough, or have courage enough, to admonish one another's sins, we fail in love.

2

TO INSTRUCT THE IGNORANT

Fill your minds with everything that is true, everything that is noble, everything that is good and pure, everything that we love and honor, and everything that can be thought virtuous or worthy of praise. Keep doing all the things that you learned from me and have been taught by me and have heard or seen that I do. (Philippians 4:8)

The life and death of each of us has its influence on others. (Romans 14:7)

What is ignorance? And what does it have to do with us? Why should we go about correcting it? The essence of ignorance seems to be a failing to notice, and then failing to notice that we fail to notice. The worst thing about ignorance is that one can remain smugly, blissfully unaware of it. If you already know that you don't know, if you are aware of your own ignorance, you have made the first great leap toward knowledge. Unfortunately, unless another person cares enough to instruct you, you can remain blind, dumb, and ignorant until you die.

Persons instruct those who are ignorant for all sorts of reasons. Secular self-interest is one great motivator. Who wants to live and work with those who know nothing? Every functioning society needs to educate its new members in order to survive. If our tribe lives by hunting and we fail to teach the young to hunt, then we will all die of hunger when the present generation of hunters grows old. And if a civilized community is wanted, then the general populace must be educated and instructed to a civilized standard. Gone are the days when powerful elites could withdraw to their protected preserves and count on safety for themselves and their children. Today, in our increasingly complex and technological world, we have to recognize our interdependence and mutual vulnerability. The ignorance of some can threaten the welfare of all. Nowadays, at the very least, someone has to be paid to educate and civilize the plebeian mobs. Barbarians within the gates can create too much havoc and destruction.

But the act of instructing the ignorant can be motivated by active love as a spiritual or personal work of mercy. The desire to instruct and relieve ignorance can spring from far more than self-interest. Even if I am not threatened by another person's limited development, when I love a human person I naturally want them to be all that they can be. I want it for their own sake, and I want it because I can't stand the waste of godgiven human potential. If we love the world and the people in it, we want to see the full flowering of all human talents. Most of all I want those ignorant of the good news of the Gospel to be liberated from the land of gloom. After all, God has created us and instructed us out of love. Jesus spent his ministry instructing his followers and inspiring them to learn from him. Should we not in our gratitude do the same for others?

When we feel grateful to those who have instructed us, we long to go and instruct others in the same way. We seem naturally impelled to give what we have received, to imitate the models we admire. Look at the child carefully giving her doll tender maternal care and lessons in good behavior. Filial piety has been considered a basic virtue and foundation of civilization because it encourages the gratitude to one's progenitors that motivates similar caregiving and instruction for the next generation. And fortunately, instruction is never just a one-way process, since when we teach we also learn. Gratitude initiates ongoing links of mutual instruction that go on forever. Life is a great school, in which we alternate the roles of student and instructor.

We can hardly avoid constant teaching and learning in all the domains of life. Human beings are organisms programmed to learn and communicate. It is the innate nature of *Homo sapiens* to want to seek truth, solve problems, and pass on the knowledge. As the rational animal, we are made in the image of a God who is infinite truth, the inexhaustible creative source of reality. Persons seek truth to fulfill their deep innate hunger to know. We want to know more and more, because there is always more to know. But the search for knowledge begins with an acceptance of our present ignorance. The more there is yet to be known, the more ignorance there must exist here and now.

One can be ignorant of culture, art, literature, logic, mathematics, and the world of science. One can lack social and political understanding of the way one's world functions. One can be ignorant of psychology and of one's self, and one can be ignorant of religion, God, and God's dealings with human beings. All of these forms of ignorance have much in common. And all processes of instruction—education, therapy, and religious instruction—are also similar. Teachers, missionaries, therapists, and parents find that they all do much the same thing in similar ways. Certain truths about teaching and instructing apply generally. But here I shall emphasize religious, psychological, and social instruction as being more personal, more motivated by active love, and, so, more prototypically spiritual.

True ignorance does not really signify a simple lack of information or facts. To repeat what was said above, ignorance is always much more serious than not having a set of facts on hand. If one knows what information one does not have, then one will have some idea of how to get it, and the battle is almost won. Real ignorance consists of not knowing that we don't know and, therefore, having no idea of how to go about finding out something that we do not even know exists to be found. The young Helen Keller was blind, deaf, and dumb and could not at first imagine that there was such a thing as language to be learned and used for personal communication. Once she grasped the miraculous concept that words could signify things, that her own primary experience of "water" could be named and communicated, her life was changed forever. Learning an innumerable number of specific new words was easy compared to her first great abstract discovery of the general principle of naming things. The gratitude Helen felt to her teacher who liberated her from dumb ignorance, lasted for the rest of her life.

But Helen's teacher did not penetrate Helen's ignorance easily. This long-ago struggle of a teacher to instruct a small handicapped child in rural Alabama has been dramatized often on stage and screen over the years and has moved millions of people. This conflict between a child's self-willed ignorance and her teacher's determination to teach, has the power of an epic, because it embodies the paradoxical challenge of instructing the ignorant. In human beings an innate thirst to learn coexists with a deep resistance to submitting one's self to the new and alien perspective of teachers who make new demands. While all children possess a natural curiosity, they also possess a bull-headed determination to do things their own way. Like many grown-ups, children can feel deep shame and humiliation when they must admit and confront their own ignorance. Self-protective strategies to avoid pain can stubbornly resist all enlightenment. Apathy and the cooling of the desire to know is one defense that can begin fairly early.

More pain can arise from the discipline and hard work it takes to learn to master something. Just as it takes patience and effort to teach, so it takes effort and patience to learn. If shame and impatience and the need to avoid pain and failure dominate, the will to learn may be dulled (if never totally extinguished). The art of teaching begins with the ability to outwit and minimize the pain and shame that can emerge in the student's confrontation with ignorance and failed attempts at mastery. Logically, it should be no shame to be ignorant. How could a person possibly know something without prior instruction or experience? But with proud sensitive human beings, shame at nonculpable, unavoidable ignorance seems inevitable. Adam and Eve became newly ashamed of their nakedness after they tasted evil in the garden. God grieved over the shame and fear that accompanied the Fall: "Who told you, you were naked?" Alas, human pride produces shame, shame produces fear, and fear casts out love and brings more shame—the enemies of truth flourish. To be able to learn about reality, one has to cease being afraid of confronting what one doesn't know.

INSTRUCTING AND INSTRUCTORS

All who wish to instruct the ignorant must overcome the paradox. A teacher, therapist, parent, or missionary knows something, and knows, too, that the other person does not know; while the other may be shamed to feel ignorant, he or she is also motivated by the innate human thirst for truth and reality. Neither the knowledge of another's relative ignorance, nor the student's innate desire and ability to learn can be ignored. A teacher must keep both of these things in mind. In our democratic times some persons overzealous for equality have resisted any recognition of ignorance and incompetence; they refuse to accept as a reality that the teacher, parent, or therapist must in some sense know more than the one who needs to be instructed. They confound our godgiven intrinsic equality as human beings with our inevitably unequal status as beginning, intermediate, or advanced students in some field. Yes, we are all learning together and we always learn from each other, but those who instruct should have advanced farther than those instructed.

At the other extreme are those instructors who refuse to believe in the inner ally and the intrinsic universal desire of human beings to learn and to grow. They refuse to build on the positive with praise and gentle encouragement. Some instructors will even champion the fear of punishment and anxiety as the only reliable human motivators. Others will defend an elite view of instruction, and regard only a few talented persons as teachable. Elitists would do well to study infants and observe the intense interest and desire of infants to learn about the world. Piaget described the infant as behaving like a small scientist in the crib, seeking, exploring, and trying to understand. More recent investigators of infancy have been even more astounded at the infant's abilities and desires from birth to encounter and understand reality. Infants do not start out in a hazy world of wish fulfillment, but with an orientation to seek and master the truth of things. When we instruct the ignorant, we should never collude with their ignorance, nor should we ever underestimate innate human abilities to learn and to grow. Our hopes for successful instructing are well-grounded in human nature.

Perhaps we teach best by keeping in touch with our own past experiences of moving from ignorance to knowledge. We can remember the joy of learning something, the intrinsic delight of mastery and new recognition of our own developing understanding and competence. Often—as, say, in learning to ride a bike—there is a long frustrating struggle, followed by a moment when we finally get it. This sudden grasp of the integrated process as a whole—of the big picture or the necessary solution—has been called the "aha" or "eureka" experience. This epiphany, or sudden rush of enlightenment or mastery, is so delightful that we forever seek its repetition through different activities. Sports, games, puzzles, riddles, jokes, crossword puzzles, and the life of the mind and science attract us because we love and adore the high of finally seeing some solution or discovering a relationship, of suddenly being able to "get it."

When we can enable another to feel this mastery, we experience their glow of success vicariously. When we help another "get it," whatever "it" happens to be, we are doubly delighted. We are catapulted back to our original good feeling when we first learned it, and we have the second experience of competence in now having successfully passed it on. A parent runs along behind the bike and finally sees the child ride away unassisted by the helping hand, no longer needing the lessons on how to balance, "that's right, go a little faster, turn into the fall." This moment of mutual triumph is a simple demonstration of what a privilege it is to teach anyone anything. The patient effort involved in instruction is rewarded a thousand times over.

Each of us can remember many such breakthroughs into mastery or insight, compounded by the later joy of passing them on to others. To this day I remember learning to tie my shoes at age four. What a triumph it was to finally succeed after the repeated frustrations of this seemingly impossible task. When the time came to teach my own children to tie their shoes I remembered my own pain—and eventual victory. To teach a child to master a complex task of daily life is indeed an achievement. The great genius Maria Montessori understood both how to teach and the joy of teaching. She was the first to systematically provide materials and a structured environment in which children could more easily master reality—child-sized furniture, rods that demonstrate fractions, large sandpaper letters. To teach another person to cook, to wash dishes, to sew, to read—any of the skills and competencies that our complicated world demands—gives riches to another. And how satisfying it is also to teach of intellectual, psychological, and spiritual matters, which are even more complex, subtle and uniquely personal.

The art of instruction is based upon the teacher's ability to put the self in the other's place and see the situation as they see it. I can only lead another to a new place if I can enter the place where he or she now is and get them to accompany me on the journey. I must cultivate the ability to jump back and forth from my perspective and goals, to the student's point of view. These mediating perspectives will have to shift constantly in the course of progress. Instructing in all its forms necessitates the double vision, how to be teacher and one's student at the same time. Empathy and the ability to take the role of the other while maintaining one's own perspective produce an effective teacher, parent, therapist, missionary—or savior. The Incarnation is the supreme model of effective mediation and instruction.

Teaching is best done by those who love their students for love induces the attention, empathy, encouraging praise, and perseverance necessary to penetrate the other person's perspective and move the other toward the common goal. Hate, vengeance, and the desire to control or break a person may inspire equally keen attentiveness, but since the goal of hate can never be a mutual good, the victim's resistance may eventually sabotage the enterprise. A successful teacher perseveres out of goodwill toward the student; the teacher's respect for the student and their mutual goal help overcome shame, fear of failure, distrust, and apathetic indifference. A teacher who loves and cares enough to pay a student sustained attention can be inspired to hit upon what will work to instruct this learner in this situation at this moment. One may always look for a "teaching moment," but the good teacher specializes in making such moments happen. What will work here and now?

Love and goodwill sustain hope for future success. If a teacher gives up in despair before starting, progress is impossible. We know now from a great deal of psychological research the enormous influence of expectancy. Those students who are expected to learn, will learn. What a teacher expects to happen shapes the outcome. If a teacher is impatient and quick to disparage, only the very quickest students will learn—and they will learn arrogant impatience along with the lesson. A discouraging impression will be made, namely, that only the most able are worth expenditures of time and effort. How different from that most loving teacher who proclaims, "a bruised reed I will not break nor a flickering wick extinguish." Since God is love, and pays constant attention, the Holy One is the supremely patient teacher. Loving patience and hope are all-important in teaching, therapy, and parenthood. Knowledge is a necessary but not sufficient condition. A good teacher or therapist or parent must be able to imagine change, inspire change, and shrewdly gauge what will make it happen.

All change has been described as a process of unfreezing, reforming and refreezing. The first stage of unfreezing, or stirring up the status quo, must take place before any new learning begins. Something must happen to stimulate a learner to focus attention, and see the inadequacy or insufficiency of the existing state of affairs. Some awareness of need, ignorance, or incompleteness has to emerge before movement is motivated. The tendency toward inertia and stasis can be disturbed by some crisis or, at the other extreme, some positive force may enter the field and induce a desire or readiness for something new and better, some awakening of the innate desire to learn more.

After instruction and learning takes place, the new patterns will soon have to withstand the counterpressure for a regression to the old status quo. In the terms of the Gospel we would say that all newly sown seed will be in danger of being choked by the return of perennial weeds. Old habits and old ways will reassert themselves. Whenever a functioning system is disturbed it tries to reestablish equilibrium. No person can have freedom diminished without some reaction aimed at reasserting the old liberty. Thus, for successful change or learning, a refreezing stage is necessary so that what one has learned is assimilated and becomes more than a temporary exercise or enthusiasm. A good instructor will try to prepare a learner for the prolonged practice necessary for new learning to really take hold. One must prepare learners for obstacles and lengthy efforts. Good teachers who love their students are interested in the long run and long-term results.

The best teachers aim to give their students ways to learn for themselves. Never give a hungry man a fish when you can teach him how to fish. The golden rule of all instruction is to become biodegradable, to pass on a self-generating process so that one's teaching is no longer needed. Every good teacher, therapist, or parent wants to induce self-guidance. Now that I've shown you why and how, go and do what you have seen me do. In Christianity we have the model of Jesus, who promised his disciples that they would do even greater works than he, after he departed. He told his followers to learn from him and sent them out to the harvest. Christians are charged to grow up into the fullness of Jesus, to be adult friends, not perpetual children. A loving teacher, therapist, or missionary wants to lead those they instruct into full equality. One starts out with inequality and ignorance and moves the learner into equality and, if possible, toward greater achievements than one's own.

In the course of becoming unnecessary instructors must prepare their students to always look for what is not obvious. One of the most important things that one can teach another is to pursue an awareness of the hidden frameworks and prior assumptions which may be constricting one's vision or confining one's range of solutions. Again this means that in overcoming ignorance we don't solely work on learning bit by bit, but focus attention instead on the process: What are the guiding principles, presumptions, and goals which will shape the larger picture? In other words, one of the most important things to inspire is the student's future search for what I don't yet know that I don't know. Humility and openness to new and different ways of seeing become the best educational policy. Socrates always spoke of his lack of knowledge and proceeded to become one of the greatest teachers of all time— without publishing a word.

While all successful teachers have much in common as they pursue the essentials, it is also the case that a variety of individual styles will flourish. Consider the great teachers, therapists, or parents that one has known, they are alike in some essentials and yet also had different talents. A variety of teaching styles can work together, much as different instruments in the orchestra can carry the same musical theme; indeed, different individuals at different times in their lives may respond best to many different approaches. Let a thousand flowers bloom seems the general rule of good instruction. All flowering species share the common processes of photosynthesis and reproduction, but there can be riotous differences in color, shape, and scent. Getting the most productive match between individual learner and individual teacher is sometimes a challenge, whether in school, therapy or religious direction.

One interesting typology of instructors can be constructed from an analogy with tribal healers in different cultures. Among many tribes in different lands one finds the recurring figures of the shaman, magician, naturalist, priest, or mystic healer. With their different methods, they can all produce change in an individual. Shamans operate with a sense of personal power, conviction, autonomy, and faith in themselves, along with a certain potential for narcissism and megalomania. Shamans bring about change on the basis of their personal influence and power, their ability to induce trust in their power. Magicians, naturalists, and priests do not rely on personal influence but on their accrued knowledge, or positions as gatekeepers.

None of the changes that shaman, magician, naturalist, or priest can bring about can match the effects wrought by the mystic healers. The mystic healer, like a good teacher, is a catalyst for change and instructs as a form of love and personal investment in the other's well-being. In contrast to the more superficial self-centered endeavors of the other types of wonder-workers, mystic healers inspire learning as a means for the other person's unique integration and fulfillment. Unlike shamans or magicians, mystic healers are those teachers who, while they may be dramatic and colorful, still do not rely upon quick tricks or props, and they seek no permanent dependents. The lessons learned from these good teachers are both simple and profound, and last for a lifetime. Mystic healers also appear in an amazing diversity, from Zen Buddhist monks to the devoted schoolmarms who populate American autobiographies. They, along with great therapists and great parents, have the power to inspire growth and integration, invoking feelings of gratitude. Like Socrates, effective instructors are unafraid of their own ignorance, and insist that their students seek to know themselves.

PSYCHOLOGICAL AND SPIRITUAL INSTRUCTION OF THE IGNORANT

But what of these even more subtle realms of psychological and spiritual instruction? How do we teach others to know themselves, or begin religious instruction about God's ways with human beings? Heretofore, the family has always been the first and most primary school for the development of character and religious understanding. But instruction continues in many different kinds of situations encountered throughout a lifetime. Parents teach their children about God and the self, but so do siblings, peers, teachers, therapists, clergy, employers, fellow workers, lovers, mates, and the family one creates as an adult. The development of the self is lifelong and emerges as the one necessary, unavoidable curriculum. Even those who have avoided or been denied all formal religious or psychological instruction will have to enter this school. When people talk about the school of hard knocks, they are referring to the fact that life is a long process of overcoming, or failing to overcome, self-ignorance and self-delusion. Today in secular circles the task which religions and spiritual counselors were traditionally assigned is often given to psychology and therapy. But the perennial questions and dilemmas remain and reappear to give trouble.

Why are we so ignorant and easily deceived about ourselves? Why don't we achieve self-knowledge more promptly? Although philosophers and mystics have always said that spiritual progress requires self-knowledge, the task remains incredibly difficult. We look around us and see such widespread blindness to self—and, of course, we have had enough painful personal experiences of entrapment in illusion and ignorance of self to recognize the condition. Intense new interest in this ancient human problem has produced a provocative new psychology of self-deception.

According to some new theories self-deception is genetically programmed into the human species. Some measure of self-deception has adaptive uses that favor its continued use in the struggle for human survival. Persons who can successfully fool themselves, may look more sincere to others, seem more sincere to themselves, and so be able to garner more of the environment's resources; they can rationalize their selfish strategies and provide advantages to their own offspring, who perpetuate the genes. Evolutionary theorists are just as sure that altruism, cooperation, and learning are also innate, so one finds a curious secular replay of original-sin theories in which human nature is mostly good, but also wounded in its propensity for self-enhancing illusions.

Other investigations of self-deception do not focus on evolutionary strategies but upon the way human consciousness functions day to day. A built-in need for self-deception is posited as emerging from the strong human drive to avoid pain and seek pleasure. Avoiding pain by not attending to it may be both an innate and learned defensive strategy. There may be physical and psychological trade-offs and adjustments between pain and attention. If I don't notice something, it hurts less; it is easier to avoid a painful reality than try to change it. The self's negative experiences of weakness, failure, and wrongdoing may be particularly painful to confront with full awareness, ergo a defensive dimming of attention or outright avoidance becomes the best defense.

Self-scrutiny and introspection have traditionally been known as painful and difficult enterprises. Research studies of attention and self-consciousness have confirmed the fact that when we become self-conscious we usually become self-critical. Our attention is turned inward upon our weaknesses and inadequacies, we notice our failures to meet our own standards. Pain and the threat to our self-esteem tempt us defensively to change or distort reality in order to be able to protect ourselves from the truth. We can learn to keep our attention dimmed or turned outward in habitual defensive strategies that prevent self-knowledge.

Habitual self-deception is possible because humans have multiple, complex, different levels of functioning and consciousness. Highly differentiated semi-independent systems are an advantage when it comes to self-correction; one system can check, substitute for, or correct the input of another. But it is also possible for systems to become isolated or fail to be integrated properly. We usually function with several simultaneously interacting systems—with a physiological system, an emotional-affective interpersonal system, and a conscious-rational symbolic system. Each system contributes to a sense of self or identity. The most familiar self that we recognize is the alert awake consciousness or "I" that seems to scan the world without and within like a narrow beam of light. When we daydream or go to sleep we can feel this beam fading and other levels of functioning taking over. When awake we direct our beam of attentive consciousness toward reality, ready to cope with daily life.

But when our coping is not successful or when we are frustrated, we can see defensive maneuvers taking place in consciousness and attention. Our dedication to reality wavers, particularly if self-scrutiny is in order. We resist turning the light inward upon ourselves because of the discomfort and critical function of self-consciousness. The habitual defensive strategies can begin. Because we are so complicated it seems possible that information can be processed but remain isolated from full conscious awareness. We become adept at hiding from full self-confrontation, in order to avoid pain, procure pleasure or block the moral self-censure of guilt or shame. The more maladaptive the process becomes and the more we hide from self-knowledge, the more threatened and defensive we become.

All psychological therapies or programs for self-knowledge or spiritual disciplines insist upon directing consciousness inward in searching self-observation. This mindfulness or sustained attention to inner reality is a painful but necessary discipline for personal change and progress. The natural tendency toward self-deception and defense has to be struggled against by equally strong efforts toward reality and truthful self-confrontation. When a person's automatic, heretofore avoided or isolated defensive processes are attended to and brought to full consciousness, a person can be free to choose in new ways what will determine his or her future life. We are told to know ourselves so that we can be freed from being driven by hidden forces with which we have colluded in self-protective strategies of self-deception. Naturally we resist the pain and the effort to overcome ignorance of the self, even while desiring to be free.

We both seek and resist enlightenment, but without the help of other persons we can never overcome self-deception. No one can experience themselves or see themselves as others do. We cannot see how we look from the back, or be fully conscious of all our unconscious habits and mannerisms, nor can we penetrate our personality all by ourselves. Others must disclose us to ourselves by their response to us. One can overcome ignorance of the self by the ongoing dialogue with the other. If we are failing to communicate, if we are arrogant or too self-deprecating, someone must tell us; are we reading the environment and other persons rationally?

We instruct one another by giving accurate responses and reactions to what is said and done. If we love persons we are forced in charity to tell them truthfully how we respond to them. Without this truthful response a person can continue in defensive self-deceptive traps. Often those who have been raised by too indulgent parents, or those in positions of great power who are surrounded by sycophants, or those who are greatly pitied or avoided, will not have the truth told to them. They do not get a proper education in self-knowledge because the human dialogue has been deficient or dishonest. Sooner or later they pay for the fact that others did not love them enough to tell them what they needed to know or to force them to confront the real consequences of what they do.

To instruct another in the struggle for self-knowledge is much like all instructing, a delicate task filled with paradox. One must tell the other when they are failing, while support-ing and affirming them. It is no favor to mislead another out of mistaken efforts at nurturing. In this culture women have often been socialized to soothe, charm, lie, and cover up the faults of the men and children in their lives. Through timidity, mistaken kindness, or inattentiveness, many persons do not get in family life the instruction in self-discipline they need. The situation is far worse if a family is at the same time too ungenerous or meanspirited to affirm an individual's good qualities and potential strengths.

In many cases it takes psychological counseling to liberate and free the self from distorted past learning which no longer applies in the present. As in other instruction, the goal is to induce self-control and ongoing self-guidance. It is possible to learn to think about one's thinking and regularly examine how one feels and functions with other people. The more self-knowledge and self-awareness, the more freedom of choice. It is possible to learn to feel and act in new ways. Action, thought, and feeling can change if we make enough effort and have enough good and truthful companions to help us overcome our ignorance of ourselves. Self-control, or self-mastery, basically seems an ability to integrate consciously all of our different systems and levels of personality so that we can choose to act as we would.

Many of us who were educated in an earlier day were taught strategies of self-control in the family. Self-discipline was part of the Calvinist American heritage that fused stoic values and good manners. One was taught to cultivate cheerfulness and self-control as a contribution to the family and social circle; one should never be so self-indulgent or so rude as to litter the communal space with surliness or bad feeling. Ironically, psychological research has now vindicated the therapeutic value of many of the personal self-management strategies that parents and schools once taught. Stop pouting, don't dwell on your troubles, get busy, and you will feel better. Stand up straight, dress up, clean your room, and you will feel better. Go talk to others and you'll stop feeling self-conscious. Learn patience, finish what you start, and you'll feel better. Do something for others, be cheerful, and you'll feel better. Such strategies worked and still work; we can make ourselves feel better and change ourselves for the better through strategic efforts at self-control. What psychology calls self-management or self-control training, we called "character," the traits which you built through persistent effort.

Character means that individuals shape their environment, including their inner environment, as much as the environment shapes them. There is two-way influence. Freely willed effort can produce transformations of the unconscious and preconscious as well. Through effort, love, attention, and discipline those parts of the personality that seem beyond direction, awareness, and control can slowly be changed. Through consciousness and effort we can change much of our preconscious and emotional life. The method seems to be to deploy attention, the capacity which gives us freedom and makes self-management possible. Those parents, teachers, therapists, or religious guides who instruct us to know ourselves, and direct ourselves, and achieve disciplined self-control prepare us to be able to cope with life—and to be cheerful while doing so.

Many young people in our post-Calvinist culture do not seem prepared to struggle with difficulties. They have been so protected by loving parents and shielded by affluence that they are not ready for the tests of character and personal integration which life brings. The need for self-discipline, perseverance, and long-term effort is a surprise to them. That marriage takes sacrifice is a surprise; that one's work and career should take so much dedication and effort is easier to understand, but still something of a shock. The difficulty of balancing work and family becomes disconcerting if not overwhelming. And few are prepared for the struggles of parenthood in a time when much of the family and community support for child rearing has vanished. Today we see many young adults struggling to come to terms with adulthood, sadly ignorant of many psychological and spiritual truths that could help them.

RELIGIOUS INSTRUCTION

Religious instruction in our pluralistic secular culture is a form of missionary activity. While most of us would never go as missionaries to Africa or China or New Guinea, we can be faced with some of the same challenges of communication here at home. Surely followers of punk rock stars, the Cosmo girls, or materialistic yuppies can seem as foreign to many of us as any distant tribe. How do we convey the good news of the Gospel to people whose culture is such a variant form of our own that it is difficult for us to bridge the gap? Indeed, the world of our own children can be quite alien for many of us raised in the last gasp of the nineteenth-century ethic of honor, integrity, and self-discipline. It's a long way from the world of Lord Tennyson, Jane Austen, George Eliot, and Charles Dickens to videos of rock stars and game shows. Confronting the modern cult of instant gratification, with its accompaniment of anxiety, violence, pornography, and the trivialization of life, can be as difficult as a mission to head-hunting cannibals.

In our evangelizing efforts to overcome religious ignorance we will face all the age-old challenges of teaching and learning. The same paradoxes of all instructing apply. We must overcome the obstacles and resistance to change. We will succeed through empathy, love, attentiveness, and reliance upon the ever-present inner ally in others. The innate human thirst for truth, love, and contact with the Creator is present beneath all apathy and can be reached through hope, love, and perseverance. Yes, there will always be martyred missionaries, whether in the Amazonian jungles or the American slum, but the greater number of successes give evidence that all human persons can be moved.

All the usual strategies, hazards, and rewards of teaching operate in religious instruction. But there are a few different factors in religious instruction that Christians going forth to proclaim the good news of the Gospel should keep in mind.

Essential to successful religious instruction is belief in one's own message. Is my faith more than a notional, verbal business? Do I give my real assent with all my heart and practice what I preach? Only the doers of the word, not the idle chatterers about the word, make an impact. In all instruction one must to some degree exemplify what one would teach, but in Christian teaching this is the crux of the matter. If the core of the message is love and one does not love, the empty gong resounds with a deafening hollowness. If one is declaiming about truth and lives a lie, the hypocrisy invalidates the message. The medium is the message in Christian instruction. All efforts to instruct well will fail if the instructor does not seek inner integrity and a Christ-centered life. One must be good to be a good religious instructor.

Also important for good religious instruction is an understanding of what is essential to the faith and what is historically conditioned. I need to know what is necessary, central, and basic to the good news and what is peripheral, culture-bound, or even a matter of my individual preference. Many great masters of Christian spiritual life have repeatedly affirmed the necessary theological distinctions between the core beliefs of Christianity and the evolving, changing interpretations of the faith in different epochs. The contention is that if the center and the core is strong and deep, there can be a great deal of flexibility, variety, and change on the periphery. Philosophy of science has also distinguished between the central tenets of a theory or scientific paradigm and the ongoing flexible accommodations in less central corollaries as new evidence appears from experimentation and discovery. Within Christianity, the certain, strong, living core of the Gospel allows flexible change and accommodation as Christianity is actually practiced throughout the world; a universal living faith can change and be embodied in various ways.

When modern Catholic missionaries go to other countries today, they no longer attempt to export their own historically conditioned nineteenth-century American or European Catholicism to other cultures. Instead they give the essential seeds and try cooperatively to harvest the strengths of the people to whom they are sent and from whom they expect to learn. One missionary to the Masai people of Africa reports,

> After having explained God and Jesus Christ to the people I had come to the end of the good news. It might seem a bit abrupt but I believe it is true. After declaiming all that God has done in the world because of his love for the world and for human beings, and after announcing the depths to which this love has gone in the person and love of Jesus Christ, the missionary's job is complete. What else is there?

The people to whom the good news has been given then must become self-guiding in the Lord. They must build up a Christian community and a Christian practice that will sanctify their particular time and place. They alone can develop their specific incarnation of God's love.

The Christian missionary, like all instructors, wishes to become unnecessary. He or she aspires to pass on the essential framework and the processes which will produce a self-generating knowledge and wisdom. The point here is to introduce a new Christian to prayer, to Scripture, to the inner light of conscience, and to the ongoing Catholic Church, or body of Christ in which a Christian life can be lived. No one can be a Christian alone. Even the hermits or those Christians incarcerated in solitary cells under oppressive regimes were formed by their Christian communities and relied on their presence as a spiritual cloud of witnesses. In a solitary life the social world remains in the head and heart, for individuals continue to think and feel in those modes given by their formative community. For those not incarcerated, a real community is necessary so that one can show expressions of love. As early monks justifying the formation of communal monasteries put it, "If you live alone, whose feet will you wash?" We also need our Christian community to confirm the new social reality we construct by our common Christian belief, language, and action. Otherwise the world's reality reasserts itself, and our faith weakens.

Catholic Christians must have a community consisting of particular places and specific people—life is with people. The parish structure is one place where we find people and receive religious instruction. If the parish does not give much support, American Catholics can find many other supplementary Catholic communities in which to grow in the faith. America has from its inception been a society that understands the creative possibilities of free association, compacts, and cooperative groups. As a consequence, Catholics in America have many, many different Church groups in which to seek instruction, even beyond the formal Catholic educational system. Intellectuals have *Commonweal, Cross Currents, America,* various newspapers and theological journals, along with a multitude of guilds and professional groups. Those who are more activist and those who are more conservative have other kinds of societies and groups in which they can participate. Third orders and institutes of every kind exist. These volunteer associations of Christians can provide some of the framework and mutual instruction that persons need for their religious formation.

As in all efforts to know one's self, there is the constant struggle against self-deception. In religious life as in other contexts, only one's fellows can help one overcome this most intractable form of ignorance. We need our Christian community to correct our own biases and predilections. This is another reason why the individual's incorporation into an ongoing concrete historical institution is important. Everyone finds certain parts of the good news easier to accept than others. The self-deception that keeps us from seeing our own faults may keep us from accepting the fullness of the Gospel. The community corrects and complements selective perceptions; no individual alone can know it all and have the definitive last word with the Word of God.

Being in the Church also instructs us in humility and irony. There are always models before us who are far ahead of us in spiritual wisdom and virtue. They instruct by their example; sometimes their entire existence is instructive. The fact that great mystics, saints, theologians, and thinkers are in the community inspires us. The knowledge that other quite ordinary persons around us are living the Gospel more fully and heroically than we are gives perspective and balance. A nice irony emerges when the large view is achieved and Christians no longer take themselves too seriously. Humble detachment, gratitude, and the catholic long-term communal perspective encourages saving wit and humor. We instruct when we are merry and full of joy, graciously humble and happy in the teeming company of fellow pilgrims. Saint Paul understood this and urged Christian apostles always to use tact and wit and to instruct others with respect and gentleness.

Christian religious instruction stresses over and over again that the loving heart is the heart of the matter. All of us need constantly to be reminded that God loves us more than we could ever love, that God has gone before us, waits for us, and is constantly eager to respond to us. We can always lift our heart to God and seek the Lord within. The divine presence within, the inner light, is intensified after baptism and entrance into the community. Since the Spirit guides an individual from within as well as through the Church, a delicate balance always has to be achieved between a reverence for individual conscience and the authority of the Church. A Christian should feel supported by the authority of the communal faith, as well as enjoying the liberty of the child of God to find his or her unique way to God. The point was tellingly made by a priest who, preaching on Saint Ignatius's arduous life, said, "And this, dear friends was Saint Ignatius's way to God. Thank God it is not the only way." There may be only one entrance, but an infinite number of paths lead us to the gate.

Whatever our spiritual path, we must learn how to read the signals of the generic self-guidance called conscience. This spiritual self-evaluation process has been called the discernment of spirits and bears a family resemblance to the inner scrutiny of psychotherapy. Such discernment involves looking into one's consciousness, emotions, moods, thoughts, images, and attitudes and trying to understand them in the light of faith. It is a way to know one's self and respond to God through the self-knowledge, another effort to overcome the snares of self-deception and defensive blind spots. Our family, friends, religious community, and spiritual mentors can help with their good counsel, but each unique individual must make his or her moral and religious decisions. We have to seek our unique and special road. What does God will of me?

An old constricted, deformed misunderstanding of Christianity discerned God's will in whatever hurt most, was most difficult or distasteful, or entailed the most sacrificial suffering. This approach now is seen as a defamation of the gentle but liberating yoke of Christ. The greatest spiritual masters, including Ignatius, understand that God leads us through happiness, desire, and inclination. Happiness and joy are signs of the Spirit. Christ promises joy, peace, rest, and the abundant life; the positive emotions are a positive sign that we are progressing in the way of truth for us.

Of course if we have persisted in grievous sin or become addicted or have long been in a dissolute or downward spiral in our moral life, it may be that a change of course will be painful and difficult. Desire and pleasure may not be a reliable guide when we are running away from God. But even in such cases the pain of our repentance will produce a deeper more peaceful quality of joy than the rather frenzied manic pleasure of dissipation. Baron von Hügel, a great master of spiritual counsel, told those he instructed to differentiate excitement from zest. He felt that while zest was good, excitement was negative. We have known the excitement that comes from

anger or from the lust for revenge or self-glorification. The evil
excitements of lust seem to exist in many more forms than
carnal desire. What Shakespeare wrote of "lust in action" is
true: it is

> the expense of spirit in a waste of shame . . .
> Mad in pursuit, and in possession so;
> Had, having, and in quest to have, extreme;
> A bliss in proof, and proved, a very woe,
> Before, a joy proposed; behind, a dream.

Such mad feelings of shameful excitement are usually a sign to
ourselves that what we contemplate is not good. Lustful excitement is also intrusive, obsessive, accompanied by contra-
dictory disordered thinking and distortions of reality.

Zest, on the other hand, is a positive desire that gives us joy
and happiness. We have zest when we feel most completely
ourselves, most completely in touch with reality. Zest seems
to be a form of passionate love and joy which is not a dream,
not shameful, not an expense of spirit. Instead of leaving us
wasted and exhausted, zest inspirits us and makes us soar and
mount up with wings to our own greatest heights. We are
high, but not fearing a fall. We have experienced these high
peak feelings—when lawfully in love, when working in white-
hot creativity, when worshipping, or when playing well. We
may be burning, but with a fire of love's peaceful and happy
flame.

Zestful feelings of desire and happiness are a signal to us
from ourselves that what we are doing is good for us. God
leads us by happiness to know what we should be doing. We
become more truly God's work of art when we are becoming
uniquely our selves, growing in heart and mind. In the discernment of spirits our positive emotions affirm the truer
deeper self that we want to become, the person we want to be
with our friends and family as well as when we stand before

God and the joyful company of the saints. Indeed, one criterion to use in appraising our present emotions, desires, and decisions is whether we think that the spiritual cloud of witnesses who surround us would approve and be glad.

Pain, anxiety, and depression will generally show us that we are on the wrong course for growth. Our negative emotions, like the positive ones, are signals arising from our emotional selves, our past experiences; they also should be taken seriously as psychological and spiritual indicators that must be evaluated. Often we can see ourselves regressing into the negative patterns of infantile thoughts and emotions that are quite destructive to our spiritual and psychological health. We can sense that our feelings of rage, despair, hate, jealousy, and selfishness are hardening our heart toward others. These feelings are experienced and directly discerned as not being fruits of the Spirit. Like lustful excitement, evil desires and fears are obsessive, intrusive, agitating, and make us conflicted and unhappy. We can feel our negative emotions drawing us toward serious sin.

The destructive power of the negative emotions, particularly of lustful excitement, has led many religious counselors and moral instructors, influenced by the stoic ideal, to recommend the overcoming of all emotion as the way to truth and perfection. The suppression of affection, particular attachments, and desire was seen as the way to freedom and self-mastery. Religious instruction and moral instruction included exercises aimed at curbing one's feelings, which were deemed either dangerous or irrelevant. A detached and completely rational approach was championed as the way the person should make all decisions. Along with the stoic philosopher, the detached and rational scientist was held up as the epitome of the nonemotional approach. Today, of course, the philosophers and historians of science have discovered that many factors other than rational deduction guide the scientific enterprise. We hear talk in science of personal and tacit knowledge, intuition, belief systems, and faithful attachment to theories, mentors and scientific communities. Science progresses by much more than exclusively rational and cognitive methods of thought.

In religious and moral instruction emotions need to be taken into account much more than has been the case. The importance of reaching both heart and mind has to be stressed in all instruction, and particularly in religious instruction. Heart speaks to heart, said Cardinal Newman. It also turns out that mind speaks to heart, heart speaks to mind, and mind speaks to mind. The dynamic interplay between our emotions and our thought, both within the self and with others, is being newly recognized as a complex ongoing process that affects all of our life. Sometimes thinking and reason should control and constrain emotion, especially negative emotions. Negative emotions such as despair or lust should not carry the day. But at the same time positive emotions and heartfelt feelings can tutor the reason.

Neither heart or mind can be discounted in instructing other persons or in self-guidance. Therapists have had to face this truth in psychological instruction and good teachers have always known it intuitively. Now religious instructors have to rethink their approach to educating the heart as well as the mind. We need to revive the practice of the discernment of spirits and meditate on the power of love to tutor the reason. Love make us attend more closely, gives empathetic understanding, and inspires hope and perseverance. Our attachment, attentiveness, and desire give us creative insight into the truth. Religious instruction has a new world to explore as we mine the rich tradition of spiritual counsel and move toward the new synthesis necessary in our psychological times.

To instruct another is to collaborate with God, the One who teaches and enlightens. There will be effort, pain, and joy in this spiritual work of mercy, but love impels us to seek truth and share what we have with others. Our God, who came to teach us personally and who instructs us from within, enkindles the fire to know and to teach in all hearts. We imitate the most loving, patient, and attentive of all teachers when we instruct the ignorant.

3

TO COUNSEL THE DOUBTFUL

When there are some who have doubts, reassure them; when there are some to be saved from the fire, pull them out. (Jude 1:23)

Simply reverence the Lord Christ in your hearts, and always have your answer ready for people who ask you the reason for the hope that you all have. But give it with courtesy and respect and with a clear conscience. (I Peter 3:15)

DOUBT

"I believe. Lord, help my unbelief." So said the centurion in the Gospels and so say we all. The first thing to recognize in counseling the doubtful is that everyone pursuing a life of faith will doubt. How could it be otherwise? Our faith is hope in things unseen. If matters were clear and evident there would be no need for faith. Faith implies a gap between what is fairly certain and what is only probable. We live in the realm of probabilities because we are not yet face to face with God, the ultimate reality.

Jesus, too, seems to have experienced doubt. The resounding cry of agony comes down to us across the ages: "My God, my God, why have you forsaken me?" Enough faith and assurance remain so that Jesus uses the words of the Psalmist to cry to the loving One who hears and cares for a son's pain, but the troubled "Why?" "Why so forsaken?" bespeaks doubt and uncertainty. If the Christ has not been spared such a troubling of spirit, then it is not surprising that we also will experience our intermittent doubts in the midst of belief, before and after belief, side by side with a sense of assurance and faith. Even faced with the resurrected Jesus, many of us, more skeptical than Thomas, would still doubt, in the midst of joy; we would think him an apparition too good to be true— we would say we might be dreaming, or perhaps experiencing a hallucinatory projection of our unconscious desires for a magic helper. The varieties of doubt, like the forms of faith and devotion, come clothed in the intellectual fabric of the day.

Faith always and everywhere is based upon the logical and psychological understanding that alternative readings of reality are possible. Faith and doubt are intertwined. However, there exists some decisive element in faith, some uncoerced personal assent of the whole person is involved, which tips the balance against inner doubt. As in a gestalt figure which can be seen as either vase or two profiles, faith emerges from the ground of doubt and dominates our perception of the whole picture. In this sense, the assent of faith is an activity, an active cooperation of perception with God's grace.

I think of the life of faith using the ancient imagery of light and darkness. Faith is a personal turning and stretching toward the sun; it is my part to open my eyes and let myself be drawn out of the dark corner where I huddle in misery. But choosing life, following the light to the sun out of the addictive land of gloom, is surprisingly difficult. To be doubtful is "to hesitate in belief, to admit of doubt, not to be clear or inclined not to believe." It is the inclination not to believe that creates the worst obstacle; there's something in us, profound inertia, that wants to subsist in darkness, taking some miserable pride in the finality of death and despair.

COUNSELING THE DOUBTFUL

Since all who believe must encounter doubt, counseling the doubtful can never be a one-way dispensing of the bounty of one's abundant faith to those without. Counseling in all its forms is much better understood as consultation or mutual deliberation, a coming together of persons with a common focus. Counsel can be taken in many ways. One can take counsel with one's self, reasoning and reflecting upon all of the different motivations and considerations within the complex personality we recognize ourselves to be. We can also take counsel with God within and without, through prayer and reflection, opening ourselves in silence and meditation. And we take counsel with other persons, meeting, discussing, reflecting, mutually considering some question or situation. As usual, the self-self interactions within, and the interaction with God, reflect our interactions with other persons, and vice versa. Those who never listen to others rarely look within. Closing off one's access to self and others will result in a closing off to God as well. Giving up on God engenders a despair that impedes reaching others. Certainly no one can counsel the doubtful who has lost touch with his or her own doubts and inner struggles, or who has lost the ability to ask for help from others. Even Jesus asked his disciples to watch with him, to support him with their presence, during his last intense inner struggle of doubt and prayer.

Would-be counselors must share their moments of hesitation and doubt with each other and take counsel and comfort from the sharing. It would be dishonest to pretend—especially to ourselves—that we do not experience doubt. Sealing off and denying doubts is the worst of all defenses, for things that are sealed off from self-scrutiny tend to gather irrational energy and often burst forth in more destructive forms. But we are also called to share our moments of certitude, joy, and faith. Fortunately, one's periods of deep doubt are not often concurrent with those of one's fellow believers or others who may be seeking counsel. It is always unsettling to think that one may be the only believer some people know well enough to approach. Who else can they ask about God, or speak to about spiritual things?

To counsel the doubtful is a spiritual work of mercy, and like the other spiritual works, it is a form of active love and care. It takes energy and time. It cannot be palmed off on priests or relegated to trained pastoral counselors or psychologists. In the broadest sense, one can see that Scripture, liturgy, and all spiritual writing and sermons are forms of mutual counseling by Christians to meet doubt. But counseling the doubtful more specifically applies to face-to-face encounters, conversations, and dialogues with persons we meet every day. When we try to love others, we move to meet doubt by the effort to extend and share our inner selves.

Counseling encounters with another may be formal or informal, very brief or extended in time. Over a long life there may be conversations we hardly remember that nonetheless affected another person. One of life's most gratifying experiences is to hear years after the event that some now-forgotten word of encouragement made a profound difference in another's life. A bit of seed fell on fertile ground and bore abundant fruit. How marvelous to hope that in the final judgment there may be a few forgotten good deeds to lay alongside the mound of failures and omissions that remain so painfully etched in the memory! Such experiences of counsel given and received defend us against the most disturbing deepest doubt of all, the anxiety that we are ultimately isolated and totally helpless to succor one another. The first requirement for counseling the doubtful is to believe that we matter to one another, we can make a difference. If we believe we are members of one another, it is worth the effort to try to connect. We must see each other through.

It seems clear that when we connect, we connect in many ways, and on many levels at once. Our words, nonverbal signals, silences, emotional messages, and deeds are all parts of communication. If counseling is the meeting of persons, all of these dimensions of a person-to-person encounter become important. Perhaps the most effective way to counsel a person who is hesitating in belief is to hold up the exemplary life of a believer or community of believers. Paul does this over and over in the New Testament. Would your doubts be persuaded? Look to your experience of faithful persons. By their fruits you shall know them. It does not take a philosophical pragmatist to understand the power of observing what works and what doesn't in spiritual matters. We test for soundness. Are persons acting on their beliefs? If they are Christians, do they love one another? Are they increasing in joy, peace, truth, good sense, prudence, good works?

The other day I was watching a film on Mother Theresa. She was confronting a group of secular officials in a struggle to enter Beirut to rescue some retarded children. I was impressed by the familiar cast of her efforts to persuade the doubting officials of her mission: "Come and see," she said. It is the ultimate Christian counsel to the doubtful. As Jesus sent an account of his liberating actions to assuage the doubts of John the Baptist, so all Christians have known that they must be ready to testify with their lives. Come and see if you would believe. Since counsel, or mutual meeting, takes place on all levels and through all modes of communication, dishonest signals and false claims become apparent. While many might disagree with Mother Theresa's approach to solving problems, few can doubt the sincerity and power of her belief in active love. Young women flock to her uncompromising order, devoting themselves to lives of hardship and service.

But Mother Theresa's community also understands that prayer and worship are necessary to keep their beliefs strong enough to continue the active practice of charity. Doubt is inevitable. A person cannot see Christ in the loathsome leper or repulsively deformed retardate unless one continues to find Christ in sacrament, Scripture, and prayer. Romantic gestures rapidly wither away without a stable source of spiritual power. The bottom line of secular wisdom asserts that human life is nasty, brutish, and short—we die like the animals and there is nothing after. Only communal worship empowers the Christocentric world view, which can overcome the doubts of the world.

If belief and knowledge are partially constructed and sustained by the social group, as sociologists of knowledge tell us, then one cannot be a believer alone. There must be others to confirm one's reality through consensual conversation. We who live in a pluralistic society, where the majority of people doubt and a minority believes, may never experience the certitude that we might have known in a time when every person shared basic assumptions and sustained each other's concept of the world. In contrast to the closed communities of the past, most of us today are forced to develop a more complicated way of believing to take account of doubt and disbelief. Counseling the doubtful and the need to be sustained by consensual conversation are both more necessary and more complex than they used to be.

But few would want to return to the parochial enclosed enclaves of an earlier day or another culture. Those narrow worlds exact their own price. Our struggles with our doubt and disbelief can produce spiritual growth, as they force us to become more complex self-conscious personalities. We can be humbly grateful that somehow through God's grace our faith is still stronger than our doubt. Gratitude helps us cultivate the saving irony and gracious detachment that keep us from taking ourselves so seriously that we become dogmatic, humorless, simpleminded and insufferable "true believers." How crude and offensive Christian fundamentalists and absolutists become. Experiencing an assault by a true believer can give a lasting lesson in how *not* to counsel the doubtful.

A woman acquaintance of mine, a divorced Hispanic lawyer and long-lapsed Catholic who was newly converted to a fundamentalist Christian group, once came to my house. Although I hardly knew her, she came on a mission to persuade me to declare myself for Christ. Thoroughly taken aback, I attempted to explain that I had been trying to be a faithful Christian for thirty years, since my own adult conversion. But she insisted that I must now profess with her my absolute certainty that I was saved and in communion with Jesus Christ, my savior. To help me overcome my doubts, she began to show me the relevant passages in Scripture (underlined by her pastor) so that I could announce my conversion and we could pray together.

A curiously embarrassing struggle ensued between us, paradigmatic of the clash between believer and true believer. I was filled with mixed emotions—simultaneously annoyed, touched by her fervor, and puzzled over what to do. I did not want to be rude or discourage her newfound faith, however aggressive, manic, and simpleminded it appeared to me. So I kept on protesting my own Christian faith and hope, while insisting that I was convinced that no one could ever be absolutely certain of one's salvation: hope, yes; assurance of God's love, yes; but *certainty*, no. I maintained that it was necessary in humility to recognize some doubt, since I was a sinful human being and God alone could be all-knowing. I feverishly quoted Saint Joan of Arc's great reply to the question of whether she was in a state of grace: "If I am, God keep me so; if I am not, may God speedily bring me to His salvation."

But my fired-up holy inquisitor dismissed my ideal of irony in the Christian life and my fear of presumption as mere waffling. She insisted and insisted that I could not be truly saved if I would not verbally profess my absolute certainty that I was saved. In the end I did pray with her and perhaps gave her some satisfaction and hope for my soul. At least I controlled my anger over her arrogant presumption toward me. She would barely listen to me. My faith and theology, not to mention my past writing or twenty years of pillar-of-the-parish efforts, were of no moment to her. I was simply a conversion opportunity in her newfound faith agenda. This basically comic experience at least made me seriously search my own conscience: Had I ever tried to steamroller others in the same way? Had I ever been as insensitive and imperious as this true believer?

The typical true believer, often met in fundamentalist cults and ideological movements, has violently suppressed all inner doubts and so has little trouble assaulting all dissent in others. After cutting off the inner dialogue, one can hardly communicate with other persons; only absolute submissiveness to the orthodox truth is acceptable. All inquiry or openness or dialogue is seen as dangerous since tight controls must be maintained at all times to suppress inner doubts. Even physically, true believers radiate tension and tightness in face and body (sometimes even tics and twitches) as they exert their defense of hypervigilance. The idea of using doubt to progress toward truth, or unbelief as a means to achieve humility and therapeutic irony is anathema to the closed mind. Nor is the human condition seen as comic; no merriment is allowed to deflect from the intensely serious struggle. Caught up in the cause, the person gains purpose and can avoid attending to the inner self or to personal problems. The true believer cannot counsel the doubtful effectively because the inner self must not be attended to; empathy for self and others fails. Self-doubt produces too much anxiety; all doubts must be displaced and projected and then countered by renewed assaults against outside enemies. The paranoid view of the world triumphs.

The great spiritual scholar and counselor Baron von Hügel wrote that some persons need to have their faith mapped out with geometric precision, with a clear and sharp boundary between belief and unbelief. He, however, espoused a more complex view. He saw himself as a person who possessed a strong center of faith and light, but he realized that as one moves toward the peripheries of faith there must be flexibility and a gradual indistinguishability of the boundaries between truth and untruth. He was a great spiritual counselor because he realized the many different ways to truth and could help individuals find the best way for them. Like all great counselors, teachers, therapists, or parents, his aim was to have the learner progress toward the ultimate goal of a mutual relationship of equals. Counselors, too, seek to be "biodegradable," to encourage the counselee to absorb what they have to give and pass it on.

As an intellectual, von Hügel also understood doubt; indeed, he recommended the pursuit of science, with its use of doubt and skepticism, as a corrective discipline for believers. (He also saw joy as a mark of the Spirit.) The case for complex irony in faith can be strengthened by remembering that Jesus himself did not claim to know or decide everything in absolute detail. He disclaimed knowledge of when the Last Day would occur and refused to be a judge in a case of brother against brother. He also refused to be called good: he knew what was in man as he knew himself. His authority and ability to counsel the doubtful contains no trace of arrogant assault, but is empowered instead by his love and acceptance of others.

When we are called to counsel the doubtful we must seek to know who it is we are meeting and value them. The ability to listen and truly learn how another sees the world is the first rule of any form of counseling. The famous rule that a counselor should tender the client unconditional positive regard and acceptance is really a secular translation of Christian charity. A true counselor will follow the lead of the Holy Spirit as Counselor. The Spirit is always working within us—suggesting, comforting, standing by us with love—in our journey through life. And if we wish to counsel others we have to make clear that we will stand by them whatever happens. Just as the love of Christ is the one thing we can depend upon, so anyone that we counsel should be able to depend unreservedly upon our love and understanding, our respect and empathy.

Each individual is a unique mystery unto herself or himself. While there are general laws and general orderings and developmental patterns in human personality, there is also something totally unique in each person. Christians believe that God has arranged it this way. Each person is made in the image of God; and God, who is infinite, is pleased to be imaged in multitudes of unique individuals—from the first human to the last—who can each be a part of the human creation in his or her own special way. In the last days, it is written, each person will receive from the Lord a white stone upon which a unique name known only to God and the self will be written. Obviously, unique persons, in their infinite variety, will believe and will struggle with doubt in many different ways. Explorations of the varieties of religious experience and belief can be matched by considerations of the differentiation of doubt.

William James is of course the classic and still reliable guide to the way different people experience belief and unbelief. He was one of the first of modern thinkers to point out that different personality types have characteristic religious experiences along with characteristic patterns of unbelief. James calls "healthy minded" those persons who believe easily and without effort; they tend to see beauty and goodness and joy and marvelous coincidences and confirmations of the good news everywhere. Evil and the darker side of life hardly exist for them; doubts do not often trouble them on their religious journey. These optimistic, happy, naturally mystic spirits are drawn to American religious movements of holistic health and Christian Science that deny the reality of evil. More pessimistic persons have great difficulty believing and overcoming their doubts; they will never rest easy in the face of the omnipresent evil and injustice they see in the world. Such tortured dark spirits find and sustain faith at great cost.

I think James is correct in his assessment of yet another set of persons who are more or less incapable of subjective religious experience. They do not believe, nor can they really be said to doubt. They are simply tone deaf to the spiritual dimension of the universe; religious questions seem meaningless. James attributes this spiritual color-blindness to innate temperament interacting with and abetted by particular cultural environments. Certainly the mid-twentieth-century dominance of a dogmatic secular humanism encouraged such persons. Faced with general working assumptions of atheism and agnosticism it has been easy for many persons to feel that religious questions are either regressive or neurotic.

I also think later psychologists following the lead of Jung are correct when they consider developmental life stages as relevant to religious experience. Personality type and individual uniqueness play large roles in faith and doubt, but so does the stage of the life cycle that a person is experiencing. Adolescence is a critical period for religious experience. Middle age and old age also force inner spiritual questions to the forefront of personal concern. Religious issues can be robustly suppressed as in youth, but the limits of life and the approach of death cannot be denied. Even after a life filled with great public and private fulfillment, with few betrayals or disillusionments, a spiritual restlessness of the heart can emerge. Oddly enough, those who have experienced the best that the world has to give are most susceptible to the vanity-of-vanities argument: How can it be that I have all of this, all of these good things, and it is still not enough? If the rich young man had been older, possessed of even more personal achievements, might not his encounter with Jesus have had a different outcome? At least his doubts would be different.

The loss of the rich young man whom Jesus grieved over, is a comforting reminder that Jesus understands that we, too, will often fail in our efforts to counsel the doubtful. The particular personality and stage of life, and the free choice of the other person, are as much factors in success or failure as our effort or level of skill. Our responsibility is to love, to care, to meet the other, to share our selves, and to do our best. In actuality we never really know what transpires in the inner spiritual journeys of even those we love and are close to. It is as delicate and mysterious a business as the comings and goings of the wind, for the Spirit bloweth where it listeth.

Henri Nouwen, one of our modern masters of the spiritual life, has remarked on how surprisingly difficult it is for believers, even religious professionals, to talk to each other about personal experiences of faith. Church politics, yes; faith experiences, no. In our culture we are much more likely to reveal our sexual lives and difficulties than we are to speak of spiritual difficulties or revelations. In some circles personal religious experience can become almost a taboo subject; only objective intellectual discourse is permitted. Are we reticent because we live in a time when the supernatural and the spiritual is denied, corrupted by television hucksters or horribly debased in various spiritualistic movements which are the staple of the tabloids? Andrew Greeley has said that in his investigations of religious believers he finds many, many people who have had spiritual experiences, but they do not tell those around them. A survey of the laity conducted by the Synod on the Laity also revealed surprising faith experiences never before revealed because "no one ever asked." Believers resist telling or talking because they fear the doubts of others and are afraid of being ridiculed or thought neurotic.

In our postpsychological age, of course, it is very difficult to achieve a balance of faith and skepticism. Our psychological knowledge of the tricks the mind can play on itself makes it difficult for us to trust spiritual experiences. We now know that persons can be deluded in their construction of meaning and in their sense of how things are related. We also know that we tend to notice what stands out in the perceptual field and ignore the background or the foundation. We tend to interpret everything that happens to us in certain biased ways. But it is also the case that we do not make up our stories out of nothing. There is evidence, there are facts, there are experiences that come in spite of other viewpoints and perspectives that we may take. Reality is partly constructed by us but there is also something out there that interacts with our constructions in convincing ways. As one secular scientist in a new area of mathematics has expressed it, the rationality of the universe has been imprinted in the human species throughout evolution. We have an innate ability to think logically and are fairly well adapted to making appropriate judgment.

Science in its most recent explosive developments has disclosed the universe in amazing ways. We have been forced to give up older pictures of a closed determined clockwork of cause and effect and confront natural mysteries concerning the open and dynamic nature of matter, time, space, and information. We know that we must function without the complete truth, while trusting in human processes of rational judgments, intuitions, and testing. In the open universe more things seem to exist than this world dreams of; but our business is to keep seeking truth and sorting things out as sensibly as we can. In common sense, as in science, we make our decisions about what to believe by looking at the big picture, the accumulated patterns of evidence, relatively weighing different explanations that we view against the rest of our life experience and personal knowledge.

The new philosophy of science demonstrates that no one in science can ever actually prove anything decisively by simple facts. Facts and evidence must be evaluated in the light of theories and basic assumptions. One is always working with tacit knowledge, communities of adherents, models, best interpretations, and the weight of probabilities. Paradigms can shift, new pictures emerge. The briefest excursions in the modern understanding of how science works is extraordinarily liberating (as von Hügel and Newman intuited) for the religious believer's understanding of what is involved in personal faith. The same complex processes of rational assent operate in common sense, science, and religious faith, although the supportive evidence differs. In religion, too, there are different ways of believing and doubting; the differences come from the qualities of the personal and reasoning processes that have gone into the outcome.

Many children and childlike adults believe in a way we would call superstitious because their beliefs are both irrational and immoral, having very little to do with the God we know as the Holy One who is Truth, Love, and the Creator of the universe. Usually, in the course of life, adolescent skepticism and rationality, in concert with religious education, will purify and refine the superstitious coarseness or sentimentality of childish immature faith. Finally, however, a mature faith culminates in what has been called "the second naiveté." While incorporating rationality and skepticism, one can also be mystical, experiential, and childlike in the good sense of what children bring to the faith. There is an acceptance of things beyond reason that are neither irrational nor immoral, things that cannot be empirically proven but that may be proven valid when tested by reason and by the good fruit they produce.

In the second naiveté, protected by the exercise of reason, one can go beyond reason and calmly accept what Blessed Cornelia Connelley called the fairy-tale elements of Christianity. We experience happy coincidences and answers to our prayers; unusual things happen that are difficult to explain in purely natural ways. I think it is important to accept these things, once called consolations or experiences of grace, without overrating them or underrating them. Though we cannot explain it, God's providence does seem to work through many small things and converging events in our lives. We don't dwell on these providential occurrences because we do not wish to fall into superstition or the heresy of thinking that evil and suffering are also sent by God. It is beyond our philosophical resources to figure out how God's love and care operate in a universe that is assumed to be structured through random chance events or laws of cause and effect.

We know that Creation is separate from God but sustained by God, and we know that our will is free. Creation is basically good but has somehow been made futile and is now groaning along with us in the painful birth process of redemption. The problem of explaining evil and unjust suffering while integrating into our faith the belief that "everything works together for good" is beyond us. So although we cannot explain it, we still have our experiences of comfort, answered prayers, healings, wonderful coincidences, little miracles, all of those little flowers from Saint Teresa of Lisieux that reassure us that God's providence and care is still operating. We continue with our "peak experiences," our spiritual highs, our epiphanies when God seems to be breaking through and coming to our rescue. If we hold to our commitment to reason and the discipline of rational inquiry, we can accept God's good gifts in gratitude. Simplicity, too, is a gift.

If Christians in the mainstream were willing to share their spiritual experiences more fully, they might help stem the tide of superstition and false spiritualism that is rising in our culture. The aridity and poverty of the secular establishment's technological world view seems to be producing a backlash against the rationality of the Enlightenment. A distorted affirmation of the spiritual dimension of reality fuels the spread of astrology, cults, drugs, satanism, and the like. Such reverberations of the spiritual have always been with us and will never be extinguished by secular materialism. When the devils have been swept from the house, something spiritually potent and positive must take up residence to avoid the invasion of a much worse set of demons. So it is all the more important that Christians share the elements of their religious experience that are magnetic enough to appeal to the imagination and love of people while they encourage sanity and health.

The issue of how much belief and doubt is appropriate came up at a recent dinner party of deeply committed Catholic intellectuals. The taboo against talking about private spiritual experiences was almost broken as we began to discuss our reactions to Marian apparitions and Marian devotion. Divisions emerged rather clearly. Some relegated the whole Marian thing to regressive superstition entwined with neurotic manifestations; since they themselves had always been left cold by Marian devotion this aspect of Catholic diversity was more or less meaningless, if not embarrassing. Another position taken by a sophisticated Jesuit was that it did not matter whether such appearances were true or not, but they were generally a good and positive thing to be valued in our religious tradition. My own argument, in this general mutual counseling of doubt, was that while I believed Mary could, would, and did appear to humankind, not all apparitions were authentic and it would be important to determine which ones were true and real and thereby valuable in our tradition. Neurotics and psychotics also have visions, and self-hypnotized power seekers, assisted by clever mentors, have been working the gullible crowds since the oracles of the ancient world. Every Marian appearance has to be tested by the complicated ways we judge the genuineness of all other claims and theories, religious or secular. We must constantly make efforts to distinguish various levels of probability and then give different levels of assent. Something may be possible, but it might not be probable or productive, given everything else we know about God, Mary, and reality. After the most cursory appraisal, I would judge the Marian appearances at Guadalupe as much more probable than the highly suspicious apparitions claimed in Queens, New York, with the Yugoslavian appearances somewhere in between.

My attitude toward Marian devotion has evolved from complete Protestant rejection to warm endorsement. I have moved from the severely purist stance, verging on iconoclasm, to deep appreciation and grateful belief. For me it has been a journey through Christ to Mary. By this I mean that devotion to Mary has grown as I was able to accept my whole embodied self as a fellow creature in a good creation. Some melting of pride and self-sufficiency has been involved in this development, some willingness to cry for a mother's help in a simple way. I firmly believe with the mystics that God is our Mother and Christ is our Mother, but this belief seems to be strengthened by devotion to Mary as Mother. In our culture, women, too, have to struggle to appropriate the traditional "feminine" qualities within themselves; women have been taught to suspect and doubt as weakness their allegiance to love, nurturance, motherhood, and feminine bonding. Marian devotion defends us against the phallic fallacies of our culture: the glorification of aggression, autonomy, and competitive individual achievement. In the world of the bottom line we need to affirm again and again that the bottom line is love. Our Mother of Mercy and Good Counsel strengthens our hope, our sweetness, and our life, slowly leavening us with love so that we can be worthy of the promises of Christ.

SPECIFIC STRATEGIES IN COUNSELING THE DOUBTFUL

Reconsidering Faith and Reason

Christianity consists of a historical institutional incarnated life, an intellectual cognitive understanding of the faith, and perhaps most important an emotional heartfelt affective assent to Christ as Lord. A full religious life must incorporate all of these dimensions but each can also be a realm of doubt. Often the emotional assent is lacking, sometimes the rational or intellectual understanding of the faith is more troubling, or the incarnated community and historical ongoing existence of the Church presents a problem. When counseling the doubtful it is important to understand what is the real difficulty and how the different dimensions may be interacting. One strategy that often works wonders is what I would call a lightening-of-the-load approach through education. Some persons have a false idea of what or how one must believe in order to be a Catholic. (They usually have misconceptions about the operation of scientific proofs as well.) Theological education is then in order and may solve many dilemmas. Educational programs aimed at correcting theological misconceptions have been very successful in reuniting lapsed Catholics with the Church.

In the post-Vatican-II Church there remain many people who think that they must believe every jot and tittle of the tradition with the same measure of assent. They were educated by teachers who were often Irish-American Catholics still under the sway of the Counter-Reformation and the modernist controversy. They think one must absolutely believe everything up to a clearcut boundary; and one step beyond the boundary is heresy. It is all or nothing, take the whole thing, relinquish all doubts, or out. Nothing ever changes, and nothing ever should change. Many rebellious ex-Catholics display a morbid nostalgia for the old authoritarian Church; they could not abide this Church, yet they wish to see it preserved in amber. But if seekers have doubts that come from an intellectual misunderstanding of what is necessary for belief, they can best be counseled through good theological instruction accompanied by a realistic psychology of the person.

Unfortunately, many pre-Vatican-II types are often trained in an outmoded psychology that cannot accommodate doubts or problems of conscience. In an older view of the person, people were divided into separated parts and faculties; this view overestimated the ability of the faculty of the will to direct the intellect. This psychology implies that one can perform acts of will in order to believe. Deciding to believe is thought to be possible. If one wants to enough, and makes enough effort of the will, one can overcome doubts and make one's self believe. Such thoughts seem to be behind the use of torture or penalties or threats against those whose beliefs are out of line. There is little understanding that a free assent of conscience wells up from an integrated whole person.

Vatican officials who demand that dissenting theologians reconsider and retract seem to be following the older psychology in concert with a conservative reading of Vatican II documents. They seem to believe that through acts of will a person can dissipate doubts or considered dissent. Other more mundane examples of the old view can appear in family life or community life. If members of the family or group stop believing or drop away or lapse from the faith, other members may demand belief, and blame the person who no longer believes. They are assuming by their blame that a person can will or force assent to the faith. This is obviously a much too simple approach to understanding how one believes, how one doubts, and how one ceases to believe.

The whole person believes and doubts and the whole person decides to assent. One cannot decide by an act of the disassociated will to override one's rational perception of what is or is not really the case. One can perform acts of love or hope or trust, but not decide to assent to reality contrary to one's considered opinion. Psychologically it is impossible to believe that what I believe to be so is not so. Yes, one can always reconsider and persons dedicated to seeking the truth must grant that subjectively they may be wrong, but in any final confrontation with oneself it is impossible knowingly to retract what one knows to be one's own view of reality at the present moment. If one happens to be in error or to be self-deceived, then by definition one cannot perceive it. After self-scrutiny and all-out efforts to seek the truth, one can only believe what one believes. God, who is a God of truth and honesty as well as love, will understand an honest person's inability to lie about what he or she truly perceives to be reality.

An impasse of faith should not be countered by counseling a doubting person to make some sort of absurd leap of faith or enter into the calculating wager on God's existence that Pascal recommended. These solutions seem either too irrational or too coldly rationalistic. To recommend irrational leaps of faith, to glory in the absurd, implies that reason and truth are not part of the divine plan, and that God does not want us to think as well as we can. Faith must be an assent beyond reason, but it is a reasonable and probable, never an irrational or absurd, step. We can reason to the point where we know that it is reasonable to hope for more than can be seen or proven, but our hope never rejects rationality or God's great gift of reason.

At the other extreme, Pascal's wager or calculation on the existence of God seems unsatisfactory in its rationalistic approach. Pascal recommends a cool cost-benefit analysis in which betting on God's existence ensures heaven, avoids hell, and produces a better human life even if death proves to be the end of human consciousness. Does this approach really overcome doubt? It seems offensive to the modern sensibility because of the impersonal, selfish calculation involved, and the implication that one can just decide to believe. Why would God be pleased by such a wager? We ourselves would not want a person to decide to marry us in order to avoid harmful consequences, or through a calculating gamble on the goods we could bestow. The motivation for taking up the wager would corrode the whole relationship. Honest doubt seems preferable to us. Besides, if anyone ever actually employed Pascal's wager it was probably because they already believed in some vague way, and lived in a culture where most people believed. In any case, it seems psychologically impossible to force mental assent *de novo* by an act of will.

A God who has put the light of reason in our minds and written an inner law of love upon our hearts would not want human beings either to deny their reason or to come to faith through force or calculation. We glorify God as the God of truth and the source of all knowledge by seeking truth, the whole truth, and nothing but the truth. Our part is to seek, to open readily our eyes and ears, to wait, to respond, and never to harden our hearts; but at the same time we must never coerce or lie to ourselves about what we think or feel. The gift of faith is a reasonable extension of the light of reason into the light of loving assent. God draws us on through the best that is in us. Someone once described religions as being not science-minus but poetry-plus. This is not adequate because religious belief is science-plus as well as poetry-plus, and love above all. I do not think one should counsel the doubtful by asking for existential wagers or leaps into absurdity. Other counsels, other strategies, and more holistic approaches to doubt can be explored.

Patience and Perseverance

Patience and perseverance are an old tried and true strategy for dealing with doubts and periods of troubled belief. Most of us never progress to the advanced stages of spirituality that are described as the mystic's dark night of the soul, but almost everyone experiences times of unusual storm and stress, or times of extreme emptiness. How should one deal with such periods when they occur in a life of fairly solid belief? The old answer is, "Wait, it will pass," and continue with business as usual. The approach of patience and perseverance is like taking shelter and waiting for the storm to pass. After all, anyone who has lived very long, or at least passed through adolescence, knows that life can sometimes resemble a roller coaster of inner and outer ups and downs. Moods and emotions may move from highs of exultation, well-being, and near ecstasy to lows of total depression and despair. Many volatile yet normal temperaments suffer such shifts of mood very rapidly. Other persons may go beyond the normal range of ups and downs and suffer the exaggerated violent mood swings of mental illness.

It is difficult to differentiate the normal from the abnormal, but extreme depression or extreme mania become so out of touch with common-sense reality that they manifest the need for professional treatment. But persons well within the range of normal still must deal with the mystery of change in daily consciousness and function. In one's psychological life, and in the life of faith, there can be cycles similar to those experienced by athletes. One may experience "hot" periods, when everything clicks, alternating with grim losing streaks, when nothing works and one is hardly in the game. Psychologists are busily researching the way we unconsciously and pre-consciously process external and internal stimuli, so perhaps we shall someday understand more clearly the natural causes behind our ups and downs, or why certain ideas or feelings seem to pop into our minds. Freud's insights into the unconscious are being submitted to rigorous experimental investigation. However since by definition we cannot be aware of our unconscious, we are still left with the problem of how to cope. Given the oddity and complexity of our minds, it is no wonder that persons have always been willing to blame evil thoughts and temptations on the Devil or demons.

Whatever their origin, a multitude of manic, depressive, doubtful, and depraved notions can beset very normal persons; such notions appear as out of nowhere in the ever moving stream of personal consciousness. Maybe I am an omnipotent god in disguise who can heal, or fly, or control all things; surely I exist beyond all good and evil. Or again, life is absolutely meaningless, ultimately unbearable, so I will kill myself. Or, I'll take revenge on my enemies and torture them slowly, or kill this innocent person for no reason. Or, I'll run away from home, family, work, and duty. Such dreadful momentary impulses come to many a mind, but the point is that in normal functioning they are jumbled in with a thousand other neutral and loving thoughts, and they disappear as quickly as they come. Our sense of reality and moral commitment dissipates our weird impulses. All we need do is wait a moment and we come to ourselves.

So, too, moments of doubt arise and pass away. In the approach of patience and perseverance, one does not panic, seek to repress doubtful thoughts, or fight back. Knowing the law of least effort, one does not become engaged with or focused upon evil or doubt by struggling with it head on in mortal combat. A better strategy is simply to quiet oneself, fully recognize the doubts as they emerge, and calmly wait. When the bedouin riding his camel meets the overwhelming sandstorm in the desert, he stops, gets off, lies down in the sand, covers his head, and quietly waits for the storm to be over. Storms do pass and doubts disappear. A wise person does not dissipate energy in a struggle when time alone will take care of a problem.

Another strategy is to continue calmly going about whatever it is that has been the subject of doubt—one's worship, prayer, job, marital life. When the storm passes it becomes clear that this was what one should have been doing. Belief returns. To keep on keeping on, to persevere, renews hope and strengthens our commitments. Fidelity deepens the bond. When we persevere through difficulties we give testimony to the fact that we trust and identify with our former self and our own past goals, roles, promises, and commitments. We learn to increase our trust and respect the self that brings us through the problematic or conflicted periods of doubt. We trust our self, the person who made those earlier decisions, enough so that we do not overturn the commitments we decided upon in an earlier time.

The human ability to make promises and commitments and to adhere to principles is based on our psychological understanding of the fluctuation and complex multiplicity of personal consciousness through time. We know that superficial inclinations, passing desires, or other vicissitudes may tempt us to give up or change purposes. So we bind ourselves for the future, staking our self-respect. When we make a promise we affirm that we can now know what we should do in the future no matter what may happen and, even more confidently, we affirm that we will be able to direct ourselves and carry through in the face of all inner and outer countervailing forces. It takes self-esteem and self-confidence to engage in commitments for the future. Self-esteem and self-confidence in one's past produces perseverance despite difficulties and doubt.

But this process of perseverance and fidelity is not a simple opposition of reason and emotion in which reason must conquer desire or emotion overcome reason. The challenge during periods of doubt can come from any dimension of my self: I might meet new intellectual problems or feel new desires. It will be best for me if the promise or past commitment or personal principle to which I now adhere emanated from an action of an integrated self. Principles, too, are not merely abstract moral rules, but can be seen as a form of crystallized, self-appropriated, chosen emotions. The principle, say, of justice embodies the best empathetic emotions I have felt; these crystallized emotions condensed into the principle will serve as a bridge over those times when I am assaulted by less welcome emotions or less admirable attitudes. I can persevere through periods of doubt because I have experienced more certain feelings in the past and remember my allegiance to

these better, stronger, truer, feelings. My heart can serve to
keep me true to myself.

Strategies of Heart and Deed

Suppose we have hardened our hearts in doubt. Is there an
acceptable strategy for counseling doubt that directly affects
our emotions and thereby counters doubt? Are there actions
to be taken that can strengthen the inner self's progress
toward faith? Ancient spiritual wisdom has always pointed to
the effectiveness of certain practices of penance and self-
purification, and the effort to change the desires of the heart
through cultivating detachment or through new attachments.
One seeks to purify and dispose oneself for higher and more
encompassing attachments; the effort is to try to detach
oneself from anything that may cloud the truth or get in the
way of progress. What in my life now impedes my desire to
move toward God's love and truth? What may be getting in
the way of someone who comes to take counsel with me?

Spiritual seekers from time immemorial have testified to
the fact that changing and simplifying certain parts of life help
a person to open up and see things more clearly in other parts
of their lives. Traditionally the demand was made for poverty,
chastity, and obedience as the great simplifiers and major
requirements for spiritual progress. Today, for the laity or
those engaged in the world, the required moves may be less
clearcut and more subtle. In most vocations persons must
spiritually progress through the affirmation of the world and
through loving commitments to spouse and family. This
means there is a need to strengthen our deepest desires for
greater commitment amid the distractions of irrelevant triv-
ialities.

Each of us must ask, What do I really want from God? To
make progress or cure doubts we may have to give up certain
kinds of slothful pastimes that draw us into things which we do

not really want to be doing. Certain social circles—or habits, such as endless consuming or procrastination—may make our inner and outer environment cluttered and confusing. Will I see more clearly if I give up alcohol or drugs that I imbibe in nondamaging amounts but that still serve as a screen from self-consciousness? Do I need more time for retreats, or do I need the sustained self-examination of therapy? The goal is not to overcontrol or do violence to the self but to use discipline to get in better psychological shape. Ascetic practices must serve the purpose of clearing the ground, making it more open to receive and give love.

Performing acts of love and hope also seems to be within the realm of will. One often has emotions that arise and overwhelm us in an uncontrollable way, but at other times we can control or deflect feelings through an inner conversation with ourselves or through willed deployments of attention. We can control attention and attention controls emotive feelings to a great extent. We are often able to initiate acts of love and affection, and to desire the good of others. Love begets more love. To love and to encourage and feed the fire of our love of God and humankind seems to help resolve our intellectual difficulties. Love helps the mind penetrate problems because with empathetic feelings of love we concentrate on the desired object, we pay attention and find it easy to persevere in efforts to understand. When we care, we will continue to wrestle with doubts without giving up.

The need to enlarge our hearts in the struggle with doubt is also behind the strategy of seeking counsel from those that we love and admire. We pay heartfelt attention to those whom we love and judge to be good. God usually leads us through persons. We learn from others by loving them and seeking to understand that which they love. The good and the wise person who is a loving person helps us resolve doubt because we try to perceive as they perceive; we also want to acquire whatever personal qualities they exhibit. The great souls who love much, inspire love and faith in others. Through the power of love persons are led from doubt to affirmation and to belief. A community of persons who inspire love and admiration is the most potent therapy for doubt.

On the road to Emmaus we have an example of Jesus counseling the doubtful. Jesus instructs the troubled disciples discouraged by the debacle of the crucifixion and the crash of their hopes for change. In an intellectual exchange he interprets and elucidates the Scriptures for them; he uses verbal cognitive instruction to make sense of their present situation. But he also reaches out to them in an affective way and induces such love that they press him to stay on with them. When he acts by breaking the bread and eating, the Lord is recognized fully. Of course, they say, did not our hearts burn within us when he counseled us? The power of intellect, love, and the communal act transform doubt into belief.

Newman, an acute philosopher of faith, spoke of differentiating a notional assent from a real assent to truth; the difference seems to be that when the affective and emotional capacity is fully integrated with the cognitive intellectual capacity, real assent occurs. As psychologists well know, without emotion and feeling integrated with an intellectual or verbal understanding, nothing is fully understood or grasped. Dissociated or verbal accounts or notional explanations can be given and make rational sense, but without the appropriate feelings, real understanding is missing. Psychopaths can verbally explain the moral rules, but they do not feel the moral emotions of guilt or empathy that produce moral behavior. A bereaved person can verbally describe a loss, but cannot really take it in until the appropriate emotions have been felt. So, too, we can intellectually explain doubts but we cannot really, deeply believe or be able to counsel another if we cut off emotion. Heart speaks to heart; the heart ensures good counsel.

FAILURE AND LIVING WITH CHRONIC DOUBT

Since our hearts are involved in efforts to counsel the doubtful, our failures inevitably produce pain. Jesus felt sad when the rich young man turned away; he was heartbroken by personal betrayal and rejection. The old-fashioned devotion to the sacred heart of Jesus acknowledges the importance of human emotions and the heartbreak that occurs when we fail to reach those we most love and care about. Often every effort to counsel the doubt of those most dear to us has been confounded. They do not respond. We must live with members of our families and with good friends who are alienated, doubting, and separated from the Church. In the old days leaving the Church was so traumatic that it was not as common as it is today. Now most families, and certainly all circles of friends, are full of those who are lapsed Catholics or Catholics by convention only. We live among chronic cases of doubt. After all our efforts have failed, how do we continue on?

Certainly we should never become defensive and separate ourselves from these doubtful persons that we love and hold in friendship. We have to avoid taking on the guise of true believers, complete with their angry and paranoid style. ("How dare you continue to doubt when I have given you my best conversion efforts? A plague on you, faithless one.!") Instead, we must stay calm and loving, continuing to talk about our own doubts and difficulties, never pretending that we are always full of certainty and assurance in order to set a good example. Being open about our own weaknesses and problems of our faith, being ironic and humorous about our faith, can keep us in touch with our own doubt and in touch with the doubtful. They must know that they are not that different from us in our own waverings and our own struggles.

But in the same way we should share our wonderful moments of certainty and happiness and joy when we feel that

God has been particularly good to us. Sometimes out of a kind of overdelicacy and discretion, believers who live with the chronically doubtful don't share their triumphs and happinesses in the faith, out of fear that it will look as though they are proselytizing or condescending to the other. A simpler, less self-conscious approach achieves a better balance. So maybe we have struggled over these questions in the past, but now I'm just going along and telling it like it is today, since this is too large a part of my life to keep in the closet.

But my openness and honesty must be above suspicion—even in my own mind. I should never be secretly plotting or calculating to convert or influence others. This kind of covert apostleship, often recommended by certain groups, such as Opus Dei, who talk of the apostleship of the luncheon table, seems repugnant in its deviousness. Christianity should be open, it should and must be transparent, liberating, and free. Needless to say, the secret manipulation of others through playing upon their irrational fears or desires is not true to God's example of loving friendship.

An attitude of respect and openness, for self and other, comes from a reverence for the varieties of individual spiritual journeys. God deals with everyone in unique ways and each person is different. What works for us and may be our way may not be the way of another. Convinced of our own uniqueness and trusting that God will help us through all our ups and downs, we can also let go, and trust that others will find their way. They are probably living as well as they can, hardly welcoming the doubt or the condition that they find themselves in. If they ever seek us out again for specific counsel, we are, of course, ready, but we don't push, coerce, or judge them to be inferior.

We can hope that those who doubt may someday believe, but our hope must spring from our perseverance in our own faith. Our main business is to live a life that day by ordinary day will witness to what we believe. Saint Paul talked about wives who sanctified and saved their husbands by their loving life in God. Parents, children, spouses, brothers, sisters, and friends can also hope that by their own perseverance and effort, their struggle to grow in love may help the beloved others who share one's life. Love overcomes all things, and God has eternity to work with. God wins, but we may not live to see it.

If and when we do see the doubtful ones return to strengthened faith, we are gloriously grateful and glad. The parable of the lost sheep is also psychologically true. But sometimes we have to be modestly, quietly, tactfully glad. We would not want to make certain sensitive prodigal sons feel guilty or bad or inferior to those who were more steadfast. We may consider steadfastness to be the most important of all virtues, the most needful thing for the service of God. But it is only through the grace of God that the steadfast stand, and continue to maintain their fidelity and equanimity. Of course if the prodigal son himself glories in the return and wishes to celebrate, then the feast can be readily joined. Such gladness is indeed a foretaste of the ultimate universal reconciliation we hope for in the marriage of the Lamb.

Doubts, trials, separations, and suffering test and prove our love. The best counsel we can give is to enlarge our hearts, seek God's wisdom, and live in the Spirit more completely. We, too, want to be able to say to the doubtful, come, come and see. God's power can transform us so that we, too, can give good counsel and our hearts pour forth living water.

4

TO COMFORT THE SORROWFUL

I will comfort you, as one is comforted by his mother. (Isaiah 66:33)

You now have sorrow; but I will see you once again and your hearts shall rejoice, and no man shall take your joy from you. (John 16:22)

CONFRONTING SUFFERING AND SORROW

To think about suffering is always difficult. We hate to suffer so much that the very thought arouses anxiety. We know that we should comfort the sorrowful if we are going to be Christians who imitate God's love and mercy, and part of us wants to do so, but still we shrink from the effort. As one young woman put it, "I always want to run away when I have to go to see someone who has lost someone they love." The urge to run away from suffering is a very basic human response.

We are ambivalent toward the sorrowful. A primitive superstitious fear whispers that we, too, may be drawn into the other person's suffering and be dragged down with them. Suffering seems to pollute and contaminate those unlucky ones singled out for misfortune; if we avoid them and turn away our face, perhaps we can avoid their fate. Irrationally we tell ourselves that if we can deny the reality of suffering then it won't have power over us. If one never goes to funerals or visits the sick in hospitals, and resolutely stays away from those having breakdowns, bankruptcies, divorces, or other crises, one may be spared similar evils.

As Americans we have other problems with suffering—especially suffering that cannot be rectified immediately. If we can do something about a problem we will readily wade in and work to fix things. But when we come up against sorrows that cannot be alleviated, they induce anxiety in a can-do people who insist on transforming the world rather than accepting fate. Our very virtues of optimistic activity often handicap us in the giving of comfort. Of course there are also more realistic problems inhibiting us from comforting the sorrowful. How can one do it adequately? Is it possible to find meaning in suffering?

The question of why so much human suffering exists, remains an inescapable problem for all believers in a benevolent all-powerful God. This difficulty has obsessed religious thinkers, at least since the writing of the Book of Job. Job's comforters did not do a very good job, but their mistaken and unsatisfactory efforts to explain and justify Job's condition with easy explanations of evil are still being handed out to those who mourn. But in reality, no simple approach can clarify the problem of suffering because it comes to human beings in so many varieties and forms, arising from so many different causes. Today some Christians have the opposite problem of Job's comforters: in a charitable age stressing the power of the external environment many find themselves unable to admit that some suffering is justly deserved and brought on by freely chosen wrongful acts.

Some sorrows being endured by a person are the direct consequences of the individual's free choice of evil. At times people actually receive immediate commensurate punishment in this life for the morally wrong choices that they make. The punishment fits the crime. There are cases where a person trying to harm and destroy an innocent person, instead brings about his or her own downfall. The movie villain in a car chase tries to kill the hero and rams his own car over the cliff. More common is the case of a person who, after leading others to take dangerous illegal drugs, suffers an overdose. How should a Christian respond to cases of justly deserved suffering? Should comfort be offered? Unfortunately these cases of just and appropriate consequences make up only a minuscule portion of the world's suffering.

More often we confront situations in which people err and do bad things but the consequences are disproportionate to the evil intent. Utter disasters often follow relatively minor acts of wrongdoing. A pilot is culpably careless and a plane full of people crashes. Someone sets a fire in frustration and anger but the fire spreads through a whole neighborhood and kills twenty persons. Drunk driving or engaging in sex outside marriage often produce terrible consequences far more serious than the bad motivation involved. Certain behavior that the culture condones as romantic or daringly rebellious can set off chain reactions. The suffering that ensues is not totally undeserved, but is disproportionate to the lapse or wrong committed and also is visited upon innocent bystanders. Much personal neurotic suffering from pride or wrong desires or inflated narcissism also falls into this category.

There exists also the huge amount of human suffering endured by completely innocent persons in totally unjust and unfair circumstances. There is no rational justification or explanation for most of the human suffering that we see in our world. In our lifetime we have seen several genocides destroy millions of innocent people: the Armenians, the Jews, the victims at Hiroshima, the Cambodians. Human inventiveness and technological mastery of nature have made human beings able to compete in destructiveness with monumental natural disasters. Worse still, the combined use of psychology and technology makes possible new forms of cruel and inhuman brainwashing and torture practiced in prisons all over the world. Weapons, terrorism, and open warfare become ever more cruel. Every time Beirut explodes or India riots we see again the sufferings imposed upon innocent victims.

Nature also regularly turns against human life in droughts, earthquakes, floods, tornadoes, volcanic eruptions, poisonous gas clouds, and tidal waves. Evil seems to exist in every form. Disease, viral illness, and genetic deformity inflict unjust suffering everywhere. Innocent children suffer because of their parents' neglect and active abuse in new and horrible ways. A disease such as AIDS, for instance, is bad enough in adults, but even more dreadful in an innocent child who is born facing a horrible and undeserved fate. Human suffering can take every shape and form, from natural disasters to the suffering of infants to the self-conscious pyschological suffering of highly sensitive individuals who may commit suicide out of depression. Confronting the human condition, many persons have despaired. How can one confront evil and still comfort the sorrowful?

We must look more closely at the psychology of suffering and the actual experience of individual persons. In acute attacks of grief and suffering, no matter what the cause or what the situation, pain seems to flood into or infuse personal private consciousness. One can feel one's self-awareness sinking into a sea of pain, either being immersed or experiencing the suffering in repeated waves. Whatever the cause, organic or psychological, human suffering quickly becomes an amalgam of physical and psychological distress. Mind and body can become one in pain, confirming that we are embodied beings. Suffering suffuses the person with its reality with only small bastions of resistance remaining as islands of high ground in a sea of distress. Mental and physical pain is acutely real, if hard to describe, and seems to throw us into a different subjective dimension of conscious reality. One can barely remember the other mode of being when immersed in a state of painful consciousness.

The subjectivity and unique experiencing of pain is important to remember. Suffering from something that is objectively or rationally unimportant can still be acutely painful and overwhelming to the person undergoing it. Taking the subjective psychological point of view seriously is a first requirement for those who wish to comfort another. An adult, for instance, has to understand that the child who is suffering, or the adolescent, or the neurotic, who is suffering over some objectively small matter, can be suffering as deeply as the strong adult broken by deep and dreadful tragic circumstances.

Suffering is also differentiated by whether it is sudden, acute, or an ongoing chronic state. The duration is important, particularly if a person is still in a state of shock. Confronting the unexpected takes its own mental adjustment. How is the person making sense of what is happening? Anyone who wishes to comfort the sorrowful has to think about how the person is interpreting the sorrowful experience. Does it seem unjust or unfair? Is the suffering seen as something unique to this particular individual or a part of the common tragic heritage of human beings? Is this suffering something that can be seen as temporary, or an irreversible tragic loss?

A particular individual may have to face a chronic condition in which his or her creativity and gifts are permanently thwarted by circumstances. We can suffer knowing that we have missed opportunities and will never be able to be as competent and creative as we could have been. Missed social opportunities may also produce isolation and loneliness. Many women and minority group members have seen their best talents wasted, through no fault of their own. Sorrows, of course, can also arise from the realization of things that were our fault—misspent years, wasted opportunities, or wrongs done to others. The sorrow arising from guilt and contrition can be oppressive. We can be forgiven by God, but often it is too late to make things right with those we have hurt. The death of our loved ones, especially deaths by suicide, produce painful losses, but can also possess an admixture of guilt. The unfinished business that we may have with another who has died adds to the complexity of the sorrow.

Then there is the pain and suffering that we experience from being actively hurt by others. Psychological sorrows arising from interpersonal conflict can be just as devastating as any larger social misfortune, or natural disaster. There is pain when one is misunderstood, ignored, or unappreciated. Struggles with those one respects and admires or loves hurt terribly. Perhaps the worst psychological suffering comes from a personal betrayal or when one is falsely accused by a beloved person. I have often thought that the greatest suffering that Jesus must have experienced was that of being betrayed and falsely accused. The rejection by those who should have appreciated him most would have been far more painful than persecution by the foreign Roman oppressors.

Sorrows between friends or colleagues or marriage partners can also arise when there is conflict and a divergence of beliefs. Good marriages may include acute moments of suffering, while bad marriages specialize in the high regularity of lower-grade miseries; since the general expectations, satisfactions, and love given are greater in good marriages, the painful hurts that do arise are more intensely disappointing. We are always more hurt by those with whom we have more in common, as demonstrated regularly in interreligious struggles, civil wars, and family struggles. Parents and children can hurt each other almost as deeply as beloved marital partners.

We also experience vicarious suffering for those we love and like. Watching others make mistakes or undergo trials when we cannot help them produces pain. Mary's suffering at the cross can be understood by every parent as an enactment of the worst the world can offer: helplessly watching a beloved child be tortured to death. At another extreme, others we love can torture us when they reject and turn against our expectations and hopes for their moral flourishing. We can be truly disillusioned and distressed by the downfall of those we admire. The concept of collective honor, or being dishonored by our own kin or clan or country is not now in vogue, but there can be a real distress suffered when one feels ashamed of one's own. This kind of sorrow becomes even deeper when a trust or common cause is betrayed. A grave public sorrow and shame can be felt over the wrongs committed by one's country or religious community or some other group with which one identifies.

Some psychologists have interpreted such public political sorrows to be in reality a screen or cover for some unacknowledged personal difficulty. This reductionism seems thoroughly misguided. While it is true that some very neurotic or even psychotic persons can latch on to public causes and distant problems as manifestations of their own illness, normal idealistic persons can be genuinely distressed over communal failures. Psychologists such as William James and Gordon Allport realized that the self extends its boundaries to identify with other people or ideals, so that larger groups and causes become an extension of the self. Those who truly identify with their country, religious group, profession, or institution can suffer when that group does not live up to its own standards.

Certainly the prophets of Israel suffered over the lapses of the people. And members of the affluent first world often feel deep shame and sorrow over what our country does or neglects to do. Anyone who lived through the Vietnam War or the Christmas bombing of Cambodia can remember the gloom that spread in our private and collective lives. So, too, the assassinations and riots in the 1960s engendered a public sorrow that those who loved their country could not shrug off. Many today suffer anxiety and near despair over the global threat of nuclear destruction and our country's part in maintaining the danger. Such sorrows are real and not a projection or symptom of personal neurosis.

The catalogue of the different forms of suffering and sorrow that exist pose for Christians a challenge that is nearly overwhelming. If we are to comfort the sorrowful we must recognize the extent and depth and differences that exist in the call. After confronting the range of sorrows we must ask what exactly we mean by comfort.

COMFORT

If suffering makes us anxious, the idea of comfort makes us uncomfortable. We are often uneasy at the thought that there is any comfort to be had; it seems a denial of the seriousness and sorrow that we experience in life. Surely, the bad news is the real news, and to believe in comfort is to succumb to the various opiates of the people, the pie-in-the-sky-when-you-die denial of the reality of evil and injustice. Is not gloom the mark of serious grownup persons who accept the sad reality of the universe? If we fully accept the sorrow and suffering of the world we should look with a steely eye on all attempts to comfort ourselves and others. Sophisticated wordly circles seem to cultivate agnosticism and a staunch stoicism at their best; at their worst, the reigning spirit of the world is one of sour cynicism.

Are we not better called to afflict the comfortable, rather than to comfort the afflicted? Certain persons courageously attempt to be prophets in their time: they exude despair and convince others of the seriousness of their purpose by their unrelieved pessimism and heavy, heavy concerns over the hypocrisy and sin of the world. Occasionally, the gloom and doom seem assigned by gender. While males despair, females offer hope and reassurance. The illusionless man journeys with the visionary maid—a perennial parable. Undoubtedly, comfort is seen as feminine because our first comfort comes from mother. Indeed, a certain level of comfort and hopeful cheerfulness is a characteristic of maternal thinking and practical nurturance; if it were not, no child would survive to become an adult.

Thus, comfort and comforting inevitably take us back to earlier dependence upon our mothers and caretakers. The comfort of touch, the comfort of love given physically, the comfort of our pleasure-giving bodily processes of eating and sleeping, are effective, early learned ways of comforting ourselves and others in distress. The joy of interpersonal attunement and emotional accord is also experienced between mother and child. Such affirmations of one's whole self may be reexperienced in adulthood in loving sexual intercourse. Sex is a comfort when all the different levels of personal being are engaged and give life to happiness. To love and be loved, with or without sexual expression, is the greatest comfort known to human beings. To be loved by those who are known and familiar, to be loved by one's own, adds to the comfort and joy. Familiar persons, routines, and places can affirm and establish the reality of the self, and so give comfort to a person torn apart by psychological distress and suffering.

It is also the case, somewhat paradoxically, that the new and unfamiliar can offer comfort. New experiences, new people, and travel have long been seen as ways to comfort a sorrowing person. As the common wisdom holds, new experiences take one out of one's self; when the self is miserable, novelty in the right dosage and context helps to turn attention outward. Work has always been known to be a comfort in the midst of sorrow, because carrying on with one's work and meeting one's obligations offer the consolation of familiar duty and providing new activities that distract.

Since we live complex lives and play many different roles, sometimes those in our more public or professional lives may not know of our private sufferings. Having to go to work and perform while one's heart is breaking can be a form of comfort, because one can become engrossed in meeting the task at hand and thus be temporarily distracted from sorrow. People mourning a parent can function when working among those who do not know of their loss, and someone in the midst of a divorce or family crisis can continue to find comfort in work. Waves of personal sorrow may well up again and again, but there are intervals when the distraction of the performance and role to be played can give some surcease. As someone very wise once said, to save face is to save oneself.

It is also fortunate that even in the midst of our deepest sorrows, when we have been absolutely devastated and are experiencing constant pain and anguish, we can know odd moments of happiness. Strange as it seems, one can laugh or joke in the midst of the deepest suffering—a form of wit aptly known as gallows humor. The humor, goodness, and beauty of life and other people seem able to peneterate every human hell and give flashes here and there of comfort. Human beings are an irrepressible species; this side of psychosis or coma, we display an innate predisposition to take comfort from anything at hand, no matter how horribly we are suffering. Something in us strives to reclaim and recover love and happiness.

Those who have gone through the worst sufferings that one can imagine—the suffering of persecution and betrayal, the agony of prison and concentration camps—have testified to the indestructibility of hope and moments of comfort. Even in the midst of hell, prisoners report taking comfort in the flight of a bird, the work of a spider, the beauty of a sunset—as well as the bravery and indestructibility of the human spirit. No matter how complete the suffering and hellish environment created by oppressors, some comforts and delight in the smallest of things seem impossible to suppress. The larger comforts of loving memories, thoughtful analysis, inner resources of cultural heritage, and religious faith also sustain persons under tortured conditions. If persons can be together in a company, then one will quickly see the resurrection of the comforts of communal life. In the Warsaw ghetto during the worst of the struggles, people still were able to play, celebrate, and engage in religious rites, taking comfort in life together.

The Christian injunction to comfort the sorrowful does not have to work against human nature; there is an innate predisposition to give and receive comfort. Empathy and sympathy are as natural to the human being as selfish survival instincts. Every viable culture reinforces and socializes the young to develop their natural aptitudes to give and take comfort. Thus one finds always and everywhere, customs, rituals, and rites designed to help those who would comfort the sorrowful. The collective institution of custom helps overcome the forces that may inhibit individuals from giving comfort. We know that to comfort another takes energy, attention, time, and effort—that is why it is a form of active love. And inertia, selfishness, and feelings of inadequacy are always present along with altruistic sympathy. Group customs tip the balance in favor of giving comfort by offering patterns to follow and inducing social pressure to overcome inhibitions.

Familiar rituals and formal rites can give great comfort in moments of deep sorrow. Funeral customs have always been an instance of the collective attempt to comfort those who mourn. Today in our pluralistic culture we have many and wide-ranging rites. One dreadful day in our town I went to two equally heartbreaking but very different funeral services. Both families had lost young adult sons, beautiful young men in the prime of their lives, through tragic senseless accidents. One funeral was a traditional Catholic mass with a large Italian family and the whole parish going through the old liturgical rites. The other memorial service was held at a mansion, now used as an educational center, and consisted of friends and family sitting in a living room, giving spontaneous remembrances of the young man and his life. The Catholic mass gave comfort through the familiar formal liturgy that incorporates death into the larger life of the Church and of Creation. The spontaneous informal memorial service gave comfort in the gathering of the company and the opportunity for the ongoing family and circle of friends to express support. Both spontaneity and formal rite were able to provide comfort for those with different temperaments and different belief systems.

Few successful efforts to comfort sorrow attempt to justify or explain the suffering. But at the same time some meaning is given to the sorrow. Why this suffering happened or had to be, is not a question that has to be addressed or fully answered before comforting. Something meaningful can be done about the suffering by offering social support in the present, and inducing hope for the future. Meaning can be discerned and suffering can begin to be transcended even when one recognizes that the suffering is totally unjust and unfair, and no possible explanation can make it right. As Jesus said when healing the man born blind, his blindness was not to be explained or justified by citing any past sin done by him or his parents; rather, the blindness served as an opportunity for the glory of the Lord to be made manifest. We give meaning to suffering by trying to alleviate it through healing love. Even our sufferings can be used for good, if we grow in love and good works.

Christians take comfort from the fact that God can give meaning to suffering by using it for the triumph of love and life. We cannot fully explain evil and suffering, but, by God, we know what to do with it. If we cannot prevent, alleviate, or heal human suffering, we can still triumph over suffering by using it to increase love and life in the world. With God's help we can imitate Jesus, who triumphed through the cross. We also take comfort from the fact that God as a innocent human being also suffered unjust torture and an unfair death as a failure. Jesus was not only tempted as we are, but he suffered as we suffer. We worship a God who understands the human agonies that we experience. The more sensitive the personality, and the more highly developed the self-awareness, the more a person can suffer; it then may well be the case that Jesus suffered more than any other human being ever has. But his suffering also was more triumphantly productive and meaningful than all others. What a comfort and joy it must be for the Lord to know that he has redeemed and liberated the world.

Traditionally, Christians have thought that they can share in the world's liberation by joining their own sufferings to Christ's redemptive suffering. Our greatest comfort and hope would be to see that the senseless human sufferings that cannot be prevented or healed, can still somehow be used by God. Nothing need ever be wasted or lost in Creation's great travail, the childbirth of the Kingdom. Saint Paul voices these ideas in his letters and sees his sufferings as having meaning; his present struggles will be joined with Christ's and so be used by God to work out the world's salvation. Jesus' words in the Gospel about taking up one's cross to follow him imply that our sufferings can be used, as his were, to bring life and love to the world.

Today some Catholic thinkers have tried to reinterpret the idea of redemptive suffering and the belief that the faithful can fill out Christ's suffering. They see a need to correct masochistic devotions of the past, with their exaggerated focus upon the cross, bloody sacrifice, and suffering. They feel the faithful were led to think that God wanted suffering in this life and did not want us to be healthy and happy; the victorious message of the Resurrection and Easter joy was obscured. Perhaps an imbalanced picture did exist in the past, in which the body, the self, the human will were seen solely as enemies of grace to be mortified, scourged, and abnegated. Christian humanism and love of the abundant life Jesus gives us in the present were overcome by a misguided glorification of failure, sacrificial pain, and the world to come.

But revisionists correcting past imbalances can go too far themselves. Christ's obedience unto the cross and his sacrifice is the way we are made one with God, and human suffering is still very much with us. While we realize that God wishes us all to be healthy, happy, and humanly fulfilled, we still have to cope with human suffering in all of its forms. The orthodox emphasis enables us to see meaning in our inevitable sorrows. It makes sense to believe in Christian hope, that God can use our suffering for the good of ourselves, our family, and our friends, and for the transformation of the world.

Our experiences confirm another unfashionable truth. We see that suffering can purify a personality, and can make a person finer, deeper, more understanding, and empathetic— as well as more merry! People full of joy and gratitude often are the same people who have known deep sorrow. There is an old idea that suffering carves out the depths of a personality so that more joy and deeper delights can be contained. At least those who have never suffered often appear superficial, blank, bland, weakened, and out of touch with the human condition. It seems true that "that which does not kill me makes me stronger," as Nietzsche said.

Those who have suffered also appear more driven to struggle against human suffering, having actually known its sting. Admittedly, too much, too early, and too prolonged experiences of suffering can stunt or destroy a person, but when suffering is transcended, it serves to deepen and connect us with our fellow human beings. Sorrow produces a profound need for comfort and it can bring the sufferer closer to God as Mother. Suffering can be turned into a positive impetus for spiritual progress. But to tell a person in sorrow what we have experienced of the long-term uses of suffering is no way to offer comfort. We comfort others in the immediate present by trying to relieve suffering and effect healing, thereby imitating the divine comforter.

Jesus tenderly comforted and healed human beings whenever he could. He desired to comfort more completely the people of Jerusalem, as a mother hen shelters her chicks under her wing. He loved his own, his friends and his people, and he tried to comfort them in the face of death, illness, and other distress. He is shown on the cross comforting those sharing his fate and comforting his mother and beloved disciple. Jesus incarnates the God who in Scripture is shown comforting his people over and over—a bruised reed I will not break nor a flickering wick extinguish. From the beginning to the end God is seen as the great comforter and savior, giving meaning and love's reassurance. God does rescue us from the depths and comforts us in every affliction. In the ultimate Kingdom, God will wipe away every tear, there shall be no more death, no more mourning and sadness. When people say religion is a great comfort to them, they are echoing the testimony of their hearts.

So many times when we go to Mass troubled, sorely beset, and distressed in sorrow, we return home comforted and strengthened. We are comforted by the promise of justice and eternal life in the liturgy, by contemplation of God's goodness and desires for us to be happy, and by the presence of our fellow Christians all struggling on their own journeys, all eating together the bread of life. To comfort also means "to give strength," and worship and prayer do renew us for the daily struggle. Whatever the trouble, whatever the distress, worship, prayer, and fellowship help make it better. We immerse ourselves in an alternate reality where love reigns supreme and we rise up refreshed. A child aroused from the power of a nightmare can be comforted by prolonged reassurances and a walk with a parent around the lighted house— it takes time to reestablish in the consciousness the dominance of the safe daytime world. In the same way, worship reawakens us to God's maternal reality and reassurance.

It is appropriate that adoration of Mary as Mother and the various Marian devotions have long been a comfort for so many Catholics. When God as Mother is obscured by God as avenging Judge, Mary's role reminds us of the maternal love in God's care for us. The wonderful Marian prayers are all prayers that comfort. The repetition, the invocations, the

assurances, the cries to our mother, induce the early dependence and experience of maternal comfort that we remember.
We need such constant reminding because it is always supremely difficult, as John says, to "put our faith in God's love
toward ourselves," and realize the comforting truth that God
is love.

Those strengthened and comforted in the assurance of
God's love are best able to give love and comfort to others in
sorrow. Once again the way we deal with ourselves and God is
entwined with the way we deal with others. One has to be
comfortable to give comfort. When we have been comforted
and have survived our sorrow, we are better able to comfort.
Comfort and joy are the sign of the Spirit's presence and God
as Comforter can give us the heart and power to comfort
others. Love is the motive, love is the message, and love is the
means by which we comfort. The great lovers and saints that
have gone before us have been wonderfully comforting. When
we consider ways to comfort we can look to their example and
to our own experiences.

HOW TO COMFORT

This is perhaps the only case where angels rush in and fools
fear to tread. We should throw ourselves into situations where
the sorrowrful need comfort and try to overcome our hesitan-
cies and our tendency to shrink from the demands of empathy.

We can find many excuses not to offer comfort. Perhaps we
even think of blaming the victim, so that through internal
debate and procrastination the moment passes and we end up
not even trying to offer comfort. Perhaps we should not in-
trude, we tell ourselves, surely there are other people who are
closer than we are. What can we possibly do to help? Won't it
seem intrusive or emotionally false? Of course, if in reality by
some quirk of fate we find that we are not able to help, we can
quickly fade away. Most often our efforts will be welcomed

and appreciated. Each of us can remember, and will remember forever, how good others were when we were comforted in a time of sorrow.

There are times of crises and sorrow when stoic pride, self-reliance, and our horror at being an object of pity no longer matter. Once we have overcome such culturally conditioned feelings and been comforted we can believe that others will welcome our efforts rather than remaining in their isolation. Pride and desires for privacy are better reserved for happy times. After we have been through the mill of life a few times we come to cherish human comfort and realize that strength also lies in being vulnerable, being able gratefully to accept help from others. After receiving comfort we become better at giving it. We learn what works and what doesn't.

The most important thing in giving comfort is to pay attention to the other person. We must enter into the other's inner state and try to grasp his or her experience of sorrow. What feelings, thoughts, and interpretations exist in the other's unique situation? Empathy is a form of reaching out and entering the experience of another person; to really listen and extend one's self takes sustained attention and emotional energy. But when true empathy is achieved, it is wonderfully comforting for the person in pain to know that another person is sharing their inner state. The ability to connect, and to see another through, begins with the ability to reach out and become attuned to the other person.

Mothers seem to attune themselves automatically to their infants. This emotional or affective attunement has been newly studied in developmental psychology and observed to take place in many ways. The mother can show that she is tuned into the inner feelings and emotions of her infant by gesture, rhythmic movements, words, or tone of voice. The message is conveyed that mother understands. When a mother does this as her part in an ongoing dialogue, the infant realizes that another self exists out there and can even share one's inner experience. The infant's sense of inner self is confirmed. The mother's response says, I am here too, I read you, I know how you feel. After this meeting of two selves, a mother may be able to move the dialogue on to other meanings or to different feelings. If the original emotions were sad or fearful, a mother can meet them, confirm her infant's experience, and move on to comfort.

In the same way we must use maternal sensitivity and affective attunement to comfort the sorrowful. One must enter into the person's sad state, attune oneself to their unique experience, slow down, be sorrowful as they are sorrowful. When an insensitive person cannot do this and brusquely insists on dismissing the pain, or puts it aside too quickly with an instant fix, the suffering person is affronted by the lack of understanding. A comforter can only begin to help after he or she has been sufficiently attuned to another's experience. Please, don't do something, just stand there—empathetic presence is what is most needed.

A comforter also has to listen with great attention to understand what is going on in the self's inner dialogue of interpreting and explaining the pain. Perhaps a person is fully in touch with reality and the comforter can simply affirm their interpretation and evaluation of what is happening to them. But perhaps a person is excessively guilty, angry, or despairing, or is projecting in some distorted way. If a comforter can see that a person's explanatory self-dialogue is not in accord with reality, it is part of the comforting role to slowly and gently offer a corrective. Otherwise, sufferers may continue to blame themselves or perpetuate destructive self-imprisonments in illusion. Iron bars do not a prison make, but the mind can thoroughly entrap and cement suffering into a person's inner world.

Of course in offering one's view of reality one also has to be aware of what another person can accept. Again one has to be innocent as a dove and subtle as a serpent. To tell an unbeliever that their suffering can be joined to Christ's redemption of the world, would be stupid as well as intrusively offensive. All effective therapy must be built slowly on what a person can understand at the time and what will reach them where they are. It is always a circular process. One's cognitive interpretations will shape the emotions one feels, and emotional feelings of love and trust will help suffering persons attend to new and less distorted views of reality. Insight therapies, rational-emotive therapies, cognitive therapies, or reframing approaches, relieve suffering by changing the explanations and world view that a person holds. Christians do the same, as do all those persons who have the gift of good counsel.

Perhaps we learn most of our lessons about comforting the sorrowful from our own experiences of tragedy. While one has many experiences over a lifetime there is often a critical incident that makes the most impression. I learned most about comforting those in pain twenty-seven years ago, when the sudden infant death of our fourth son catapulted our young family into crisis and grief. One minute I was a happy nursing mother, with four children, contentedly celebrating my birthday (ironically the feast day of Saint Colette the patron saint of mortally ill infants as well as of Felicity and Perpetua the martyred young mothers). Suddenly, within minutes, I was a grief-stricken young mother streaming tears and milk, in the throes of agony, panic, guilt, and near despair. This searing experience of sudden loss and devastation taught me a great deal.

Some persons we knew were so pained and upset that they could say nothing and so avoided us out of dread of doing or saying the wrong thing. The most successful comforters came and stayed and did not try to explain or justify or interpret, they were simply present to offer love and support. One wonderful woman, the mother of six children herself, heard the news, called a baby-sitter, called a taxi, and came immediately to our house. To grieve together, to share, and to feel the support of friends and neighbors mean everything in a crisis. People also used all the tried-and-true nonverbal ways of giving comfort, bringing food, sending flowers, arranging a funeral mass.

Two thoughtful women friends came and took down the crib and took away all the baby clothes and furniture. Unfortunately, they missed the baby food still in the icebox, nor could anything be done to stem the flow of milk or tears. Wave upon wave of pain overwhelm those who grieve; how much mourning and weeping there is in this valley of tears. Those people who are not upset by a person crying are by far the most comforting: friends who could face death and sorrow as a part of life that can be talked about, were able to talk to me. The priest who came was wonderful in the sense that he was comfortable enough with death to be able to talk about it and give comfort. As fellow Catholics we could affirm some meaning in offering up one's suffering as a sacrifice. Belief in the Resurrection means that death and the desolation of separation cannot be seen as final. Faith does not make the pain less, but it does stave off despair, self-pity, and the temptation to give up on life.

How our family and community rallied to support us! Although everyone who mourns can at times become annoyed at the inadequacy of efforts to relieve pain, still the main response has to be overwhelming gratitude. The horror of being pitied, in need, struck down, and no longer self-sufficient, quickly gave way to thankfulness for the offering of so much love and support. My husband and I clung together along with our three remaining children, all under five. My friends stayed with me for days and suffered through the repetitive compulsion accompanying all traumas, going over and over the circumstances in an effort to finally accept and master what happened. Even my awesome Uncle Tom, a general, wrote an emotional and loving letter. (One is always surprised by the resources people display in a crisis.) He sounded a resurrection theme as old as David's cry in the Old Testament; when David lost his infant son, he voiced his hope that he would go to him and once more see him again after death. Having lost a child makes one sensitive to all similar losses, in the news, among one's friends and family, in Scripture, in literature. Suffering always sensitizes us to similar events. One also takes renewed comfort in the promise that in the future Kingdom of God, there will be no death of infants, and every tear will be wiped away. The belief in immortality and heaven is important for those who lose their loved ones. It is central to our faith to know that our God loves his own and would never leave us alone and lonely.

I also learned how not to comfort by experiencing the unwitting pain that some persons caused when they tried to be consoling. One person did not help when she said that maybe it was better for the baby to die now, since he might have died in an automobile crash as a teenager. The well-meaning lady who said that all infants would be twenty-eight in heaven, seemed in her certitude about the afterlife to be less than reassuring. Nor should we ever tell a sufferer that a disaster is God's will, for who can know? And though it is true that time will heal, no one should be told that at a time of crisis. I have learned never to talk about what might have been or what might be in the future when trying to comfort another's sorrow. Nor should comparisons to other sorrows be offered. An overwhelming situation which brings a person suffering is so present, so uniquely personal, so suffusing of consciousness, that any talk of what might have been, what will be, or what others have suffered can only be seen as a denial and rejection of what is. Even knowing that time does heal and that one will someday recover does not much mitigate present suffering.

It is also important not to cut off one's grieving prematurely. In misguided efforts to be stoic and have faith triumph over misfortune persons can be left with unresolved sadness. I can see now that I should have grieved more and allowed myself to be comforted even more. But as a young person who had mostly experienced triumphs in life, I did not know that one has to thoroughly immerse oneself in a grief and mourn enough to leave a sorrow behind. Nowadays when parents lose children, they are allowed to see and touch and hold the child's body in fully experienced acts of grieving. We have learned a great deal about the pyschology of mourning and grief. Healing takes more time than I allowed. In the past there was an element of trying to deny and undo what happened by prematurely getting up and getting on with life.

Lack of psychological understanding—and a false sense of stoicism, heroism, and the need to be strong—can keep many people from seeking the help that they need to recover thoroughly. Many conscientious souls cannot help but experience a deep sense of guilt for having failed to avert their misfortune. It is far too easy with little-understood and rare occurrences to sink into irrational orgies of self-blame. The residual irrational guilts which many of us carry over from earlier times of our life, can make the comforting of sorrow much more complicated. One has to pay close attention to the inner explanations that a person gives for what has happened. Comforting must always be attuned to external reality as well as the other person's inner state.

A POSTSCRIPT ON OVERCOMFORTING

What if a person brings suffering upon themselves, so that in any moral accounting they deserve the suffering that they experience? What then? Can there be exceptions to our mandate to comfort the sorrowful? Perhaps there are times when the most loving action would be to refrain from attempting to alleviate sorrow; there seem to be cases in which one should not rush to offer comfort. We hear a great deal today about infantilization, overnurturing, enabling, and the necessity of confrontation and tough love. The contention is that you can in reality harm people if you don't let them suffer the consequences of their bad behavior and thereby learn that they can and must help themselves. It seems true that there can be times when someone is suffering good guilt or true remorse, and to try to alleviate their immediate pain would be counterproductive for them in the long run. They may need the pain to be in touch with reality, and to be induced to change and amend their life. The prodigal son suffered in many instructive ways before he came to his senses and decided to return home and restore his life to happiness.

The need to suffer valid consequences is emphasized in much of the self-help and how-to-help-others literature. The philosophy of Alcoholics Anonymous and the books for women who love too much are examples of this message. Many other books on dealing with people with drug problems or coping with rebellious adolescents have talked of reality therapy and learning to give tough love. Tough love is based on letting people grow up and take responsibility for the real consequences of their own behavior. Many people have always had persons who have protected and enabled them to keep on hurting and harming themselves and others. The overnurturing parent, spouse, or employer constantly assumes responsibility and shelters the guilty or sick person from the consequences of his or her behavior.

The suffering and sorrow necessary to learn responsibility or to be impelled to seek help, may never be fully experienced or confronted. A delinquent child, drug addict, or abusing spouse is never forced to learn what other people have learned. Ironically, a nurturing caretaker's natural urge to rescue can become an impediment to wise nurture. A rescue fantasy, or a desire to excise another's pain once it has become too much for us to bear, can sometimes impel us to do over-protective things that enable the other person to continue on a self-destructive course. In these situations a person who truly loves another has to be strong enough to allow another's pain and sorrow to be experienced. Comfort would be only false comfort.

One other exception to the mandate to comfort arises when someone uses unhappiness and sorrow to hide from other emotions. Sometimes depression, sorrow, and a sense of failure serve a hidden purpose in an individual's life. There is a need to be unhappy, a need for failure, and a clinging to sorrow so that one will not have to face other aspects of one's life, such as justifiable anger, fear of success, or a drive to achieve more. Any number of things can be hidden: the fear of being envied, the fear of living more fully and joyously, and so on. Psychologists have found that sorrow is used often as a self-defeating strategy and is quite different from the way it may appear on the surface. In such cases to comfort the sorrower and not see the other underlying factors would be to support the stunting of a person instead of challenging them to grow in a new way.

Fairly subtle problems of discernment can arise. Confronted with a person's suffering, we must ask whether this is a case where the sorrow should be challenged or unmasked? Is this a sorrow that needs to be felt and experienced in order for the person to grow up and mature? Or is this a sorrow that comes to all people, could never be avoided, and should simply be comforted as an act of love for another? As always in trying to love wisely, one has to discern by careful attention and listening exactly to what is happening in a person's inner life. Sometimes the very best thing one can do for others is to challenge them or help them let their sorrow go. Sometimes the best thing that one can do for others is to let them truly sorrow and grieve. They may need to allow themselves to fully experience the pain for the first time in an extended way.

Such problems of discernment will never be solved easily.

One guide may be how much someone can do on their own about reversing the situation or the events that are creating their sorrow. Some things can simply never be undone. Those people who have done horrible deeds and are sorrowing, or those people who have brought upon themselves dreadful fates, should be fully sympathized with and comforted when they repent. In the end one looks to the example of God and Jesus, who seem to reach out to everyone good, bad, or indifferent and offer love and comfort. Perhaps we should always err when in doubt on the side of offering as much comfort and love as we can. In our individualistic selfish culture we should probably take our chances with offering comfort until we have clear evidence that it is harming another. After all the God whose love we seek to imitate never fails and constantly goes beyond reasonable bounds in loving us.

In the end the greatest comfort is knowing that no matter what, God loves us. As Saint Paul says the one thing certain is that nothing can separate us from the love of Christ. A true comforter will offer love in a thousand different ways, over and over, with subtlety and finesse. Love provides the ultimate meaning of life and if we cannot understand why or how things are working out, we can understand what it is to be loved. Some of the greatest mystics have repeated over and over very simple words of comfort. Dame Julian of Norwich constantly reminds us, "All will be well, all will be well." She invokes Christ as mother and reassures us of God's maternal care. If we are truly loved everything can be borne.

5

TO BEAR WRONGS
PATIENTLY

*If you put up with suffering for doing what is right, this is
acceptable in God's eyes. It was for this you were called, since
Christ suffered for you in just this way and left you an example, to have you follow in his footsteps. He did no wrong; no
deceit was found in his mouth. When he was insulted he
returned no insult. When he was made to suffer, he did not
counter with threats. Instead, he delivered himself up to the
One who judges justly. (1 Peter 2:20–25)*

To bear wrongs patiently. In an age of liberation movements,
revolution, and assertiveness training this work of mercy
makes us wince at its apparent endorsement of fatalism and
masochism. Have not generations of the poor and oppressed
been kept down and made submissive by the idea that they
should bear wrongs patiently? Today, we do not see patience
as a virtue; it is impossible to imagine parents naming their
daughter Patience in admiration of the attitude. Patience now
is equated more often with passivity and long-suffering, an
undesirable condition to be overcome.

Part of our problem with patience may stem from our
American spirit. America has always been the land of ideal
supermen who run faster than a speeding bullet. We are the
people who wish to hurry up everything and provide instant
relief, in medication, in fast food, in the fast-track career. At
the same time we are programmed *not* to stand for wrongs, or
as one state motto warns, "Don't Tread on Me." If you do, you
will be instantly sorry. We won't tolerate delay, obstacles, or
oppression—"Give me liberty or give me death," right this

second. We believe that the impossible can only take a little longer; individual liberty and rights to self-defense (enabled by the possession of guns) are our paramount values. This American cultural conditioning makes it difficult for us to relate to spiritual counsels commending patience.

Feminists, blacks, American Indians, and other oppressed groups have also balked at traditional spiritual interpretations of the need for patience. Accepting suffering and injustice in the name of love has been labeled the "Uncle Tom response" that holds back liberation movements. Induced female masochism has been seen as a chief obstacle to women's progress. Indeed, masochism is much on our mind these days and has long since escaped its narrower meaning connected with sexuality. Masochism in its general cultural form applies to persons who are apathetic, resigned to suffering, and expect poor treatment from others. Their self-defeating behavior correlates with a low sense of self-worth, an inadequate sense of personal rights, and a lack of hope that things can change for the better. Who am I to deserve more or make waves? I am doomed to suffer, and besides, as a suffering victim, I may be able to garner some psychological advantages for myself, or at least avoid danger.

Self-defeating behavior can become a way of life. The martyred, long-suffering mother, the put-upon wife, the overburdened worker or middle manager—even male versions are available. Psychoanalysts have described lives in which a person manifests a persistent need for failure or the idealization of unhappiness. One can observe regularly the puzzling cases of the competent persons who, despite their innate capacity, can never quite make it and who repeatedly self-destruct, snatching defeat after defeat from the jaws of victory. An unconscious or preconscious program or script appears to have been established in early life such that unhappiness and defeat appear psychologically necessary for safety and security. Success, happiness, or victory may have become identified as dangerous for unconscious reasons—fears of provoking retaliatory jealousies or losing love, and guilt over outshining one's parental figures. Only personal defeat, suffering, and inhibition feel safe.

In self-deprecating long-suffering, a person defensively adopts the habit of abnegation. Is this psychological condition the same as bearing wrongs patiently? No; neither masochism nor fatal resignation are meant when Christians speak of bearing wrongs patiently. Christians believe that fatalism can be fatal, indeed a form of despair. When one gives up hope, self-respect, and a sense of internal agency, one gives up the struggle to change. We cannot make the Kingdom come when we have become resigned to suffering and think that nothing we can do will make any difference. We need to reconsider patience, and rethink what it means to bear wrongs patiently. How is this activity related to love? What is patience? What are wrongs?

WRONGS

What are wrongs? How does a wrong differ from injuries or from sins, the other negative things that we must cope with in the traditional list of the spiritual works of mercy. As compared to injury or sin, a wrong seems more general, less specific, less intentional, less often directed with premeditated malice toward a particular individual. The time framework is also different, in that wrongs often are long-term chronic conditions as compared to acute attacks or brief episodes. A wrong is more socially institutionalized and impersonal. Wrongs are definitely immoral and unethical in the sense that the innocent suffer, but they lack the characteristic of specific injury or specific intentional rejections of God through consciously evil action. Things should be otherwise, should be just—some things are unfair, unjust, terrible—but wrongs seem less personal than either sin or injuries.

Examples of wrongs to bear might include prejudice against one's race, sex, religion, age, class, or condition. To be subject to dislike as a member of a stigmatized group would be an example of a wrong or violation of justice. This wrong would not be directed at oneself specifically but would be a form of structural social oppression. We can think of many wrongs that exist even in our relatively free American society. To be old and denigrated is certainly one wrong that many in the society can look forward to. To be poor, homeless, or deprived of health care or other basic needs and rights is also a wrong. Other wrongs one might have to cope with include being imprisoned wrongfully, being dismissed from a job unjustly, and being wronged in some other transaction with the world or social system. Wrongs and injustice also arise from human errors, flaws, and failings.

Wrongs do not include acts of nature such as earthquakes, floods, or disease. One could not say that one has been wronged by an earthquake or pneumonia. Of course if one has intentionally been given a disease, such as AIDS, by someone who through deception spread the infection, then one could consider the suffering incurred as a wrong. Wrongs are essentially social betrayals and failings toward an individual, infringments upon justice, equality, and human dignity. In countries where one can be arrested, imprisoned, or tortured without recourse to the law there are, of course, many more wrongs to be borne. We are indeed fortunate to live in a society that does not require most of us to bear as much injustice as most people have had to bear.

But, say the skeptics, America is a land in which justice more or less prevails because Americans have never accepted the counsel that we should accept wrongs patiently. Have we not always taken arms against a sea of troubles, with the firm conviction that we could overcome difficulty and injustice through effort. The idea that God helps those who help themselves and that human beings can solve their own problems, has been at the root of our satisfactory condition of life. We have always been willing to fight for our rights. Not for us the sentimental glorification of suffering, or the excusing of failure and retreat! We are the can-do people who will try ever harder when an obstacle or wrong is in our way.

BEARING WRONGS

But does *bearing a wrong* mean passively accepting the wrong? Not when we pay attention to the meaning of *to bear*. To bear means "to support and move, to carry, to sustain, to hold up, conduct oneself in a given manner," and, of course, it also means "to produce a child." These are all intensely active human functions. Bearing is not passive after all; weak delicate persons given to apathy or masochism cannot bear up, cannot bear down, cannot bear much of anything. Other active meanings of bear are "to exercise as a power" and "to assume something." All of these activities take strength and depths of human resources. The power to sustain something, assume something, or bring something forth, requires strength and courage. This has nothing to do with fatalism or passive submission.

Once we see that bearing is an active exercise of power, we can begin to understand what we are called to do in this spiritual work of mercy. To bear wrongs patiently is an active enabling form of love and power. It is having the firmness to hold ourselves and others up, through strain, stress, and evil times, without causing more suffering and evil. One can best see this spiritual work of mercy as a call for toughness, strength of will, and strength of purpose. It is a display of firmness and fortitude rather than weakness. Is one strong enough to bear trials, to bear up when things are not working out, when things are not going one's way, when one is being oppressed or having to suffer unmerited wrongs? Passive, weak persons faced with difficulties either collapse or are driven to violent outbursts in which the wrong done them is taken out on others. Self-pity and tantrums, including the tantrums of sullen silence, are often the reaction of the childishly immature. They pass on their distress to others, often with violent abuse, and thereby multiply injustice, escalate misfortune, and magnify the amount of suffering and evil in the world.

How well one bears the wrongs one encounters in life is a true test of strength of character. Some wrong will have to be faced by almost everyone, since injustice is inherent in the disorder of the present world. If we cannot bear wrongs with fortitude, we fail in our responsiblity toward those with whom we live. Everyone knows those who cannot bear stress, who cannot cope when obstacles or problems arise. Often they are people who have never had to struggle before, or people who, despite superficial indulgences, seem not to have gotten enough love or discipline.

A person needs past experience in coping in order to be able to cope when injustice or wrongs are encountered later. This aptitude seems to have less to do with physical health or strength than with psychological attitude. A certain humility, gratitude, and sense of reality is needed. When one is still a childish, self-engrossed, narcissistic person, one demands that the world conform to one's whims and wishes. Everything one encounters should be fair, just, comfortable, and instantly solvable. When reality does not oblige, the immature person disintegrates. Or alternatively, a person who has struggled to succeed, can become gradually corrupted by power, comfort, and flattery so that he or she falls into narcissistic expectation of omnipotence. A person with power can begin to ignore reality and the needs of others, slowly regressing to infancy over the course of four or five decades. Psychological strength is revealed by how well a person is able to cope over the long haul.

It is instructive to look at extreme cases in which people have had to bear wrongs, cases all too prevalent in our modern era of concentration camps, preventive detention, disappearances, and torture. Victor Frankl, the noted psychologist who was incarcerated in the Nazi concentration camps during the Second World War, was one of the first to draw pertinent pyschological and spiritual conclusions from his observation of individuals in extreme situations. He saw that persons react to stress and persecution partly in common patterns determined by the horrible situation; but, more crucially, their behavior was also partly determined by their individual character. Some people were not able to cope, or bear up under the pressure. They broke down morally, spiritually, and physically. Others mustered the strength to keep their humanity alive in the grim situation, while still others were truly heroic. As Frankl reflects, "It becomes clear that the sort of person the prisoner became was the result of an inner decision, and not the result of camp influences alone." There were always decisions to be made:

"Every hour offered the opportunity to make a decision, a decision which determined whether you would or would not submit to those powers which threatened to rob you of your very self, your inner freedom: which determined whether or not you would become the plaything of circumstance, renouncing freedom and dignity to become molded into the form of a typical inmate."*

Personal attitude makes the difference in situations of stress. Wrongs that we encounter will offer this test, this challenge of whether we will be conformed to the world or will be able to overcome through our inner resistance. We

Man's Search for Meaning (New York: Simon & Schuster, 1963), p. 104.

bear up and sustain and carry wrongs because we believe with Frankl that "man can preserve a vestige of spiritual freedom, of independence of mind even in such terrible conditions of psychic and physical stress." The poeple who have experienced the worst demonstrate that "everything can be taken from a man but one thing: the last of the human freedoms—to choose one's attitude in any given set of circumstances, to choose one's own way." When people give up choosing, give up hope, they can no longer cope psychologically, nor long survive physically.

Despair is born in many ways. One of the most insidious ways is through acquiescence in one's mind to the claims and world view of those who inflict the wrongs. To be persuaded by and accept the viewpoint of one's oppressors or torturers, to give up one's inner moral and spiritual resistance to evil, breaks the human spirit. As one young woman poet writes of her struggle to resist the guards in her Siberian prison, "Well, we'll live as the soul directs, not asking for other bread." If one begins to inwardly accede to evil, if one becomes callous to the wrongs inflicted upon oneself and others, then the oppressor has won a convert to their system of injustice and immorality. In the Gulag prisons, as the young poet proclaims, it is "the best in all the world, the most tender, who don't break." Their virtue, tenderness, and alertness to the unjust wrongs being inflicted upon the innocent, help them withstand torture and bear wrongs without succumbing. Those who harden break because they no longer care enough to nurture and support themselves or other sufferers.

It is important to remember that Christians, knowing that they are made in God's image and redeemed at great cost, are instructed to admonish sinners and to struggle as in childbirth so that God's love and justice can be born in the creation. However it is obvious that success can never be achieved instantly. Before the final victory one must be able to bear the wrongs that still exist in the midst of the struggle. This is true in the political communities and the larger social groups in which we live, and it is also true as we struggle and work out our salvation together in family and personal life. It is essential to get the right balance.

One must bear wrongs patiently while at the same time admonishing, resisting, and working to right the wrongs. Bearing wrongs patiently is not an instance of religion serving as the opiate of the people, or pie in the sky when you die. It has nothing to do with a pietism that retreats from the world in order to avoid conflict. In fact the spiritual resistance to injustice may precipitate or increase conflict: struggles to overcome evil with good are not compatible with certain gnostic approaches to life in which evil is thought not to exist and wrongs suffered are only an illusion. In the tradition of the Old Testament prophets, we must accept the presence of evil and recognize injustice before we can bear it or initiate change.

A belief that the status quo represents a just world has been seen by psychologists as the royal road to blaming victims and abdicating social responsibility. Since there is something in us that wants the world to be just, the temptation is always there to believe that the world is just. If the world were just, the victors would deserve their spoils and the losers would deserve what they get. When persons believe this it meets all sorts of psychological needs. If victims have somehow brought suffering on themselves, our responsibility to help them is lessened. The rest of us in a just world can also more easily deny that we, too, could be victimized. This belief serves as a protection against accepting the irrationality and injustice that exist in life. How upsetting it is to realize the truth that good people have terrible things happen to them that they certainly never deserved.

To face the disorder of the world produces deep anxiety. We try to deny it. But the counsel to bear wrongs patiently helps break through our denials by reiterating and reminding us that wrongs do exist and that the innocent and righteous suffer. We belong to the human community who endure unmerited wrongs. We cannot avoid it, nor separate ourselves from the unlucky persons who suffer.

PATIENCE

Patience is an active exercise of power. Patience is to be expectant, to act strongly without complaint, to act with equanimity. It is the ability to continue efforts undisturbed by obstacles, delays, or the temptation to quit. Perseverance and patience are related. To expect that victory and success will come in the long run is the basis of patience and perseverance. And perseverance, as Saint Paul points out, brings hope. The activity of *keeping on* keeping on produces the change in viewpoint. One's own activity reveals to oneself and others that activity is possible. Each step that one takes changes one's position in the world.

One is patient because one believes in the future and in the ultimate victory of good. As Christ was sure of God, the One who judges justly, he could return good for evil. The ultimate triumph of justice means that one can be patient as one makes interim efforts. As Saint Teresa of Avila said, "Patience obtains all . . . all things pass, God alone suffices." When we look at the patience of the saints imitating the patience displayed by Jesus, who bore his wrongs with calmness, equanimity, and courage, we see that they were all able to act in this way because of their utter confidence in the ultimate outcome and victory. God's will *will* be done, justice *will* come. In the end all wrongs will be righted by God's power. This belief that the Kingdom will triumph and that in the end a new Jerusalem will be created gives the assurance and power to bear wrongs in the present with patience.

Victor Frankl also observed that only those people who were able to discern meaning in their suffering and thus sustain hope were able to bear wrongs patiently. To see meaning in their suffering meant that they could bear it without despair. Christians are not the only ones who have had the ability to be patient and bear wrongs; other believers have also been certain of meaning in life. Marxists and communists, for instance, have seen themselves contributing to the inevitable forces of history—and they, too, held up well in concentration camps. All believers in transcendent meaning are given strength in the present by their belief in ultimate spiritual vindication. The American Indians who could sing their victory songs while being tortured were as great a witness to the psychology of conviction as were the Jesuit martyrs whom the Indians tortured. Both groups believed that their courage was not wasted.

The conviction that suffering is not wasted helps us to act bravely and bear wrongs patiently. The ultimate despair in the modern world arises from the fact that nothing seems to have meaning when "the best have lost all conviction." Then the wrongs that we suffer are simply random occurrences in a chaotic world that has no purpose and no connection with ultimate values. This lack of meaning leads to the collapse of young persons and adolescents who so often commit suicide in the midst of material abundance. They have no sense of meaning, no sense that the wrongs they must bear might have a connection to the rest of the universe. Without a hope that God can use their suffering in some way or that they can transcend this suffering or that ultimately the forces of right will triumph, they despair and end their lives. It's also important to note that few children today are ever instructed in the virtue of patience. In a world in which immediate satisfaction is touted (go for it, and so on), where would one find a model of patience that would be admirable to a young person?

With patience we can work to right wrongs, but we know that it cannot happen immediately. Even Christians confident of final victory still have to get through the intermediate time between now and then. While we are patient in hope and trust that eventually justice will triumph, what should be our attitude toward those who are working with us, or toward those who are the oppressors, and who are creating the wrongs which we have to bear? If we take seriously both the commandment to love and the need to forgive the sins of those who oppress us, there is only one answer to this question. We must be patient and full of graciousness, kindliness, and positive joyful strength. The other alternatives are sullen apathy or varying degrees of rage.

When one gives into wrath, anger, and—even worse—bitter resentment, it means that the enemy or the oppressor has conquered one inside as well as outside. When one hates an oppressor, the outer coercion that one cannot prevent has overcome one's inner freedom as well. Patience differs from masochism: masochists who suffer entrap themselves in the suffering insofar as they feel that they should be suffering, should be unhappy, and are unworthy to be happy. But those who bear a wrong patiently know that it is unjust, know that it is wrong for this wrong to be existing, and yet refuse to let this wrong make them miserable or enraged. When one is patient one can be joyful in the midst of the oppression. A heart that is filled with love and kindness toward one's self, toward one's fellow victims, and toward one's oppressors cannot be counted as crushed. This magnanimity and kindliness and graciousness produce the spirit of a person who is a victor and no longer a victim. It is the ultimate triumph of the inner spirit over the wrongs being inflicted. But, of course, such a victory is not easy to achieve.

Here, again, an extreme case history can be instructive to us in meeting the challenges of more ordinary experience. A woman who had been tortured in a Russian prison reported on her struggle to find an effective way to respond. As she was being subjected to systematic torture by an expert at breaking down every defense she searched for ways to find meaning in her absurd and horrible situation. When she tried to shrink into a negative posture the torturer came on stronger as bullies usually do when they sense weakness. However, if she tried to fight back in anger she also whetted his sadistic appetite. In the midst of this she prayed and tried to permeate the situation with spiritual consciousness. With this she felt that she began to understand the other person's self in a new way. But if she became in the least sentimental or overly indulgent toward her torturer, he would brutalize her all the more. Also if she became self-pitying or overindulgent of herself, again displaying weakness, the same thing happened. Slowly she found a balance between indulgence on either side, a way of serenity that she felt was founded on the "divine rock." In the presence of God within her, the core of her personality and foundation, she was able to find the strength to resist and transcend each new act of brutality. She was so grounded in God that she grew perfectly quiet despite the pain. Realizing that he could not disrupt her serenity the torturer lost interest—the sadist was freed from his obsession and she was freed by her centeredness in God.

Now most persons will never be tortured in prison, but many people have had to bear unavoidable psychological persecution in some form, often from a family member. A person under the influence of alcohol, a person being cruel in defense of his or her anxiety or guilt, or a person trying to avoid emptiness and depression can actively persecute a friend or family member.

Just as in physical torture, there can be malice and efforts to confuse and to cause pain through lies and verbal abuse. The effort can also be made to destroy a person's sense of self and confidence in their perception of reality. Objective reality threatens the psychological torturer's power, so it must be distorted by every means at hand. When this horrible kind of suffering and wrong is visited upon an individual the only defense is to seek the serenity and spiritual centeredness that

can give one the power to patiently bear the wrongful persecution. In ordinary circumstances one has to seek the same
balance as a person under physical torture: one can neither be
indulgent and superficially forgiving of what the other person
is doing nor self-pitying and self-defeating, wallowing in sweet
sorrow. It is necessary to seek confidence in oneself as God's
child, and confidence in one's view of the world and reality.
Centeredness on God gives the patience and love needed for
detachment and the transcendence of anger and bitterness.

Many of the self-help books and self-help movements that
have helped so many sufferers teach the same spiritual lessons
of unsentimental love and balanced detachment. A well-
known example of this is the famous serenity prayer of Alcoholics Anonymous which beseeches God to grant me the
serenity to accept that which I cannot change, the courage to
change that which I can, and the wisdom to know the difference. This serenity is a form of patience for those who
cannot avoid suffering a wrong; it helps them to center themselves and not be consumed by bitterness and the fruitless
effort to change and control the uncontrollable.

Other self-help books take a similar spiritual approach.
They emphasize praying for the persons who are provoking so
much sorrow and trouble, thereby letting them go in order to
center upon oneself and one's own spiritual affirmations and
belief. This "letting go" through the cultivation of patience
includes love, detachment, hope, and confidence in one's own
view of reality. Bearing wrongs patiently gives peace and an
ability to survive and bear the unbearable one day at a time. If
one fights back and becomes angry and wrathfully obsessed
with the other's wrongdoing, one allows the persecutor and
oppressor to be victorious. Once again, they have made you
play their game, and you lose. By fighting back one also
sustains the distracting game in which wrongdoers can take
refuge and justify themselves. Instead of facing their own
difficulty, their own wrong, and the reality of their own be-

havior, they have in their victim's counterattacks and reactive anger a continuing excuse for their own aggression. All oppressors and wrongdoers love to provoke violence so that their own suppressions and original violence will seem justified to themselves and to others.

If one keeps one's serenity and lives up to Christ's example of patience and love, then no matter what happens one's inner spirit has not been violated by aggresive hate. It is what actively comes out of a person that defiles and disintegrates personality, not what is done to a person without consent.

It is also the case that bearing wrongs patiently may be the most prudent and shrewd course of action to accomplish one's goal. When Christ says that the meek will inherit the earth, he may be making a descriptive statement as well as giving spiritual counsel. A Christian does not bear wrongs patiently *in order* to be more successful in the world, but it often turns out to be an effective life strategy. Even those who do not share the Christian motivation have championed the advantages of nonviolent strategies to achieve certain goals. If they are not innocent as doves, they are at least wily as the serpent.

WHY THE MEEK MAY INHERIT THE EARTH

Bearing wrongs patiently may work better than anything else one can do in a struggle or conflict. It works because in order to plan and think effectively, one must be calm and able to take time to assess all the factors in any situation. Wrath and anger and the gusts of near madness one might feel when being mistreated can keep one from being able to think clearly or see the oppressor or aggressor as they really exist, that is, from their own stance and point of view as well as from one's own viewpoint. Bearing wrongs patiently has sometimes been interpreted as meaning to bear with wrongdoers patiently, and this larger understanding is important.

While trying to support and love an oppressor one will cultivate empathy and take account of his role as he sees it. This alternate point of view keeps one from subjectively over-estimating or underestimating the other's power or position, as hate and fear induce one to do. What is important to this other person or to this other group's world view? What in his system is being threatened in our particular conflict or struggle? Loving my enemy I must pay sustained attention to his point of view; through careful attention I will inevitably and easily penetrate psychologically to his goals, fears, strengths, and weaknesses. As the mother knows her child, and the lover knows the beloved, so I can know my oppressor through sustained empathetic efforts to love him.

Once I know through patience what I could never know through violent hate, I can better devise a means to solve our problems. Love is creative in its free play of the mind, while hate narrows thinking into the obsessive circuits around revenge. If I would seek the best for my enemy along with the best for me and mine, I must be free, confident, and loving in my strategic actions. I can enter a dialogue willingly, for I, too, am concerned with what will serve my oppressor's best interests, including, of course, his moral well-being as well as pyschological and material welfare. If he is ensnared in wrong-doing and injustice, I want to help liberate him. How can we together use what Gandhi called soul-force and truth-force to lead us to a new creative solution that will do justice to us both? When my opponent sees that I am concerned about him as well as steely in my concern for justice for myself and my people, new options become possible.

Gandhi said that means are ends in the making, and this is certainly true when one is bearing wrongs and struggling to right them. If you foment acts of aggressive violence, or collapse in self-pity back into fatalism and masochism, there is little hope for a new peaceful future. Violence begets more violence, masochism invites sadism, apathy begets inertia. If I do what my enemy does in retaliation, I become my enemy. Violent revolutionaries who come to power repress in their turn.

We are just beginning to plumb the resources of nonviolent social action in the world today. The civil-rights movement, Solidarity in Poland, the Philippine revolution, and other grassroots campaigns for peace and justice are pointing to new realities of the way power is exercised. Power always depends to some extent on the cooperation of others. Waging peace instead of war is slowly becoming a real option in the world. But training and mobilizing for nonviolent action may take more discipline and sustained effort than old-fashioned warfare. What remains to be seen is whether such strategies can work without prolonged efforts to achieve high levels of collective spiritual discipline. What works for individuals and small communities should be adaptable to larger numbers but it will be a challenge to devise strategies for a whole society.

LEARNING TO BEAR WRONGS PATIENTLY— CULTIVATING PATIENCE

For a Christian, progress in bearing wrongs patiently can only mean growing in wisdom and truth. Becoming more Christlike in our own lives is the only Way to go. Once one has tried to do good to enemies and had the bitter experience of failure, one is forced to admit that it is impossible without God's help. God wins, because we learn that one cannot learn to bear wrongs patiently without being sustained and transformed by God. Only through the empowerment of Christ and the Holy Spirit helping us from within the depths of our personality can we cultivate the centeredness to become patient. We need a great deal of meditation and quiet prayer. At the same time we must have worship in community, participating in the sacraments to strengthen the bonds and beliefs which give us faith that justice will come. Only love begets love. If we do not patiently grow in love among our own that we see daily, we surely will not be able to love wrongdoers who oppress us.

We must also cultivate loving patience toward ourselves. We have to be patient with ourselves before we can be serene and patient with others. As with all our spiritual transactions, the way we treat others is intimately tied to the way we treat ourselves, which depends in turn on our relationship to God, the ground of reality. Bearing our own faults, and limiting our own self-destructiveness and suffering are prerequisites for bearing the faults of others and supporting them so their wrongdoing is limited. We can overcome evil only by good, through the real and deep understanding that God loves us and accepts us just as we are. With all our faults and failings we are not able to bring about instant justice and right all wrongs immediately. It takes time for the leaven of patience to work, for the seed to grow. Once we understand that God lovingly accepts our efforts and will bring about final victory, we can accept ourselves more completely. We know we're not perfect and that we fail often, just like those whose wrongdoing we must patiently bear. Perhaps one of the best ways to think about ourselves and our oppressors as we bear wrongs patiently is that we are all developing and growing—hard as that is.

All creation is groaning to be born and trying to come to the fruition that God desires. We now know that the universe is hurtling through space and that expansive change is the only constant surrounding us. However, certain things, such as our bodies and many of the material things around us are changing at such a slow rate that they seem hardly to change at all. So, too, the wrongs that we are trying to right can seem unchangeable, but if we think about the history of our world and the fact that so much change has already taken place over the centuries we gain hope and patience. Seemingly permanent structures are really only temporary crystallizations, slower in their transformations than other aspects of the universe. Our bones seem solid compared to the food that we eat but this is only because our bones change more slowly. So, too, with the mountains and the inner core of the molten earth, as well as with the explosions of the stars—everything we know from science points to a universe of perpetual movement. I make all things new, says the Lord. Surely the human spirit and our social consciousness and social worlds are also in motion.

But nothing in our human sphere happens without human effort. Only after working can we rest in God, and after rest and restoration we return to work out our salvation. We must prepare the ground of our personality so that God can act through us. This preparation and pruning require discipline. Discipline and the tools of discipline that many have spoken of are ways of training and painfully pruning, so that we are able to live in fuller happiness and joy in the long run. We cannot become patient without a certain amount of discipline and asceticism; it is the training that is necessary to run in the race. We have to learn delayed gratification. We have to learn to give up illusions and fantasy for the sake of truth and reality, and we have to learn to admit our responsibility for those things that we do and cause. We also have to become flexible and no longer rigidly fixed on perfection and the desire for absolute control. We would like to be gods—we constantly thirst after perfect and absolute order according to our will. Training ourselves in patience and serenity is much like training the body for sports. It is slow. It requires constant individual effort combined with constant reliance upon creative forces beyond us to bring about a new birth.

It is instructive to remember that in actual childbirth a form of patience is also the best of all strategies. Similar principles seem to operate in pain management. To fight the pain or to fight the body's birth contractions, to flail about in fear and loathing, to writhe and grimace and struggle, makes the pain more horrible and intense. The way to conquer is through acceptance of the body and through efforts to transform what is happening. One must concentrate mentally and simultaneously exert controlled efforts to relax in order to float through the process as a swimmer rides a wave. The body seems to follow certain laws that operate in the psyche as well. According to the "law of least effort," it is better not to struggle and focus upon a goal, but to focus upon something else and imperceptibly float toward one's goal bit by bit. In trying *not* to do things one should not focus upon the thing one does not want to do, since that only brings it to mind more acutely and makes it more difficult to resist.

The best way to bear pain and to bear wrongs is to jog along patiently, in a sense of moment-to-moment calmness and acceptance, attending to the good, and confident of eventual victory. Struggling to control a chaotic situation can only result in pain, frustration, and stress. Some unfortunate personalities (those with so-called type-A behavior) spend their lives struggling against the constraints of time, the frustrations and obstacles of matter, and the inability of the world to function perfectly. Their driven quality produces intense stress, making these persons irritable and more subject to heart disease and other stress-related diseases.

So many persons in our society suffer physically and psychologically because they have never learned even the first lessons of patience. It is such an un-American virtue. We are all too familiar with the experience of burnout, in which people struggling to help others and to right wrongs simply have to give up and quit. They have not been able to persevere in patience and hope because of the continuing frustration of their desire to see wrongs righted; they become angry, irritable, and emotionally drained; finally a condition of emotional numbing is induced. Such numbing can happen to idealistic teachers, nurses, social workers, health workers, and others who must struggle against injustice and the wrongs of the world.

When techniques for "stress reduction" are offered to over-stressed modern persons, they turn out to be secularized versions of spiritual techniques and spiritual disciplines. One changes behavior by changing thoughts and feelings, and one changes thoughts and feelings by changing behavior—all at the same time. Imagery, behavioral rehearsals, and physical strategies involving breathing exercises and health habits are used to help persons relax and to restore their sense of well-being. How hard it is for Americans to cultivate serenity, when it is so alien to our culture and to our most admired heroes!

It takes a long time to discipline the mind and the heart and the body. While techniques such as role playing or behavioral rehearsal sound like mere jargon, they are simply old and tested means of using the human imagination to help become the way one wishes to be. By playing out new scripts and scenarios, either actually or in one's mind, one can prepare for future challenges. Watching films of the best tennis moves improves one's next game. Liturgical re-creations of the Gospel inspire one's next moves in a larger game. The spirituality of Saint Ignatius, in concert with many other schools of spirituality, have known all about the power of imagination.

But alas, one cannot simply perform one's way to inner spiritual strength. We really cannot do this alone. For the Christian, the path to such strength must include prayer and worship and actual practice of certain kinds of virtues. Only through practice and the deeds that produce new habits of the heart can God act to transform us into the selves we wish to be. Christians change themselves by asking God to transform them: Give us a new heart, one that is no longer apathetic and hardened. Indeed, make us desire to be given a new heart capable of love. When we have grown in God's love, we will be able to bear wrongs patiently.

6

TO FORGIVE ALL INJURIES

Bear with one another: forgive each other as soon as a quarrel begins. The Lord has forgiven you; now you must do the same. (Colossians 3:13–14)

To forgive all injuries—this spiritual work of mercy may be the most difficult of them all. If every spiritual work of mercy is an act of love freely undertaken by a person's conscious self, this particular work is the hardest to come by naturally. Human beings do not forgive easily. Indeed, most legal and moral systems do not ask people to forgive injuries—as though recognizing it to be an impossible task. Among certain pagan religions it was even an impiety to forgive an enemy, especially an enemy who has harmed one's kin or country. Forgiving an enemy would have been seen as craven cowardice and an affront to the gods, who rightly demand vengeance and blood sacrifice.

The more common moral norm in the human species seems to be the crude justice of an "eye for an eye," "a tooth for a tooth." This attempt to establish an equilibrium of hurt and retaliatory payment seems to satisfy some deep and primitive concept of fairness. Those who make others suffer should suffer equally in return; appropriate retribution should be meted out as a debt should be repaid. Small children immediately take to this approach, with little or no instruction. "It's only fair," says the child; harm that has been done should be repaid by equal punishment for the offender. This strong innate feeling for the rightness of retributive justice still fuels our legal system and the recurring campaigns to retain or restore capital punishment. A life for a life—nothing else will do. A person should suffer in equal measure for horrible crimes committed against the innocent.

Satisfying the natural thirst for just retribution for wrong-doing, can serve socially to control the equally natural human lust for revenge. Persons can long for a totally destructive vengeance in which tenfold harm is returned for an injury. If you kill one of ours, we will wipe out your whole family, your people, and your country, plowing over your fields with salt. The desire to take excessive vengeance is also natural to the human heart. At least fair retribution combined with the safeguards of due process restrict human aggression and desire for immediate vengeance. The lynch mob or feuding clan must bow to the authority of the courts and the law; this is as much justice as most societies can manage.

Fairness may even be programmed into the natural order. It has been shown by computer programming of game theories that a game called Tit for Tat eventually leads to advantageous cooperation. In the Tit for Tat computer program players return only what has been given to them. One never initiates injuries or makes the first harmful move, but one always returns in equal measure an injury that has been given. Following this systematic program the eventual outcome of the game is cooperation and a condition of mutual advantage. This computer model has been used as evidence to explain the evolution of cooperation in everything from animal to human organisms.

So why does Christianity burden us with the impossible demand to forgive all injuries? This seems impossible to do if the common wisdom of the ages or our developed systems of justice can be believed. Is the command to forgive all injuries only to be followed by Christians as a supererogatory course for believers? Does it have any practical or common-sense justification as a way of life for ordinary people in our society?

For that matter, how can anyone succeed in this incredibly difficult task that goes so much against the grain?

We often do not have a clear idea of what forgiveness entails, nor do we think enough about how to do it. To struggle with these questions of why and how to forgive I will begin by reflecting on the why questions and work through to the how questions. Along the way I will focus on what injuries are, and what forgiveness is. Thinking about what hurts us and why it hurts, helps us grapple with what must be involved in acts of forgiveness.

WHY MUST CHRISTIANS FORGIVE ALL INJURIES?

The question of why we should forgive has pragmatic answers which will be addressed below, but the theological dimension of the question must also be considered. For Christians there is simply no escaping God's demand that we forgive injuries. While the Old Testament's message about forgiving and holding no grudges, may be seen as ambivalent when placed alongside of biblical accounts of divinely approved vengeance, Christianity makes forgiveness of injuries a clear commandment for a follower of Jesus Christ. We must forgive injuries because God has forgiven us and we are commanded to be holy and perfect as God is perfect. Christians must forgive injuries because Jesus has testified in word and deed to the ultimate importance of God's demand that we forgive our enemies. In saying after saying, parable after parable, command after command, Jesus reiterates the demand summed up in the Lord's Prayer that we must forgive those who trespass against us.

Paul's letters, the rest of Scripture, and the testimony of the saints, martyrs, and mystics instruct and reinstruct Christians to forgive, to love their enemies, to return good for evil. Naturally this Christian teaching has always been a great stumbling block, a perpetual offense to good pagan common sense. Clearly, the Christian faith comes with this demand, a command that cannot be avoided, reinterpreted, or demythologized. This command points to the strait gate, the narrow way. Hard and unnatural as it is, forgiveness seems to be at the heart of the Gospel. Obeying this command to return good for evil must clearly differentiate the followers of Jesus: Christians, to be Christians, must freely forgive all injuries.

We must forgive all those who injure us, but worst of all, we must forgive those who continue to persecute us with no show of repentance. We must forgive those who are not about to ask our forgiveness. Christian forgiveness does not wait upon the enemy's repentance or request for restored relations. Of course it is wonderful if through repentance, interpersonal peace and community is restored. But the Gospel demand seems clear. Often forgiveness must be unilateral and a one-way process. We are told to forgive our injuries, even though the other person does not deserve it, is not sorry, and has not asked to be forgiven. Indeed many of the people that we have to struggle to forgive are those who have injured us in the distant past. Such persons are either no longer available or even alive, so they can be forgiven only unilaterally. Since injuries inflicted and hurts delivered can linger long after the injurers have departed, forgiveness must often be a one-way process.

WHAT ARE THE INJURIES AND TRESPASSES AGAINST US?

What constitutes an injury we are commanded to forgive, and what counts as a trespass against us? How do you hurt me? Let me count the ways. Injuries come in all varieties. But a real injury is rarely physical, nor does it come by accident.

The essence of an injury inheres in the negative psychological intention or motivation on the part of the injurer. Intended malice or evil directed toward our person produces the real injury, whether anything physical is involved. An accident, which by definition is not intended, can be fairly neutral in our psychological life—as long as it is not the result of criminal negligence or reckless self-indulgence. Accidents, along with natural disasters, can be seen more as misfortunes, or as the residual evil of disorder and chaos of the world; they are hardly injuries directed at us and calling for acts of forgiveness. If I am harmed by an earthquake or caught in a tornado, I am not offended or injured in a personal way. Real injuries are those acts that are aimed at us, as specific known persons, alive and operating in the world in this particular time and place. The perpetuators personally intended, or did not prevent when they could have, the particular harm inflicted upon us.

Our sense of injury increases in proportion to the amount of voluntary control and exercise of personal will that is involved in the harm. If someone carelessly falls asleep and causes us injury, even a great injury, this is of a different order from a case in which someone has plotted and connived to make us unhappy or to bring evil into our lives. Serious, freely enacted sins against us are the injuries that are most difficult to forgive. Of course, many people find it difficult to believe in sin, and therefore cannot accept that people could desire, plan, or carry out evil actions directed toward others. Some of these skeptics deny free will, or deny persons enough control over their lives to carry out malevolent projects, or deny that people could ever truly desire evil. Such doubters will stoutly maintain that there is no such thing as a deliberate injury aimed at another, necessitating personal acts of forgiveness.

Our concept of injury is inevitably related to our concept of the human potential for evil and sin. The idea of injury is also dependent upon an acceptance of the existence of a real self that can truly suffer. Those philosophies and religions that deny the reality of the self can also deny the reality of evil and treat personal injuries as simply another illusion. There can never be anything to forgive because there is no reality to the evil and suffering that is being falsely perceived. So, in a paradoxical sense, when one accepts the existence of injury and suffering as real phenomena, it is an affirmation of the reality of the individual self that can suffer, and an affirmation of another individual's freedom and power to will evil. Accepting a divine savior's real suffering upon the cross validates our own human existence as nonillusory individual conscious selves who experience nonillusory suffering inflicted by nonillusory other selves intending to do us harm.

But how difficult it is for certain proud persons to accept the reality of their own personal injury and suffering. Strong characters are inevitably attracted to the stoic ideal of transcending all suffering through strength of will and superior detachment. To admit that they have been injured is a confession of weakness and vulnerability. It hurts to recognize that one is hurting, or that one is weak enough to be hurt by another. Trapped in their desire for omnipotence, a defense that perhaps begins in the child who has to use this strategy against suffering, proud persons can simply deny that they are being injured. They continue to maintain that nothing hurts and that no one has succeeded in penetrating the self's defenses to inflict harm or pain. No one can "get to me."

To recognize the pain and the injury is a necessary first step in being able to forgive. Sometimes the recognition of pain and injury is absolutely necessary for safety and future survival. Individuals can so deny injuries that they fail to take necessary steps to flee imminent danger. Bruno Bettelheim talks of the Jews of Nazi Germany in the 1930s who simply refused to recognize injury after injury; they could not accept the signs that so much evil was intentionally being directed toward them as a group. Their "pathology of hope" and denial

of malice helped them eventually to perish. Women, too, have
denied and excused the pain and injury of physical abuse by
their husbands and have paid with their lives. Ironically,
extremes of either arrogance or innocence can lead to dangerous denials of pain and injury.

Once one accepts the existence of injuries it is easy to see
that injuries can come in many ways. Each of these varieties
or categories necessitates different efforts and involves different capacities in order to forgive. One dimension of injury
is how close it comes to the innermost being of a person. The
self is experienced as a physical self and a social self and a
spiritual self with many different facets. Each of these dimensions of the self can be injured in different ways. The more
important the dimension attacked, or the closer to the center
of the self, the more hurtful the injury will be. Injuries aimed
at external nonessential parts of my life or being can quickly and
easily be forgiven. Injuries to my deepest self, my sense of
well-being, my self-esteem, my sense of honor and integrity,
or my deepest commitments will hurt more and be much
more difficult to forgive. The rather enigmatic saying of Jesus
that he who calls a person a fool shall be in danger of hellfire,
makes sense when one thinks of how much it hurts to be
called a fool and have one's sense of self, or competence and
worth, publicly insulted.

Since I invest my self in others, vicarious injuries also hurt.
Since I identify so closely with those I love most in the world,
injuries done to them are injuries done to me. Injuries done
to one's beloved spouse or children or parents or friends may
sometimes be more difficult to forgive than injuries that are
done to one's self. This human propensity to take umbrage at
the injury done to one's family and friends fuels the ongoing
feuds and vendettas that have marred the world's history.
One's communal honor, or group self-esteem, can also be
injured by insult and indignities. Especially in traditional
societies, group identification can be very strong. In some

cases communal honor can be injured by shameful behavior on the part of a member of the group. Honor killings are committed in revenge for a betrayed group's shame.

Detraction or bearing false witness may be among the worst injuries because personal repute lives on in a community, residing for prolonged periods in the minds of others. To have one's good name or honor or integrity or virtue impugned among one's peers is a grievous injury. We are communal beings who live with others and are ever conscious of the fact that our character is considered by others. We seek social esteem far more than material goods. It would take almost superhuman detachment not to be hurt by a malicious attack on one's public reputation and character.

Another dimension in the categorizing of injuries is that of time. There can be one-time injuries that were done long ago and are over and done with. Then there are injuries that once initiated, continue on and become chronic problems. Another dimension of injury is the inducement of anxiety and dread—a favorite tactic of torturers. The onset of an injury in time also affects its quality. There can be slowly developing problems that are so obviously signaled that the eventual injury is expected. Then there can be totally unexpected and shocking injuries delivered out of the blue. The unexpected injury is difficult to bear because in addition to the injury itself, the victim has to deal with the shock and surprise of the attack or sudden betrayal. Sudden injury or betrayal is particularly traumatic because one's belief system is turned upside down. Rape victims, for instance, find the suddenness of the assault particularly upsetting, and the subsequent mistrust and anxiety are difficult to bear.

Who injures me is another crucial factor in injury. When an enemy or acquaintance or a distant colleague injures me, this does not have the impact of an injury done by someone I have loved and trusted. The more intimate the relationship, the more ideals and values are shared, the more the injury will hurt. The old saying that you always hurt the ones you love is true, because a love relationship makes a person more vulnerable to injury. The closer the injurer is, the more the injury and hurt is felt.

The most hurtful injury of all may be the betrayal of trust by a beloved person who has shared one's life. So marriage partners and family members and intimate friends can hurt each other more than anyone else. Next, perhaps, come comrades and those who have fought together and shared a mutual investment and struggle for a common cause. Civil wars and fighting among alienated political allies can be most bitter. We react so strongly when those who are close and beloved hurt us, because besides the hurt, we are forced to doubt our past life together. Has this person changed, or did I not really know him as I thought I did? Was I totally wrong in my estimation of his character and our relationship?

Perhaps the worst part of an injury from a beloved person is that it can penetrate our habitual defenses and diminish our innermost selves. If the person I love and identify with injures me, I am drawn into my own victimization through my intimate union with him or her. If you repudiate me, I inevitably begin to see myself through your eyes and feel diminished; I am not only hurt, but feel demeaned and maimed by the self-repudiation you have induced in me. When deep betrayals by beloved persons occur, a person can be nearly annihilated by the injury; the shared life, the mutual love, and all the ideals and values that have formed the committed bond of the past are trampled upon and called into question. Perhaps a completely self-confident, self-sufficient person would not be deeply injured or hurt in such a situation, but any person so invulnerable to hurt would also be detached from love and interdependency.

The fact that victims can be led into their own victimization produces the potential for all types of chronic abuse. Many abusers convince their victims that nothing wrong is happening. If anything seems to be the matter it is the victim's fault and the result of their own wrongdoing or weakness. Injury is compounded by the deceptive efforts to confuse, project blame, and keep the victim from escaping the psychological bind. A person's very sanity can be threatened when such subtle assaults are prolonged. Since people who sin usually project and protect their sin to avoid their own guilt, they can spend enormous energy blaming, persecuting, and attacking the person who is truly the victim. The need to escape guilt impels a persecutor to make the victims feel that their perception of reality is completely distorted. The injured victim is then not only betrayed but forced into destructive self-doubt and self-repudiation. Unfortunately, this kind of ensnaring evil takes place frequently in marriage and family life.

A dreadful injury takes place when a beloved spouse betrays his or her marital partner with infidelity. Such injuries are horrible because every level of one's being is betrayed. The belief in one's world is overturned, the trust that one is beloved and that one is the object of loyalty is destroyed. When betrayal is discovered suddenly and shockingly after much deception and the kind of lies that accompany such betrayals, the hurt is compounded. The sense of desperation, sorrow, hurt, and annihilation inflamed by jealousy and desire for revenge, produces an injury that is unique. The injured spouse cries out, "How could my beloved do this to me? Indeed, how could this person I trusted and admired do this at all?" Every dimension of self suffers, from sexual validation and self-respect, to one's commitment to promises and good faith.

The hurt and suffering brought about by infidelity in a marriage becomes almost overwhelming—and the better the marriage the worse it is. The sense of despair and pain is psychological, but soon can be manifest physically. Betrayed, bereft persons lose weight, become physically weak, or contract illnesses. A broken heart is not just symbolic. The common experience of human beings in every age validates this symbol of deep injury as that most difficult to forgive. One can see why this image of the betrayed spouse was used in the Old Testament as the ultimate injury and challenge to loving forgiveness. The people of Israel are depicted as the unfaithful spouse of the Lord; the people sin and yet receive God's free forgiveness. It is far easier to understand injury than it is to understand forgiveness.

FORGIVENESS

What exactly is meant by forgiveness? What do we do when we forgive the sinner? It is ironic that millions of Christians every day pray for forgiveness and speak of forgiving trespasses, yet are not quite sure exactly what is involved. Is to forgive to totally forget the injury, or is it to so understand that one excuses the injury? Before going on to discuss how one can manage the act of forgiving injuries, it would be well to know what it is one is aiming for. When we are told to forgive one another as God has forgiven us we need a more distinct concept or sharper focus upon what it is we are about to attempt.

Since injury is a phenomenon of many dimensions it may be that forgiveness is equally complex. There are different levels and types of forgiveness with differing developments and courses. There are times when one has been able to forgive on a very rational symbolic level, but has not really, truly, deeply forgiven with one's whole being. Without the emotional follow-through the forgiveness remains at a superficial level. Sometimes the symbolic cognitive forgiveness only initiates the long process that will finally result in full and complete forgiveness. A happier discontinuity can also be experienced when one finds that one has already forgiven on a deep emotional level when at a conscious verbal level one did not know one was yet able to do so. People sometimes find themselves mysteriously making up, long before they thought they could be ready.

One can guess that those people who have a hard time accepting that they have been injured are the same people who have trouble forgiving from the heart. They habitually operate on a very rational level quite removed from the deep springs of their personality. They are too proud to admit injury, but when forced to do so they use the same pride to forgive—on a certain level. Their forgiveness serves an aggressive need to dominate by being morally superior. The high tone of the person too willing to forgive an injury too lightly felt, has an artificial and disquieting effect. A full, deep act of forgiveness can only come after a full acceptance of how hurt one has been, and how the injury has taken its toll. One has to go down deep into the injury and accept the full measure of pain before one can truly begin to forgive.

Does true forgiveness mean that one finally forgets the injury? A friend whose spiritual judgment I respect says with absolute certainty that "to forgive is to forget," indeed, it is the only way that one can truly forgive another. Many others champion this amnesiac approach to forgiveness. But the idea of equating forgetting with forgiving doesn't work. It is too simple. After all, my memory, my consciousness of existing through time, my personal history, must necessarily be maintained as a part of my present identity, my present self. Therefore I cannot simply blot out sections of my past or painful episodes and still retain all that I have been, which is the foundation for all that I have become today. The past cannot be denied or undone. If we use our defenses to seal over past problems with denial or repression rather than facing up to the painful reality, we incur another psychic cost. I think direct confrontation and working through what happened is the better way to forgiveness.

In this world, time is irreversible; it flows in only one

direction. An injury, even a long-ago injury, much less one that is recent or chronically present, cannot simply be erased from one's personal history. Something much more complicated than amnesia has to be effected in an act of forgiveness. But what? Is perhaps the better way a deliberate strategy of minimizing through an effort to explain away the injury? Knowing that to err is human, many would hold that to understand all, is to forgive all. In this understanding approach, one basically equates forgiving with excusing. If only one could understand how insecure the person who injured you was, how deprived, how stressed, how handicapped by upbringing, and so on, and so on. A true understanding all of the relevant factors and variables will lead one to see how what happened at that particular time came to be—indeed, given all the variables, was practically inevitable.

Unfortunately, the excusatory environmental approach takes away moral responsibility from a person. In the process of explaining evil acts through some soft social determinism, it explains away freedom and choice on the part of the person who injures, and, by implication, my own moral responsibility. Why or how, then, can I be expected to have enough freedom to forgive an injury? Admittedly, at times some people do act involuntarily and are not in control of their actions. But it is also true that many human choices remain in every situation, and that the past free choices of a person have helped shape their present situation. In many cases, persons freely choose to harm one another. Their evil intent may be far greater than the harm they succeed in doing. Explanations may occasionally be a road to forgiveness but they can never be the whole story. To forgive someone who knows not what they do is one thing. To forgive someone who knows very well what they are doing, and does it anyway, is the real challenge.

Forgiving, then, is neither forgetting, nor excusing. The reality of the injury remains in memory. Its seriousness and the actual evil intent is neither denied nor excused in some misguided effort to deny the reality of sin and free will. But the past reality must now be transformed in the present by a free act of love and forgiveness. Forgiveness essentially means restoring one's relationships to wholeness, giving to another goodwill, love, and care, despite the other's efforts to rend the relationship. The reality of another's malice is not denied, but the inner personal reality of present goodwill and hope for a loving future transforms the past. God's love, which can remove the sting of death, can remove the sting and bitterness of a past injury. The memory of the wrongdoing and suffering remains intact but the anger and wrath or sorrow and despair of the past no longer accompanies the recollection.

After full forgiveness the memory of the injury is divested of its agonizing emotional component because the present emotions of goodwill or love or care or hope are stronger than the negative anguish that was experienced with the injury. It is as if the injury recedes far, far away in time, or shrinks in perspective in proportion to the whole picture. What was overwhelmingly in the foreground becomes another part of the background, the insistent searing quality of a still-throbbing injury fades into the overall design. The restoration of wholeness, as in physical healing, re-creates psychological networks, new patterns that overlay the gaping wound. Something that was broken is mended. The breach that seemed impossible to bridge is overcome.

Consider the worst case, the injury inflicted by the infidelity of a marriage partner. Here there is a betrayal of trust, with marriage vows and promises broken; moreover, lies, manipulation, and deceit usually accompany the rejection of the spouse. Such treatment hurts horribly, especially if it is accompanied by hostility. Often a guilty party will try to justify his or her actions by attacking the innocent spouse in a classic case of blaming the victim or scapegoating. After such breaches of trust, forgiveness requires an inner healing of the wounds. The betrayed spouse must be restored to self-esteem and wholeness, if he or she is to begin to see the injury and injurer differently. If repentance is sought and the guilty person wishes to be forgiven and to continue the marriage, the restoration of the breach will mean rebuilding together. To do this, the marital love that exists in the present and can continue to exist in the future, will have to seem more of a reality than the past betrayal and injury. With forgiveness, the past no longer poisons the present or future relationship. While the past can never be undone, forgotten, or explained away, it will no longer call the tune for the present relationship. Forgiveness restores goodwill, friendship, and loving hope; positive emotions are dominant in the mind and heart of the wronged person.

When forgiveness occurs, the present and the future dominate the inner stream of consciousness. Loving concern reigns, instead of despair, hurt, bitterness, or wrath. If actual mutuality is restored and the partner is back in the relationship, then each day's action can demonstrate the new focus. Resurrections of marital relationships are possible.

There are some very sorrowful cases in which an injured person may have to separate himself or herself from an unrepentant chronic abuser. Often separation is necessary for physical or psychological survival. In any event, forgiveness must be achieved if the victim is to survive and grow. The restoration of wholeness will still involve a transformation of attitude toward the other, now absent, partner. Past injuries must be worked through and emotionally resolved, even if the other person refuses to cooperate. Let the dead bury the dead. A person who forgives is interested in love and life now. There just isn't enough psychological energy left for bitterness, or enough time left to be wasted on wrath.

Our knowledge of forgiveness comes from understanding how God forgives us our sins and repeated failings. God forgives us, though our sins be scarlet they shall be white as snow. The whole imagery of washing and whitening implies the transformation and restoration possible through God's saving love for us. Jesus, through his healing actions and teaching, confirms in our hearts and minds God's love and forgiveness to the sinner. Most important is the Resurrection and the coming of the new Jerusalem and the marriage of the Lamb. God is a God who makes all things new, a God of love with the power to transform the past into a redeemed present, full of abundant future. We are to love in the same re-creating way. Yes, love always means being sorry and asking forgiveness, but receiving forgiveness also means caring and wanting the best for the other person. One actively desires to see the other flourish. The essence of love is harmony, communion, joy, and attention to the happiness of the beloved.

God transforms us and the world through love and forgiveness. The God of power and might seems intent on the ultimate victory embodied in the restoration of loving relationships. Forgiveness is the only means to make this marriage feast of reconciliation happen. Imitating God, the loving person forgives; he or she is even unbecomingly excessive in eagerness to forgive and restore the broken bond. In Jesus' story of the father and the prodigal son, the father sees his son from afar and runs to meet him. The feasting and joy that mark true forgiveness, from finding lost sheep to lost children, are perennial themes in the Gospel good news. Our hearts burn within us when we hear these stories because we have known the joy of forgiving and being forgiven, the joy of reconciliation.

The ultimate exemplary model for our forgiveness can be found in Jesus' forgiveness of those who crucified him, freely given while in the midst of agony and pain. The magnanimity and large-heartedness of this ability to forgive inspires us to do the same. Nothing that we sinners suffer can be harder to forgive than what Jesus clearly forgives at that moment of torture and death. One wonders if this supreme act of forgiveness includes those acts that Jesus seemed to have had a harder time forgiving during his ministry. His words about those who have misled the little ones, or hypocritically put burdens upon the already burdened, or made life more difficult for the poor, seem to confirm that forgiving those who hurt those who are dear to us is a most difficult task.

Forgiving those who injure me may be easier than forgiving those who injure my child. But yet we must forgive, and transform all relationships that have been broken. If not, the cycle of vengeance and retribution goes on forever. Evil triumphs in acts of continued vengeance, as demonstrated by the deforming hate in the Middle East or Northern Ireland. We must not only do good to those who injure us but also to those who injure those we love. This is what we mean by "going the second mile." This is truly obeying and imitating God who gives goodness to the just and injust. Ironically, our consciousness and ability to remember, which is basic to our human identity, makes it harder for us to forgive. Caught as we are in resurgent memories and anger, we need help in our efforts to forgive.

HOW TO FORGIVE ALL INJURIES

Our knowing that we must forgive injuries doesn't make it any easier to do. In fact, forgiving injuries is perhaps the hardest thing that we will ever have to do, the severest test of our Christian commitment. The difficulty of this ordinary challenge of everyday life surprises us. Given what we know of the horrors of modern warfare, many of us might imagine that the ultimate test of our faith and character would be whether we could stand up under torture or behave with dignity in a concentration camp. Yet as we pass into middle-class American middle age, it seems unlikely that we will ever be tortured or have to face incarceration in a camp or totalitarian prison. For us, as it turns out, forgiving those who injure us becomes the most difficult test of our faith and character.

Forgiving all injuries is so completely against our human nature that we give up in despair and recognize that we are unable to do it by ourselves. We simply can't do it without God. The strength of our evil desire for vengeance is, for many of us, the most convincing evidence we have experienced firsthand of the human need for God's grace in order to avoid evil and do good. Only God's power and Christ in us can help us to restrain ourselves from evil and truly forgive. We may never have known how pagan and unconverted our hearts really were, until faced with a grievous wrong done to us. Then bitterness, anger, despair, and the desire for revenge rise up like a tidal wave and threaten to overwhelm us. The assault of these waves of bitterness and wrath and sorrow and pain are all but overwhelming. One can almost feel oneself being pulled down and beginning to drown in pain and fury and plans for revenge.

Once one sinks into this state it is a long time before one can rise to the surface again. But as one begins to go down sometimes the descent can be averted by the fervent invocation: "Jesus Christ, liberator, save me from this madness, pain, and hate." If the invocation is given too late and one sinks anyway, then all that can be done is to try to remember Jesus Christ crucified and hope that one's self-control can at least keep one from doing anything more overtly evil than succumbing to one's inner rages of vindictiveness and wrath. God can at least keep one from drowning in the confusion and evil as the inner storm batters on. No wonder the anchor was an early symbol of Jesus Christ. It is also understandable that Christians considered these losses of control and overwhelming desires to do evil to be temptations by the Devil. One can almost feel oneself being seduced into evil and feel the temptation to give way to pain and anger. How delighted Satan (if he exists) must be with these falls into wrath and bitterness.

Not only has evil been done by the injurer, but the victim is also ensnared in evil desires, with ensuing bouts of distress and self-loathing.

Not to forgive injuries is hell. To carry the anger, wrath, pain, and distress that accompany a sense of injury is to remain in confused chaotic turmoil. One flails and writhes in pain and hate, feeling tortured, torn apart, and impotent. An odd conflict can arise for the good person who is caught in a peculiar bind. A person can know that they could never let themselves exact vengeance, yet they still lust to inflict punishment upon their tormentors. It is even more galling to realize that a wrongdoer may escape retribution within one's power because it would be a greater evil for one to seek revenge. Good persons can be trapped by their own strength of character and self-control, too obedient in conscience to take revenge, but not Christlike enough not to want to. After experiencing such divided and tormented states, a Christian can give ready assent to the truth that all the way to hell is hell.

Experience gradually convinces us that God's commands are always for our good; Christ's yoke is light indeed compared to the burdens of evil. Undergirding the commands of faith and duty, there exists a moral reality that arises from the psychological laws of our human nature. From a purely secular point of view, it is important to be able to forgive our injurers for the sake of our own health and happiness. The stress and turmoil of bitter anger is bad for the heart, both literally and figuratively. When one cannot or will not forgive an injury one remains in the position of battered and bitter victim, constantly aroused and hurting, constantly impaired, constantly maimed, because one is constantly conscious of the injury as it dominates and permeates the present. Nursing one's anger and nestling down into injury guarantees the victimized condition, the defeated state of weakness and pain. How can one escape? How can one be liberated?

When one enacts a spiritual work of mercy or tries to love another, a threefold attention must take place: one must attend to one's relationship to God, to one's relationship to others, and to one's inner self. Wherever one begins, one must get around to the other factors before things can change decisively. To forgive an injury one can begin with a cry to God for help. Faced with one's failure to be able to love and forgive, one is driven to faith. Only God's love is stronger than hate, stronger than anger, stronger than natural pride and the desire for vengeance. With God nothing is impossible. Through faith I can hope that I can be healed. If Jesus Christ rose from the dead and conquered death and hate, Christ in me can conquer this living death. In misery I long for the peace of Christ which comes through forgiveness—for me, for my enemy, for us.

But as in all psychological struggles for control, a curious condition is recognized in both theology and secular psychology. The more one struggles to conquer and fight an evil urge, the less one is able to do it. Psychologists talk about the law of least effort in which one is best able to change or to direct consciousness through the most minimal effort needed. Large-scale frontal assaults provoke reactions and defensiveness and thereby are more likely to fail. The image used in illustration is that of the swimmer who only by gently floating above the incoming wave can surmount it successfully; the person who fights the wave head on is knocked down, bruised, and perhaps even drowned.

The paradoxical psychological process seems to work because measures of attack provoke countermeasures of resistance. In addition, as one struggles to control evil, attention is focused upon the temptation or evil desire or habit, and such an attentive focus magnifies and strengthens its object. If, by contrast, attention can be directed elsewhere and a quiet sense of trust and confidence can be maintained, a person can gently float over or bypass the obsessive problem. Ironically, giving up the struggle and turning to a higher power in trust, can achieve what a determined effort cannot. Many self-help movements, beginning with Alcoholics Anonymous, make giving up and turning one's life over to a higher power the first step in regaining power to change. It is almost a secular version of justification by faith.

When my trust is focused upon God's power as the ultimate source of energy in the creation then I believe I can be transformed by Christ within me. God and Christ and the Holy Spirit within can empower me to forgiveness of an injury that would otherwise be impossible. I must let go and ask God to heal me, an act which is very difficult for strong, self-sufficient persons. Attending to God one tries to identify with God's point of view. Thinking of God's goodness we inevitably recognize that we, too, are sinners and have injured others. We ask forgiveness for our own trespasses. Realizing our own sins and injuries delivered to others gives us some sense of fellow feeling with the person who has injured us. Going to confession more frequently helps in this process. My enemy is not the only perpetuator of evil; we both share this ability to hurt. (In some cases we may have even hurt our present injurer in the past, a circumstance that can make present forgiveness somewhat easier.) Thinking God's thoughts we must also remember that this person who has injured us also has Christ within, and is also one of the beloved children of God. We may begin to look at them and then feel toward them the way God must feel toward them; we pity them and feel sorry for their sake. How sad that they have erred and strayed and offended God and their better selves! It is hard to feel sadness and hate at the same time. With much prayer, sadness may triumph over our anger.

Of course, change toward another cannot happen without a revolution of one's own inner life. An inner transformation must accompany the transformation of the relationship with others. The reconciliation with another that is desired has to begin with an inner reconciliation. The injury, hurt, and sorrow, have to be overcome with an inner healing. After all, the injury has made one feel hurt, repudiated, attacked, and lowered in self-esteem. The vulnerability and weakness that we all have, have been touched and we have been trampled on in some way. In the condition of turmoil to which the injurer has brought us, we cannot be free to rise above our bitterness or feel strong enough to love. We have been hated and deeply hurt, half-convinced of our enemy's scorn and repudiating acts. Our self-esteem may be nearly in shreds.

In such times of agony and conflict, we can truly cry out the words of the Psalmist (words which may have seemed excessive before we needed them): "Oh, God, my God, come to my rescue, comfort me in my affliction, do not let me be put to shame in the presence of my enemies." It is imperative that we begin to look at ourselves as the beloved child of God. We must give real assent to the reality that God loves us and wishes to comfort us, and will do so if we can open ourselves up to His love. The Great and Holy One will rescue us from this evil.

We need to dwell again and again on the Gospel words of love and assurance to help ourselves believe that God really and truly does love us so much. The sacrament of the Mass helps us believe. Slowly one can begin to feel whole again. One forgives oneself for feeling anger and indignation and desire for vengeance, realizing that while this is sin it arises from part of our nature, a part which in appropriate circumstances helps fuel the thirst for justice. Forgiving ourselves and beginning to see ourselves as loved by God, also begins to repair the damage that has been done to us. The most hurtful things happen when we have believed what the person who injured us has tried to tell us by their injury—that we are inferior, that we are unworthy of good treatment, that we are nothing. Beginning to feel loved we can begin to trust ourselves, to have self-confidence, and to trust others enough so that we can begin to forgive. We look at others as we do ourselves; in forgiveness we can look at self and others in a benign way. Then we are truly healed and whole and re-collected, once more at peace.

We regain our peace, our sense of wholeness, our sense of self-love and love for others by taking God's point of view and asking God to help us love ourselves and others as He loves. But achieving this reconciliation may be a long and difficult process with many complexities. Just as injury is complex, so is forgiveness. Time and repeated efforts may be necessary. Bitterness may come in cycles and surge up again and again. Perseverance in forgiveness is necessary so that the new trans-formed peaceful self becomes permanent. There is usually an acute phase of suffering after an injury and then the immedi-ate shock and trauma give way to a longer more chronic cyclical condition. Different strategies may be appropriate at different times. A full immersion and catharsis in hurt may seem less appropriate as time passes and the upsurges of anger and hurt become less frequent and less powerful and potent. A simple dismissal and affirmation may work. As grief and mourning have its phases so do acts of forgiveness. The capacity to love and forgive can become more fully and com-pletely a part of our life.

In a sense our life as it progresses is a continual process of forgiving past injuries. As one grows older one can begin to forgive the past injuries that have been done to almost all children by almost every parent. Since we are all sinners, in every life there have been injuries in the past that need to be healed in order to achieve present and future wholeness. Even if the people are no longer present the healing process of forgiveness needs to be carried out. In certain cases where real injuries are continuously present this process is much more difficult and becomes a case of bearing wrongs patiently. If old injuries are not forgiven they have a horrible way of being repeated in one's own life as though some unconscious programming has been laid down to be followed in the future, even to the next generation.

Life is full of forgiveness and in a sense we become better at it as we learn to love more deeply and more fully through deeper responses to God's love for us. Gradually we learn to let go more and more of our past injuries, hates, and troubles, which have knotted us up and depleted energy from the present and the future. We become more liberated from all injury and inferiority and know joy and peace. To forgive is to be forgiven, to be forgiven empowers forgiveness; love begets mercy and mercy begets more love.

7

TO PRAY FOR THE LIVING AND THE DEAD

Pray all the time, asking for what you need, praying in the Spirit on every possible occasion. Never get tired of staying awake to pray for all the saints; and pray for me. (Ephesians 6:18)

We are quite confident that if we ask him for anything, and it is in accordance with his will, he will hear us. (John 5:9)

There is no need to worry; but if there is anything you need, pray for it, asking God for it with prayer and thanksgiving. (Philippians 4:6)

QUESTIONS ABOUT PRAYER

We have been told to pray and we have the example of Jesus and the saints and the Church constantly before us. We have experienced the power of prayer in our lives and so continue to pray on pragmatic grounds as well as through faith. But do we understand what is happening? Reconsidering prayer and attempting to understand why and how this is a work of mercy will help us persevere. If we do not have an image or an insight into what we are doing it is more difficult to believe in our activity and keep doing it day after day. We need a better intuition of how prayer works, a clearer approximation of what happens. Traditionally, Christians have prayed for themselves, for others, and for the dead, but what does this mean in a world no longer tidily divided into earth, purgatory, heaven, and hell? Hard questions abound and induce new struggles to understand how prayer can make a difference.

I will start with some reflections on the case of personal petition and then move to the more difficult problems of praying for others, first the living and then the dead. Problems with prayer, especially the effectiveness of intercessory prayer, bring us to central questions about how God relates to the created order. How can there be divine interventions in a lawfully created universe? We know that the redemptive victory has been won by Jesus but that final battles continue in this time before the end. We live in an interim time described as "already but not yet." We believe that at the Creation God set the stage for our drama and that he has determined the finale of the script, but the middle acts seem to be open to the co-authorship of God and humankind. (Theological arguments turn on just how much human improvisation is demanded.) In any event, human beings are responsible for the dominion, stewardship, and exercise of freedom we have been given. God wins, we know, but *how* that victory of love will be consumated depends upon our human acts in this time of "not yet." Indeed, the whole Creation is groaning in the birth process of the Kingdom.

Those of us who have children of our own can begin to understand why God chooses to limit His divine power for the sake of human development. Parents do not wish to give their children only ready-made passive pleasures, but desire rather to enable their children to participate in the greater human pleasure of creating, achieving, growing, and developing through their own initiative and activity. Parents have to "let go" to give their children growing room for their own developmental struggle. Similarly, one of the greatest joys of being God must be the divine creativity, having the loving power to bring lives and worlds into being; so surely God desires similar creative joys for the beloved human beings made in the divine image. As Paul says, "we are God's work of art." Jesus has told us that we shall do greater works than he in Jesus' name; he has called us to be friends and join in the redemption of the world.

But to be truly creative and able to produce our own works of art, our freedom must not be illusory. God does not coerce. So we are free, with all the potential for harm and good that freedom brings. The Creation, although good, is separate from God and not divine, though God sustains it and the Spirit penetrates throughout, especially in human beings and within the community of the Church. Human beings and the Church are not divine, although, as the mystics say, we are God-seeds and have the potential to grow into adulthood as God's people. Into this separation and simultaneous interpenetration, into this space between the already and the not yet, the free activity of prayer can move. But how does it make a difference?

PRAYING FOR OURSELVES—PRAYERS OF PETITION

Many books are written today to instruct the faithful in prayer. Recordings and films, complete with music for meditation, exist as part of the current renaissance in spirituality. Pastoral courses are offered in all the many different kinds of prayer in the Christian tradition as well as new ways to mine the ancient treasuries found in Eastern spirituality. There exist a variety of ways for any individual to pray. But it is clear that we also are praying collectively and never simply as isolated individuals. We are members of the Church and pray within and through the Church. Even if we are not taking part in a public liturgical worship service, we are members of Christ's body and our prayers rise as members of that community. We should take to heart Baron von Hügel's admonition that in praying it is important always to "realize you are but one of a countless number of souls, a countless number of stars." All over the globe throughout each minute of every day the Church is praying.

We are also told in Scripture that the Spirit and Jesus pray for us to the Father. This divine giving and receiving of love and communion within the Trinity is the model for our own communication in prayer. But if the Spirit prays for us and we participate in the prayer of our high priest Jesus, why pray individually and privately beyond communal worship and the Eucharist? If prayer is a fundamental disposition of our whole being turned toward God, does overt explicit individual prayer add anything? Yes, indeed; surely an individual response of prayer is also called for, since we are separate self-conscious individuals who are able to communicate privately with thought and word and deed at the same time that we are members of one another and of the Church. One is still an individual, while being a member of a family.

We would never want to be like those family members who never talk because they assume that the others must already know what they would say, so they see no reason to speak of love and gratitude. Love by its nature seeks expression and is increased by expression. Besides, prayer is a way of specifically lifting heart and mind to God in adoration, gratitude, and petition and then listening for God's response. In a unique individual life there must be time for specific individual communications devoted to particular concerns. We must listen for our own special whisperings from the Spirit in answer to our prayers. We also know that in the act of thinking and communicating and voicing things, we discover new things that we did not know we knew. The process of active communication with others gives us new access to ourselves as we communicate. When the other listener is the divine Other, our communication can be even more creative. Although God knows everything and all our thoughts in the future as well as the past, we don't. Voicing our prayers entrains new thoughts and new ideas, by directing our attention to God.

Psychologically the way prayers of petition seem to work to transform our lives is through the operation of attention. Attention is that light of our consciousness which we can focus at will. As William James and others have noted, the one ultimate act of freedom at man's disposal is his ability to "keep the selected idea uppermost." When we attend to God and the divine love and goodness and truth, we are drawn into joyful adoration and loving attachment. These states produce more prayerful attention and induce desires to imitate God and pursue God's will in our lives. Slowly we become transformed as our habits of attention and attachment inevitably shape our thoughts, feelings, and behavior. As we grow in love for God we are more and more assured of God's love for us and so begin to be able to love others better. God's love for us overflows in love for others.

Consciousness of the fact that God loves us creates more love for the self. Self-esteem grows from being esteemed by another, and what an Other we discover in God. The amazing good news gradually sinks in; truly we have been created, redeemed, and cared for so that every hair of our head is numbered. God really does love us dearly, more ardently than any other person or parent could. This raises our sense of self-worth, even as it makes us humbly grateful for such excessive benevolence. Through prayer we begin to value ourselves in a new way so that the intertwined relationships of self to self, self to God, and self to others become transformed. Great lovers of God become increasingly aware that God is in each person and so begin to love and attend to the Christ in others. Love multiplies in bountiful profusion.

In prayer, the direction of consciousness and thought and emotion and action toward God is a movement that infuses in us the energy of God. God's zest, God's spirit, and God's power can come to us when we ask to receive it. Prayer is the way we participate more fully in God as Reality. Prayer is the way we open ourselves to the divine and ask that we, too, may become hearts from whom living water flows. A prayerful person rises up like an eagle and has youth perpetually renewed. I have also found that human beings much given to prayer *look* different, despite their original physical endowments given in the genetic throw. There is something particularly light and clear around the eyes. I do not think this is just my imagination operating, because reliable new psychological research on facial expressions shows that emotions habitually displayed in the hundreds of facial muscles can, over time, shape the way a face looks. As Abraham Lincoln long ago noted, after forty a man is responsible for his face. Moses' face shone with light when he had talked with Yahweh, and to this day reflections of a similar shining seem to appear in God's friends.

Unfortunately, the opposite is also true, the light can go out of a face—and a life. If we do not pray we cut ourselves off from the vine and begin to wither in our power and capacity to love others. Sometimes we may think that we do not need prayer or our communion with God to function and to live in the world. But over the years, we and those who live around us see that the withering has begun. In middle age a person begins to reap what has been sown. Once the youthful ego has either obtained satisfaction or been deeply frustrated, we see that it was ego that kept us striving, even in supposedly doing good for others. Without private prayer persons can become cut off from the spiritual source of life. They are not living abundantly.

We also need corporate prayer of course, prayer with our community. Both kinds of prayer are needed to keep our liveliness, to keep our merriment, and to restore our joy as life inevitably begins to take its toll and grind us down. The Spirit within us needs infusion from the Spirit of God. We need that communion to bear fruit. Without prayer we dry up and

become dead before the body dies. The thirst that we think
we can quench through work, worldly success, and a busy life
with friends and family cannot be quenched by any other
means than by drinking at the fount of the living water.

As we go through the various trials and tribulations of life's
struggles we find our prayer life expands and changes according to our need and life situation. However, the basics for
many of us who pray remain simply, "help, help, help," and
"thank you, thank you, thank you." These cries of the heart
are, of course, supplemented by all the great formal prayers of
the Church, and especially by the great Our Father, which
Jesus taught. We also can pray the Scriptures and the Psalms.
Marian devotions help many of us pray, just as the prayers of
the great saints or other traditional prayers, such as the Jesus
prayer, work for different individuals. Today we also have
access to other mystical traditions, such as the prayer of quiet,
and centering prayer. As we learn more from Zen and Yoga we
can see that in the West we must recapture a sense of praying
through the body and the physical dimensions of what has
been identified as the core self. Breathing, prayer postures, and
bodily actions can be used in prayer. These insights from afar
help us reconsider in our own tradition those physical acts
used in devotion that heretofore have been rather conde-
scendingly relegated to the folk-religion aspect of Catholicism.

If we can pray with all of our bodily being then climbing a
holy mountain, lighting candles, or standing vigils can be acts
of prayer. New efforts to incorporate prayer into daily life may
evolve. A woman I know uses quilting as an act of prayer for
her father. This seems a modern equivalent to the ancient
process of painting on cave walls, which was considered a form
of prayer (drawing over earlier drawings did not really matter
since the process rather than the product was most important
in the act of worship). In many other eras repetitive rhythmic
recitations, such as mantras, chants, or rosaries, have been
used for prayer. It is difficult to find something truly new

when it comes to human beings seeking contact with their Maker. I go to a health club and finish the exercise routine in the steam room. I thought I had discovered in the steam room, with its all-enveloping warmth, a new place to pray; as the steam rises up, so do prayers. But then I found that certain American Indian tribes had created similar prayer rituals with steam huts, using hot water and rocks to invoke the spirits, cleanse themselves, and allow their prayers to rise with the steam. Probably those who pray in the hot tub or during television commercials or during car trips can also find ancient precedents for what they consider totally modern practices.

Certainly it is most natural to pray in surging moments of great physical joy and triumph and delight. It seems appropriate to praise God at moments of orgasm, or when giving birth. David danced naked before the Ark of the Lord as an act of exhultant worship, and we can understand his motive. I can remember a need for a Deborah-like song of victory when my first baby was born and I was wild with excitement and ecstasy. Such peak experiences or natural highs induce prayer just as do quieter times of nursing or other wonderful embodied moments of feasting and joy. Knowing that Creation is good and really believing it, we can see that prayer at such moments of physical love or pleasure is fitting. Those enchained in the old dualisms of matter and spirit cannot see the positive dimension of praying through the flesh; they understand only fasting and painful disciplines as ways to pray with the body. Asceticism works, but the prayer of embodied joy also magnifies the Lord.

All of the different ways of prayerfully communicating with God expand the self and keep us in touch with what we need to live the liberated life. Prayer is a fundamental orientation before it is a specific act, but the acts are important as one lays one's own concerns before the presence of God. The thing to remember is 'to pray often and as one can, not as one cannot.'

Many pray as they would speak to a friend quite informally. Others have more of a sense of awe and distance, and pray more formally. I think that many women, sensing God as Mother, pray in informal intimate ways. When one looks at the great female mystics, for instance Julian of Norwich, one sees that the homeliness of women's experience gives them an ability to capture and understand the homeliness and sweetness and graciousness of the way that God deals with us. When God becomes a friend, nothing is too small to bring to the divine comforter. The little way in prayer means that prayer can be constant, unceasingly leavening the details of life with the inner dialogue.

We know that the continued process of prayer psychologically transforms a person, but is its power limited to the subjective domain? Yes, prayer makes me different, but does it make a difference otherwise? Can prayer transform reality beyond its influence upon the individual? The question of whether, or how, the petitions of prayer can intervene and change things or change others is a difficult one. Jesus prayed privately and personally but he also raised the dead, healed the sick, and successfully prayed for Peter's salvation, telling his followers to imitate him in their own faith and good works. Great saints comply and religious orders devote their lives to intercessory prayer, but we in the ordinary secular scientific world have difficulty grasping how to go about acts of intervention. Our problem is moving from the more easily explained subjective effects of prayer to understanding the effects of prayer in the objective world of matter and other people.

PRAYING FOR THE LIVING—INTERVENTIONS IN CREATION

The easiest thing to accept about intercessory prayer is that as in the case of praying for oneself, prayer will change the person who prays. Praying for another, especially an enemy, changes one's own attitudes and consequent behavior. When we pray for others we recognize them as fellow creatures beloved by God, and so we must seek God's will for them as well as for ourselves. This realization immediately transforms the way we attend to other persons. When we take a God's-eye view we have to enlarge our own narrow perspective and break out of the egocentric point of view. The distant and longer view immediately changes our attitude. If someone has hurt us or is an enemy and we wish to seek revenge, then prayer for them will eventually quiet our fury and dissolve our resentment. We cannot hold on to our enmity and at the same time pray that God's love should be in those who hurt us. Prayer creates a reconciliation and realignment in the subjective relationship we have with others.

Our prayers for those with whom we have a positive relationship loosen our needs to control or have others act as we will them to act (for their own good, of course). We give them into God's hands and so give up our obsessive anxiety over their welfare, a repetitive stabbing of sorrow that can destroy all composure and ability to think and act productively. To pray for another is to be healed and to be made whole, to come to a deep peace in one's subjective attitude. Experience shows us that praying for others works for us. Prayer heals, reconciles, changes, and enlarges our perspective toward them. Prayer reinforces the belief that another possesses dignity as a child of God; they are fellow family members with us in the human community. Our mutual dependence and our mutual origin in God's love and purpose are made manifest to us when we pray for these others. And the change in attitude bears fruit in changed behavior.

This changing and enlarging of perspective also works, of course, in the collective prayers of the Church when we pray in the liturgy of the Mass. We are moved out of ourselves into a more spacious, gracious, and beauty-filled world of love and truth. We come up from the gloomy confinement of our desires or despairs or detestations into the enormous vistas of God's perspective. The alternative reality gives us rest.

When we pray for others we help ourselves immensely, but can we be helping them? At the very least when we pray for others we create a network, a community of concern, a reaching out to others in a way that symbolically connects us in the minds of those in the community who are praying together. Consciousness, both individual and collective, is certainly being changed in a real way and will predispose us to different actions in future encounters. Yes, prayer can change another through my changed behavior toward them in direct encounters, but the problem is whether change can take place at a distance.

Changing the collective consciousness could affect an object of prayer only if there are interconnections between all persons and objects in the universe and if the heretofore understood physical laws of the universe are not immutable in their operations. Since faith is informed by reason and grace builds upon nature so it is instructive to look at the present state of the question in our present knowledge of nature. How connected are people? With the growth of the science of genetics we understand that we are all connected in our species membership, our common DNA going back to our earliest origins as a human group. There appears to be a common ancestry for all human beings so that we are all members of one another in sharing our genetic heritage. We can also see that as a species we share certain mental and bodily structures that result in common developmental patterns.

Perhaps most important is the new evidence that individual infants develop a sense of self and self-consciousness in orderly patterned ways that result from innate programs and early social nurturing. Studies of infants show that from the earliest experiences of being cared for, each infant seeks to orient and order reality and also seems to produce a generalized "evoked companion" who becomes incorporated into the human personality. This evoked companion, of course, invokes in a religious person thoughts of Jesus and the Spirit within, but in the eyes of child psychologists it is seen as the self-governing "significant other" or "generalized other" whose social response gives a child a maturing sense of self and individuality. We are all innately social as the self is created. We are "selved," to use Gerard Manley Hopkins's phrase, in wondrous ways from the very beginning. In a sense we do create ourselves as a human species, in physical procreation, in social ways as we evoke the affective self, and finally in cognitive and symbolic ways as we share language and rational communication. The idea that we exist as a common human family has strong rational support. The belief in a universal human nature has had a resurgence in recent decades.

Psychologically, each of us is a member of the family and group that has created us, starting from the mother-child bond, and growing to include the father, the nuclear family, the kinship group, the community, the neighborhood, the linguistic-cultural group, and so on. By thinking the same thoughts in the same way and sharing feelings and actions we do have within ourselves all the persons who have influenced us psychologically and socially. As William James and Gordon Allport and other great psychologists say, we are socially a part of many other persons' lives and they are a part of ours. The social self always consists of others through the inner dialogue and imagined audience. But this communal consciousness, as far as we can ascertain, still resides within the body, skin, and brain of the individual person. While followers of a psychologist like Jung have posited a collective unconscious, and others have insisted that links between individual consciousnesses exist, the evidence is not yet convincing enough for a skeptic to accept.

Psychologists have tried to prove that telepathy does exist and that communication can occur between persons at a distance. So far the evidence suggests no more than chance occurrences. Yet almost every person has had experiences of remarkable coincidences in which some contact seemed to be coming into the individual consciousness from a distant person. Religious traditions witness to such phenomena. Family members, lovers, and twins regularly claim such experiences. But the problem is whether these experiences are just examples of what has been called illusory correlation, in which two events seem related when they really are not. Our human perception and memory is so biased that we remember hits and successful incidents and often fail to take account of all the times when we are mistaken, or have intuitions that are not later confirmed. Believers in ESP retort with the observation that such experiences would, of course, be too particular and personal to be captured within the confines of scientific method.

But direct face-to-face social influence is incontestable. Social psychology has experimentally demonstrated group phenomena such as emotional contagion, mood shifts, conformity, norm setting, obedience, attitude shifts, stress reduction, and suggestion, to name only a few. Since communication can take place through many channels beyond words, the social influence of other persons in the environment is a powerful force. Human beings are always mutually influencing others in interesting systematic ways. Social rituals, rules, and signals given and received, constantly affect behavior even if we are not conscious of these nonverbal interactions. Social systems exist beyond individuals and role expectations can shape individual behavior. Families are now seen as small social systems with smaller social microenvironments within them. The systems approach to intervention and change is established: the presence of others and groups of others does affect us.

New understandings of the influence that others can have upon us in direct interaction can help explain the form of face-to-face intercessory prayer known as mediation. When a person is being prayed for in the presence of another or others, there can be effects socially conveyed in the same ways other group influence can be exerted. This influence may be particularly potent if there is physical contact. In the newest nursing research, and in behavioral medicine, there is an interest in investigating the operation of what is called "therapeutic touch." The role of touch, perhaps correlated with relaxation responses, hypnotic suggestion, and stress reduction, has proven effects. In traditional religious practice there has always been an emphasis upon prayer along with the laying on of hands, anointing, and healing touch. As science examines the mysterious workings of social influence and the relation of the body and immune system to other aspects of the person, the reported effects of direct face-to-face intercessory prayer do not seem so alien.

Face-to-face intercessory prayer of mediation can be understood as an act of love and charity for another. This aspect of this spiritual work of mercy assumes that the other who is present has asked for the prayer and is receptive to its influence. A fellow believer or believers can open themselves together to the transforming effects of prayer. But there is still the problem of intercessory prayer for those people or events at a distance. Suppose these persons are not believers, or don't know or don't care that they are being prayed for. Are they as removed from our interpersonal social influence as are, say, weather patterns or other parts of the natural world? In a way praying for rain and praying for persons at a distance present similar problems of intervention in the created order.

As regards praying for rain, when we think it absurd or impossible we are assuming that matter has its own immutable determined laws separate from human consciousness, and/or that God would not intervene in the lawful universe to change things for specific persons or events, since God loves all equally. Today, the old problem of matter and its lawfulness is being reconsidered by science. Old assumptions about the universe as a stably running machine with determined laws of cause and effect have vanished. While we still don't really know what matter or antimatter is, new respectable theories emphasize dynamic movement, relativity, openness, and the mysterious interconnections of all existing things. Elementary biology texts inform school children that every atom now in their bodies was once a part of the stars; humans living billions of years after the big bang are made of actual stardust. New theories of superstrings as the way matter is organized are even more amazing, for they emphasize anew how dense and interconnected all things in the universe are.

If matter is a form of active energy it makes sense to hypothesize that matter cannot be totally different from consciousness or mind that can activate the brain's energy fields. While we don't understand the whole picture, the universe seems to be differentiated by how fast the energy of things is changing. Everything is energy and everything is constantly changing, but some things appear solid to us simply because their rate of change is so much slower than our own. Even the earth is not solid but seething and bubbling at its core; rocks and bones and buildings look permanent to us because they change more slowly than soap bubbles. Computers compute like lightning because they use electricity, but their hardware also changes and will eventually decay. So far, in brain research it appears that our thoughts and consciousness are more like lightning, but with the involvement of the body's biochemistry far more complex than any computer.

With new research scientists can see the change in magnetic fields within the brain when attention is deployed in various ways. When told to pay attention to a song and ignore another concurrent stimuli one can detect a visible amplification of the electrical signals in the appropriate site in the brain—this demonstrates the human freedom to keep a selected idea uppermost. In other new research we see superconductors effecting magnetic fields so that heavy objects hover above a surface, as superconductive railroads will soon enable passenger trains to do. (Traditional reports of saintly levitation or walking on water do not seem so absurd when we have seen objects levitating in the lab.) It is not beyond reason to hypothesize that in a universe which seems to consist of electrical energy, the energy of directed human consciousness might be a force that could intervene in the energy patterns of matter. Russian psychological research has long been attempting to scientifically prove such telekinesis or direct influence of mind on matter. While all such attempts have so far been unsuccessful, such efforts, as in the equally unsuccessful efforts to provide conclusive evidence for ESP or telepathy, are not irrational.

Behavioral medicine has certainly concluded that human consciousness and emotional states affect the body's workings and have much to do in particular with the workings of the immune system. Just as we have always known that the body can affect the mind and brain, as in diseased and drugged states, we now know that causality can be a two-way path. As human individuals, we are self-conscious organic wholes made up of mind and body, always interacting with our environment in complicated ways. Our ultimate environment, the universe, increasingly seems to be a vast open changing system undergoing dynamic processes that are as yet poorly understood. Who knows to what destination Earth and the distant galaxies are hurtling through space, or what new forces or dimensions may exist beyond those we now know?

Instead of a giant machine, the universe seems better pictured as a dynamic, evolving open organism in which time itself is a relative dimension somehow interdependent with space. The thought that as we look out at distant galaxies we are looking at the youthful past of the universe boggles the mind. We can no longer look at time and matter in our old plodding way as fixed external constants. Laws of cause and effect must also be reconsidered and now the rational order of nature seems less deterministic and more like a varying range of patterns and probabilities. Influenced by evolutionary thinking, scientists emphasize the ways in which openness, chance, and change are built into patterns and events. There is both a lawful pattern and an openness in the processes of development that reveal themselves in the making of each unique snowflake as well as in the creation of each human personality, even perhaps in the earth as a self-regulating organism, or in the life and death of stars. Random chance and probabilities exist making various open combinations lawful and possible.

Such reflections about the universe must inform my intuitive understanding of intercessory prayer. To pray for rain or some other intervention in material events is not to pray for a complete overturning or contradiction of nature's laws. It can be better understood as an effort to affect or fix or focus the already open probabilities of the universe, which is constantly evolving and changing. Intercessory prayer at a distance when a person or group is facing some material confrontation—a drought, storm, disease, or journey—is an effort to ensure that certain benign combinations of probabilities take place rather than other possible combinations that may be destructive. The hope is that the energy of individual or group consciousness can interact with the energy inherent in matter so that chances and open probabilities in an evolving system can be affected for the good, through God's good grace.

The moral problem of why God would respond to specific requests or allow them to make a difference is also a difficult one. It seems that God has created a universe subject to law but that these laws include openness and change. We have been told in Scripture that in this "not yet" time before the Kingdom, the Creation, too, is groaning in its birth pangs, just as we are gradually being transformed or Christified. We have also been told to pray unceasingly for all things and to imitate Christ's works performed through intercessory prayer. Such struggle seems necessary because of the Fall: some wound in nature or the enslavement of Creation is evident, as we see evil prosper and the persistent reign of death and decay in our unjust, suffering world.

Perhaps, as in the parable, an enemy has sown weeds in the good fields of earth and we really do struggle, as Paul says, against spiritual forces of evil. It has long been argued whether a Devil or other fallen angels exist, or whether beliefs in personified evils are but symbolic ways of demonstrating the effects of the absence of good and of humanity's refusal of God's grace. Inertia and the absence of good, or the effective force of corrupted human abilities, can go a long way toward explaining human evil and suffering. But the demythologized explanations of evil do not account adequately for natural devastations, genetic accidents and disease, or the seemingly "demonic" violent outbreaks of collective human perversity and sadism. Whatever the origin of evil, a person who prays for others will have to confront evil ensconced in human actions and in natural forces and mischances.

There exists no fully satisfactory moral explanation of why, if God is all good and all powerful, so much evil and suffering suffuses the human condition. The only beginning we can make in accepting suffering is to see that the Creation is separate from God and that this separation is the condition of freedom necessary to achieve the separate identity of human beings who must live and grow in the limitations of time and space. The potential for evil is the price of our freedom. We have been given stewardship of the created world even though God permeates and sustains the universe in which we live and move and have our being. We can imagine that God is all around and throughout the Creation but separated and self-limiting enough so that separate human wills and actions will be free to make a real difference. God's noncoercive policy may mean that only human beings can freely invite and freely open their own human sphere to God's active power. God constantly broods over the Creation and is seeded within each human being. God longs to be invited to help. To ask is already to find. God is everywhere, but freely initiated human cooperation seems necessary to focus, activate, and magnify the divine force of love and power.

Prayer, especially intercessory prayer, may by its own god-given energy affect the world and at the same time directly infuse the universe with God's active love. Specific human requests in specific instances work because then God is invited into the human condition and separate creation, and the divine power can work overtly. The divine ground or horizon always sustains the whole creation, but specific events in our time and space are affected by free human acts and initiative. As human beings our every deed, thought, feeling, and prayer has its effect. The intercessory prayer of individuals and the Church may well be co-creating and co-redeeming the evolving universe. Teilhard de Chardin had such an understanding of human initiative, as have many poets and creative spirits. I love Annie Dillard's idea that each act of artistic creation and each act of ordering done by a human being, whether seen by another or not, helps create and sustain the universe. Convincing images of intercessory prayer contribute to our perseverance in prayer.

In Scripture we have been given many images of prayer. There is the familiar image of a child making requests from a loving parent or the other way around, as in the case of Mary at Cana. Other interpersonal images of intercessory prayer are those of the beseeching beggar, or the request for a superior authority's command (as in the case of the centurion). Prayers are also pictured as incense ascending or voices raised on high. For us today, nonverbal images of the operation of intercessory prayer are perhaps more powerful. Images of light, energy, and water are particularly appropriate to represent God's power and love. Intercessory prayer can be seen as operating like a magnifying glass that can focus and intensify God's light upon a particular point. While light is everywhere such an intensifying of light can start fires. The more persons praying, the more God's light and power can be focused upon a situation.

Another image of intercessory prayer is that of a magnet that enters and changes the magnetic fields and so attracts God's power to a particular event. A magnet refocuses energy already there. Images of opening a cloud cover, providing a prism, or tuning into sound waves for transmission, get across the same ideas about intercessory prayer. Images of water are also used. Prayer for others can be seen as an opening of flood gates or providing new channels of irrigation so a parched terrain can be watered with God's love and power. One wishes to bathe and renew another in the living waters, giving them drink and refreshment. Other ancient images are that of breath, wind, and fire. One breathes the Spirit upon a person, fans the winds of the Spirit, or fans flames of fire toward a frozen situation or an ice-cold resistant heart.

To pray for a change in another's personal intentions, or to attempt to convert the heart and mind of others, presents its own moral difficulty. Since God does not coerce, we cannot try to use the divine power in some magical way to override or overwhelm another personality. Voodoo, spells, and sorcery try to coerce others, bypassing the assent of the individual's will. And all who have loved another and seen them in the throes of self-destruction can well understand the temptation to use any means. I have many times been so desparate that a Mephistopheles or Witch of Endor could have had my soul for the price of my child's safety and salvation—a feeling Saint Paul seems to have understood. But for Christians, the freedom, conscience, and free will of the other person or persons are at stake. The self and personal conscience are sacred, for they are the ways in which human beings express their nature as made in the image of God. A self remains free either to choose good or to choose evil. How can intercessory prayer change the consciousness of another? How does one pray for the conversion or change of another's inner self?

First of all if one is praying for a person to turn to the true and good or to grow in God, then one is praying essentially for an increase in their personal freedom or liberty. Turning toward truth, goodness, and love as the divine reality, can only empower and liberate a personality. The reality principle always betters human functioning. But a person can only become more liberated by their own free act. Thus one must pray for an increase in their opportunities to hear and see God's invitations. One prays that the light will be focused more brightly and be revealed more obviously to the person in need—perhaps through chance encounters wtih others or critical experiences. One also prays that the Holy Spirit within the person may whisper more loudly. I refer to this as upping the decibel level of the Spirit's still, small voice, which is already prompting and inviting from within. The individual is free to attend or not, to harden the heart or not, but in intercessory prayer we hope to change the probabilities for paying attention.

It is important here to remember that we are told that we are members of one another, all created as the children of God imprinted with the divine image. While we may not be able to prove interconnections of human beings and human consciousness from a scientific perspective, we do believe in this union by revelation. This communal unity in the Spirit means that we are vitally connected at some deep level irrespective of differences in space or time. My prayer for you in the Spirit, with the Spirit, and through the Spirit communicates with the same Spirit within you. As a member of the human community I can add my own vicarious invitation for the increasing presence of the divine voice in your consciousness. Our

elder brother Jesus always prays for you but we have also been
told that a group gathered and praying in Jesus' name can help
the Kingdom to come.

The whole Church formally prays for the world and all the
sheep and lost lambs throughout the liturgical year. Other
groups, from large religious orders to small communities,
constantly engage in intercessory prayer. Groups devoted to
intercessory prayer often make efforts to discern specific
needs and pray for these, while at other times they pray for
others in a more general way. Often one must pray that the
best combination or most positive combination of events will
take place, because one is not able to discern where the good
lies or what evil should be avoided. At other times our prayers
are more clearly focused. Some intercessory prayer groups
keep logs and journals to record their prayer life and to keep
track of results.

Those who pray experience the effectiveness of intercessory
prayer. Persons and events are seen to be affected, often
through the workings of improbable coincidences that skeptics can almost always consider "mere" coincidence. Only
when the probabilities of an event become astronomically
unlikely do we label it a miracle. Yet reports of miraculous
cures or other miracles continue and often seem to be sub-
stantiated, although illusory correlation, the will to believe, or
mass suggestion can obviously explain many accounts. Since
God has once initiated a reentry into Creation in one great
redemptive miracle, there is no reason other extraordinary
unilateral miracles may not happen on special occasions in
order to communicate symbolically. But it is well to remember that even the redemptive reentry into Creation was
contingent on Mary's free assent and cooperation as a human
being. Thus it more often may be the case that even in "big
miracles" it is the intercessory prayer of the human faithful
that makes a difference in a world given over to human stewardship and dominion. Jesus himself often pointed out the

need for cooperative human faith as a necessary condition for his own works of healing.

On the other hand, lack of faith or insufficient intercessory prayer is not a ready-made reason for what may appear to be unanswered prayers. Many other explanations may apply. When prayers seem to be unanswered it may be because the specific intervention requested would not be best in the long run. Even in our own histories we can remember when we prayed fervently for something that would not have served the good of others or ourselves, although we could not see this at the time. Other situations may also arise in which the lawfulness necessary for a separate Creation, albeit one in dynamic process, has already evolved to a point where change cannot take place without disrupting the separate integrity of the created order. Death having entered into Creation, death comes to all, despite intercessory prayer. But God does appear to be the master of the contingency plan: we give God the cross, God gives us the Resurrection.

We are kept going in prayer by our experiences of directly answered prayers and by the way unexpected better solutions keep popping up when we pray about something (the contingency planner again). New doors do open and unanticipated things happen when one deals with the God of surprises. Playful surprises, too, keep us merry. No one prepares Christians to encounter the Lord of Hosts, as the master of the sporting life, full of wit, joy, parry, and ironic touches. Prayers can get answered in delicious ways, as in this small instance. A woman I know prayed to Saint Joseph for help in her large family's financial emergency. A sympathetic acquaintance heard of this and was moved to ask her husband at work to withdraw some money from their savings account and mail it anonymously. The husband sent off an arbitrarily chosen amount, leaving some money in his own account to start again, only to discover later that he had unknowingly sent the *exact* amount of the distressed family's monthly mortgage payment. "But how could anyone have known?" asked the mystified woman. Obviously, Joseph and Son are a firm that deals in little jokes, just as Teresa of Lisieux likes to scatter flowers here and there. The spiritual life is comic as well as tragic, and God acts in many ways.

PRAYING FOR THE DEAD

Why pray for the dead? If they are really dead, then we Christians are to be most pitied in having believed in the Resurrected One's promise of life after death. Perhaps there are stoic spirits who do not yearn for eternal life, but ordinary Christians do. We have hoped in the good news of an eternal life with God and our departed friends and family, a life with all suffering and injustice routed. If the good news is true then the dead are not dead but only changed; and if the dead are now with Christ and God, why do they need our prayers?

Praying for the dead can, of course, be seen as a means to reconcile ourselves to their death. Acts of intercessory prayer for our departed friends and family can do a great deal for us. Each of us must eventually come to terms with our past and in new versions of the virtue of filial piety, forgive and understand our families and early caretakers. Those persons practicing the healing of past memories through imaginative efforts to achieve reconciliation with those dead and gone, are practicing a form of praying for the dead. But does such a use of guided imagery and loving goodwill benefit the other persons as much as it does our own spiritual condition? How can the dead who are now with God need further acts of mercy and charity from us?

To pray for the dead makes us confront the mystery of the last things. While we have been told that no eye has ever seen nor mind imagined what God has prepared for us, human beings have never given up the effort. We keep seeking imaginatively to penetrate beyond the ultimate veil in order to understand our own future and to consider our present responsibilities toward the living and the dead. What of purgatory, heaven, and hell, which have played such a part in our past cultural history?

Are prayers requested for the dead because they are now in some intermediate state or purgatory in which individuals must do penance and achieve further purification or transformation before taking on the weight of glory? Most religions have believed in some form of the afterlife and religions such as Buddhism and Hinduism have been very definite in their assertion that an individual soul or self must progress through many stages and reincarnations on the way to final enlightenment. While belief in reincarnation has spread in the West, even among Christians, it remains unconvincing to those committed to the eternal reality of a separate human identity and self. How could an individual continue to be the same self while coming back in cycles of reincarnation without historical, self-conscious memory?

Memory and conscious continuity of experience through time are essential to our individual self-identity. To keep our individuality, identity, and moral responsibility, our self would have to retain conscious memories of all we have lived through. Besides, if some purifying extended journey to God is necessary there seem to be better ways this could be achieved. When viewing the breadth and density and explosive dimensions of the universe it would appear that if we must live many lives in a purgatorial way, there could be individual and group destinies other than repeated returns to this small star.

Those persons and things that we have lived with and invested in are inherently a part of our identity. Sociologists speak about reference groups and cohorts; we see how hard it is for elderly persons when the social world that was once one's own is gone. Even if, as an individual, one could be frozen and thawed in a thousand years, could one have an identity or happy life without one's own community? Thinking about how important both our individual identities and our communal social selves are, Christians imagine different versions of the last things. Dante seemed to be on the right track when he peopled the afterlife with everyone he had ever known or heard of, but he possessed a particular scientific world view and a particular version of classic culture that he integrated into his artistic and theological synthesis.

One problem with medieval images of the last things resides not so much in accepting the immortality of the individual soul, but in the fact that in our universe time and space have disappeared as eternal constants. The immortality of an individual self or soul can still make sense to us, since knowledge of DNA reveals our bodies to be basically an information program, form (soul?), or gestalt that reproduces itself by repeatedly shaping an ever-changing turnover of molecules. Even as the visible body gradually disintegrates, the programmed patterns of information and energy that make up an individual organism could well continue in a different dimension. Science fiction plays with such notions all the time. In real science we see persons who experience real pain in phantom limbs that exist experientially in built-up patterns in the brain long after the physical limb has been amputated. One can imagine a similar buildup of experiential identity and patterned information continuing after death's disintegration and dissolution of the physical body. But how all things and persons could exist simultaneously beyond time or space, or what we could experience in an afterlife, challenges our imagination.

It suddenly came to me one day that the greatest heaven that God could give any of us would be time, endless time to live the fullness of life that we enjoy right now. One hears of the mystical "eternal present," but cannot quite grasp it until facing the disappearance of one's allotment of time. Indeed, heaven could well begin here and now; it could consist of having enough time to do all of the things that one loves to do with all the people that one adores. All the way to heaven is heaven, said Teresa of Avila. Heaven could hardly be some totally alien new place apart from all the people and things that have made us what we are and that we have loved. Surely God would be more clearly manifest in heaven and the whole world would be redeemed of suffering and injustice, but heaven may be this life exploded beyond the confining limits imposed by the choices and sacrifices now necessary in time.

In this down-to-earth heaven of total fulfillment in the eternal present here and now, one could continue living and have all of the experiences that one could not have before. All of one's potentialities for creativity could be expressed and developed in cooperation with God and one's friends. One could also have all of the friends and intimates that one could not fit into this life because of family obligations or other constraints of time and place. All of the places that one wished to explore yet never could and all of the good experiences that one had to miss would finally be possible. In other words, God's incarnational heaven would be an endless time of being able to do all those things we know how to do and love to do and would like to learn to do, if we could overcome evil, our own self-limitations, and the restrictions of the external environment.

In a dark time I have also had a distinct vision of purgatory. This unwelcome insight into purgatorial suffering came to me while undergoing the most severe psychological trials of my adult experience. As I suffered a cycle of repetitive torments full of sorrow, jealousy, hate, disillusionment over betrayal, and lust for revenge, it became clear that purgatory and hell also can begin here and now just as heaven can. All the way to hell is hell. A penetential purgatory could be no worse than the psychological sufferings we undergo. In a final purifying reckoning experienced outside linear time, a person could first undergo all of the suffering that he or she has caused others. It would be an appropriate form of justice if each of us were to experience the pain, torment, and trouble that our weaknesses and mean-spirited cruelties have visited upon other persons.

After such a purgation there might follow a further purification by the final experience of all of the unworthy emotions and degrading thoughts that we have wallowed in during this life. Evil thoughts torment us and keep us from the peace of Christ, as those raging in jealousy, anger, and desire for revenge know all too well. Guilt, shame, despair, and anxiety are other painful symptoms of our separation from God. It would be fitting and appropriate to experience all of the painful dross of a lifetime in one great cleansing passage to freedom and God's love and truth. How wonderful to shed all one's hatefulness and finally have the power to live in God's light and joy.

But, of course, since human beings are free, it would be theoretically possible for persons to refuse God's grace and remain in a self-chosen hell. An individual could choose isolation and elect to remain in unending suffering. When time is no more, of course, everything one chooses would be unending. Instead of shedding past suffering in order to be one with God and humanity, a person could cling to the self-torture of hate and the desire for revenge. Hell's stubborn gnawings of anger, hate, and revenge have been aptly depicted as a state of frozen despair, icy hardness of heart, and cold, proud isolation. The hellish moments we experience here and now give us a good picture of what hell is like; we need no embellishments of hellfire or demons. Our inner boredoms and despair, and the pain and nausea of no-exit torments, provide experiential previews of what human damnation might be like. Our century has already provided a plethora of examples of humanity's penchant for creating hells for the self and others.

Our intuitions about life after death stress the continuity of human experience. We have listened when Jesus says that one who sees Jesus sees God. Our experiences of human happiness and joy are the seeds of heaven just as our experiences of hell are continuous as the self and identity we create moves into the expanded dimensions beyond this world. Theologians speak of the fundamental option open to us at the moment of death, so at this critical juncture of transition we have a chance to make an even clearer, freer choice than those we have made before. The process of dying may be a birth into a newer more clearly chosen consciousness. As in the human birth process, the support of fellow human beings should be helpful. In other words, to pray for the dead is really to pray for the dying, as a support for those making the transition.

How disorienting it may be to die! The anxiety of all new and unknown journeys and endeavors must be multiplied to the millionth power. How most of us shrink from the moment, even if we are believers and expect to meet a loving and gracious Lord, and enter into a more abundant life. For those who in this life have resisted all things spiritual and all of God's promptings, it must be a traumatic shock to find oneself surviving death. Surely these persons could use the prayer and support of their fellow human beings on earth, and even more perhaps, the help of those who have already gone before. The communion of saints must take on great importance during the dying process. Christians have traditionally sought Mary's maternal aid in the childbirth they must negotiate at the moment of death. But others we have known must also be willing to help us. If in heaven we do what we love to do, surely the saints large and small who love helping others, must be ready and eager to nurture and guide their fellow human beings. Everyone could at last be a catcher in the rye, rescuing those in peril and working for the redemption of the world with all one's powers and gifts.

Christians have always had a confidence in the support and companionship of those who have gone before them in the

Lord. Stephen looked up and saw Jesus at the moment of martyrdom. It later seemed only natural to conclude that the martyrs would be ready to love and help their fellow Christians at the moment of death, as well as in the daily struggles of life. The human species has always had a lively consciousness that one's ancestors or the spirit world remain involved and concerned with their successors. As Christians we ask the saints to pray for us, just as we would ask our friends, community, parish, or prayer group for intercessory prayers. Invoking the saints, along with Mary, is a sure way an individual Christian can garner a group, or a cloud of witnesses to pray. If we love to exercise stewardship and creative nurturing efforts toward our kith and kin in the present world, why should we lose interest after death? Our cooperation with God in redeeming the world would be intensified as we became transformed and able to love the world as ardently as God does.

So in praying for the dead we are really praying for those who are dying and are being born into the human company already living and loving with God. In such a transition, there is a very fine line between praying *for* someone who is dying, and praying *to* someone who can now pray for you. Those great individuals who are on fire with the love of God before they die, have rarely been prayed "for," but instead almost instantly been prayed "to" for help. They accomplished prodigies of charity and good works in this life and obviously must be bent on continuing to do God's will in heaven. They have already been so transformed in Christ that their transition must involve an instant access of more freedom and power to do good.

Somewhere between those persons that we would immediately pray to and those persons that we would feel a real need to pray for, are those more ordinary persons who seemed on the way to adulthood in Christ's friendship but remained fairly mired in the struggle when they died. For these fundamentally good people we find ourselves praying for a certain length of time as a support and help in their dying. But we do not pray for them forever. After a while we begin to sense that we should rather be asking for their intercession. They can become one with the larger groups of persons who are prayed for collectively in the liturgical prayers of the Church. The purgatorial transition to eternity may be accomplished in a flash, but since we live in time our consciousness only gradually adjusts to our beloved dead's new status.

CONCLUSION

Intercessory prayer for others is an act of love that, like all the spiritual works of mercy, takes personal energy and effort. To pray for the living and the dead makes sense in the interdependent world revealed through God's love. But we need faith to believe in God's good news; when we flag in faith or imagination our prayers for one another also wither. Prayers of personal petition give immediate comfort and immediate results from the very process of praying, but intercessory prayer, being once removed, requires greater love of others in God, and more fidelity to the unseen. Of all the spiritual works of mercy, intercessory prayer is perhaps the most arduous because it is done with less evidence, or at least concrete evidence, to support the exertion of energy. It is always possible to doubt and consider the results of prayer to be coincidence. And in our prayers for the dead we do not even have any obvious results to turn to. Thank God the great saints have provided us with inspiring examples of perseverance in intercessory prayer. We ordinary folk are then more moved to ask the Spirit within to increase our ability to pray for the living and the dead.

EPILOGUE

Reconsidering the seven spiritual works of mercy brings to our attention the many forms of active Christian love that can exist in person-to-person encounters. Several themes have recurred in this reflective meditation. One dominant theme is the need for the Church to explore the Christian understanding of the human person in dialogue with the different disciplines of psychology. In our self-conscious era a new synthesis must be achieved if Christian spirituality is going to be effectively practiced in daily life. We have to grapple again with the basic questions, "What is human nature?" and "Is there such a thing as a Christian personality?"

In answer to the second query, I would hold that yes, certain personality characteristics will regularly appear in Christians. The spiritual works of mercy, rooted in Scripture and tradition, can only be practiced by certain kinds of persons who display certain attitudes toward other persons. Individuals who actively attempt to love others in imitation of God's love for humankind, will resemble each other in their attentiveness, patience, graciousness, kindliness, and dedication to reality. In living out their faith Christians will seek to reach out and help remedy a neighbor's ignorance, doubt, anger, bitterness, sorrow, callousness, or apathy. These personal efforts to love and care can be done in a thousand different ways, but they also display essential patterns. All those who attempt to live in Christ and with Christ, and to be a Christbearer, will begin to possess a certain family resemblance.

Another important theme emerging from these reflections is the importance of personal transformation and change. Christians are committed to constant growth in their search for perfection and fulfillment in Christ. The spiritual works of mercy are efforts to change one's self and others through specific personal transactions of love. Change comes about by individual effort and by God's initiative and freely given power. As Karl Rahner once noted, it can be hard to understand "how it is that we beg of God something that we ourselves must do." We accept through faith and love that we are in the hand of the all powerful and gracious God, and then work out our salvation in fear and trembling. We trust God, and hope for salvation, while constantly trying to change ourselves and the world. Our efforts are the sign that God is working in us.

One tries harder and harder in all kinds of ways. But the main effort we make is to open ourselves through acts of faith and love to God's power. By asking and believing that we will receive, we do receive and are slowly transformed. Our gratitude for God's gifts precedes the getting of more gifts, and these new gifts beget more gratitude and love, and so on, in endless ascending circles of giving and receiving. Those who have, get more; the grateful in gratitude give more, and end up getting even more. The spiritual economy of the Trinity is based on infinite plenitude and what the mystics have called "God's fecund nature." As Blesed Jan van Ruysbroeck says, "And this work is ever new; beginning, operating, and being fulfilled; and herein we are blessed in knowing, loving, and being fulfilled together with God."*

The Seven Steps of the Ladder of Spiritual Love (London: Dacre Press, A. & C. Black, 1952), p. 61.

The Spirit within moves us to love and open up to other persons in need. As we try to reach out we are ourselves transformed. Over and over we see that the relationship of self to other is dependent upon our inner relationship of self to self, which is in turn dependent on the self's relationship to God. There are three elements in this interacting system which cannot be separated. To minister to your need, I must acknowledge both my own need and my own help from God and my fellows. To comfort you I must have suffered, been comforted, and be comfortable. To instruct your ignorance I must be in touch with my own ignorance, my present knowing, and the movements needed to obtain enlightenment. And it is the same with our personal confrontations with human doubt, anger, bitterness, and apathy. Knowing one's self, finding one's self, and expending one's self for another are intertwined activities. Love of self, love of God, and love of neighbor are interdependent.

Gradually and painfully we become psychologically integrated and whole as we grow up into Christ. As we become healed we can heal. In the beginning we may only be able to ask for an increase of desire. Never mind the difficulties involved in doing good, just help me to *want* to be good. The ancient religious cry of the heart is perpetually renewed, "O Lord, give me a transformed living loving heart instead of this hard heart of stone." It is probably true that with God's grace we can be as holy as we want to be, but wanting to be holy is the crux of the matter. Much of our prayer life and worship is devoted to attentively kindling the flame of love and desire, which then makes all effort seem effortless.

A final theme emerges from meditating on the spiritual works of mercy. While the corporal works of mercy are basically aimed at the restoration of health, the spiritual works of mercy are aimed at making human beings happy. Happiness and joy are the marks of the Spirit. Christ came to give us joy and happiness, even though this Gospel message always seems too good to be true. The reason Christians must work to overcome sin, ignorance, doubt, sorrow, anger, bitterness, and despair is that God wants us to be happy and live fully and abundantly. Only as we grow together in love will we be able to leave the sadness, gloom, and anxiety of sin behind. We are drawn by the Spirit to the warming fire of joy, and the lure of the divine work to be done. God works through us to perform the spiritual works of mercy. With each person's transformation achieved, "Amazing Grace shall then prevail, in heaven's joy and peace."

POPULATION

THE CAMBRIDGE ECONOMIC HANDBOOKS

General Editors:

J. M. KEYNES (Lord Keynes)	1922–1936
D. H. ROBERTSON (Sir Dennis Robertson)	1936–1946
C. W. GUILLEBAUD	1946–1956
C. W. GUILLEBAUD MILTON FRIEDMAN }	1956–

POPULATION

IAN BOWEN

Formerly Fellow of All Souls College, Oxford

DIGSWELL PLACE
JAMES NISBET & CO. LTD.
CAMBRIDGE
AT THE UNIVERSITY PRESS

The first Cambridge Economic Handbook on
POPULATION was written by Harold Wright
and published in 1923

First Published 1954

Reprinted . . . 1955
Reprinted . . . 1960
Reprinted . . . 1964
Reprinted . . . 1966

James Nisbet and Company Limited
Digswell Place, Welwyn, Herts
and the Cambridge University Press
in Association with the University of Chicago Press

INTRODUCTION

TO THE CAMBRIDGE ECONOMIC HANDBOOKS
BY THE GENERAL EDITORS

Soon after the war of 1914–18 there seemed to be a place for a series of short introductory handbooks, "intended to convey to the ordinary reader and to the uninitiated student some conception of the general principles of thought which economists now apply to economic problems."

This Series was planned and edited by the late Lord Keynes under the title "Cambridge Economic Handbooks" and he wrote for it a General Editorial Introduction of which the words quoted above formed part. In 1936 Keynes handed over the editorship of the Series to Mr. D. H. Robertson, who held it till 1946, when he was succeeded by Mr. C. W. Guillebaud.

It was symptomatic of the changes which had been taking place in the inter-war period in the development of economics, changes associated in a considerable measure with the work and influence of Keynes himself, that within a few years the text of part of the Editorial Introduction should have needed revision. In its original version the last paragraph of the Introduction ran as follows:

"Even on matters of principle there is not yet a complete unanimity of opinion amongst professional economists. Generally speaking, the writers of these volumes believe themselves to be orthodox members of the Cambridge School of Economics. At any rate, most of their ideas about the subject, and even their prejudices, are traceable to the contact they have enjoyed with the writings and lectures of the two economists who have chiefly influenced Cambridge thought for the past fifty years, Dr. Marshall and Professor Pigou."

Keynes later amended this concluding paragraph to read:

"Even on matters of principle there is not yet a complete unanimity of opinion amongst professional students of the subject. Immediately after the war (of 1914–18) daily economic events were of such a startling character as to divert attention from theoretical complexities. But today, economic science has recovered its wind. Traditional treatments and traditional solutions are being questioned, improved and revised. In the end this activity of research should clear up controversy. But for the moment controversy and doubt are increased. The writers of this Series must apologize to the general reader and to the beginner if many parts of their subject have not yet reached to a degree of certainty and lucidity which would make them easy and straightforward reading."

Many though by no means all the controversies which Keynes had in mind when he penned these words have since been resolved. The new ideas and new criticisms, which then seemed to threaten to overturn the old orthodoxy, have, in the outcome, been absorbed within it and have served rather to strengthen and deepen it, by adding needed modifications and changing emphasis, and by introducing an altered and on the whole more precise terminology. The undergrowth which for a time concealed that main stream of economic thought to which Keynes referred in his initial comment and to which he contributed so greatly has by now been largely cleared away so that there is again a large measure of agreement among economists of all countries on the fundamental theoretical aspects of their subject.

This agreement on economic analysis is accompanied by wide divergence of views on questions of economic policy. These reflect both different estimates of the quantitative importance of one or another of the conflicting forces involved in any prediction about the consequences of a policy measure and different value judgments about the desirability of the predicted outcome. It still remains as true today as it was when

Keynes wrote that—to quote once more from his Introduction:

> "The Theory of Economics does not furnish a body of settled conclusions immediately applicable to policy. It is a method rather than a doctrine, an apparatus of the mind, a technique of thinking, which helps its possessor to draw correct conclusions."

This method, while in one sense eternally the same, is in another ever changing. It is continually being applied to new problems raised by the continual shifts in policy views. This is reflected in the wide range of topics covered by the Cambridge Economic Handbooks already published, and in the continual emergence of new topics demanding coverage. Such a series as this should accordingly itself be a living entity, growing and adapting to the changing interests of the times, rather than a fixed number of essays on a set plan.

The wide welcome given to the Series has amply justified the judgment of its founder. Apart from its circulation in the British Empire, it has been published from the start in the United States of America, and translations of the principal volumes have appeared in a number of foreign languages.

The present change to joint Anglo-American editorship is designed to increase still further the usefulness of the Series by expanding the range of potential topics, authors and readers alike. It will succeed in its aim if it enables us to bring to a wide audience on both sides of the Atlantic lucid explanations and significant applications of "that technique of thinking" which is the hallmark of economics as a science.

C. W. GUILLEBAUD
MILTON FRIEDMAN

April 1957

PREFACE

The connection between economic development and population change is not simple, nor necessarily constant over the years. The classical economists bravely undertook to define the connection; when their generalizations had been exposed by events as over-simplifications, economists began to drop the discussion altogether, or merely to re-state the older doctrines. Nevertheless, a connection probably exists, and this short study attempts to outline how the student of economics, or the general reader, might now approach the problem. References in the text have been kept as brief as possible. Full references are given at the end in the select bibliography, which may serve as a guide to further reading.

I am much indebted to my friends and critics at Hull, who have helped in the planning and production of this book, especially to Miss Joyce Bellamy, Mr. George Maxcy, Mr. Leslie Smyth, Mr. Martyn Webb and to my wife; and for the secretarial assistance provided by Miss Olive Bevan and Miss Barbara Wood.

IAN BOWEN

HULL, 1954

CONTENTS

PART I—INTRODUCTORY SURVEY

CHAPTER I

POPULATION AND ECONOMICS

CHAPTER II

WORLD POPULATION

CHAPTER III

BRITAIN'S POPULATION

PART II—ANALYSIS

CHAPTER IV

THE MALTHUSIAN THEORY

CHAPTER V

THEORIES OF STATIC EQUILIBRIUM

CHAPTER VI

EQUILIBRIUM AND WORKING POPULATION

CHAPTER VII

THE EXPANDING ECONOMY

CHAPTER VIII

INTERNATIONAL MIGRATION

PART III—FUTURE PROSPECTS

CHAPTER IX

GREAT BRITAIN

CHAPTER X

WORLD POPULATION

POPULATION

PART I

INTRODUCTORY SURVEY

CHAPTER I

POPULATION AND ECONOMICS

§ 1. *The Economic Criterion.* The question how many people there ought to be in any country can be answered in many ways, according to the values to which the answer has reference. In this study, the size, and the rate of growth, of the British (and Northern Irish) population in relation to its economic welfare, even though this concept is itself inexact and difficult to define, are the chief subjects to be discussed. But the British population is especially vulnerable to changes in world economic conditions, and these conditions are in turn linked inexorably with world population changes.

The difficulty of defining a value criterion for the subject arises in an acute form, since what has to be discussed is not merely one population but at least two (the British and the rest of the world)—and many more according as other countries and continents have to be considered as separate problems. If values are consciously sought the discussion may become excessively philosophical, while ignoring the issue may lead to the unintentional adoption of unnecessarily biased assumptions. What size and rate of growth ought the British population to have over the next fifty years? Is it to be 2 per cent or 4 per cent of world population—fifty or a hundred or twenty-five millions? Any of these sizes might be consistent with preserving life and conserving *some* British influence on the civilized life of the world. Some additional criterion is required by which to test these alternatives.

Professor F. W. Notestein, in reviewing[1] the (British) Report of the Royal Commission on Population,[2] remarks on the "in part almost mystical, but universal and probably healthy, reluctance to see one's own group dwindle in size". He goes on to maintain that the Commission's arguments on the question of British emigration to the Dominions were "based more on sentiment than on a rational calculation of national or commercial advantage". Yet even Professor Notestein himself is here introducing unconscious assumptions, his underlying notion seeming to be that "commercial advantage" is "rational", while "sentiment" is "irrational", a value judgment that is itself open to dispute. The immediate object of any state may be material wealth, but it would be a special and peculiar society wherein material wealth was the sole objective; historically most societies have pursued other ends as well, with material wealth regarded as a means to attaining those ends, or to their fuller realization, and it is a fallacy to suppose that men need television sets in order to receive only advertisements for better or different television sets. The sounder line of criticism of nationalistic bias in population theories is that it conflicts with values which may be more defensible.

The way in which the Royal Commission itself tackled the problem deserves some attention. The Commission began its report by sketching the history of world population since 1750, and of British population in relation to it. The Report remarks[3] that "Great Britain's share in the population of the continent [of Europe] rose from 5·7 per cent in 1801 to 9 per cent in 1900 . . . if her population had not been growing, and growing rapidly, her

---

[1] *Population Studies*, Vol. III, No. 3, p. 237, and cf. Hubback, 1947, p. 116.
[2] Cmd. 7695, published by H.M.S.O., June 1949.
[3] Cmd. 7695, 1949, par. 21, p. 8.

leadership could not have endured more than a few years"
—hence, it is argued, the *economic* development of the
world (including that of Britain itself) would have been
lower in 1949 than it then was. Furthermore—and at
this point the Report's "political" values become more
explicit—"the influence of Britain and of British ideas
would be far less extensive than it is to-day". As a
perhaps rather unexpected example of this influence the
Report refers to "the expansion of the United States as
an English-speaking nation" which was "greatly encouraged by the large emigration of Britons" in the
nineteenth century.

This approach, like Professor Notestein's, is of considerable interest because of its implications. To the authors
of the Report "British ideas" is a term that includes
"American ideas", in 1949, a date at which the distinction
between them was often considered to be significant.
How much weight indeed ought to be given to such concepts as "British ideas" or "the American way of life"?
It may be natural that groups should wish to see ideologies,
to which their own group-name is attached, flourish and
expand their influence. But experience has shown
patriotic fervour to be a misleading and destructive force,
as well as, at times, a noble and preserving one. What
do we understand, in any case, by "British ideas"?
Whatever these are now, they were different in 1950 from
what they were in 1900, and the population movements
under consideration span the centuries. Or is all this
talk of "British ideas" (or French or American ideas) a
mere rationalization, as Professor Notestein has hinted,
of a primitive urge for group survival, and for national
self-preservation? Primitive urges are not necessarily
to be condemned; without them there would be no
problems of population, and perhaps no population. But

in this instance they might be rationalized by each nation in such a way as to legislate for perpetual warfare, for if the members of each separate population, or a sufficient number of them, consider that it has a sacred mission to expand (invoking the law of the ultimate survival of the fittest, and deeming their own special characteristics to be relatively the best) then international anarchy and strife are inevitable; for the power to expand numbers is very considerable.

Fear of this impasse has toned down the explicit recommendations of most populationists, populationists being defined as those who maintain that some degree (usually a high one) of continuing net natural increase in the numbers of their own nation is a desirable objective. Because of it they have taken refuge in rather vague reference to "ideas", "ways of life" and so on, rather than advocate primitive group expansion. Their argument has then run somewhat as follows. Certain ideas are good; these ideas have been preserved and developed best by certain national groups (for instance the French), and have been best expressed in the French language; therefore it is good for these ideas, this civilized mode of life, to spread. But, of course, the rational objector may here interpose, these ideas might be spread by education and not by birth. At this point the populationist appeals to history; without demographic forces to maintain it, he will argue, a civilized mode will decline and perish—this we know inductively from endless instances. For example, M. Marcel Reinhard writes of the French Canadians [1]:

"Un peuple est né, il a sauvegardé ses traditions et ses croyances. Ce triomphe est du à sa vitalité, frap-

[1] Reinhard [1949], p. 389.

pante illustration du rôle de la démographie ou, plus
exactement, de la natalité . . . Les Canadiens français
forment, en effet, environ le tiers de la population du
Dominion : 3·4 millions sur 12·5 . . . En 1763 ils
n'étaient guère que 65,000, mais déjà remarquablement
prolifiques.''

And in similar terms the same authority deplores the
decline of the French birth-rate in France, and the in-
effectiveness of the legislation designed to arrest it and to
ameliorate social conditions.

Populationism in its extreme form has always been
repugnant to humanitarian critics, because of the false
values on which it has seemed to rest. It has always
seemed to be based on blind, and ultimately mutually
destructive, group loyalties. Fascists have been notable
populationists, and so have militarists of every persuasion.
So too have been, and are, the more obscurantist religions
of the world, those that rely on faith rather than on
reason or on the wider forms of education. Considerations of agricultural space or raw material supplies or
social hygiene will not deter them, perhaps because there
are always many of these supplies in the possession of
unbelievers.

But the existence of these extreme views should not be
allowed wholly to discredit the notion that births may
be too low in some societies for the realization of a good
end. That end, for the purposes of this book, must be
defined as broadly as possible, and from the point of
view of the world as a whole. It will be assumed that it
is right to think of the world community as a single large
group; it will be assumed that this group is composed
of individuals who want (or would want if sufficiently en-
lightened) economic sufficiency, security and advancement,

as a means to exercising their physical and intellectual powers for improvement of mankind's quality of life. These assumptions are not necessarily realistic—it may not even be true that the majority of men are yet capable of regarding themselves as citizens of one world; but the assumption is nevertheless made.

It is not suggested that national and religious differences will not continue, nor that they will cease to be important. One difficulty in the formula just proposed is that there can be no general agreement on what is meant by "improving" the quality of life, and members of some groups will interpret this as attainable only in terms of the extension of their own beliefs or practices. But an assumption on values has to be made, and the one made here is that such differences of view will be, in principle, less important than the common agreement (open or tacit) of many individuals that there are some common values for the world community as a whole. This is not a treatise on political science, so the means of expressing popular will on these values need not here be discussed.

Evidently this assumption still does not provide an exact measure against which to compare possible different population rates of growth. There may be, by this test— which is necessarily rough—more than one "right size" or "best rate of change" for the British and for the world populations. But the subject can be rescued from vagueness by the fact that not all paths of advance are open to the world, or to the national economy. The range of choice is severely restricted.

§ 2. *Classification of Factors affecting Population Change.* The economic criterion discussed above was defined in terms of (economic) "sufficiency, security and advancement", and the ideas that these terms represent perhaps need to be explained a little further. All three words have meaning only in relation to existing conditions, and to various individuals' points of view; what is "sufficiency" to a British civil servant might be gross poverty to an American business man, and what a Belgian coal-miner regarded as "security" a British docker might take to be uncertainty of employment. But though the terms are necessarily relative, each of them indicates unambiguously a direction in which the economic system may, or may not, move.

There is an approximate, though not complete, correspondence between the three objectives and the customary division of time adopted by economists. Very roughly economic "sufficiency" (which might also be called the "optimum level [1] of real income per head") is an objective to be realized in the short or medium term; economic advancement is a long-term concept; while economic security for the most part (though not exclusively) means avoidance of the hazards of periodic, or cyclical, fluctuations in employment.

Whether or not a particular size of population satisfies the economic criterion depends upon the point of view. The definition of an "optimum" population is therefore a matter of some difficulty, and the question is discussed at much greater length in chapter five.

It is part of our task to examine not only what size and composition a population should have, to meet some criterion, but also how it came to be what it is. The factors which determine the size and the rate of growth of the population of any particular place, whether of the world or of some political unit, are almost certainly very numerous. Fortunately, it may be reasonable to classify

[1], I.e., the highest income that is attainable without a more than proportionate violation of some other criterion which can be valued.

them at the outset, and so to introduce an order into
our thinking, without however prejudging which of the
factors, or groups of factors, are most important.

The factors which affect population growth may, like
the economic criterion, be divided broadly into three:
long-term, short-term and cyclical. Into the first of these
classes must come such influences as a slow change in the
size of families such as follows, for instance, the spread of
knowledge of contraception; into the second come sudden
migratory flows due to war or natural disaster; into the
third, those rises and falls in the birth-rate or in the
migration rates that have been demonstrated, in some
instances, to occur in times of boom and slump. The
reader will no doubt have observed that these three
examples are each of a different *character*, however, not
only in respect of time-scale but because *family size* is
largely demographically determined, *war* is mainly
political in origin, and *booms and slumps* are economic
phenomena.

The factors have been schematically represented below,
and are divided horizontally into three rows representing
Demographic, Economic and Political factors, these in
turn being divided according to whether they are affecting
population growth in the Long-term (decades or centuries),
the Short-term (single years or less) or Cyclical (more or
less regular intervals of a few years). Thus as a first
approximation it may be useful to think of nine main
types of factor that determine the size, or rate of growth,
of population. Let p summarize the combined effects of
nine separate factors, a to k. These factors are not
necessarily independent of each other through time.

This representation is merely schematic; the letter
shown in each "box" represents one type of factor at
work on one time-scale. For example, a slow but steady

Table I

	Long Term	Short Term	Cyclical	Total Category Effects
Demographic . .	*a*	*b*	*c*	*d*
Economic . .	*e*	*f*	*g*	*h*
Political . . .	*i*	*j*	*k*	*l*
Total time effects .	*m*	*n*	*o*	*p*

decline in the intention to have large families would be classified under *a*, as a long-term demographic factor. A steady trend downwards (unfavourably) in the terms of trade of a country would be listed under *e*, as a long-term economic consideration (in this case inimical to population growth). The election, for a short period of office, of a government with an exceptionally generous family allowance scheme in its party platform would be counted as a *j* factor, and so on.

All this may seem obvious, and the mere systematization of a truism. But there are three reasons for introducing the scheme at this stage of the argument. First, this truism is one that is often mentioned verbally, especially at the beginning of treatises, and then in fact ignored. The demographic specialist mentions the importance of economic and political factors, but tends to regard them as ripples on the slow, steady tide of the demographic swell. The political theorist (or historian) sometimes ignores the demographic and economic cross-currents. Even the economist is not always wholly immune from the specialist's arrogance. The present study, partly because it is by an economist, will stress the importance of economic factors; but this is not the only reason for stressing that—the other reason is that in many discussions of population problems the economic factors have tended to be grossly under-emphasized.

Secondly, the scheme will serve to remind us not to fall into the opposite, and equally egregious error, of concentrating attention on economic factors to the *exclusion* of the weighing up of more or less independent demographic and political factors, which at certain points of history have the greatest importance for population growth.

Since the factors represented by the different letters are not necessarily independent, a short-term "political" event, say a war of short duration, with heavy casualties, may not only affect population directly but may also affect some other factor, for instance b (by creating a surplus of females over males and a lower marriage rate), or even c, since the aftermath of the war may be an exceptionally high birth-rate for a few years, which will tend to cause every twenty-five to thirty years thereafter a cyclical bump in the average birth-rate.

Any one of the classified factors may have an effect on any other, and hence eventually a feed back effect on itself. The problem of determining how population growth has occurred is the problem of writing down correctly all these functional relationships. In practice this is well beyond our present powers of analysis. The most that can be hoped for is that the chief functional relationships can be picked out, and perhaps the second order, or even third order, effects in certain instances.

To discover the functional relationships for any particular period would not necessarily mean (even if it were feasible) establishing their value for all time. In some circumstances an economic factor, say a lowering in the standard of life, may have a quite different direct effect on population growth than in others; sometimes an economic change will provoke a major political change, and at others be quite neutral in its political effects; sometimes demographic changes have immediate economic results, and sometimes their results work out only over several decades.

The scheme may be given whatever degree of precision is required. The terms Demographic, Economic and Political may be defined as we choose, so long as they provide an exhaustive basis for classifying the factors that affect population change. Demographic factors are intended to include all matters relating to size of families to physical health of individuals and communities, and to changes in the structure or functioning of the human organism; economic factors are those which arise from the organization of human beings as producers and consumers, and from the scarcity of raw materials to satisfy their needs; and political factors cover all residual items, such as the influences of the forms of society and of government, of the pursuit of power, and of the institutions which owe their origin to habit or imagination.

§ 3. *Outline of Treatment to be Followed.*   The first part of this book is intended as a survey rather than as an analysis, as will be seen from the chapter headings.   Nevertheless, it may be useful to look all the time for scraps of evidence which bear both (a) on the criterion of judging "success" (i.e., whether a population is of the right size), and (b) on the factors which have made population what it is.   In Part II, the analysis of population growth is first considered historically (including the explanations of Malthus and others); then the economic criterion of "success" is discussed in detail (Chapter V); and in Chapter VI the same ideas are broadened to cover rates of growth as well as size. Finally, international migration is both surveyed and analysed in relation to the preceding discussion.

In Part III the future prospects of Britain and the World are surveyed.

Before turning to later chapters, the reader might find it useful to try to classify into one box or another of Table I the factors which, in his experience, seem principally to have affected changes in the population of his own neighbourhood, county and country, or of other divisions well known to him. It is likely to become apparent to him that many factors other than " demographic " seem prima facie to have been operative. (In this chapter the word " demographic " has been applied in a somewhat loose sense, though one justified by usage ; " demological " would perhaps be a more accurate substitute.)

CHAPTER II

WORLD POPULATION

§ 1. *Population Estimates and Extrapolation of Trends.* It is evidently necessary to know how many people there are in the world, where they live and their likely rate of increase in the future, in order to discuss population problems at all satisfactorily, and some fairly well established estimates and forecasts are fortunately available. But estimates and forecasts are by their nature uncertain, and their credibility and hence the validity of using them require careful assessment.

Anyone who has filled up a census return knows that some slight inaccuracy may quite easily be recorded on it; even conscientious citizens may fall into unintentional error, and not all citizens are conscientious; some are not literate. In some countries a majority of adults may well be indifferent or even hostile to enumeration, nor are enumerators immune from fallibility and inexactitude. Despite these expected shortcomings census returns are regarded as, at present, giving the best count of human beings that can be obtained, and as being, for the practical purpose of discussions of broad issues, sufficiently exact.

But not all "countries" (that is, separate political units) have even a census.[1] For those with no censuses, estimates have to be made on the basis of such non-censal statistics as seem to be relevant. Hence the recorded total of world population in 1950, for example, contains

[1] For instance the Belgian Congo, Morocco, Mauritius and the British Cameroons, to pick out a few. The "type of estimate" column of Table I of the United Nations' Demographic Yearbook for 1949–50 gives some details of the basis of the estimates in a convenient form.

a considerable margin of error.   The error is much greater for Africa, Asia and South America than for Western Europe and North America.

The possible error in the totals increases for earlier dates.   The estimates even of European population in the seventeenth and eighteenth centuries are notoriously insecure.   The figures for Asia, Africa and South America in 1900 have also been hotly debated, and frequently revised.[1]   The technical details of these disputes need not be described, but the possibility of error must be mentioned since it limits the effectiveness of arguments based upon the trends in the estimates.

To look to the future, population figures must be extrapolated, which means writing down figures in a sequence justified by the rate of changes in rate, observed in a past sequence.   Evidently this justification may assume that the past rate (or change of rate) will persist.   By varying the assumptions (that is by choosing different rates as the "key" rates) different extrapolations, or guesses, as to future population can be made.   But if the assumption is that the governing rate will be very different in the future from past and current rates then arguments have to be adduced to support the likelihood of the change assumed.   The past history of population includes instances of very important and large changes in birth-rates, death-rates and other vital statistics directly affecting the change in total population.   It is a matter of judgment whether to predict any further large change in human habits affecting births and deaths.

Most extrapolations, or guesses, about the future size of population are based on assumptions not of substantial

[1] For example, a World Health Organization publication (see Swaroop 1951) gave an estimate of the population of Africa in 1900 as 141 million, whereas a publication of the U.N. Department of Social Affairs (Population Division) gave an estimate of 120 millions.

/53925

Table II. ESTIMATES OF WORLD POPULATION BY CONTINENTAL
DIVISIONS, 1650–1950

	Estimated Population (Millions)				
	1650	1750	1850	1900	1950
World total . . .	470	694	1,091	1,550	2,406
Africa	100	100	100	120	199
America	8	11	59	144	328
North of Rio Grande .	*1*	*1*	*26*	*81*	*166*
South of Rio Grande .	*7*	*10*	*33*	*63*	*162*
Asia (exc. Asiatic U.S.S.R.)	257	437	656	857	1,272
Europe and Asiatic U.S.S.R.	103	144	274	423	594
Oceania	2	2	2	6	13

Source: *Population Bulletin No. 1*, United Nations, December 1951.

changes in current vital rates but of the persistence of
some existing rates.   This is the best approach at the
start.   Demographers have, moreover, done intensive
research to discover which are the more fundamental and
stable statistics, on the grounds that the more stable
existing rates provide the best basis for extrapolation.

In the absence of all independent evidence this approach
would no doubt be the best.   But it must be observed
that other evidence may well be brought to refute what
is not a completely logical assumption; for a rate (say the
birth-rate) may have been stable for fifty years or more,
and yet be due for a change (e.g., if all potential mothers
are known to have suffered from famine in youth) which
if not strictly predictable can at least be thought likely;
and the same is true of net reproduction rate, or the size
of family rate, or whatever statistic is being used.   This
somewhat laborious warning is necessary to prevent too
ready an acceptance of whatever happens to be the
fashionable basis of extrapolation.

3

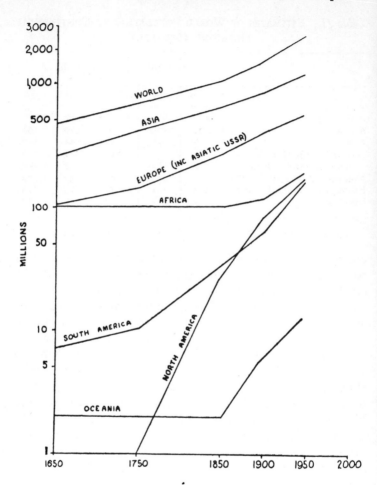

Diagram I. THE GROWTH OF WORLD POPULATION
BY CONTINENTAL DIVISIONS

Source: *Population Bulletin No. 1*, United Nations, December 1951.

There are, indeed, *two* weaknesses about any extrapolation of trends. First the errors in the basic estimates and the doubts engendered thereby. Secondly, the doubts created by the fact that in the last analysis we just do not know how many babies future generations will have, nor whether those generations will behave in the least as their predecessors have behaved, or even as they behaved themselves in earlier years; the same argument applies, though with rather less force, to their rate of dying. Mortality may be analysed under several headings. There are the deaths taking place soon after birth owing to the non-viability of the organism, there are the "normal" deaths for any environment which are an increasing function of age (from the age of about ten years onwards in Great Britain), and there are the more or less hazardous deaths due to accidents, epidemics and wars. All three are in different degrees statistically predictable for a given set of circumstances, but improvements in the different types of mortality may take place at discontinuous and at rather unpredictable rates.

Evidently, if there is a very great stability of behaviour over recent years, it is not too unreasonable to assume that this stability is quite likely to persist. But the further ahead the extrapolation is carried the greater the uncertainty attached to the hypothetical prediction; and in fact extrapolations of several centuries ahead are more or less senseless in view of the uncertainties involved.

For example, the latest available estimates[1] show that the population of the world has been changing at an *average* rate of change, cumulatively, of rather less than 1 per cent per annum (0·9 per cent per annum, or 9 per thousand) for the fifty years 1900–50. World population has been estimated at 1,550 millions in 1900 and 2,406

[1] See *Population Bulletin No. 1*, United Nations, December 1951.

millions in 1950 (see Table II) from which this rate of change has been deduced (see also Diagram I). A simple assumption, and one that may well be justified, is that the rate of change for *world* population over the next half-century will remain at approximately the same average; or in graphical terms that total world population will rise at the same slope, on a logarithmic scale, in the future as in the past. The several parts of world population have been increasing at varying rates, so this assumption is only justified if the very high rates of increase in some large portions of the globe slow down, as well as being offset by continued decline in the rates of increase experienced elsewhere.

According to the estimates given in Table II world population totalled 470 millions in 1650, a figure which statisticians have ventured to compare with 350 millions in the year A.D. 0, and two humans only (Adam and Eve) in 25,000 B.C.[1] However that may be, the average annual rate of increase in population from 1650 onwards has exceeded any previous long-period world rates, so far as these can be guessed. Moreover, the rate has increased with each half-century. From 1650 to 1850 the average was about 0·4 per cent (4 per thousand); from 1850 to 1900 about 7 per thousand, and from 1900 to 1950, as already seen, 9 per thousand.

But the rates of growth have varied very much in different parts of the world. The average annual rate of growth for the different regions over a recent period (1920–50) is shown in Table III.

The estimates suggest that American population (apart from the small population of Oceania) is the one that has advanced the most astonishingly in the first half of the twentieth century. South American population has

[1] *Ibid.*, pp. 1–2.

Table III

Region	Reliability of Estimates	Annual Average Rate of Growth, 1920–50 (%)
World	Mixed	0·9
Africa	Poor	1·3
America	Mixed	1·5
North (of Rio Grande) . .	Good	1·3
South (of Rio Grande) . .	Fair	1·9
Asia (excluding Asiatic U.S.S.R.)	Poor on the whole	0·8
Near East	Poor	1·0
S. Central	Fair	1·1
Japan	Good	1·4
Rest of Far East . .	Poor	0·5
Europe (and Asiatic U.S.S.R.) .		
N.W. Central . . .	Good	0·6
Southern	Good	0·9
Eastern (and Asiatic U.S.S.R.)	Fair	0·7
Oceania	Good	1·4

Source: *World Population Trends 1920–47*, Population Studies No. 3, United Nations, December 1949.

advanced by the amazing annual percentage of 1·9, and North American by 1·3 per cent per annum (over thirty years). It is important to reiterate the caution that the statement about North America rests on far firmer foundations than the statement about South America, where the margins of error for these estimates are much higher. But accepting the statistical picture, for the moment, as broadly correct, it would appear that America and not Asia is the continent of "teeming" millions. If America's current rate of increase in population continued to the end of the present century that continent would contain 732 million souls (316 millions in the U.S.A. and Canada), and perhaps form a higher percentage of the world total than to-day. It would, of course, be rash in the extreme to predict that any such development will take place.

Annual rates of growth in population may very well decline in some parts of the world and increase violently, at least temporarily, in others. Some of these changes for the world taken as a whole are likely, however, to cancel each other out.

§ 2. *Vital Rates for Different Regions.*   The natural increase of world population was not only greater in the first half of the twentieth than in the previous half-centuries; it appeared to be accelerating in every "normal" period. For example, natural increase in the years 1946–48 was somewhere between 1·1 and 1·4 per cent per annum, while in the years 1936–38 it had been below 1·4 per cent, and perhaps as low as 0·8 per cent (more exact estimates are impossible, and "normal" has a relative meaning only).

Over the world as a whole the natural rate of increase in the years 1946–48 was due to a birth-rate averaging some 36 per thousand, and a death-rate averaging somewhere between 22 and 25 per thousand. These average world rates, both birth and death, greatly exceeded the rate for Europe or North America.

The regions of the world may be divided into three distinct groups.[1]   For Group I the birth-rate was about 22 and the death-rate 12, giving an annual rate of increase of 10 per thousand. The group as a whole had a much lower birth-rate than the other groups, but also a much lower death-rate. But its natural rate of increase was much greater than it had been in the recorded past. Fears for a decline of, or stability in, the populations of these regions sprang from a persistent decline in the birth-

[1] Group I consists of north-west, central and southern Europe, North America (as defined in the table) and Oceania; Group II of Latin America, Japan, Eastern Europe and Asiatic U.S.S.R.; and Group III of Africa, Near East, South Central Asia and remaining Far East.

rate. The increase in that rate that followed World War II was held by many observers to be due to purely temporary causes.

Within Group II, which included about 22 per cent of world population, the rates varied very widely. Some of its countries had death-rates in the range 15–17 per thousand, and its birth-rates varied from 28 in Southern Europe to 40 in South America. Its death-rates were on average moderate, neither low nor high (in relation to the world average), but still likely to decline. Its birth-rate was on average fairly high, though lower than the higher figures estimated for Group III, so that its natural rate of increase was 1·5 per cent per annum.

Group III, which was by far the largest (58 per cent of world population in 1950), was the group of both high death-rates and very high birth-rates. The latter ranged from 40 to 45 per thousand, while the death-rates varied from 25 to 30 in Africa to 30 to 35 in the Near East. The natural rate of increase was lower than in Group II, at about 1·2 per cent (12 per thousand).

Thus we have:

Table IV

	% of World Popln. (1950)	Natural Increase %		Hypothetical 1950–80 rates per thousand	
		1946–48	1920–50	"High"	"Low"
Group I (low birth- and death-rates) .	20·2	10	9	10	4
Group II (medium birth- and death- rates) . . .	22·2	15	11	19	10
Group III (high birth- and death-rates) .	57·6	12	8	13	7
World . .	100·0	12	9	14	7

Source: *Population Bulletin No. 1*, United Nations, December 1951.

While the natural rate of increase has risen for the world as a whole, it has been rising for Group III faster even than for Group II, and much faster than for Group I.

For Group I a natural increase of 10 per cent would be "high" over the thirty years to 1980; for Group II a "high" rate would be 19; for Group III perhaps 13 or a little higher, according to the views of the United Nations' statisticians. The differences are due to the demographical history of the countries in the three groups; Group II countries have the most obvious power of increase in the next few decades, because their death-rates may well continue to fall faster than their birth-rates. Group III may, however, still prove to be able to reduce its death-rates, and the "high" estimate of 13 looks too low in the light of medical developments. If we put in a "high" figure of 15, this might be nearer the possibilities. Similarly each group has its appropriate "low" estimate.

On these assumptions world population would be 3,000 millions in 1980 ("low" estimate) or 3,600 millions ("high" estimate), all the "highs" and all the "lows" being assumed to operate together. By using the same methods world population in A.D. 2000 would be between 3,416 and 4,792 millions; these figures merely illustrate the effects of applying a fixed rate of increase over a long period. The most that can be said is that no present observer would be surprised if world population were as high as 4,000 millions fifty years hence. It might be a great deal higher than this. On the other hand, birth-rates may fall much more rapidly than anticipated, in which case world population at the end of this century may be no more than 3,000 millions. This is not to say that there is any particular likelihood of its being between these figures. The important point is the order of magnitude of the increase that *may* take place, which on these figures is from 1,000 to 2,400 millions.

The immediate problem for the world is to find in the next fifty years food and other resources for perhaps nearly twice as many *extra* people as were added to the world's peoples during the preceding half-century. Evidently if these very crude projections prove to be at all near the truth, the task of world agricultural expansion and perhaps reorganization will be by no means a small one, and vast social changes may be one necessary condition of meeting the increased needs of the world. (See § 7.)

§ 3. *Reproduction Rates.*   So far only the simplest population rate—the percentage rate of change itself—has been considered.   Changes in birth-rates and death-rates were the first refinement to be introduced; thus extrapolations could be based upon assumptions of continuing the trends in these rates.   But these in turn were considered too crude in the 1930's, since they ignored the age distribution and the proportions of women of child-bearing age in the population.

The purpose of the device known as the net reproduction rate was to eliminate the so-called "distorting" effects of the age-structure of the population.[1]   The surviving girls who would succeed each 1,000 girls born, on the basis of current fertility and mortality rates, were calculated for each specific age [2] (for females the N.R.R. on this basis was 810 per thousand for Great Britain in 1935–38).   On the basis of the low (maternal) N.R.R.

[1] See section III of Appendix 3 to the Royal Commission on Population Report (Cmd. 7695, June 1949).

[2] *Ibid.*   This rate differed considerably from the male rate, i.e., the "paternal" instead of the "maternal" rate, owing to the excess of males over females in that period.

some very gloomy forecasts were made, extrapolations of this particular rate being used to demonstrate that British and other North-West European populations were doomed to decline; or "doomed to die out", in the phrase invented by Dr. Kuczynski. This, indeed, must logically be the fate of any population with a N.R.R. below 1. The statement that such a population was "doomed to die out" was mathematically correct, but no more so than the statement that a population with a tendency to

Table V. NET REPRODUCTION RATES FOR SPECIFIC COUNTRIES 1939 AND 1944–49.

	U.S.	England & Wales	Belgium	Denmark	Finland	Norway	Sweden
1939	0·992	0·808	0·859	0·940	1·040	0·849	0·830
1944	1·171	0·996	0·851	1·242	1·036	1·073	1·140
1945	1·144	0·909	0·879	1·297	1·245	1·075	1·176
1946	1·359	1·103	1·022	1·319	1·382	1·221	1·161
1947	1·524	1·205	1·002	1·269	1·408	1·164	1·133
1948	1·462	1·070	0·996	—	1·403	1·126	—
1949	—	1·023	—	—	—	—	—
1950	—	0·986	—	—	—	—	—

Source: United Nations, *Demographic Yearbook 1949–50*. For England and Wales 1949 and 1950—*Annual Abstract of Statistics*, No. 89, 1952.

increase by nearly 1 per cent was doomed to disaster. Both statements are based upon a long-term extrapolation of trends, but the assumption that such trends will continue indefinitely is unjustified. Trends depend upon human habits and institutions; these endure, sometimes through most catastrophic shocks. But human habits can also change, and the brief recorded history of population includes some notable examples of modification in birth- and death-rates, and for that matter in the net reproduction rate as well. Even within a decade the net reproduction rate varied by as much as 40 or 50 per cent in some countries, as may be seen from Table V. The years illustrated by the table happen, it is true, to include the period of World War II, but almost equally violent short-term fluctuations could be shown if other years had been chosen, and in any case the figures establish the limited point that twentieth-century populations have the power to vary their rates of increase substantially within short periods; so far as the reproduction rate is concerned, the one lesson that experience teaches us is that it is not necessarily constant. About the same time as female reproduction rates (gross and net) began to reveal considerable instability, demographers discovered that these rates were open to several objections as a basis for forecasting. Net reproduction rates, calculated as surviving girls born to mothers, fluctuate because of changes in the marriage frequency. Such changes may, or may not, be of a temporary character; in the well-known case of World War II an unforeseen rise in marriage frequencies, due to marked changes in social behaviour, upset the stability of the reproduction rate. Or, again, the female net reproduction rate may be misleading if, for more or less accidental historical reasons, there is a surplus of women and so a low marriage frequency among them; the net reproduction rate will rise over the years as this surplus readjusts itself even though fertility among married women stays constant.

Demographers have therefore looked for other evidence of a pattern of stability; in the case of Britain in particular, as will be seen, they have developed the concept of "completed family size". For the world as a whole such refinements, whether useful or not, are quite impracticable for lack of sufficient information on the age distribution of mothers, nuptiality and other necessary particulars.

§ 4. *Logistic Curves and their Limitations.* At one time it was hoped that the fitting of mathematical curves to data of the total size of population would help to solve, in a rather simple way, the problem of how to project what different populations would "naturally" tend to become. *If* it can be assumed (which it cannot) that the rate of reproduction remains constant, then ultimately the size of a population increases (or decreases) in a geometric progression.[1] On the other hand, any such logarithmic rate of increase must be curbed because of a deficiency in the rate of increase in the supply of food or of some other necessity, or because of the simple fact of spatial limitation, so that the assumed rate of growth may further be assumed to have a diminishing rate itself. The growth equation must, then, be modified, and a "logistic" S-shaped curve will represent the projection.[2]

In the early 1920's Yule worked out an estimate of the projected population for England and Wales based on a logistic curve, and Pearl and Reed produced similar calculations for America. Bowley calculated the future size of the British population on the basis of mortality rates (those for England and Wales 1910–12) and the average number of births from 1921–23. According to Yule's logistic curve the population for England and Wales should have become 51 millions by 1951 (it was actually 44 millions) and he regarded Bowley's estimate of 49 millions by 1971 as much too low. But, as Bowley pointed out, the logistic was not the only curve that could reasonably be fitted to the data for the past populations of the different countries.

[1] and [2] See Cox, 1952, p. 82 ff. If the population at a moment of time is P_t the first assumption can be expressed as $P_t = Ce^{rt}$ where C and r (the rate of growth) are constants, t is time, and e is the exponential; r will be reduced by a value that is a function of P_t if a ceiling of some sort is further assumed.

Mr. Cox remarks [1] that it would "not be impossible to obtain plausible results by joining two or more logistics together or by using more tortuous curves", but he adds that "not much confidence could be placed in their predictive power unless special regard was had in choosing them to the present age-structure of the population and the current tendencies of birth rates and death rates". But can any confidence be placed in these curves even if Mr. Cox's condition is fulfilled? The whole weight of the argument once more rests upon the discovery of an alleged "current tendency" in the habits of reproduction and dying, and on an act of faith (or reason) that any such tendency will continue in the future.

The factors affecting births and deaths are economic, sociological, agricultural, political and so on, and embrace all the material and spiritual influences that affect human behaviour. Many different disciplines have to be consulted. The assumptions made finally demand an act of choice, or, indeed, of political judgment.

The logistic curve has not provided very successful projections because it was based upon some over-simplified assumptions. It seems probable that there is no single mathematical "law of growth" that is followed by human populations, or if there is a simplifying principle of this kind, it remains to be discovered.

§ 5. *Population Projections of the 1940's.* Since earlier attempts to study population growth had proved so unsuccessful it might be thought that economists and statisticians would refuse to risk their reputations upon further projections based upon necessarily arbitrary assumptions. But the pressure of necessity is too great; there are many practical reasons why projections of

[1] *Ibid.*, p. 88.

population should be required. Most writers of any repute distinguish between "projections" and "predictions", and to make the distinction valid offer several projections each based on a different set of hypotheses. But the possible number of hypotheses is, in theory, infinite. Each writer presumably selects that set of hypotheses which is in his view more probable than all the infinite sets that he neglects to mention. A projection is, therefore, a prediction—with an extra danger sign attached.

A simplifying principle in the history of population growth began to be discerned in the 1930's and became accepted doctrine as the basis of the projections worked out in the next decade. The principle might be called the theory of three demographic stages in civilization. The first stage, that of more primitive societies, is a so-called "natural" stage of high birth-rates and high death-rates; this was the stage from which Western European peoples began to free themselves towards the end of the eighteenth century. The second stage is that which follows the introduction of some medical, sanitary and hygienic improvements, and is a stage of falling death-rates with birth-rates still remaining high. This stage is one of rapid natural increase. The third stage is begun when urbanization, social ambition and other factors have combined to reduce the size of families by reduction in the birth-rate, and is finally reached when birth-rates are falling faster than death-rates. The ultimate consequence of this stage is a falling population.[1]

The three stages theory is apparently founded upon the history of growth of the Western European communities from about 1790 to 1940. Other populations have, more-

---

[1] The three stages correspond roughly to the three Groups—Group III being in the main in stage one, Group II in stage two, and Group I in stage three.

over, appeared, in respect of declining death-rates, to follow suit, and the three stages theory has become a kind of orthodoxy; for example, it is often assumed that a country like Japan will pass through a period of rapid expansion, and then, like Western European countries that have been industrialized, experience a falling birth-rate and reach relative stability of total numbers.

The theory of the three stages underlay the interesting projections of population that were made by Professor Notestein and his colleagues in the 1940's. They were careful to observe that they had no proof that history would repeat itself in the manner that the theory implies, but in the absence of any better guide they turned to past experience, and built their projections on the assumption that each major section of the world's population would progress more or less consistently through each phase of development.

According to the three stages theory the world's population problem is essentially acute but short-term. As each "backward" country, or region, moves from the primitive to the second stage its population will increase alarmingly, that is to say much faster than it can, with existing techniques, increase its supplies of food. Each country will in turn seem to have to face a period of population crisis such as was experienced by Britain in the early nineteenth century and is being faced by Japan in the twentieth. There will be problems of emigration, of raising capital from abroad, of imports and of urbanization at home. But fortunately a third stage will eventually supervene, and if the critical stage, the hump as it were, can be passed, an easier period will lie ahead, as family limitation begins to have numerical effect.

This general picture of the future of world population growth is still, perhaps, the best that we have, but there are several flaws in it of marked importance to economists. The major difficulty is that in this, as in some other population theories, movements in population growth are treated as independent variables, or as variables dependent only upon such relatively simple factors as "medical improvements" and "family limitation". In the real world even these two simple factors sum up and include complex developments, and furthermore many other factors, including economic, may be relevant to the extent to which these factors operate.[1]

The three stages theory is based upon historical experience, and upon the belief that European experience will be repeated for other nations. But there is a sense in which the only lesson of history in this matter is that of the uniqueness of the circumstances surrounding each development. The most striking conclusion, to be derived from Table II (and Diagram I), is that world population history has in a very special sense been unique, and on this point there must be general agreement. There has been no repetition and there are no precedents to apply of a simple and direct kind.

At least four major factors affected European development, which may not again be present—the existence of sparsely inhabited land to exploit in temperate zones of climate, the discovery of raw materials to mine in sufficient quantities to support a particular type of material urban civilization, the successful introduction of the social and political changes that enabled hygiene to play its part in reducing death-rates (as well as striking medical

---

[1] Of one version of the Malthusian theory it is often said that it ignores the "middle term"; the (geometrical) increase in population is treated as quite independent of the (arithmetical) increase in food. In fact the important point is just how the two increases are interrelated. This is a similar criticism to that here developed of the "three stages" theory.

advances in attacking epidemic diseases), and technical developments such as railways and roads which required large labour forces to construct and maintain. These are only examples and not an exhaustive list. The point is that these, and other important economic and social factors, are very unlikely to repeat themselves; the question at issue is whether there will be sufficient substitutes for them. If there are, then backward populations may develop on much the same lines as the European populations which first exploited the resources of industrial civilization. But there is no certainty that populations will automatically repeat these developments.

To begin with, the movement from stage 1 to stage 2 is taking place under very different circumstances from those that ruled when the Western world was first heavily industrialized. The decline in the death-rates then, even now not fully understood, certainly depended in part upon social as well as medical improvements. Now that advanced education is available to administrators medical improvements may be introduced into "backward" areas with little change in the social arrangements.

The movement from stage 2 to stage 3 is even more critical, and still less likely to be a simple repetition of the earlier European decline in fertility.[1] The desire to limit family size arises only in certain social circumstances (again, not fully understood even for Europe), and those circumstances may well not prevail in the expanding areas of the twentieth century. On the contrary, it is possible that quite different factors may operate. Recent studies of Ceylon,[2] for example, an area with high birth-rates and comparatively low death-rates, show that while there

---

[1] Those who have predicted a movement from stage 2 to stage 3 have leaned rather heavily on an argument from analogy with the demographic history of Japan.

[2] Taeuber, 1949, p. 302.

4

Table VI

Continents and Countries	Population (millions)			Annual % Rate of Growth	
	1900	1939	1949	1900–1949	1939–1949
Africa					
Egypt . . .	10·3	16·6	20·0	1·3	1·9
Gold Coast . .	1·6	3·5	3·7	2·1	0·6
Union South Africa	4·7	10·2	12·1	2·0	1·7
Others . . .	124·1	144·7	162·1	0·4	1·1
TOTAL . .	140·7	175·0	197·9	0·6	1·3
America					
Argentina . .	4·8	14·4	16·8	2·8	1·6
Brazil . . .	17·0	40·3	49·3	2·2	2·1
Canada . .	5·2	11·6	13·2	2·0	1·6
Chile . . .	2·9	4·9	5·7	1·4	1·5
Colombia . .	3·5	8·9	11·0	2·4	2·1
Cuba . . .	1·6	4·5	5·2	2·7	1·5
Ecuador . .	1·4	2·9	3·4	1·9	1·1
United States .	76·0	130·9	149·2	1·4	1·4
Honduras . .	0·5	1·1	1·3	2·1	1·7
Jamaica . .	0·8	1·2	1·4	1·0	1·6
Mexico . .	13·6	19·4	24·4	0·9	2·3
Peru . . .	4·6	6·9	8·2	1·0	1·7
Puerto Rico . .	1·0	1·8	2·2	1·5	2·1
El Salvador . .	1·0	1·7	2·2	1·4	2·6
Uruguay . .	0·9	2·1	2·4	2·2	1·4
Venezuela . .	2·5	3·6	4·6	0·9	2·5
Others . . .	13·7	17·8	20·3	0·7	1·2
TOTAL . .	151·0	274·0	320·8	1·5	1·6
Asia					
Burma . .	11·8	16·0	18·3	0·8	1·4
Ceylon . . .	3·5	5·9	7·3	1·4	2·1
China . . .	357·3	450·0	463·5	0·6	0·3
Korea and Formosa	13·2	27·8	36·3	2·0	3·8
India and Pakistan	282·5	380·0	420·4	0·8	1·0
Japan . . .	43·8	70·9	82·1	1·3	1·5
Philippines . .	7·5	16·2	20·4	2·0	2·3
Thailand . .	7·8	15·0	18·0	1·7	1·8
Indonesia . .	35·0	69·4	72·0	1·7	0·3
Others . . .	76·5	110·8	115·2	0·9	0·4
TOTAL . .	838·9	1,162·0	1,253·5	0·8	0·8

Table VI.—continued

Continents and Countries	Population (millions)			Annual % Rate of Growth	
	1900	1930	1949	1900 – 1949	1939– 1949
Europe					
Belgium	6·7	8·4	8·6	0·6	0·2
Bulgaria	3·9	6·3	7·2	1·3	1·4
Czechoslovakia	12·1	14·7	12·5	0·5	– 1·6
Denmark	2·6	3·8	4·2	0·9	1·0
Finland	2·6	3·7	4·0	0·9	0·8
France	40·1	41·3	41·6	0·1	0·1
Hungary	6·8	9·2	9·2	0·8	—
Ireland.	3·2	2·9	3·0	– 0·2	0·3
Italy	33·4	43·1	46·0	0·7	0·7
Netherlands .	5·1	8·8	10·0	1·4	1·3
Norway	2·2	3·0	3·2	0·8	0·7
Portugal	5·4	7·6	8·5	0·9	1·1
Spain	18·5	25·5	28·0	0·8	0·9
Sweden	5·1	6·3	7·0	0·6	1·0
Switzerland .	3·3	4·2	4·6	0·7	0·9
United Kingdom .	37·9	47·8	50·4	0·6	0·6
Total . .	188·9	236·6	248·0	0·6	0·5
Others .	100·0	165·9	144·8	1·3	– 1·4
U.S.S.R. .	126·0	170·5	200·0	0·8	1·6
Total (Europe)	414·9	573·0	592·8	0·8	0·3
Oceania					
Australia	3·8	7·0	7·9	1·6	1·3
New Zealand	0·8	1·6	1·9	1·8	1·7
Others .	1·6	2·4	2·6	1·0	0·8
Total . .	6·2	11·0	12·4	1·5	1·2
World . . .	1,551·7	2,195·0	2,377·4	0·9	0·8

Sources: World Health Organization, *Epidemiological and Vital Statistics Report*, April 1951, Table II. United Nations, *Demographic Yearbook 1949–50*.

is no apparent difference in the birth-rates of the large and small cities (Colombo and the rest), there is a higher than average birth-rate in the rural areas. But parts of Ceylon which were once fertile are under-populated, and to win more food these parts must again be inhabited. As, further, Ceylon has little immediate prospect of rapid industrialization, more of its energies must be directed to raising food. It cannot expect to gain an "automatic" reduction of birth-rates as people move to the towns, as to some extent a reverse flow is necessary, nor is there sufficient time for the small family pattern to spread from cities to rural districts. Thus, if a demographic crisis is to be averted, as Irene Taeuber points out, there must be a *direct* development of the small family pattern in the rural areas, which means that Ceylon's demographic evolution must vary considerably from the Western precedent. But Ceylon's case is paralleled all over Asia. The problem is how to populate the, at present, badly irrigated areas without worsening instead of improving the ratio of population to fertile acreage.

Unless it can be assumed that there is a unique relationship between population change, social and economic reorganization, and the population change again, it cannot be deduced that each stage of population development will be followed by the same type of successor. The projections for different parts of the world may turn out to be approximately correct, but there may be many surprises yet in store. The most knowledgeable forecasters in 1950–51 varied in their guesses of future world population in the year 2000 by a factor of at least 25 per cent (a figure of 3,000 millions being mentioned about as frequently as 4,000 millions). If the higher figure is used, the increase in population in half a century would amount to 1,600 millions on 2,400 millions, that is 2 persons more for every 3 alive in 1950.

No great importance can therefore be attached to our own rough guess of an increase of something like 1,600 millions. The movement in the sum total of world population is the result of varying rates of change in many different countries, and the reasons for these changes in the past are not so certain that predictions about the future have any serious reliability. All that can be said is that for the world as a whole a very large increase in numbers between 1950 and 2000 seems to be likely, and that the increase will very likely be greater than the whole world population existing in 1900.

§ 6. *Differing Percentage Rates of Increase.* While there seems to be no reliable general "law of population" on which to base prognostications about the future of the world as a whole, certain key statistics can be worked out for individual states which may be thought to throw some light on the problems of the next fifty years. In Table VI recent percentage rates of change in total populations are shown in contrast with the rates of change for the same areas recorded for the first half of the twentieth century. In many cases the more recent change considerably exceeds the earlier average. (Only those countries for which fairly reliable census figures are available have been shown.)

Many parts of the world have annual percentage rates of change that clearly cannot be sustained for any long period of time because of all sorts of limiting factors, including the obvious one of physical living-space. Any country which is increasing at a natural rate of 2 per cent per annum or more (Puerto Rico for example) would seem quite likely to be heading for a food supply problem unless it can either (*a*) export enough to increase its food imports, (*b*) increase its farm productivity by a very high factor, or (*c*) arrange for large-scale emigration (legal or illegal). In the actual case of Puerto Rico emigration seems to be the solution adopted. It would be very satisfying if a simple generalization could be reached, namely, that any percentage rate of change above some critical level (say 1½ per cent) represents a "catastrophic" increase, and implies a crisis in the affairs of the country concerned. Unfortunately no such tidy division of the world is at all legitimate.

For consider the countries which do in fact, undeniably, have a rate of change that cannot for ever be maintained. There are at least three groups among those above the 2 per cent level. First are the still "empty" countries with agricultural land far from fully exploited by Western European standards. These include Australia, New Zealand and Argentina. Their increases are in two cases due to immigration, not to natural increase. But what is sauce for the goose is sauce for the gander, and if 2 per cent is too much *on principle* it is too much for these countries as well as others. In fact this group of countries is demographically not ill situated. More population will strengthen them economically by improving their industries and their agriculture.

The second group of countries are the large semitropical countries like Brazil, Algeria, Colombia and Mexico which, too, in certain favourable conditions, may well support much larger populations than they do at present. Their way ahead is not so plain as that of the new (mainly temperate zone) countries, but granted that tropical agriculture can be increasingly exploited their futures would seem to be reasonably secure. Finally there are the small, already crowded, territories like Ceylon and Trinidad, islands and small states, where the density of numbers to land has given rise already to urgent social problems. But for these countries, too, the immediate outlook is far less certainly unhappy than is sometimes depicted.[1]

Again and again it is necessary to remind ourselves not to confuse the long-term *impossibility* of certain rates of increase with the short-term *desirability* of these (or even higher) rates. It is all very well to write (of Ceylon for instance) that "a rate of population increase of even 2·5 per cent per year *far into the future*" would lead to inconceivably high figures. This is beside the point, in relation to policy for the next fifty years. It would seem that a rate of increase of 2·5 or 3·0 per cent, or any other percentage, is perfectly in order until such time as the present seven million inhabitants of the island are increased to whatever is the highest figure that the island can, in modern conditions, sustain. Certainly we cannot be sure that 2·5 per cent is too fast a rate of increase for Ceylon, or Australia, or New Zealand, or Brazil, unless we study first their economic and social possibilities.

Thus, the world possibilities of a large increase of population depend partly upon how the relevant, but complex, problems of the differing rates of change affecting different national groups are solved. How great an increase the world can support can be calculated in several ways, according to the way in which the increase is distributed.

There is no sound basis for projecting world population ahead far into the future regardless of the economic and agricultural developments that are expected to take place. Moreover, it must be remembered that changes in total

[1] *Ceylon:* "Potentially the population problem is acute, but there are agricultural areas for expansion, lands which can be more intensively utilized, and some industrial opportunities. Ceylon has enough time to undertake the research essential to discover . . . how to solve her population problem by inducing a reduction in the size of families." Taeuber, 1949, p. 303.

population for particular areas depend upon migration as well as upon births and deaths.

Approximately, then, it may be thought that the large increase in world population up to A.D. 2000 will divide itself between the groups at rates similar to those estimated for 1950–80 in Table IV. A rough alternative guess may be made by simple extrapolation of the lines shown in Diagram I. Many refinements can be introduced into these calculations for individual countries, but they are based on equally arbitrary assumptions; for a first view of the possibilities the above projections may suffice.

§ 7. *World Population and Food Supplies.* (*a*) Great alarm has been expressed from time to time at the rate of growth of world population especially in relation to the food supplies likely to be available.[1] This anxiety has been intensified by the Malthusian theories of population, which will be discussed in a later chapter. The present section will be used to afford a brief first view of the orders of magnitude of the problem under discussion.

Leaving aside, for the moment, the structural economic difficulties,[2] one fact is indisputable, namely, that there is

[1] For example, Michael Roberts opened his book, *The Estate of Man*, 1951, with the remark that:

(p. 13) "If all the 56 million square miles of the earth's land surface were shared out equally among its 2,350 million people, we would each have about 15 acres, including roughly 5 acres of jungle, or forest, about 4 acres of dry desert, another 2 acres of semi-arid land and 2 acres of polar snow. . . . Over the world as a whole, the area actually cultivated amounts to just about one and a half acres per person. . . . A century ago, the estate would have been twice as large. . . . At the present rate . . . each of us is losing about an acre every ten years."

(p. 18) "Wheat is of crucial importance: it is the staple food of nations such as Britain and Belgium which depend largely on imported grain; it is the alternative to which the Asiatic countries turn as they outstrip their own supplies of rice. . . ."

[2] The structural difficulties include those arising in the production of food, the organization of farming, the degree of education and state

no *physical* difficulty to be seen in the way of increasing food supplies at least as fast as population over the next fifty years. Enough is known, on a sufficiently firm basis, to state categorically that for that period at least there is enough land and enough knowledge of techniques already ascertained to support a world population that increases at nearly 1 per cent per annum for another fifty years. Table VII illustrates the increase in yields per hectare and per person secured in many parts of the world after the war-time setbacks.

Professor Le Gros Clark has surely summed up the position correctly with the remark [1]:

"The knowledge that we have is, in our view, sufficient to guarantee the increased agricultural production we need during this century; after that the outlook is unpredictable."

The point is that the knowledge *we have* is sufficient; no allowance need be made for inventions or unforeseen improvements in agricultural technique. As far as sheer physical quantity of food is concerned, to keep the world in the year 2000 no hungrier on average than it was in 1939, and perhaps a little less hungry than it was in 1951, the existing techniques, applied on a wider scale than in the middle of the century, would suffice.

Two major economic matters have to be considered. First there is the immense question of the economic and social structures necessary to ensure that the potentially fertile areas of the world are in fact brought into

policies in regard to agricultural development, technical education and nutrition, and also the complex problems arising in the distribution of food. Among the latter are difficulties due to the distribution of agriculture as between continents, and also of course both between and within individual countries.

[1] Le Gros Clark, 1951, p. 1.

Table VII. Agricultural Productivity by Continents and for the World Pre-war and 1947–48

(In Metric Tons)

	Yield per Hectare					Yield per Person in Agriculture				
	Pre-war	1947–48	1950–51	1947–48 as % of pre-war	1950–51 as % of pre-war	Pre-war	1947–48	1950–51	1947–48 as % of pre-war	1950–51 as % of pre-war
Africa . .	0·77	0·73	0·83	95	108	0·12	0·12	0·14	100	117
Asia . .	1·26	1·20	1·19	95	94	0·24	0·22	0·23	92	96
Europe . .	1·51	1·34	1·60	89	106	1·04	0·88	1·02	85	98
North and Central America .	1·07	1·50	1·53	140	143	1·80	2·57	2·46	143	137
South America .	1·28	1·39	1·31	109	102	0·58	0·48	0·45	83	78
Oceania . .	1·06	1·20	1·47	113	139	1·94	2·38	2·28	123	118
World . .	1·24	1·30	1·36	105	110	0·42	0·42	0·44	100	105

Data based on the production of eight crops, wheat, rye, oats, barley, rice, maize, sugar and potatoes, expressed on a wheat basis.

Source: F.A.O., *Food and Agricultural Statistics*, Washington, September 1949.

Data for 1950 calculated on same basis and using same weights.

NOTE.—In Africa, and to some extent in Asia, the low figure for production per person in agriculture arises in part from the fact that these eight crops play a lesser part in the food production of these continents. No reliable figures are, however, available for the other crops.

cultivation, or improved in yield, before any major disasters occur in the way of famine or economic breakdown. Second is the question of cost. Even if cost per unit of output does not rise exorbitantly, the conservatism of peasant and farming communities, and difficulties of distribution of food due to the division of the world into national states (two political factors), may slow down the effective rate of increase.

More intensive application of fertilizers, and the wider use of improved techniques, would substantially increase the output of land that is already cultivated. Mankind will thus not necessarily become worse off, in the next fifty years, merely because of its continued expansion in numbers. But the required increase in demand implies in turn adequate channels for distributing the output of agriculture. A closer analysis of the distribution of food is therefore necessary if any realistic impression is to be formed of the economic pressures likely to be set up by the expansion of population.

Nutritionally, as in other ways, the world is, as Mr. Colin Clark once observed, a wretchedly poor place. The point can be established in two ways—on the basis of over-all statistics of food consumption per head of population in different countries, and by looking for special symptoms of malnutrition. Neither method is wholly conclusive nor satisfactory, for reasons that will appear. There are, however, sufficient facts to support the view that food consumption is either abominably or moderately insufficient for most people in most parts of the world, and that increasing populations with rising standards of living may well impose a much greater strain on the supply elasticity of agriculture than on that of any other industry except perhaps building and construction.

Out of the 1,778 million people for whom rough calculations of calories per head per day could be assessed, 1,226 millions in 1949–50 were estimated to live in countries with less than 2,400 calories per head per day average consumption. Only 267 millions lived in countries where the average daily consumption of calories was 3,000 or better.[1]

If the average daily need of calories is about 3,000, large sections of the world's population rarely obtain so much. Their stature, their health and their chances of life are thereby prejudiced.

The question thus becomes not merely whether food supplies can increase at the same rate as population, but whether they can increase faster. There may be no good reason to fear that the world as a whole will be necessarily much worse off for food in the year 2000 than it was in the year 1950, but can it be any better off? And for the population theorist this raises a supplementary and still more disturbing query: has the population of the globe *already* outrun the available subsistence? Is the only possible remedy for the shortages that exist a reduction in the total of the existing population?

The scientific study of nutrition and the discovery of such substances as vitamins are recent developments, and no doubt much remains yet to be discovered. Dogmatic statements as to how much an "average man" needs in the way of energy food daily, or of the forty nutritional elements at present thought necessary to maintain his organism "in balance", must be interpreted surely as relative rather than absolute in their application, however learned their source. For medical researchers have in mind a certain standard of "health", and relate their experiments to this standard, yet the standard may

[1] *F.A.O. Yearbook 1951*, Vol. IV, Part I, Table 77, p. 161.

itself be raised if new scientific possibilities of lengthening life, or increasing human energy output, are made. The standard is in practice probably set by unconscious social assumptions.

Subject to this important qualification, the known "needs of man" may be approximately described, wide variations between individuals, and perhaps between groups, being admitted as a further possibility. In the way that our knowledge is at present organized, malnutrition is divided into three kinds: first a shortage of the energy foods, second a deficiency of any of the chemical elements necessary to balanced replacement of the human organism (i.e., replacement to a "normal" level), and, thirdly, deficiencies of the elements to such a degree as to provoke visible symptoms of disease. Thus, as an example of the first kind of shortage, if prisoners are fed on a diet of 1,000 calories a day, as in the Nazi concentration camps, they will become living skeletons and perish prematurely. The second kind of deficiency may produce no visible symptoms, but may predispose its victims to the onset of various diseases, while the third or more extreme kind will produce special diseases associated with insufficiencies of the required elements.

The third kind of deficiency would seem to be the easiest to identify, and there are certain specific diseases associated with particular shortages. Thus lack of vitamin A produces blindness, of vitamin B_1 beriberi and pellagra, of B_2 eye congestion and other diseases, of D rickets and osteomalacia.[1]

---

[1] As Mr. de Castro points out, diagnosis is not always easy. Often several vitamin deficiencies exist at once, and there are visible symptoms of the lack of necessary elements, such as digestive disorders, minor skin ailments, insomnia and so on, before the characteristic disease has appeared. There are now at least twenty vitamins identified, and a number of mineral salts and fats, all required in a balanced diet.

Shortages of vitamins A, B_1, B_2, D and C are those at present known to have the worst effect on great masses of human beings collectively.[1] Their full effects have usually been discovered as the result of some unintentional "experiment" with human beings, such as sending a ship round the globe without supplies of meat, milk and vegetables, or feeding a large section of the inhabitants of an island on polished rice, or providing the pioneers in an Amazonian rubber boom with tinned food only. From disasters due to such specialized diets much has been learnt as to the necessity of balanced feeding, and it is possible to identify broad categories of deficiency in areas of the world where no such specialized conditions exist.

Regarded from this point of view, what are the hunger areas of the world? The F.A.O. report for 1948 [2] remarked that: "As regards the energy value of the food supplies, the current situation shows that apart from Argentina, Oceania, Canada, the United States and a few European countries the food supply of any single country would be nutritionally inadequate even if distributed evenly throughout the population." The position since 1948 has not yet fundamentally changed,[3] and uneven distribution inside most countries ensures that the poorer sections of the populations concerned fare very much worse than the national average.

The hunger areas of the world fall into three classes: the low-income and densely populated countries in the Far East and the Middle East, and to a lesser degree in the Caribbean and in eastern Europe; the low-income but sparsely populated countries, chiefly in Africa and South America; and the "special areas" of hunger that crop up

[1] De Castro, 1952, p. 50.
[2] F.A.O., 1948, p. 7.
[3] F.A.O., 1952, p. 17.

all over the world, even in high-income and relatively well-fed political units. The degree of hunger or malnutrition varies enormously. In Chile perhaps 50 per cent of the country's inhabitants are said to get less than 2,400 calories a day. In almost every country of South America calorie intake figures were said to be very low. This fearful hunger and chronic under-nourishment occurs in a half-continent which from a demographic point of view would not appear to be ill-situated. It includes 16 per cent of the world's habitable land and only 6 per cent of the world's population. One important point is that "this hunger is nothing new"; it has come from the past, from the period of the earliest discovery of the New World.

Hunger, of course, exists in both senses of the term throughout China and India, and in some parts of Africa.

The facts as they stand neither support nor refute the view that a persistently rising population has at all times led to a worsening in food supply (apart from any alleviation due to the introduction of new methods of farming).

What they do show, however, is that, historically, starvation is by no means an experience occurring for the first time in recent years; it has been rife in many parts of the world for a long time. The shortages that now exist do not even seem to be worse than those of the past, except for the post-war experience for a few years of some war-devastated countries.

In certain places population *has* increased faster than food supply could be economically increased, and such increases might indeed be "independent"[1] (for instance,

[1] With regard to the "independence" of population growth the "Group of Experts" reporting to the U.N. on "Measures for the Economic Development of Under-Developed Countries" in May 1951 wrote that: "The rate of growth of population is now first and foremost a function of the extent to which medical knowledge is made available

because of the introduction of an extraneous medical improvement), and the ensuing food shortage, however temporary, might be called the consequence of the sudden spurt in population. A case of this kind that is often cited is that of British Guiana.[1] But starvation exists in regions where there has been no such sudden spurt; there is malnutrition in lands where there are ample resources of land if so organized as to meet the population's requirements. The facts do not therefore fit in with the theory that over-population is the sole cause of hunger.

There is no happy future foreseeable for an increasing world population on the scale under discussion, if social and economic institutions are not susceptible of change and adaptation. The F.A.O. as long ago as 1946 made some calculations of the percentage increase in the world production (i.e., 70 countries included in their survey) of

to the people. . . . Medical knowledge will spread, and the population will increase, whether economic development takes place or not." This is perhaps too strong, but contains an important grain of truth.

[1] In this colony the introduction of insecticides in 1945 is alleged to have resulted, in one suburb of Georgetown, in a spectacular decline in the infantile mortality rate; and for the whole of Georgetown DDT is supposed to have diminished, in the short space of a few years, the killing effect of malaria as a form of population control. For the suburb in question the birth-rate doubled between 1938–44 and 1947. (See Tizard, 1948.)

British Guiana, if these statistics were typical for the colony, may have achieved a 10 per cent annual rate of increase in the population. This has been quoted as a single example of a world-wide change towards an ever-increasing rate of growth of population. (See R. C. Cook, 1951, pp. 69 and 319, where Sir Henry Tizard's speech has been written up, but not quite accurately.)

But British Guiana (a) had a surplus of potentially cultivable land in relation to its population, (b) had absorbed East Indian immigrants in the past quite successfully, and some in the West Indies looked to it as a further outlet for possible immigration, (c) had and has substantial agricultural and mineral resources available for export, (d) had no time for social adjustments to the DDT innovation. By no stretch of language could this tiny colony of 400,000 persons in 1948 be accurately described as an instance of population pressing hard against rapidly exhausting resources of nature (cf. the Year-Book of the West Indies, 1951).

certain food supplies necessary to reach its minimum
nutritional targets by the year 1960. These ranged from
a 12 per cent increase in sugar production to 163 per cent
increase in the supply of fruit and vegetables.[1] The
worst fed countries required an increase in food supplies
of some 40 per cent to reach the F.A.O.'s nutritional
targets for their existing populations, and of some 100 per
cent to allow for their increasing populations. In the
high-income countries something could be done by redistribution, but for the low-income countries production
was the most essential requirement; although an even
distribution of the consequent result would be just as
necessary—a point perhaps not sufficiently emphasized
even by the F.A.O. Both the enormous expansion of
production, and the guarantees of reasonably even distribution, imply institutional growth or change in many of
the seventy countries considered and co-operation between
their various governments.

The nutritional "targets" laid down by the F.A.O. in
1946 have been derided by critics who pride themselves
on realism and dislike an apparently altruistic proposal
to give a "glass of milk to every Hottentot". But the
figures just studied do not leave the question open as to
which is the more realistic approach. If the nutritional
targets are not attained, the scale of the crises of malnutrition and famine will be greater than any that have
hitherto been experienced. It is difficult to believe
realistically that these disasters will fail to spread, and

[1] The figures were:
Percentage Increases over Pre-war Food Supplies to meet 1960
Requirements

Commodity	%	Commodity	%
Cereals . . .	21	Pulses . . .	80
Roots and tubers	27	Fruits and vegetables	163
Sugar . . .	12	Meat . . .	46
Fats . . .	34	Milk . . .	100

that the existence of vast hordes of ill-nourished individuals in some countries, and smaller groups in others,
will not bring unpleasant consequences even to those who
at first have an adequate standard of life. Adequate food,
at least, would seem to rank high among the objectives of
international policy, although the precise standard laid
down by the F.A.O. may be challenged by some; for
there are many who would argue that the standard should
be lower than the full nutritional diet proposed by that
organization. Whatever standard is adopted (an adequate
one or a deliberately insufficient one) output and distribution have to be improved, unless population growth is
to be a principal cause of political disaster.

§ 8. *Population and Raw Materials.* What are raw materials? As distinct from manufactures, they may be defined as those goods which are acquired directly from
man's environment, without processing, for the purpose
of being worked up into products with an exchange value,
but they exclude any of those goods destined to be
consumed as food.

Raw materials are normally regarded as a different
class of commodity from foodstuffs. They include, among
organic items, cotton, wool, rubber and natural fibres such
as jute or flax. But there are some which are both raw
materials and foodstuffs, like whale oil and certain kinds
of alcohol, oilseeds and nuts, from which industrial as well
as edible products can be made. For some purposes it is
desirable to treat tobacco as a raw material, for others as
a part of "food and drink" consumption. The organic
raw materials often directly compete with food production
for land as well as for labour and capital.

A second main class of raw materials includes all the
useful minerals.

There is no complete record of world raw material production since 1900, so it is not possible to give a comprehensive estimate of the percentage increases (total and per head of population) in raw material usage that have taken place over the last half-century. But the figures shown in a graph in Chapter X below confirm the general view that the percentage increase in the use of raw materials since 1913 has greatly exceeded the percentage increase in population. (Raw materials are not shown directly in the graph, but as the "mining and manufacturing" index is some 220 per cent greater than it was in 1913 a corresponding raw material index, if it could be compiled, would probably have moved upwards by a somewhat similar rate of increase, except in so far as economies in raw materials have been effected.)

Whatever the exact figures, it is obvious that the huge rise in raw material use since the beginning of the century is out of all proportion to the increase in population. It is not, then, population as such that is pressing upon the raw material supplies of the world, but the tendency towards a greater usage per head. This might be described as an "income factor", a rise due to the general rise in real incomes. The description is only partially true, for it may be that real incomes could have been increased in a number of different ways. The increased raw material usage per head is due to an increase in real incomes by a particular developmental route.

A full analysis of that route would demand detailed statistics, analysed for several countries over a long period. For the present purpose it will suffice to pick out some outstanding reasons for the higher use of raw materials. The first one is that the highly industrialized countries, in particular the United States, have since 1918 geared their development to the principles of mass production, standardization and rapid obsolescence (critics call this conspicuous waste and protagonists call it efficiency). The modern economy relies very largely in its growth on a policy of rapid scrapping of machines and of the products of the machines.

This particular kind of economy draws more heavily each year on raw materials than one which has advanced along conservationist lines. Whether this is a good or bad thing is a somewhat debatable question. The point here is to note that it has happened.

The result of this development, and of the prodigious increase in real national income that the United States enjoyed over the thirty-five years from 1918 to 1953, has been an ever-increasing demand for raw materials in that country. In 1950 the United States used over 50 per cent of the wood pulp production of the free world. The use of "industrial lumber" only (i.e., excluding wood used as fuel) is also extremely high in the United States; in the free world generally its use is considered to be likely to rise by something of the order of 40 per cent by 1975 (on the basis of certain assumptions as to population increase and of usage per head).[1] But the use of some of the other organic materials might not increase so fast, as synthetic products, made of industrial lumber, are expected to cut down the demand for certain wool, cotton and linen goods. The possibility of organic raw materials competing against each other is important.

The uneven distribution of raw materials between different countries makes it impossible to generalize as to the future course of raw material development. It may be that fears of over-all shortages as populations increase are not fully warranted, for as the very advanced countries move on to new industries and new raw materials the less

[1] Materials Policy Commision, vol. V, 1952.

advanced may take up some of the more traditional materials such as cotton, flax and wool, which are no longer so strongly in demand by the richer countries, or they too may move direct from a primitive technique to a highly advanced synthetic process.   The choice between these two methods will depend on the relative costs and returns anticipated.   Whatever choice is made, the world should be able to "support" its increasing population, though not necessarily to give it the standard of life many of its members would like to see established.

CHAPTER III

BRITAIN'S POPULATION

§ 1. *Estimates and Trends*. The 1951 Census count recorded a total population for England and Wales of 43,745 thousand persons,[1] and for Scotland of 5,095 thousand persons.[2] The preceding census took place in 1931. Mid-year estimates of population are made annually by the Registrars-General, and one of the purposes of the Census counts is to check these continuous records; the discrepancy revealed was only 0·2 per cent. The total of 48,840 thousand persons (50·2 million including Northern Ireland) was the highest recorded population since the decennial censuses [3] began to be taken in 1801.

From 1801 to 1841 the decennial rate of increase of the population of England and Wales varied between 14 and 18 per cent; the average decennial rate from 1801 to 1841 was 15·5 per cent. The rate varied over the decades from 1841 to 1911 between 11 and 14 per cent and on a logarithmic graph a straight line indicates a fairly continuous advance slightly reduced after 1841 (Diagram II). But in 1911 there was a second, and much more marked, point of inflexion. The rate of nearly 11 per cent (1901–11) fell to 4·50 and 4·78 per cent for the decades 1931–41 and 1941–51.

---

[1] *Census 1951, England and Wales, Preliminary Report*, H.M.S.O., 1951, p. x.

[2] *Preliminary Report on the Fifteenth Census of Scotland*, H.M.S.O., Edinburgh, 1951, p. v.

[3] The series is broken by the omission of the census in the war year of 1941.

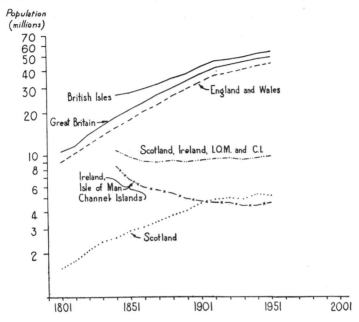

Diagram II.   150 YEARS POPULATION CHANGE, BRITISH ISLES

Source: Table VII, *Census 1951, England & Wales, Preliminary Report.*

The Registrar-General remarked of this series that [1]:

"The important features of the series . . . which cannot be too strongly stressed at the present time, having regard to the frequency of statements concerning the onset of stationary or declining conditions, are that the population continues to grow, that there has been little change in its successive rates of increase for the past forty years, and that so far there is no sign of any tapering away of the successive increments such as

[1] *Census 1951, England and Wales, Preliminary Report,* p. xi.

would normally be expected to herald the early approach of an ultimate population maximum."

Some demographers might well quarrel with this use of the word "normally", since the niceties of their mathematics are designed precisely to reveal trends concealed by movements in the total figures. The Registrar-General's duty is to record facts, however, and to be guided mainly by those facts; refinements imply further assumptions. With regard to England and Wales the facts are indeed very striking, and if the trend were to continue in a slightly modified form,[1] those countries together would have a total of 45·7 million persons in 1961, 47·8 in 1971 and nearly 50 million in 1981, or, say, 56 million for Great Britain. This projection represents a greater percentage increase than any suggested for Great Britain as a whole by demographers or official committees, who have usually tended to extrapolate the falling birth-rate, and to assume that the effect of net migration will be neutral or slight or unfavourable. Two only of the sixteen interesting projections worked out in the Royal Commission's selected papers [2] allowed for net inward migration (only of some 100,000 persons in all). Several of the Royal Commission's projections assumed the fertility of 1935–38, and all have used a constant or declining mortality. On the basis of their various assumptions, the Royal Commission arrived at a total population for Great Britain in 1982 ranging from 46 million to 55 million, and in 2002 (on the same assumptions) from 41 million to 57 million. The point is that a steady rise of $4\frac{1}{2}$ per cent per decade gives a result outside the range of those projections which the Royal Commission seemed to think worthy of detailed discussion.

[1] E.g., a decennial increase of $4\frac{1}{2}$ per cent.
[2] Selected papers, Vol. II, 1950, p. 213 ff.

It does not follow, however, that the projection is absurd or unlikely. The population for England and Wales has advanced at a different rate from that of Scotland, or that of the rest of the "British Islands", in which are included the whole of Ireland, the Isle of Man and the Channel Islands. The population of this remainder (i.e., the total excluding England and Wales) has remained practically stable since 1851, going down slightly in economically unfavourable decades and up slightly in others. This apparent stability, however, conceals the different trends in Scotland and the rest of the British Islands (principally Ireland).[1] Scotland alone of these units increased until 1911. Thus, populations in Scotland, Wales (and Monmouthshire), Northern Ireland, the Isle of Man, and the Irish Republic all declined between 1921 and 1931, for example, so that in that decade, while the population for England alone rose by 6·0 per cent, that for the U.K. plus the islands and the Irish Republic (called for convenience the British Islands) rose by only 3·9 per cent. However, the Registrar-General's remark on the smooth growth of the population curve is equally applicable to the total population of these "islands of the British seas" simply because England and Wales is numerically the most important part of the total. If the same simple projection were made to the "islands of the British seas" as to England and Wales it would appear that the 53 millions of 1951 might increase to some 56 millions in 1961, 58 millions in 1971, and so on for some decades. This projection is less likely to be realized than the first, since the stability in the growth of England and Wales was paralleled in the rest of the area by a stability not of growth but of total population; simple projections are of less plausibility, as the rate of development of the

[1] See Diagram II, p. 55.

outer areas of the group might more easily vary from their past rates in either direction, up or down.

During the decade 1921–31 there was a net migration from Scotland of 392,000 persons, and even during the twenty years from 1931–51 Scotland lost some 220,000 persons net by migration. Similarly, Ireland has persistently lost population by migration, especially to England and Wales. These countries gained no less than 525,000 net by immigration from 1931 to 1939, of whom a substantial proportion came from Ireland.

Since 1945 net migration into England and Wales has apparently revived. For the whole period 1939–51 there would, indeed, appear from one Census table to have been a net loss by "migration" of some 20,000,[1] but this particular census table includes war deaths occurring outside the country under the heading "loss by migration". When allowance has been made for war deaths, it appears that there was a net inflow of migrants into England and Wales of 220,000 in the period 1939–51 (745,000 in all from 1931 to 1951).[2] Net migration of 745,000 covering all forces affecting the size of population other than birth and death, can be compared with a "natural increase" (i.e., excess of births over deaths [3]) of 3,048 thousand over twenty years, and works out at nearly 20 per cent of total net increase. Because net migration represents a small figure in relation to *births* the fact that it has been a substantial fraction of the total net increase in England and Wales is often overlooked.

Predictions of the future of migration are naturally very hazardous; in any case, its volume and direction will depend partly upon governmental policy, both in this

[1] *Census 1951, England and Wales Preliminary Report*, Table C, p. xv.
[2] *Ibid.*, p. xiii.
[3] Including war casualties.

country and in those countries to which our emigrants go and from which our immigrants come. But are there not some rather deep underlying economic factors which will help to determine the lines that policy is likely to follow?

There are still a number of overseas countries which hope to benefit economically by the influx of British emigrants, provided that these arrive at a rate at which they can be comfortably absorbed. Details may be left aside at this stage of the discussion. The point, here, is that some emigration is likely to continue for at least the next twenty-five years.

On the other hand, there seems to be no good reason for supposing that those economic factors which resulted in so heavy a net inward migration into England and Wales have yet exhausted themselves; for they were the very factors which are obscurely working to produce the same surface symptoms the world over—rapid growth of urban centres, industrialization, accompanied by de-population first of the less urban areas and finally of the city centres themselves. The phenomenon was systemati-cally treated by Weber in the 1890's although it had been the subject of statisticians' debates at an earlier date.[1] It has continued at an accelerating rate ever since, and shows no sign of losing its momentum. The influx of population into England and Wales was part of a general rearrangement of population within these islands, taking place at the same time as a rapid general increase.

The Report of the Royal Commission [2] was very cautious on the subject of migration. It argued that "there is even less question here than elsewhere of choosing a single assumption as representing the likely course of development". It mentioned the fact that the

[1] More particularly in the 1880's.
[2] Cmd. 7695, 1949, par. 231.

balance of net migration for Great Britain was "usually outward" in the last century (i.e., 1847–1948) although inward after 1931. The Report concludes that "it seems safe to say that emigration has so far predominated", statistically, that is, and setting off the inward movement of recent years against the net emigration of the previous century or so.

If it is considered that the real national income of Great Britain may, despite the difficulties of overseas trade, rise slightly, then continued industrialization and urbanization of the country may be assumed. The precise form of that development is indeed very uncertain, nor is it predictable in exactly which places the greatest increases will take place. But that there will be a continued growth of certain types of town and of some of the conurbations (to be described presently) is more likely than not. From this assumption net migration into England and Wales seems practically certain; whether or not there must be net migration into Great Britain or the "British Islands" depends upon how far the rest of that area continues to provide an excess population for England and Wales.

The Registrar-General's optimism applies not only to migration but to the birth-rate; the Commission's Report was, on the other hand, professionally pessimistic on this subject. On this point the Report so far committed itself as to conclude: [1]

"One future development . . . we *can* forecast with a good deal of confidence, namely, a substantial decline in the annual number of births over the next 15 years."

Estimating the figures in 1948, the Report's authors guessed that average annual births for the period 1947–52

[1] *Ibid.*, par. 201.

in Great Britain would amount to 804,000. The recorded total has in fact been 836,000, so that their figure was some 4 per cent too low.

The basis of their projections was their belief in the stability of the size of the family. As they put it,[1] "it is clear that the size of the family will be decisive for the future number of births in Great Britain". The reverse is also true, since the future number of births will be decisive for the size of the family. The Royal Commission were not, however, indulging in an empty truism, since their point was that the important variable nowadays was the size of family determined upon by the average married couple. Thus, on their view, the number of births in any one year, or group of years, might be misleading if it was due not to a change in the intentions of married couples but only to the fact that marriages had been taking place at an earlier age.

The Royal Commission gave a useful rule of thumb to assist speculation on this difficult topic: the figure of 700,000 births annually for Great Britain. If the annual number of births remains greater than this figure, the total population will continue to show some net natural increase; at about this figure, stability of population will gradually be established; below it, a decline would eventually set in. Up to 1952 the decline had not yet resulted in births below the critical figure.

But the question still remains how far "average size of family" is itself a variable that is going to remain stable, and evidence that it has been stable in the recent past is not necessarily conclusive, or even very relevant. Social habits have changed quite rapidly in some recent decades in many countries. It is necessary to find the principal variables which will determine size of family—or, more

[1] *Ibid.*, par. 207.

directly, the total number of births each year—in the future.   Arithmetic is only incidental to any prediction. In any case the size of "completed families" can only be known some decades after marriage.

The factors that are going to affect the total number of births in future are innumerable, but some of the principal ones are undoubtedly economic.   Others are such specific factors as the availability of particular resources, and others again are social factors such as emulation, fashion and family attitudes generally.   In trying to guess how all these are going to work out, it is well to remember for how short a time certain social changes have been accepted, for example a national health service, the social goal of full employment, school meals and special milk for children, family allowances and so on.   The experiment of living in a world of full employment has not long been tried; as for living in a world of general economic security, the experiment has yet to be made.

Two objections have been made to the view that improved economic conditions would slow down the fall in the annual number of births; the first is that, on the contrary, the differences in the birth-rates of the higher and lower (i.e., richer and poorer) social classes in the past indicate that economic advancement makes for a limitation of size of families, and the second objection is that such correlation between economic change and birth-rates as can be observed in the past has been of short duration (in the main, cyclical) and therefore of little importance in relation to a long-term downward trend.

The first of these objections may be met in two ways: observation suggests that the differential birth-rates of the different social classes has been modified in recent years.[1]

---

[1] See "Family Anatomy", *The Economist*, 22 November 1952, p. 520 (article based on the second volume of the sample report of the 1951 Census for Great Britain).

Secondly, in a more equal society, with certain social services fully maintained and domestic life thus more firmly established on a workable basis, a slight improvement in the standard of life might well be expected *a priori* to result in rather larger instead of rather smaller families. The past is very little guide as to whether this would be so or not. The rewards of social advancement have tended often to be taken in various forms of display expenditure, but in a social system where these were discouraged a different reaction might be more common. Economic encouragement of a specific kind for large families might assist this process.

Special conditions of the past may, too, account for the apparently short-term correlation between the birth-rate and economic prosperity. To assume that rising standards of life necessarily imply smaller families is to project past experience into a future in which social relationships may have very profoundly changed.

It seems unfortunate to have to remain agnostic on this important issue, but at this stage of the argument the most that can be said is that a rise in the number of births is almost as likely as a continuing fall, and that a long-term positive correlation between real national income and size of family may quite possibly, with a suitable social background, establish itself. The future growth of the population, on this view, is to be determined by (as well as partly determining) the rate of material progress of the economy as a whole.

§ 2. *Urbanization.* Cities grow in two ways, by natural increase and by immigration; and in two senses, by an increase of numbers and by the extension of their boundaries. The economic and social boundaries often advance more rapidly than the corresponding administrative extensions, so that, for a growing "conurbation", the urbanized district extends over a wider area as time goes on, although administrative changes often lag behind the fact itself.

Exact statistical measurement of the growth of urbanization is for these reasons very often impossible. At any given moment a boundary is arbitrary, since people beyond the boundary have some economic links in their daily lives with those within it, and the boundary, however defined, ought sometimes to be re-drawn. Yet the spread of cities has been as important a change as the fluctuations of their own populations.

The effect of the extension of a city's influence in the later stages is seen in the form of a depopulation of the central districts (a decline in the numbers of those who sleep there, that is; the day-time population may remain stable or even rise) ; although, of course, this same depopulation may also be the symptom of a general decline.

Some indication of how these movements work out in Great Britain may be discovered in the census figures for the principal conurbations. There are six such conurbations officially listed for England and Wales, and their population as a whole rose from 1931 to 1951, though more slowly than the population of the whole country (by 3·1 against 9·5 per cent for England and Wales). If each of the conurbations is divided into an inner and outer ring, the inner rings lost no less than 11·5 per cent of their population in twenty years, while the outer rings (including their smaller urban areas) gained 21·2 per cent. By 1951, indeed, the population in the outer rings of the conurbations (8,900,000) exceeded that in the central areas (8,000,000), nor is there any reason for supposing that the process is at an end.

Much has been made of the social disadvantages of

conurbation, such as congestion of traffic, bad atmosphere, poor living conditions due to overcrowding, the creation of "blighted" inner areas as the town expands outwards, and of distress in other parts of the country if all new industry is attracted elsewhere. All these evils require remedy, but they are not in themselves evils arising from general over-population. Some of them arise from failure to adjust the social capital of a central urban area to its new functions, as the built-up area which it regularly serves becomes more densely inhabited, and indeed physically wider. The remedy for this must be sought (and is being sought) in re-planning. But despite the need for quite elaborate control and prompting by government authorities to promote the correct changes, and to mitigate their incidental hardships, it cannot be soundly argued that the growth of urban civilization is in itself a tide that ought to be dammed or rolled back, by the British any more than by any other government.

This is a similar conclusion to that of Professor Dennison in his well-known minority report to the Scott Committee,[1] when he looked at the obverse side of the same coin—the alleged loss of amenity accruing as a result of the decline in the agricultural population; he looked to "more effective planning" for a remedy rather than to a new set of "principles", always provided that (town and country planning) control was not restrictive or inelastic. His main thesis was that the economic welfare criterion should not be left out of account: "It is clearly desirable that the people should have as high a material standard of life as possible." [2]

The difficulty remains of how to assess the non-economic criteria, the relative advantages of different

[1] Cmd. 6378, 1942, pp. 100–123.
[2] *Ibid.*, p. 120, par. 67.

6

"ways of life", for example city *versus* rural life from the point of view of culture or social development. Much depends not only on subjective judgment on these matters but on the objective conditions in which the different ways of life are to flourish. If the growing urban areas are inadequately drained, lighted and policed, as in some manufacturing towns of England in the early stages of the industrial revolution, the social price paid for moving from the country to the town may be high. If a well-planned modern city is compared with a well-planned and prosperous rural area the relative advantages are not so clear. The growth of garden suburbs, and of "commuting" to dormitory villages, suggests that many people, given a choice, prefer to live in rural or semi-rural conditions, even at the cost of some material disadvantages, such as the cost of fares and the wear and tear of travelling.

A specialized literature has been created by protagonists of different views as to what the "city of the future" should be like, and views range from those who want to see modern civilization build round the indefinite extension of the garden suburb idea, so that towns are ultimately dispersed more widely, the siting of shopping centres, etc., being related to the assumption that every family is to own its car or cars, to those who want multi-storey dwellings erected on the outskirts, or even in the centre, of existing urban conglomerations.

§ 3. *Age and Sex Distribution.* In the Census count of persons in Great Britain in 1951 there were 25·4 million females and 23·4 million males, a "surplus" of 2 million females due to the exclusion of the armed forces overseas from the count, to the superior chances of life of females and to historical causes such as two world wars contribu-

ting to further excess than would otherwise have existed.
Over the country as a whole there were 109 females for
every 100 males at that time.

But, as is usual in urbanized countries, there was a
greater percentage excess of females in the urban than
in the rural areas. In the conurbations there were 112
females to every 100 males, and in other cities of 100,000
inhabitants or more the proportion was 111:100. The
concentration of women in the urban areas applied
to all age groups, though much more to the oldest than
to the youngest group. In the two most active age
groups, (a) 15–19 and (b) 20–64, the excess was for (a)
very marked and for (b) just noticeable. In the 15–19
group, for example, the national ratio was 105, while in
the conurbations it was 118, in the next group of cities
125. In the rural areas, where males were in excess, the
figure was as low as 74 women per 100 men for this age-
group. Females aged 20–64 lived in conurbations in the
ratio of 111 to 100 males, and in the rural areas in a ratio
of about 100 to 100.

If a comparison is made between the birth-rates of the
great conurbations and other urban areas of England and
Wales, and the rural areas—both being divided further
to show the Northern and North-Western Regions
separately from the rest of the country—it will be seen
that the North and North-Western cities have a crude
birth-rate that exceeds the average (by 7 per cent in this
case). The other groups had birth-rates a few per cent
less than the average for the country, which has been
equated with 100. To generalize: the northern towns-
man's proclivity to have children offsets the declined
families of the country people everywhere, and of the
cities and towns in the midlands, the east and the south.

One reason for the crude birth-rate in the rural areas

being below the average is that there are, on the whole, fewer women of child-bearing age (say 15–49) than marriageable men (say 15–64) in the country districts; as column three of Table VIII shows, there were only 89 women (of these ages) to 100 men (of these ages) in the rural districts all over the country. The "refined" rate referred to in the table divides total births by numbers of women in the age-group 15–49. This "refined birth-rate" was 7 per cent greater in "southern" rural areas, and 3 per cent in northern, than the national average ("southern" here referring to England and Wales apart from the Northern and North-Western regions).

This table brings out several other points of interest. If "refined birth-rate" is plotted against "female/male ratio" for England and Wales exclusive of the northern regions there would be three points:

Conurbations . . . . 92 : 105
Other urban areas . . . . 100 : 101
Rural areas . . . . . 107 : 89

giving an apparent negative relationship. The districts with higher female/male ratios have a relatively low birth-rate. The cities attract women into employment rather than into marriage and motherhood; the country districts have a low proportion of females to males, but a relatively higher birth-rate.

The figures for the northern districts follow a distinctly different pattern, apparently because of the relatively higher birth-rates in the conurbations of the north-west and north-east, a differential due perhaps to social and religious differences.

Such analyses as these suggest that projections of future population change, even in terms of natural increase, must imply, or be based upon, assumptions as to the social

Table VIII.—COMPARISONS BETWEEN THE BIRTH-RATE AND THE FEMALE/MALE RATIO FOR SELECTED AREAS IN ENGLAND AND WALES.

(Index numbers: Average for England and Wales = 100)

	Birth-rates expressed as Index numbers		Female/Male Ratio (Females 15–49/ Males 15–64)
	Crude Birth-rate (Births per 1,000 of Total Population)	Refined Birth-rate (Births per 1,000 of Females Age 15–49)	
England and Wales (excluding Northern and North-Western Regions):			
Conurbations	96 ⎫	92 ⎫	105 ⎫
Other urban areas	101 ⎬ 98	100 ⎬ 96	101 ⎬ 103
Rural areas	99 ⎭	107	89 ⎭
Northern and North-Western Regions			
Conurbations	109 ⎫	108 ⎫	103 ⎫
Other urban areas	104 ⎬ 107	105 ⎬ 107	100 ⎬ 102
Rural areas	98 ⎭	103	89 ⎭
London and South-Eastern England	93	89	107
Remainder of England and Wales .	103	104	98

Sources: Births from *Registrar-General's Statistical Review*, 1950. Population data from *Census of Great Britain 1951*; *One per cent Sample Tables*.

patterns of future living. It is evident from any study of the nineteenth century that the distribution of the female population throughout the country was profoundly affected by the changing economic demand for different types of female labour. In the twentieth century, not least in the decade of the 1940's, there were further substantial modifications in these employment opportunities.

The further reduction in domestic service, and the war-time employment and mobilization of women, affected their geographical distribution, their marriage opportunities and their social attitudes; and it would be extremely rash to predict, or to imply by a projection, that further changes in these factors will not take place.

The birth-rates of the towns, and especially of the outer rings of the conurbations, encourage the presumption that urbanized populations are capable of reproducing themselves by natural increase, although their present and future numbers are, and will be, partly determined by net immigration.

The power of population, that is the numbers of potential parents (adults physically capable of reproduction), does not seem to have been gravely impaired in Great Britain, nor likely to decline below a critical level for some time to come. If any series is considered which shows the curve of numbers of females coming into the child-bearing age-group, this fact becomes clear, especially if falling mortality rates and improved chances of life are considered too. This does not mean that the number of births will necessarily rise, or remain above the level of 700,000 annually for many more years. All that can be reasonably well established is that the power of population, in the sense defined, still exists.

§ 4. *Distribution by Occupations.* The main changes in the proportions of the occupied population in the forty years from 1911 to 1951 are summarized in Table IX. The "occupied" population included children as young as 10 years in 1911, but no younger than 15 in 1951; the total rose by 20 per cent for males and 27 per cent for females over this period. Among males the percentage of those occupied in agriculture or fishing fell from 10 to

6 per cent, in mining and quarrying from 10 to 5 per cent, in textiles from 5 to 3 per cent, and in personal service from 2 to 1 per cent. The percentage employed in the distributive trades is also thought to have fallen, but the figures are estimates only. The metals and vehicles occupations, chemicals, building, contracting, public administration and the professions all showed increases. For females most emphasis must be placed upon the heavy percentage declines in personal service, textiles and clothing, on the proportionate rises in the importance of metals, engineering and vehicles, the distributive trades, and the professions. The figures summarize a chapter of social history: the decline of the female servant class, the decline of the textile and clothing industries relatively to other occupations, and the rise of the shop assistant, the female industrial employee and the office worker or professional woman—these changes have been identified with the progressive political and social emancipation of women although it would be a gross over-simplification to suppose that the one change implied the other.

Thus in 1911 women's employment was concentrated in four groups (textiles, clothing and the various kinds of service adding to 69 per cent of the total), but by 1951 these accounted for only 34 per cent of the total occupied females.

According to the Family Census of 1946 the average size of family of professional and administrative workers in Great Britain was about 1·6, while that of unskilled labourers was at least twice as large.[1] A fertility enquiry also reported by the Royal Commission showed that for a certain group of marriages between 1920 and 1934 non-manual workers with "higher" education (above elementary school standard) had smaller families than those who

[1] Cmd. 7695, par. 408, p. 152.

Table IX.—Analysis of the Occupied Population in England and Wales by Industry Groups.

(Per cent of total occupied in each case)

Industry Group	Percentage of Total Occupied							
	Males				Females			
	1911 10 and over	1921 12 and over	1931 14 and over	1951 15 and over	1911 10 and over	1921 12 and over	1931 14 and over	1951 15 and over
1. Agriculture and fishing	10	9	8	6	2	2	1	2
2. Mining and quarrying	10	11	8	5	*	*	*	*
3. Non-metalliferous metals	1	1	2	2	1	1	1	1
4. Chemicals, etc.	1	1	1	2	1	1	1	1
5. Metals, engineering, vehicles	12	16	13	21	2	5	4	11
6. Textiles	5	5	4	3	14	13	11	8
7. Leather goods	1	1	*	*	*	*	*	*
8. Clothing	3	3	3	3	15	10	10	7
9. Food and drink	3	3	3	3	3	4	4	4
10. Wood and cork manufactures	2	2	2	2	1	2	*	1
11. Paper, printing	2	2	2	2	2	2	3	3
12. Other manufactures	1	1	1	1	1	1	*	1
13. Building and contracting	7	6	8	9	*	*	*	*
14. Transport	10	10	11	10	*	1	2	3
15. Distributive trades	14†	13†	14	10	7†	15†	15	17
16. Insurance, finance	3†	1†	2	2		1	1	2
17. Public administration and defence	6	8	7	10	4	7	3	4
18. Professions	3	2	4	4	7	7	9	13
19. Personal Service	2	2	2	1	26	20	22	6
20. Other services	4†	4†	5	5	14†	10†	11	13
	100%	100%	100%	100%	100%	100%	100%	100%
Occupied population	11·5 mn.			13·8 mn.	4·8 mn.			6·1 mn.
Index of increase (In occupied labour force; aged 15 and over in 1951, but 10 and over in 1911; 1911 = 100.)	100			120	100			127

Source: Relevant Census statistics. N.B. The figures for the four dates are not completely comparable owing to changes in method of classification and in the various age limits.

* Less than 1 per cent. † Estimated.

had had less education, and similarly for manual workers (who had larger families than non-manual in both categories).[1] These, and similar facts, have long been observed and recorded, and have given rise to doubts as to the future quality of the British population. The main fear that has been expressed is that, although social differences in fertility may narrow, they will still remain, and that the consequence will be the over-breeding of persons with less successful social characteristics (less successful in every respect, that is, but that of the biological act of breeding itself), and that hence there will be a relative decrease in each generation in the numbers of those likely to inherit qualities which lead to social success and esteem.

One such quality is sometimes held to be "intelligence", an abstract quality which is believed to be partly hereditary and partly subject to environment (that is, susceptible of being hidden by adverse educational influences). The argument is then re-stated as follows. On the whole, according to intelligence tests taken at schools, children of greater intelligence come on average from smaller families than the less intelligent. Since, by this hypothesis, intelligence is partly a hereditary characteristic, each succeeding generation of children will tend to be, on average, less intelligent. Each generation the general level of innate intelligence of the nation is bound to decline. This is an alarming proposition, which has been supported by many distinguished scientists, and not merely by historians theorizing about the "decline of the West", and it deserves very serious attention.

Many tests seem to have established the general proposition that, on average, the less intelligent children have belonged to the larger families in British schools where

[1] *Ibid.*, par. 410.

varying tests have been applied since before World War I. What the tests have failed to show is that the average intelligence of schoolchildren is declining. The question is what interpretation to put on these facts.

The first point to observe is that the actual predictions made by the early enthusiasts for the technique of intelligence tests have not in fact been fulfilled. They predicted unequivocally that the intelligence of the nation would fall, and, according to their own techniques (incidentally modified considerably over the years), this verifiable fall has not taken place. While it may still be true that *innate* intelligence is falling (if there is a scientific basis for the distinction between "innate" and "total" intelligence) observed total intelligence, as evidenced by behaviour in intelligence tests, shows no corresponding decline.

The argument that intelligence is mainly hereditary seems closely analogous to the similar argument that bodily stature is also a mainly hereditary characteristic. A school of thought exists which questions the validity of the statistical methods used in many of the so-called "proofs" of the hereditary influence.[1]

In the standard statistical textbooks tables are often given of the heights of fathers and sons, and second degree statistics (e.g., correlation coefficients) are used to demonstrate the hereditary influence. But a first degree statistic, average height, for example, is often neglected, although this may be compatible less with a hereditary theory than with the simpler theory that improved diet and environment improve stature. Both influences are undoubtedly at work; what is fallacious is to ignore the lesson of first

[1] See Barnet Woolf, 1952. I am indebted to Professor 'Espinasse for calling my attention to this, and the subsequent reference in this chapter.

order statistics showing increasing stature with each generation.   Similarly of intelligence.

In about thirty years the average intelligence of Scottish schoolchildren rose by about twice as much as it was expected to fall according to the genetical theory.   These results some writers have attempted to explain away as due to the better practice at intelligence tests alleged, or supposed, to be indulged in by modern schoolchildren, but this argument tacitly admits the factor of environment as being of importance; and environment correlates with home conditions, which are affected by size of family income.   There seems little reason for the plain man to doubt that level of income and environment raises the standard in the community both of intelligence and of bodily stature.

An *a priori* argument of Professor Penrose [1] may also be considered; if a hypothetical population is divided into three groups in respect of intelligence, say I.Q.103 for the best, comprising 90 per cent of the fertile population, a small group with I.Q.73 comprising 10 per cent of the population, which is more fertile than the first group, and a fractional third group with very low intelligence and low fertility as well, and the extreme assumption is adopted that intelligence is due to a single perfectly additive pair of genes called A and a, the upper group will be all AA, the small inferior group Aa, and the weaklings aa.

On the assumption of two types of mating only, $AA \times AA$ will produce nothing but slightly superior offspring.   In the inferior group $Aa \times Aa$ will, on orthodox genetic theory, produce $\frac{1}{4}AA$, $\frac{1}{2}Aa$ and $\frac{1}{4}aa$.   It can be calculated that this population will be in perfect equilibrium in respect to the (assumed inherited) characteristic,

[1] Penrose, 1949, p. 124.

intelligence, *if* the birth-rate of the inferior group is rather more than twice that of the superior group. Thus a considerably higher birth-rate is required to prevent the inferior group from gradually dying out. The particular result follows, of course, from the figures chosen by Professor Penrose for his example, but the result is instructive.

The general argument follows from the assumption that a fraction of the reproduced offspring of the "mixed" group (*Aa*'s mating with *Aa*'s) turn out to be sub-lethal *aa*'s, incapable of survival. On the other hand, another proportion of the same mixed group's offspring replenish the ranks of the *AA*'s who would otherwise tend to diminish in proportion of total population because of their own lower birth-rate. Furthermore, it may well be, for all that we can easily state, that some societies, and particularly modern industrial societies, require for their operation a large mass (or a small mass—in either case a pre-determined proportion) of only averagely endowed individuals. This will evidently be the case when the techniques of production absolutely require fairly large numbers of unskilled, or only semi-skilled, workers.

The differential class birth-rates observed in our societies may then be, in part at least, the consequence of social pressures tending to lead at least partially to the "correct" numbers of individuals being born of given grades of intelligence. Of course, it would be absurd to pretend that the adjustment of labour supply to demand can be exact in the long-run, that is, over the long period of years required to raise and educate a family. But if demand for trained skilled "labour", right up to the top professional and managerial grades, is persistently high, the working-class may in favourable conditions react by throwing up a proportion of persons with first-class brains, who can be sent at the expense of some sacrifice by the family to be educated or trained for a higher social class. All this is speculation; the point that has been established by Professor Penrose is that even on the most extreme assumptions as to the importance of genetical influences there can be no *a priori* case established for predicting a general decline in national intelligence. This does not, however, mean that measures, or circumstances, which discourage the more intelligent members of society from reproduction are not deplorable in their effects.

PART II

ANALYSIS

CHAPTER IV

THE MALTHUSIAN THEORY

§ 1. *Malthus as a Publicist.* Thomas Robert Malthus, the second in a family of eight children, was born in 1766. His father, Daniel Malthus, was a country gentleman, with dilettante intellectual interests, who was honoured .to receive David Hume and Jean-Jacques Rousseau as guests at his house near Dorking one month after the prodigious Thomas Robert had seen the light. Daniel Malthus admired the eighteenth-century enlightenment, and caused his children to be brought up by private education, sending Thomas Robert in due course to a tutor who prepared him for Cambridge. Robert Malthus entered Jesus College in 1784, took orders in 1788, and became a fellow of his college in 1793, a fellowship which he held until he resigned the post on his marriage in 1804. He accepted a curacy in 1796, and wrote an insignificant political pamphlet, attacking Pitt's Government, in the same year. Two years later, after the celebrated argument (described in the preface to his essay) with his father, who defended Godwin's views set out in *Political Justice* in favour of the possibility of Utopia, T. R. Malthus published the first edition of his *Essay on the Principle of Population as it affects the Future Improvement of Society, with remarks on the speculations of Mr. Godwin, M. Condorcet, and other writers.*[1]

As a publicist, Malthus was enormously successful. He

[1] These biographical facts have been taken from Dr. G. F. McCleary's *The Malthusian Population Theory,* 1953, from which the reader may derive a full, accurate, but wholly favourable view of Malthus's population theories.

set out to attack the poor laws, and he lived to see them repealed.   On this subject he converted Pitt, who dropped the New Poor Law Bill of 1800.   His first essay was intended to refute Godwin, and Godwin's eclipse was complete.[1]   In 1811 Shelley was to hear with "inconceivable emotion" that Godwin was not yet "enrolled in the list of the honourable dead".[2]   Other social forces, public and personal, contributed to Godwin's period of oblivion; Coleridge, for example, had ceased to hymn Godwin with any ardent lays, and Southey and Wordsworth were living to regret the naïve optimism with which they had welcomed Godwin's quiet but effective attacks upon superstition and the abuses of the established order of government.   Godwin's utopianism, like that of others, though effective in its attack on abuses, and attractive in its confidence in human enlightenment and reason, was open to deadly counter-thrusts in many of its positive propositions, such as the famous views on marriage which were easy for critics both to distort and to deride.   Through Shelley himself, and through his earlier influence on Place and Owen, and indeed on generations of radicals, Godwin's influence was perpetuated. But he was doomed to be practically ineffective in his own lifetime, although he outlived Malthus, dying in 1836 in his eightieth year.

Many strands were joined in Godwin's thought, both of rationalist and dissenting ancestry.   The principal point which Malthus selected for attack was his belief that human institutions, rather than the intrinsic vices of

[1] As Godwin admitted in the preface to his "Enquiry" of 1820: "the Essay on Population has gotten possession of the public mind." (Godwin, 1820, p. viii).   The first edition of his *Enquiry concerning the Principles of Political Justice* was published in 1793, the second in 1796, and the third in 1798.

[2] Rodway, 1952, p. 45.   Shelley was not, apparently, ironical in this passage, but had genuinely believed that Godwin was no longer alive.

individual human beings, were the main cause of the evils of mankind; he looked forward to an imaginary period of reforms ending with the dissolution of government—the final "withering away" of the state.[1]

Godwin wrote:

> "With what delight must every well-informed friend of mankind look forward, to the auspicious period, the dissolution of political government, of that brute engine, which has been the only perennial cause of the vices of mankind. . . ."

This was the somewhat extreme and flaccid optimism that Malthus discerned in his own father's presuppositions, and which, as a young Cambridge intellectual of some capacity as a mathematician, he set out to deflate and refute.   Malthus wished to show that owing to his "principle of population", vice and misery must always be with mankind, in accordance with the Biblical text about the poor, except, according to the qualification of his second edition, in so far as "moral restraint" was exercised, and in his view it was unlikely to be exercised very extensively.   He succeeded in making his point, and, from his day to this, vice and misery have never been wholly dissociated in the minds of Western civilized persons from high birth-rates among the poor.

As the study by Mr. Kenneth Smith[2] very well shows, almost every logical objection that can be brought against Malthus's arguments was publicly expressed, and often well and trenchantly expressed, by critics such as Hazlitt, Booth, Place, Grahame, Weyland and a host of others,

---

[1] This aspect of Godwin's thought derives perhaps from his own sensitiveness to the brutality of the state's methods in most of the countries of contemporary Europe rather than from any particular literary source.

[2] Smith, 1951.

in Malthus's own lifetime.[1]   Yet it was Malthus's doctrine
that survived to be discussed, and not that of any of his
critics.   The revival of Malthusianism at intervals of
some thirty years (for instance in the periods 1885–93,
1918–25 and 1946–52) is a subject for separate study.
What cannot be denied is that Malthus himself was, on
his chosen ground, a most formidable controversialist.
From what sources came the strength of his position?

Malthus, unlike Ricardo, did not wish to usher in the
new phase of rapid capitalist expansion already heralded
by the earlier technical developments of the industrial
revolution, but rather to defend a society dominated
economically by land-owning and land-holding classes.
In two little discussed pamphlets he warmly defended the
Corn Laws.   But his population theory fitted into the
intellectual structure of the Ricardian system very well,
or, at least, it could be adapted to Ricardo's ideas, and
provide the basis for his theory of wages and of profits.
The general thesis that population tended to outrun
subsistence pleased nearly everybody, capitalist apologists
as well as those who defended the landed interest.   One
element in his strength is that all schools of classical
economists adapted his theory to their own ends.   Even
Engels thought that Malthus was "right in his way"
(i.e., with reference to bourgeois society) in asserting that
there are always more people on hand than can be maintained from the available means of subsistence; but of
course he and Marx gave a different explanation from
Malthus for this phenomenon.   But they fully recognized
the importance of the Malthusian theory of population,

[1] Dr. McCleary dismisses Hazlitt in a footnote referring to that great
writer's indiscreet *Liber Amoris* (see McCleary, 1953, p. 101).   That even
modern apologists for Malthus have recourse to such irrelevancy exposes
them to the accusation that they have no better argument to put
forward.

which they thought had been "invented" to reconcile the otherwise inexplicable phenomena of capitalist society.[1]

Malthus's population theory needs, moreover, to be read in relation to the preceding population theories of the eighteenth century; they were many and various.

Cantillon's theory,[2] for example, was elaborate and subtle, and evidently based upon careful observation. He thought of the landowners as the controlling class of society, and of land as "the source whence all wealth is produced". Population growth depended, in the main, upon the subsistence produced at the behest of the landed proprietors, the proportion of this which those proprietors made available for the hire of labour, and the standards of life current among the wage-earning and land-owning classes respectively.

Thus population depends, in Cantillon's view, upon what might now be called the "strategic decisions" taken by the landed proprietors. If the proprietors live far from their land "Horses must be fed for the transport into the city", and "the more Horses there are in a state the less food will remain for the People". The number of inhabitants in a state depended chiefly upon the means allotted to them for their support, and the amount of these means in turn depended chiefly on the "Taste, Humours and Manner of Living of the Proprietors of Land".

He thought, further, that the population of a country would tend to be increased or diminished as a result of

---

[1] When pressed to answer whether over-population could arise under communism Engels admitted " the abstract possibility " of a necessity to impose limits on numbers, but added that if regulation of numbers ever became necessary only a communist society could carry out such regulation successfully. (See the letter to Kautsky, quoted in Meek, 1953, p. 108.) Some occasions for testing the correctness of this opinion may occur if communist societies survive.

[2] Cantillon, 1755 (reprinted 1931).

international trade, according to the degree to which that trade resulted in a net import of necessaries. For example, the import of Brussels lace into France would tend to diminish the French population if wine were exported to buy the lace, since the wine would cost France the use of many thousands of acres.

Cantillon thus linked the size of the population with the amount of food and necessaries available, as Malthus did in a much blunter form with his first postulate (that food was necessary to man). But he had no conviction that Malthus's second postulate on the geometrical ratio of population increase operated unrestrainedly—or, putting the matter another way, he fully understood as a result of observation the phenomenon described by Malthus as "moral restraint".[1]

Quesnay and the Physiocrats also believed that population tends to grow as the supply of subsistence expands, and they, in their turn, began to concern themselves with the procreative instincts of man which, they feared, resulted in a downward pressure on wages. But they seemed, on the whole, to think that such downward pressure was self-adjusting, since the excessive misery temporarily engendered would lead to a reduction of population by emigration and a fall in the number of births. As agriculture became more prosperous, on the other hand, real wages might rise above a mere subsistence level, and the tendency towards over-procreation was by no means an inexorable law.[2]

These schools of French writers failed to anticipate

---

[1] If there were not sufficient necessaries, Cantillon thought "the People will diminish in number. Some will be forced to leave the country for lack of employment; others, not seeing the necessary means of raising children, will not marry or will marry late . . ." (Spengler, 1942, p. 116).

[2] Spengler, pp. 208–9.

Malthus, except in the very general sense of discussing fully the relation of population to food supplies, and the dangers of too great a rate of procreation.

Thus on *two* essential points Malthus's views were diametrically different from those of many earlier writers. On the first point he was opposed to Wallace, one of the British writers who most closely foreshadowed some of his arguments.[1] Malthus clearly owed very much to Wallace's exposition.[2] But there was this important point of difference, that Wallace, like his French contemporaries, thought that any evil day of over-population lay ahead at some unpredictable date in the future, whereas Malthus often insisted that it had already arrived.

On the second point, too, Malthus's theory was sharply different from that of any of his predecessors. They were willing to discuss the "defects of government" in Wallace's phrase, or the shortcomings of absolutism in France, as obstacles to a greater population; in other words, to treat human institutions, like the state, as variables that could be changed to meet changing social needs. Malthus was concerned to point out a "principle of population" which was, in his view, immutable and inexorable, and which rendered most proposed "improvements" of social

[1] Wallace had written in 1753: "Indeed had it not been for the errors and the vices of mankind, and for the defects of government and of education, the earth must have been much better peopled, perhaps might have been overstocked, many ages ago; and as these causes operate more or less strongly, the earth will be better or worse peopled at different times." He had added in 1761, that: "Under a perfect government, the inconveniences of having a family would be so entirely removed, children would be so well taken care of, and every thing become so favourable to populousness, that though some sickly seasons or dreadful plagues in particular climates might cut off multitudes, yet in general, mankind would increase so prodigiously, that the earth would at last be overstocked, and become unable to support its numerous inhabitants."

[2] Wallace wrote clearly of the forces making for a reduction of any surplus population that there was "no need of miracles for this purpose. The vices of mankind are sufficient."

institutions valueless and nugatory. The deeper significance of his position as a publicist is well explained by
Dr. Spengler, who points out that Malthus's predecessors
were, on the other hand, chiefly concerned with the
discovery (and diffusion) of means to dissolve the evils
of political absolutism.

Malthus took up the defence of property and of (to a
large extent) the social *status quo* at the very moment
that technological progress was making itself felt. Increased opportunities for the growth of incomes seemed
to be about to occur; real wages could then rise, and
many established relationships would become obsolete,
and disappear with or without some violent social upheaval. Malthus was essentially a lover of a well-ordered
society, stable and beneficent, and governed by recognized religious principles. Some kinds of progress there
might be, but any advance in living standards must be,
he hoped—and he believed that he had discovered that it
would be—associated with the exercise of moral courage
and restraint. The task of governments was to protect
property and prevent its abuse, to discourage pauperism
by abolishing such expedients as the Speenhamland
system, and in every way possible to link real incomes
with effort and work, treating idleness as a social crime.

§ 2. *Malthus's Postulates and Arguments.* Malthus's principle, in its deductive form, was derived from two postulates and one assumption. The postulates were that food
was necessary for the existence of man, and that sexual
passion was a determined and unchanging force sufficiently
strong to maintain some geometrical rate of population
increase. The assumption was that the production of
food could be increased only in the ratio 1, 2, 3, 4, 5, 6,
7, 8, 9, that is in an arithmetical ratio, at the same time

as population tended to increase, or had the "power" to increase, in the geometrical ratio 1, 2, 4, 8, 16, 32, 64, 128, 256 and so on.

The assumption of the arithmetical increase in food was subject to the qualification that "fresh starts" in agriculture, that is improvements due to reorganization or the introduction of new techniques, could from time to time raise the level from which the increase began.

Reasoning from the postulates and the assumption Malthus concluded that, unless marriages were postponed, or restraint on reproduction otherwise introduced, population would always tend to outrun food supply; hence some "checks" would be imposed by "nature", or as we should perhaps say, would arise from the situation itself. These checks could in general be described as "vice and misery". In the second edition the possibility of "moral restraint" was admitted, by which term Malthus meant the kind of prudence with regard to marriage more clearly and objectively described by Cantillon.

As Edwin Cannan shrewdly remarked:

"The soundest economists will hesitate if asked directly, 'What is the principle of population as understood by Malthus?'" [1]

Cannan answered his own question with the statement that:

". . . It seems probable, it would be rash to say more, that in the first edition of the *Essay* 'the principle of population' is that the growth of population must necessarily be checked by misery or prudential motives."

Certainly there can be no doubt of the position adopted

[1] Cannan, 1924, p. 134.

in the first *Essay*, as this was purely deductive. The argument in the *Encyclopædia Britannica* of 1824 [1] was fundamentally unchanged. From the two postulates as set out in the first edition verbatim which were:

"that food is necessary to the existence of man"

and

"that the passion between the sexes is necessary, and will remain nearly in its present state"[2],

Malthus argued that "the power of population is indefinitely greater than the power in the earth to produce subsistence for man." The jump in the argument from the postulates to the conclusion depends, of course, upon the assumption. In the next paragraph the assumption is stated:

"Population, when unchecked, increases in a geometrical ratio. A slight acquaintance with numbers will show the immensity of the first power in comparison with the second . . ."

The postulates and the assumption may fairly be identified as Malthus's major contribution to the subject, [3] and if Malthus was wrong either one or both of the postulates must be rejected, and/or the assumption about the ratios. The later editions of the *Essay* "explained" his position, however, with many qualifications.

But before turning to the *qualified* theory it may be worth while first to explain the merits of the earlier

---

[1] Malthus, 1824.

[2] Modern apologists for Malthus sum up his principle as being that it is "easier" for mankind to produce children than to produce subsistence (see McCleary, 1953, p. 157). But precisely what does "easier" mean in this context? And, however defined, can such a statement be universally valid?

[3] Sir James Steuart, in his *Inquiry* of 1767, had fully explained the relation of populations, both human and animal, to food supply (Vol. 1, Book I, chap. 3).

deductive statement and secondly to examine reasons
for supposing it to be false.

Malthus argued that, because of his postulates, there
must be "a strong and constantly operating check on
population from the difficulty of subsistence". Ignoring
for the moment the social implication of this statement
(which Malthus at once stated—"this difficulty . . . must
necessarily be felt by a large portion of mankind"), its
brilliance as a wide generalization needs to be observed;
for at one blow Malthus placed mankind on the same level
as the other species of creation. He put man in relation
to the restraints of his environment, and it was this aspect
of his work that supplied Charles Darwin in 1836 with
the germ of the idea for the theory of evolution. For
Malthus's very next paragraph gave a classic basis to
ecological thinking:

> "Through the animal and vegetable kingdoms, nature
> has scattered the seeds of life abroad with the most
> profuse and liberal hand. . . . Necessity, that imperious
> all-pervading law of nature, restrains them within the
> prescribed bounds. The race of plants and the race of
> animals shrink under this great restrictive law. And
> the race of man cannot, by any efforts of reason, escape
> from it. Among plants and animals its effects are
> waste of seed, sickness, and premature death. Among
> mankind, misery and vice . . ."

No one, after Malthus had written, could ever view the
human population problem out of relation to the problems
of food and other supplies provided with the assistance
of "nature". The ecological point had been made.[1]

Food is necessary to man; there is no reason to dispute

---

[1] But see the reference in footnote 3, p. 90.

this postulate. But several observations on it are relevant.

First, food is not the only necessity of mankind; water, clothes, shelter and warmth are in different degrees prime necessities. Clearly, if the standard of life is to rise, the output of necessities must rise faster than the increase in population. Historical experience now affords, and had already afforded in Malthus's time, many examples of the production of food and other necessities increasing faster than population, and that without any distinct symptoms of increasing "misery and vice", but rather of their diminution.

It is important not to overlook necessities other than food. As a contemporary critic remarked, the absurdity of Malthus's doctrine might have been seen if he had stated it in respect of clothes.

The amount of food necessary to man varies, as is now known, within fairly narrow limits; even so, the limits widen according to the activities of the persons concerned, the climatic conditions and other factors. The *kind* of food required is of great importance. Improvements in dietary technique may be viewed rather like improvements in the arts of raising crops; better food is put into human beings, and they become more efficient animals. Thus the food (and other necessities) made available may affect the second postulate, interpreted as meaning the proclivity to have children in an imprudent manner, and also the conditions of the assumption that food production cannot be rapidly expanded. The postulates and the assumption are thus not independent of each other, as it is essential for Malthus's argument that they should be.

The second postulate, in the sense originally meant, was abandoned by Malthus himself when he admitted the possibility of "moral restraint". Those who refuse to class the extension of birth control, among married people especially, as vice, admit a further large class of exceptions to the generalization.

Once Malthus had admitted the check of "moral restraint" (which in his view consisted of virtuous abstention from marriage) the use of "the principle of population" as an argument against the ultimate perfectibility of mankind was no longer valid. Entirely different arguments had to be adduced, based on allegations as to the inability of working-class groups to exercise such restraint.

Malthus's argument against systems of equality thus changed its basis between the first and the later editions of his essay. Once he had admitted the possibility of checks to population growth which were neither miserable nor vicious his case against the "reform" of existing institutions, and his defence of the institution of private property, rested on the argument that prudential checks on population were in fact only possible in the context of the right kind of institutions. He argued that equality and common ownership of property were not conducive to moral restraint.[1] In this he may or may not have been right; the interesting point is that his case was now explicitly a *political* case (an instance of *i* in the notation of Table I above) and no longer rested on inexorable demological tendencies.

Despite these admissions, Malthus clung to his assumption of a geometrical population increase, which he claimed, in both the first and all later versions of the theory, to be consistent with observed fact. It was based, indeed, on the report that the population of certain colonies in North America had doubled in twenty-five years. Long after he had conceded the theoretical possibility of

[1] See Robbins, 1952, pp. 124–5.

moral restraint, Malthus clung to the belief that doubling in twenty-five years was the *natural* rate of increase of a population from which the special preventive checks associated with a shortage of food were removed. The article on "Population" in the *Encyclopædia* of 1824 returns to this same argument in more detail. "In an endeavour to determine the natural power of mankind to increase", the article states, ". . . we can have no other guide than past experience." We should expect, the article argues, the greatest natural increase where "room and nourishment were the most abundant". North America is a case in point; statistics for 1790, 1800 and 1810 confirm the view that natural doubling takes place in less than twenty-five years. This, then, is the "natural" rate of increase which any population will have.

Be it noted that Malthus in quoting these facts is not "reasoning from facts"; he is assuming that the one instance of an observed geometrical ratio is the "natural" ratio for all populations. He is assuming that this ratio would at once be attained by any other population with the like conditions of "room and nourishment". He is generalizing from a single instance. Thus a single instance of a population which had sufficient "room and nourishment" to multiply naturally at this rate, and did not in fact do so, would suffice to refute the assumption; and so would sufficient evidence of social forces capable of restricting the rate of natural increase of populations below his assumed rate, even though no instances had yet occurred. Little is still known of the precise social and economic forces affecting natural increase, but there is a wide enough experience of falling birth-rates among economically advanced populations to make it certain that his assumed geometrical ratio is wholly untrustworthy as a generalization of universal applicability.

The assumption of the ratios had to be abandoned by Malthus when he admitted that subsistence had in fact increased at times in a geometric ratio. As Cannan wrote: [1] "Deprived of the theory that the periodical additions to the average annual produce cannot possibly be increased, or, as Malthus preferred to put it, that subsistence can increase only in an arithmetical ratio, the *Essay on the Principle of Population* falls to the ground as an argument, and remains only a chaos of facts collected to illustrate the effects of laws which do not exist."

Cannan was perhaps too optimistic in thinking that the essay "falls to the ground", since Malthus had provided himself with the escape clause of allowing for "new starts in agriculture" (to explain "temporary" rises in standards of living).

But so long as "new starts" (i.e., improvements) continue to provide a higher standard of living, and to increase food and other necessities faster than the natural increase in population, there is no reason to regard growing population as the cause of inescapably increasing misery and vice for a large portion of mankind.

Perhaps an inkling of the reasons for Malthus's success as a controversialist may already have been gained. Although he abandoned the universality of his second postulate, and that of his assumption on the second ratio, he reiterated the universal applicability of his theory that there was a "tendency" for population and food supplies to grow at different rates, incompatible with each other.

§ 3. *Peculiarities of the Malthusian Doctrine.* Malthus's theory has thus two main aspects; it was conceived by a brilliant publicist who wished to attack existing social legislation, and also to attack "speculations" upon the

[1] *Op. cit.*, p. 144.

possible improvement of existing institutions of government and property; and, on the other hand, by a "philosopher" who first saw the importance of the limiting
factors of environment on human material progress.

Malthus attached the highest importance to the
geometrical and arithmetical ratios.

Marshall interpreted Malthus much too favourably
when he stated that the arithmetical ratio was "really
only a short way of stating the utmost that he thought
any reasonable person could ask him to concede. What
he meant, stated in modern language, was that the
tendency to diminishing return, which is assumed throughout his argument, would begin to operate sharply after
the produce of the island had been doubled. Doubled
labour might give doubled produce; but quadrupled
labour would hardly treble it . . . etc." [1]

The law of diminishing returns was not so modern that
Malthus was unaware of it; on the contrary, Malthus himself enunciated the doctrine in his *Observation on the effects
of the Corn Laws* in 1814 [2] a few months before West
invented its "modern" name. He had a good reason for
clinging to his "ratios" even in the later editions of his
work on population. Diminishing returns might have
been discussed in terms of facts—returns are sometimes
diminishing, sometimes not. The ratios, on the other
hand, can be asserted to be "tendencies" whether or not
they are observable in a specific period.

Moreover, the concepts of diminishing returns in agriculture, and of the arithmetical ratio, are not quite the same
thing. The arithmetical ratio applies to the total produce
raised. What has to be asserted is that this total cannot
be indefinitely doubled. The law of diminishing returns

[1] Marshall, 1938, p. 179, footnote.
[2] The date is given as 1815 in Sraffa's Introduction to Ricardo.

refers to the produce raised per head of labour, as more and more poor land is brought into cultivation to meet the needs of a growing population.   Diminishing returns may operate without a failure to double the total produce.[1] This is quite possible, and the income per head of a growing population may in such a case still rise if there are increasing returns in manufacturing, so releasing enough labour to offset diminishing returns in agriculture. Malthus's ratio, crude as it was, looked beyond any such "temporary" improvement; indeed, without reliance on the ratios he could not have been sure of his inevitable "misery".

Malthus's doctrine was not produced inductively but deductively.   Thus, for example, as Malthus wrote: [2] "One ingenious writer has remarked that I have not deduced a single original fact from real observation to prove the inefficiency of the checks which already prevail. These remarks are correctly true, and are truisms exactly of the same kind as the assertion that man cannot live without food.   For undoubtedly as long as this continues to be a law of his nature, what are here called the natural checks cannot possibly fail of being effectual."

Yet Malthus's later claim to be reasoning from the facts deceived so acute a critic as Alfred Marshall, whose piety towards his forerunners on this point outweighed his judgment.   He wrote of Malthus: [3]

"By a careful study of facts he proves that every people, of whose history we have a trustworthy record, has been so prolific that the growth of its numbers would have been rapid and continuous if it had not

[1] Indeed, as re-stated by Ricardo, the L.D.R. operated mainly when "wealth and population" were both increasing.

[2] See Cannan, 1924, p. 137.

[3] Marshall, 1938, p. 178.

8

been checked either by a scarcity of the necessaries of
life, or some other cause, that is, by disease, by war,
by infanticide, or lastly by voluntary restraint."

The transitions in Malthus's argument from a deductive
theory to an inductive one included a series of qualifications to the original theory. These were very fully
developed in the later editions of the essay. The resulting
modified theory was, however, incapable of either disproof
or verification.

Malthus, in his first essay, had *assumed* that population
always "tended" to increase faster than food "unless
there were checks", and he had *assumed* further that food
determined (with certain qualifications elaborated later)
the rate of growth actually observed. These assumptions
are in principle unverifiable. It is not necessary for
population ever to increase faster than food for his theory
to be true; indeed, as he sometimes remarked, according
to the second of these assumptions in his own theory, it
could not do so. The "tendency" of the population to
increase faster than food could therefore never be observed. The only tendency that could be observed was
that population always increased at exactly the same rate
as food. But, according to Malthus, observations on this
point were not really necessary since the truth of it was
self-evident.

What, then, of the numerous examples that could be
brought of rises taking place in the standard of life? At
this point Malthus introduced one of his famous after-
thoughts. It appeared that, after all, social custom and
the institutions of society had some effect on the amount
of food that the average working-man consumed. As an
example of a rise in the standard of living *not* offset by an
increase in population, the history of rural England in

the early years of the eighteenth century might well be quoted.

What is rather astonishing is that Malthus quoted the example himself:

> "It is well known," he wrote,[1] "that during this period the price of corn fell considerably, while the wages of labour are said to have risen. . . . From 1720 to 1750 the price of wheat had so fallen, while wages had risen, that instead of two-thirds the labourer could purchase the whole of a peck of wheat with a day's labour. . . . This great increase of command over the necessaries of life did not, however, produce a proportionate increase of population."

How did this fit into the Malthusian theory?   Because, of course, there *must have been* "prudential habits" among the workers, attributable to "civil liberty", which in turn depends upon "political liberty".[2]

Thus Malthus did not assert that the output of food could never increase faster than the growth of population. He merely asserted, and assumed, that when it did so the explanation must be "prudence" (i.e., the preventive check) or the fortuitous onset of some of the positive checks (wars or epidemics).   He defined a situation where (a) the standard of life was rising, and (b) there were no positive checks as an instance of the preventive check at work, and having thus assumed his result he could never be proved wrong.

The Report of the Royal Commission on Population states [3] that Malthus's argument rested on "two assumptions" not in fact realized, namely, (1) that technical

1 Malthus, 1820, chap. iv, Sec. II, pp. 253–4.
2 *Ibid.*, p. 251.
3 Cmd. 7695, par. 264.

improvement in agriculture could only proceed very slowly, and (2) that imports would only make a minor contribution to a country's food supply.

Malthus would not for one moment have conceded that his argument rested on either one of these assumptions, both of which he considered quite fully at various points in his work.

It might, of course, be argued that Malthus's conclusion could only be justified if assumption (1) was true, in other words that Malthusianism only made sense if, historically, the law of diminishing returns was operating continuously. But this would be to change Malthus's doctrine completely and make it a historical statement on the law of diminishing returns. The *Encyclopædia Britannica* [1] article on "Population" states his position well:

> "It has already been stated, that while land of good quality is in great abundance, the rate at which food might be made to increase would far exceed what is necessary to keep pace with the most rapid increase of population which the laws of nature in relation to human kind permit. But if society were so constituted as to give the fullest scope possible to the progress of cultivation and population, all such land, and all lands of moderate quality, would soon be occupied; and when the future increase of the supply of food came to depend upon the taking of very poor land into cultivation, and the gradual and laborious improvement of the land already cultivated, the rate of increase of food would certainly have a greater resemblance to a decreasing geometrical ratio than an increasing one. The yearly increment of food would, at any rate, have a constant tendency to diminish . . ."

[1] Malthus, 1824, p. 313.

The useful word "tendency" is later reiterated in italics:

> "While improvements in agriculture, accompanied by a great demand for labour and produce, might for some time occasion a rapid increase of food and population at a later period, in the same manner as if cultivation had been in an earlier stage of their progress."

(Malthus would have been in no way abashed by a period which he did not "foresee", since he was convinced on *a priori* grounds that "after a period" the pressure of population on food would show itself again.)

> "These variations," the article continued, ". . . obviously arise from causes which do not impeach the general *tendency* of a continued increase of produce in a limited territory to diminish the *power* of increase in future."

Thus Malthus conceded [1] that there was a possibility of "fresh starts" in agriculture, that is of technical progress. But he held that if this possibility was realized the day of reckoning was merely postponed, and perhaps aggravated in its effects, since each "fresh start" would, other things being equal, give rise to an even greater population. (This was a position in flat contradiction to his view that the crisis had already begun.)

Before leaving this point, it must be granted to the authors of the Royal Commission Report that undoubtedly they are giving a fair picture of what was *probably* Malthus's view of the immediate future. To quote again from the *Encyclopædia* article:

> "If, setting out from a tolerably well peopled country

---

[1] Moreover, he made the same point at greater length in both early and later editions of the Essay.

such as England, France, Italy, or Germany, we were
to suppose that, by great attention to agriculture, its
produce could be permanently increased every twenty-
five years by a quantity equal to that which it at
present produces, it would be allowing a rate of increase
decidedly beyond any probability of realization. The
most sanguine cultivators could hardly expect that, in
the course of the next two hundred years, each farm
in this country would produce eight times as much food
as it produces at present. . . . Yet this would be an
arithmetical progression, and would fall short, beyond
all comparison, of the natural increase of population in
a geometrical progression, according to which the
inhabitants of any country in 500 years, instead of
increasing to twenty times, would increase to above a
million times their present numbers."

This passage, and others similar to it, suggest that *probably* Malthus took a gloomy view of the future agricultural
capacity of the world. But he, at least, and later many
neo-Malthusians, were careful not to tie down the argument to any particular figure or to any particular forecast as to the actual rate of agricultural progress. It cannot be too often reiterated that his argument was *a priori*,
and general, depending upon a dogmatic statement that
a geometrical ratio would apply to humanity's natural
increase, while an arithmetical ratio applied to the increase in the food supply. That he *probably* foresaw an
early calamity can hardly be questioned—he would not
otherwise have had the brashness to forecast a disaster
to Godwin's system "within thirty years", and there are
many passages which suggest that he thought that
humanity in Western Europe and England could double
its numbers in twenty-five years successfully, but might

fail to double again in the next twenty-five; but he did not base his theory on any specific forecast, but used these figures illustratively. Had his theory been concerned with two periods of doubling only, as logically it should have been,[1] the argument would have been much clearer, and could have been afterwards tested by facts.

Malthus is sometimes supposed to have "taken for granted" that "imports would only make a minor contribution to a country's food supply". It seems odd that Malthus, who was in close private discussion, correspondence and public controversy with David Ricardo, and other leading economists, for at least ten years, on the subject of the importation of "corn" into Britain, should have been supposed to have given no consideration to this possibility. Malthus, of course, fully entertained the prospect of a heavy increase in food imports. He argued, however, that any alleviation to his "principle" gained in this way would be "temporary", meaning by this yet again that, at best, such a remedy would only postpone the evil day. In an early edition of his work there occurs the passage about "corn from America",[2]

---

[1] Because the famous geometrical ratio could not in fact operate beyond the third term (Malthus himself admitted this) according to the first postulate of his own argument.

[2] "In the wildness of speculation it has been suggested (of course, more in jest than in earnest) that Europe ought to grow its corn in America, and devote itself solely to manufactures and commerce . . . But even on the extravagant supposition that the natural course of things might lead to such a division of labour for a time, and that by such means Europe could raise a population greater than its lands could possibly support, the consequences ought justly to be dreaded. When upon this principle America began to withdraw its corn from Europe, and the agricultural exertions of Europe were inadequate to make up the deficiency, it would certainly be felt that the temporary advantages of a greater degree of wealth and population (supposing them to have been really attained) had been very dearly purchased by a long period of retrograde movements and misery."

while the maturer statement of his views in the *Encyclopædia* states:

> "It will be said, perhaps, that many parts of the earth are as yet very thinly peopled. . . . This is unquestionably true. Some parts of the earth would no doubt be capable of producing food at such a rate as to keep pace *for a few periods* [i.e. for some 'periods' (length unspecified) of doubling] with an unrestricted increase of population."

Those who think that Malthus ventured on a prophecy that has since been falsified are underrating his skill as a controversialist. This would be a point of mere historicism were it not for the consequence that neo-Malthusians may correctly claim that their forerunner has not been refuted by the facts. The facts cannot refute Malthus, since his theory was either:

(*a*) a statement based upon assumed postulates. In this case the only relevant argument is as to the universal applicability of those postulates. Once they are shown not to be universally true the theory loses all force as an inexorable law; or

(*b*) a modified and qualified historical generalization that is in principle unverifiable.

§ 4. *The "Qualified" Malthusian Doctrine.* There were three important qualifications,[1] finally, which distinguish the Malthusian doctrine from a strict historical prophecy or forecast. They are very difficult to pin down because they were stated many times with different variations.

First, there is the very loose definition of the "checks"

---

[1] Just how early these qualifications were developed by Malthus is a point of textual criticism that may be left aside; undoubtedly, in the course of controversy greater emphasis was placed on them.

on population, both preventive and positive. Once the existence of "checks" of varying force is admitted the doctrine ceases to be a statement about what *will* happen, and merely a statement about "tendencies". The existence of loosely defined checks then allows the Malthusian to fit any set of facts into the theory. A "tendency" for all populations to increase "geometrically" is alleged, and any instances to the contrary can be dismissed, without further enquiry, as cases of the operation of a positive check, or perhaps of a preventive check. After all, the degree of misery and vice in a community cannot readily be measured; if the main reason for the failure of the population to increase at the geometrical rate seems to be a low birth-rate the preventive check can be assumed, and if the reason is a high death-rate a positive check is invoked. Ah, says the Malthusian, that merely proves that the theory fits all the facts. Unfortunately, it fits too many facts; it fits, indeed, all *conceivable* facts. The "tendency" of the population to increase at a fixed geometrical ratio is alleged whatever the rates at which actual populations are growing in any circumstances. If, for example, there is abundant food available and yet the natural increase falls short of Malthus's assumed maximum rate, and the death rate is low, then *by definition* the preventive check must be operating, and so on for any other example that may be chosen.

Moreover, the positive checks are just as elastic (and circular in reasoning) as the preventive. Examples of what may be called "misery and vice" can no doubt be found in all human populations. So long as "premature death" exists in any form whatsoever (and in a sense all deaths are premature), the Malthusian apologist can claim to discover positive checks that operate to prevent population increase from reaching its "natural" maximum.

Godwin had very much the worst of his arguments with Malthus because of this defensive strength in the Malthusian position. In his first counter-attack, indeed, he even conceded the "principle of population". When he returned to the attack in 1820, though aided by the statistician Booth, he adopted the wrong approach. He asked,[1] "if Mr. Malthus's doctrine is true, why is the globe not peopled?" and devoted chapters to the different major portions of the globe to investigate this issue at length. But the existence, *by definition*, of either preventive or positive checks provided an answer to this line of attack.

Much more effective and subtle were Nassau Senior's letters to Malthus.[2] He raised the much more awkward dilemma of how, if Malthus's theory were generally valid, the standard of life in many countries had gone up over the centuries. He wrote:

"... the only difference between us is one of nomenclature. You would still say, that in the absence of disturbing causes, population has a *tendency* to increase faster than food, because the comparative increase of the former is a mere compliance with our natural wishes, the comparative increase of the latter is all effort and self-denial. I should still say, that, in the absence of disturbing causes, food has a tendency to increase faster than population, because, in fact, it has generally done so, and because I consider the desire of bettering our condition as natural a wish as the desire of marriage."

Malthus replied that:

"Whether population were actually increasing faster than food, or food faster than population, it was true

[1] *Op. cit.*, 1820, p. 20.
[2] Quoted by Smith, 1951, p. 184.

that, except in new colonies, favourably circumstanced, population was always pressing against food, and was always ready to start off at a faster rate than that at which the food was actually increasing."

Any improvement in food supply, he thought, would "soon" be swallowed up in increased numbers.

This brings the argument to the second of Malthus's major qualifications of his doctrine, the period within which it was supposed to become demonstrable to all.

In the first essay, and indeed in all later versions of the theory, Malthus insisted that the evils consequent upon the "principle of population" were already pressing and urgent.   Thus the *Encyclopædia* article of 1824 states: [1]

"The pressure arising from the difficulty of procuring subsistence is not to be considered a remote one, which will be felt only when the earth refuses to produce any more, but as one which not only exists at present over the greatest part of the globe, but, with few exceptions, has been almost constantly acting upon all the countries of which we have any account."

This would seem to tie the theory down to a historical generalization that could be tested.   The actual broad facts of history were the reverse, as Nassau Senior pointed out.

Simultaneously with the view that population pressure was always observably pressing on food, were the arguments about "tendencies", about a prisoner being restrained by the walls of a prison even though the walls were not touching him, and about "periods" of doubling —it being a matter of no moment whether one or two

[1] *Op. cit.*, p. 316.

had to be conceded before the crisis arrived. Indeed the very same *Encyclopædia* article on population spoke of the principle in terms of farms not being able to produce on an average more than eight times their present output over the next two hundred years.

Thus Malthus introduced the qualification that his principle might not work out for some hundreds of years, and stated the ratios in such broad terms that they could not be justified except over hundreds of years; yet at the same time he remained dogmatically convinced that the time of reckoning had already come and that the "checks" had always operated.

This double position is not formally a self-contradiction; it *might* be true that the ratios worked out infallibly only over centuries, and also that there was already population pressure everywhere. But the two are really quite separate arguments, and Malthus's qualifications succeeded in inextricably muddling them together. *If* the problem is one of centuries, then the real questions are: just what are the forces making for population doubling (increasing at a given rate) and for food and other necessaries doubling (increasing at a given rate)? This question can hardly be settled by a dogmatic assertion that the one always "tends to" double faster than the other (in the absence of increasing vice and misery).

If, on the other hand, the problem is a current one, that population increase has outrun the supply of food and necessaries, then the correct question is: what has caused this ill-balance? Can any humane steps be taken to remedy the situation? Do laws need to be passed, or institutions improved? No, says the earlier Malthus, because any improvement is short-lived; and in any case laws and institutions are but froth on the deep irresistible stream of the life forces making for population pressure.

But now comes Malthus's third qualification.[1]

Surprisingly, in view of the original purpose of his work, he emphasized the dependence of the actual level of population upon the laws, institutions and habits of each society. Indeed, he went so far as to invoke these factors to account for the present "*scanty* population of the earth",[2] remarking that there were few large countries where the population might not be double, triple, ten or a hundred times what it actually was "if the institutions of society, and the moral habits of the people" had been favourable to such an increase (meaning to a sufficient increase in food cultivation).

This concession gave away everything that had originally been at issue. Hazlitt's question, reiterated in a different form by Nassau Senior, now became unanswerable; how could the "principle" be an answer to Godwin and others? Are we to believe, in Hazlitt's words, that "if reason should ever get the mastery of all our actions, we shall then be governed entirely by our physical appetites and passions, without the least regard to the consequences"? Has reason no power over the impulse to propagate?

If, as Malthus had to concede, the arithmetical rate of increase can be laid aside, why assume that the *numerical value* of the rate of population increase would be insensately, and not temperately, increased to meet the changed circumstances?

Malthus's argument really now boiled down to two generalizations (current and future population pressure) based on the one instance of the North American population. It was as though an investigation were carried out into the "natural appetite" of men. Ten

[1] Malthus, 1820, chap. iv, sec. II.
[2] *Encyclopædia*, 1824, p. 316.

men would be set down in front of large dinners; one of the men would have plenty of room for his food, having had a morning of heavy exercise—he might eat 1,200 calories. The other nine would eat varying less amounts (and might be provided with less amounts). Malthus concludes that "natural appetite" is 1,200 calories. All men would eat 1,200 calories if it were placed before them. If, then, in a second experiment the 1,200 calories are placed before the other nine and they do not eat it they are alleged, by definition, to be either sick (owing to misery or vice) or capable of unusual moral restraint. Natural appetite as a concept is not re-examined.

The power of increase of population is thus thought of as something that is given and unchangeable; in Malthus's system it is only *revealed* when food is plentiful, but it is not a *function* of plenty of food. Its force is the same whether there is plenty of food or not. Malthus's theory was not based on belief that a population's power to increase was a function of changing food supply, but that *actual* population increase was a function of this variable.

Since Malthus's time no *theory* of population has been invented. It has for many years been recognized, for instance, that modern war is not a check to population in the Malthusian sense at all.[1] Yet the teaching of Malthus is still often assumed to apply to modern society. But if war is not a check on population, is it wise to assume that "misery and vice" in all their forms are checks either? May not the power of increase of population be an increasing function of "misery and vice" (or, at least, of some specific forms of misery and vice)? In this case a more direct attack on these things, even by way of mere alleviation in the first instance, may be a good way of reducing any existing pressure of population upon food.

[1] See Wright, 1923, p. 136.

Steps, however small, towards a more "perfect" human society may be far from impracticable, and indeed the only sensible steps to take to meet the world's population problems.

The clear alternative to Malthus's theory is the hypothesis that economic as well as social conditions affect the growth and size of populations, and that sexual passions operate only within the restrictions or stimuli imposed by these conditions.

§ 5. *Neo-Malthusianism.* Neo-Malthusians sometimes argue that there is perhaps a lessened moral obligation on Western nations to provide scientific aid to backward nations because it can probably be demonstrated that a sudden increase of population in those nations will lead to disaster.[1] Such an obligation, it may well be agreed, is not to be regarded as unconditional *if* it can be shown that the result of such aid would be an increase in population so sudden that famines of an incurable kind would result.

India is the example that is most frequently cited. But can anyone argue that India's increasing population has, mainly because of its increase, been a prime cause of international tension and disorder? This purely political argument could hardly be sustained from the record of international exchanges at the United Nations Assembly. There is no doubt that the rapid increase of India's population creates a problem for India, and for its neighbours and for other countries, but that this is one of the major causes of the international tension in the world since 1945 is not demonstrable. It might of course become so, but so might a number of other demographic changes, and all sorts of degrees of demographic

1 Hill, 1952, p. 93.

pressure have been made the excuse for expansionist and aggressive policies. But the increase in itself does not necessarily demand a warlike solution. Indeed, the other neo-Malthusian argument which is most frequently encountered is precisely contrary to this; namely, that a sudden increase of population will undermine the physique of the people concerned, and impoverish them. This is a more realistic fear.

The Axis powers used population pressure as an excuse for aggression. But the objective of their rulers was power, not room for peaceful expansion. The Germans and Japanese wanted to acquire territories in which the birth-rate was higher than their own, and so did the Italian government to a lesser extent. The Japanese allowed Manchuria to fill up with Chinese faster than with Japanese, as being a more readily exploitable labour force; the Germans fell back on genocide, not to find room for unemployed Germans but to establish strategically placed loyal populations in conquered territory. The rulers of two of these countries encouraged a high birth-rate to further their ambitions.

When Western publicists express the fear that the increase of Eastern populations may make it hard for "civilization itself to survive" it is difficult not to entertain the suspicion that they are identifying "civilization" not with defined and recognizable qualities of life but with the predominance of certain social groups. Otherwise it is difficult to make any sense of the fears that they express as to the needs of the backward areas. How, they sometimes ask, can India be supported if its population rises in the next thirty years to 700 millions? [1] For if the

---

[1] This was the figure mentioned by Professor Hill in 1944 in an address to the India-Burma Association on "India: Scientific Development or Disaster." Quoted by Bertram, 1949.

Indian standard of life goes up, as it well may, and mortality rates fall, more food per head will then be needed, and India will consume some three times the amount then that it consumes to-day (in 1944 the population of India was put at some 430 millions).

Evidently it is no longer the welfare of the Indian that is at stake. His standard of living has gone up, *ex hypothesi*, and his mortality rate has gone down. The argument is political, and not economic or biological.

Yet another form of the same neo-Malthusian reasoning is the inappropriate comparison between Oriental and American methods of production and standards of living. This argument takes two forms: first, how can world resources possibly meet the enormous claim on raw materials that will arise if these numerous Eastern peoples raise their economic requirements per head to anything approximating the present consumption per head of the average U.S. citizen?

And, secondly, how can an Eastern farmer (say a Chinese) be induced to get any benefit, on his subsistence farm, from a tractor, or modern agricultural machinery, when he produces virtually no cash crops at all?

Both of these arguments usually come from physical scientists with little or no training in economics or the social sciences generally. It is very useful that they have raised these questions, since puzzling over the issues that have to be settled may not be unprofitable. But the notion that the questions in themselves provide *a priori* proof of over-population is not strictly tenable.

Why should the economic advance of any backward country, say India, follow the same path as has been followed by the United States? Reflection suggests that this is historically quite impossible. Because it is impossible there is no likelihood that India will absorb

9

raw materials per head at the same rate of increase as the United States has exhibited. That particular phenomenon can hardly be repeated in the Argentine or Brazil, let alone in the Far East. Is there, then, any excuse for deliberately withholding medical or scientific knowledge from India in order that its mortality rate should be maintained?

For reasons of social organization, which has varied from country to country, many economically "backward" countries have been organized on the basis of the family, and on the basis of the large family; there have been social checks placed on unlimited multiplication (marriage restrictions, sometimes infanticide, and sometimes practices of abstention) for centuries, but it so happens that social organization has been in many places framed to encourage population increase.[1]

Farming in parts of China reached very high levels of output per acre. It is true that the Chinese peasant farmer, in an almost cashless economy, could not afford a power disc, a battery of grain drills, a combine or a fifty horse-power machine,[2] or even to hire an aeroplane to sow his seeds from the air, but he could raise twice the product per acre of the American farmer with all these advantages. Some parts of China suffered from erosion, but the farmer on the loess soils could produce crop after crop (like his Western European opposite number) without exhausting the fertility of the land, even without the aid of manures.

This is not to say that the Chinese farmer was on balance efficiently organized. In the long history of China the social forces had strongly favoured an increase of population to a point that was very high indeed in

1 Pan, Chia-lin and Taeuber, 1952.
2 Smith, J. R., 1949, p. 359.

relation to the land politically and geographically available for peaceful cultivation.   But the balance of advantage as between him and his American equivalent was less obviously on the American side than the purely neo-Malthusian argument allows.   The American farmer needed a vast industrial organization to back him up, and this organization, too, had its bottlenecks.   In so far as the germ of truth (which becomes distorted in neo-Malthusianism) is that "bottlenecks are to be feared" then it is not certain whether, in the long run, the highly mechanized farmer or the subsistence farmer (if he is on good soil) will feel the worse pinch first.

Are there really any good reasons, Malthusian or otherwise, for agreeing that medical and scientific knowledge should be withheld from the backward populations? Various counter-arguments, in addition to the humane considerations so obvious as to be unnecessary to mention, can be brought against any such suggestion.

First,[1] it is much easier to make a vaccine for a million people than to re-equip them economically, or to educate them to operate new production and agricultural techniques.   This cuts both ways; it raises the danger, so much emphasized by the neo-Malthusians, that the health reform will be unsound, resting on "fragile foundations", since the necessary social changes that should have gone with it will not yet have taken place.   But, on the other hand, since this type of reform is easier to introduce than a more radical change, that in itself makes medical advance a good starting-point for a much wider programme of reform.

Moreover, the fight to reduce mortality will reduce

---

[1] In these two paragraphs I am much indebted to the summary arguments put forward by Professor Sauvy (*Théorie Générale*), 1952, p. 32.

morbidity as well in most circumstances.   This ought to have the effect of increasing the productivity of labour. Secondly, to save a young man of eighteen years of age is to save an important capital investment (the economic waste of high death-rates among young people is often overlooked), and, thirdly, medical progress may indirectly reduce the level of fecundity.[1]   Fourthly, until health conditions have been improved in backward communities little serious technical developments of other kinds can be expected, for the simple reason that the technicians will not be there (if they are in short supply they will seek employment elsewhere).   Medical reform up to a certain standard is a prerequisite of economic progress.

The effect of a sudden reduction of mortality will raise different problems for different populations according to how they are already situated.   It is true that where the standard of living is already low, and alternative means of employment difficult, a reduction in mortality by reason of a medical reform may cause an acute population problem, at least for some decades.   But where the population is sparse, or where economic development of industry is possible, or where emigration is feasible, no such embarrassment need ensue; furthermore, in these circumstances a rapid decline in mortality may itself lead to social conditions in which fertility also rapidly declines.

Neo-Malthusianism goes much further than the reasonable claim that a sudden spurt in the size of a population *may* cause a decline in the standard of living.   In its more extreme forms it claims that an ultimate decrease in the

---

[1] "The Indian born in 1931 had a life expectation of 26·5 years; the Englishman in the same year, a life expectation of 61 years.   This meant that pre-war India spent 22·5 per cent of its national income on raising children who would make hardly any contribution to production, while England spent only 6·5 per cent of its national income on the raising of children."   (See F.A.O., *The State of Food and Agriculture*, 1948, p. 31.)

standard of life for the world is inevitable, and this view is based on postulates analogous to Malthus's, if more severe and improbable.

The neo-Darwinian version of neo-Malthusianism starts from the proposition that man is a wild animal.[1] The machinery of the theory is the use of a limitless time-scale (a "million years", or, in other words, infinity—as long ahead as is needed for the result). But the conclusion from the theory is not timeless, or related to a remote future; it is related to present policy. For at any given moment, particularly the present, it is found convenient to divide the world into advanced ("good") populations, which multiply slowly and so secure and preserve a relatively high standard of life, and backward ("bad") populations that multiply fast, so threatening the existence of the good, civilized, small-family peoples. (Strictly speaking, the neo-Malthusians should count the Americans as a "bad" population since they have been historically among the fastest growing of peoples, but this is always ignored in their expositions.) The policy of the good civilized peoples must therefore be to check the increase of the backward peoples for the greater glory of civilization.

The modern neo-Malthusian has to explain how it is that standards of life have risen in large parts of the world despite an immense percentage increase in population, and why it is that populations in more primitive societies have not yet exhibited that wild animal rate of increase to which they are held, *a priori*, to be prone. On the first point they have to admit that what they call "local" or "unstable" advances in the standard of living have been gained, unstable because, *ex hypothesi*, any "good" population making such a gain will sooner or

[1] Darwin, 1952.

later be reduced again to penury by the multiplication in numbers of some inferior breed. The first population will then be crowded out of existence by the second, owing to the Gresham's law that bad populations drive out good.

Why cannot, even on these assumptions, some agreement, open or tacit, be made with the rising tide of lower type humans? Because, on the neo-Darwinian view, man is ultimately and always a wild animal that cannot be tamed, except in a very superficial and incomplete way. If such an agreement were made and kept, there would be always some more savage (more natural? at any rate a wilder) group which would take advantage of the truce to gain its ends by multiplication.

The whole case rests then, not on scientific experiment nor on observation, but on a doctrinaire view.

Once it is granted that man (or some man) has (and always will have) an incurable impulse to multiply regardless of consequences, the rest follows from the further supposition that ultimately food can only be available at an arithmetic increase, while (over a long enough period) man will multiply geometrically. But all that this shows is that man cannot double his numbers twice, unless food can double twice in the same intervals; as has already been seen. And if mankind once tried the experiment of multiplying faster than its maximum rate, with a consequent loss of income, it might, in most people's view, learn something from the experience. Even without the experience there seems no good reason to suppose that peoples multiply with the crass disregard of supplies that is assumed. Whole societies have learned to limit their numbers (as even the neo-Darwinians admit) and it cannot be proved that other societies are inherently unable to learn the same lesson.

The strength of the neo-Darwinian case lies in the resuscitation of the indefinite time-scale. However clearly the social scientist demonstrates that one population after another has been able to limit its rate of growth, the neo-Darwinian can always retort: "Well, maybe this time, or next time, or the time after; but what if world population reaches ten-fold its present size? Then, you must concede, things will be getting pretty awkward, and if not at ten-fold then at some multiple my case must be allowed, and I can go as high as I please."

This argument is spurious because it assumes what it is necessary to prove. Hypothetically, it may be conceded that there is some size of population which would be too great for the world's resources to maintain since these are believed to be finite. But what is not conceded is that the inevitable doubling process should be indefinitely followed. During even the next fifty years mankind's economic and educational institutions and his social structure may well be modified along lines that are now quite unpredictable. We cannot say anything very useful about these institutions as they will exist in one hundred years' time, although we may speculate upon them. When the time-scale is extended to a thousand, a hundred thousand, or a million years, prediction is still more unreliable. It is not only pointless, but unworthy of science, to pretend that man's behaviour in the matter of reproduction can be predicted for centuries ahead.

§ 6. *Equality of Population with Food.* Food is in general a relatively perishable commodity, and only in recent years have methods of long-period storage become practicable. It follows that food is one of the goods that have to be produced concurrently with consumption, except for such storage as is necessary to tide over from harvest to harvest. In this respect food differs from clothes, books, wine and houses, and from most forms of capital goods used in production.

The agricultural industry has, moreover, always tended to be highly competitive.

For both these reasons it is usually uneconomic, and sometimes disastrously so, for the producers, to produce more food in a year than can be currently consumed. It follows that, in reasonably well-organized economies, the food production is roughly equal to the available effective demand. So long as all members of the community have a sufficiency of purchasing-power, the amount of food produced will usually satisfy need, but, for the reasons given, will not greatly exceed it. Thus, historically, in all periods of reasonably "viable" economic organization, the food supply will be roughly sufficient to equal the needs of the population; it is an illusion to suppose that, for this reason of equality alone, the population must have adjusted itself to the volume of the food supply.

This illusion is one all neo-Malthusians are prone to mistake for reality; of course, an equality of population with food *might* be due to an adjustment in population, but the point is that such an equality is by no means a proof that such an adjustment has taken place.

For most civilized communities there is fairly strong contributory evidence to suggest that the adjustment is of food to population and not the other way round. In all but the most primitive communities there are considerable economic resources devoted to many other satisfactions lower down in the scale of necessities than food, even for the consumption of the poorer classes, and still more so for the better off and the very rich. These populations might sacrifice some of their relatively luxurious consumption rather than starve, or support a "starving margin". If they choose a set of institutions which allows a starving margin to exist side by side with resources that could be used to produce food but are not so used, it is a stretch of language to argue that the starving margin is the consequence of an unconquerable difficulty in producing food, and those who hold that, on the contrary, bad institutions are the cause of misery, vice, starvation and war would seem to have the better of this particular argument.

§ 7. *Neo-Godwinianism.* Many writers and thinkers of to-day ascribe starvation, famine, high death-rates among children, and disease not to population maladjustment but to the inefficiency and injustice of the social institutions operative in the regions concerned. This approach may, with some historical accuracy, be labelled neo-Godwinianism, because although there is a diversity of views on how to reform society there is a common Godwinian standpoint taken up in response to the neo-Malthusian challenge; all such writers agree that human institutions and not the inexorable laws of nature are at fault wherever grave social evils are found.

In its crudest form neo-Godwinianism can degenerate into a theory as circular and non-operational as the modified Malthusian theory. Godwinianism of this kind can be neither supported nor refuted by any conceivable set of facts. If it is alleged that all human ills are the consequence *by definition* of some human institution that is unjust (or of some flaw in the working of a just institution), then there is no more to be said. The definition of an unjust human institution has been given, and no instance of it can be proved to exist, or not to exist, as a consequence of finding with it the characteristic by which it is identified.

Some writers who attack in particular a social institution which they name "Colonialism" come dangerously near to this kind of circular reasoning. Malnutrition in an existing colony they can readily ascribe to colonialism; but what of Brazil or Calabria in Italy? To explain malnutrition there they must refer back to the results of colonialism that ceased long ago, or of a colonialism that is deemed to exist surreptitiously because of the social structure of the South of Italy. The cases of evident short-term over-population in Italy and Japan are, indeed, especially difficult for the anti-colonial theorists to explain, and they must have recourse to a definition of "Colonialism" so wide as to deprive the term of any precise meaning.

The neo-Godwinian view has the merit of recognizing that human institutions should be treated as a variable in the problem of population. It can hardly be denied that what is an "optimum population" for one set of institutional circumstances may be greater or less than what would be the optimum for a different set of circumstances, even though the raw materials available and the technical means of production remained the same.

But this only means that the problem of population is much more complex than it is made out to be by those who neglect the fact that social institutions are mutable. It does not mean that there is no population problem; it means that the problem may take many forms.

At some date in the future, possibly fifty, a hundred or a thousand years hence, the rate of population increase will have to slow down. Common sense indicates that it is possible that it will slow down without tyranny, misery or vice, in such a long period, since in many countries, with fairly tolerable social conditions, it has already slowed down.

Common sense indicates also that tyranny, misery and vice will be hard to eradicate.   However, this gives rise to a very different degree of fear from that which is due to the belief that, however hard people try, these social evils must always be with humanity, in a steadily intensified degree.

CHAPTER V

THEORIES OF STATIC EQUILIBRIUM

§ 1. *The Idea of a Maximum Population.* There can be only one optimum size of population, if the terminology of economics is correctly derived, although opinions will differ as to the criteria for it. But first the even more fundamental concepts of "maximum" and "minimum" populations need to be explained, and their usefulness discussed.

A maximum population occurs, in an isolated community, when the death-rate rises to the same level as the birth-rate, or more exactly, when the two rates come into equality with each other. Most people, whether Malthusians or not, believe that there is some definite upper limit to the size of population that a given "country", with given techniques of production, can support. What is implied is that at some point natural increase falls to zero.

Let us suppose that actual population, at any given time, is ON_1; then the common assumption that populations have a maximum can be expressed by saying that there is some larger size of population, say ON, beyond which further population increase is impossible. What is implied, then, is that as population expands to ON natural increase falls to zero, so that over some of the population range from ON_1 to ON natural increase must be a decreasing function of the size of population.

How would this come about? There are many possible causal links between size of population and birth- and death-rates. For biological or economic or political reasons death-rates may rise as population expands; or birth-rates may fall; or both movements may occur.   The only assumption that has to be made is that *BR* meets

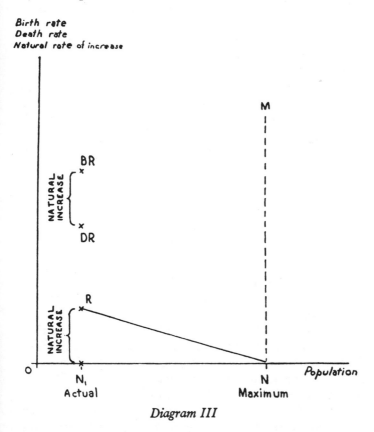

Diagram III

DR somewhere on the vertical line *NM*, which represents a population of the maximum size *ON* (Diagram III).

The analysis is timeless.   What is considered here is the functional relationship between vital rates and sizes of population. How long any particular adjustment would take to complete is a separate question.

The cases most commonly feared are those in which natural increase is reduced to zero wholly or partly because of a rise in mortality rates, this rise being due to a severe decline in the standards of living. With most age-distributions, this implies a rise in crude death-rates before maximum population is reached. A population that reached its maximum for this reason would be forced into a temporary (or if the situation persisted, a "permanent") stability of size, a stability clearly less favourable than one attained by population planning.

Equality of birth- and death-rates is a necessary but not a sufficient condition of a maximum population, for such an equality could be gained by a population which "chose" some point short of the maximum size, and maintained it by restricting its birth-rate to the ruling level of the death-rate.

Where equality of rates is enforced by circumstances—that is, where a maximum has been reached—savage restrictions on life must have been imposed. A condition prevails that there will literally be one extra death for every extra birth that occurs. This probably would mean either a very high infantile mortality rate, or infanticide, or an appalling disease rate among the old and helpless.

Thus the degree of misery implied by the "true maximum" is worse than that suffered in either India, Egypt or China, where all the populations still seem, after all, to be on the increase. The populations of these and other countries may be far nearer to the true maximum level than any humane person would want them to be, and far closer than is either desirable or necessary, but even so, these populations are not, as a whole, suffering the frightful conditions which a maximum would imply.

Emigration is the classic remedy when desperate or bold solutions are needed, and is perhaps in some cases analogous to the swarming of certain animal species. The "realized maximum" will be less than the "true maximum" if emigration takes place, and is reached when net emigration rates plus death-rates come into equality with the birth-rates (Diagram IV).

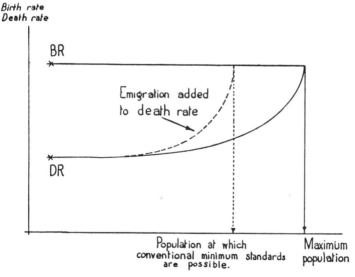

Diagram IV

Italy seems to have reached some kind of "realized maximum" about 1910, and Ireland in the 1840's and 1850's. Where any maximum actually occurs depends partly upon the conventional standards of living that people regard as tolerable before they emigrate. Evidently, although in the nineteenth century England and Wales, Germany and other European countries were

sources of net emigration their populations still grew, and
were far smaller than either the "realized" or the horrific
"true" maximum.

The economic problem of the real world is not, then,
in practice that of meeting the imminent danger of a
maximum being reached, but that of meeting the needs
of a greatly increasing population wherever it happens to
be expanding.   For such a population seeks not only food
but employment, not only clothes but sound government,
not only water supplies but amusement and transport;
it has to be housed, if only in hovels or caravans, at least
on land, either within the state's existing boundaries in
new urban expansions or conurbations or in more densely
peopled agricultural districts, or abroad amid some alien
culture.

No wonder that the torrent of natural increase has led
to some signs of panic among those upon whom leadership or responsibility has fallen!   But the problem has
to be looked at as one of reorganization to meet a current
increase in numbers, not as one that is intrinsically insoluble, despite the complexities that it raises, which will
no doubt strain human ingenuity very seriously.

§ 2. *The Idea of a Minimum Population*.   The problems of
the isolated community offer several parables of much
wider application than to the special issue of rural de-
population.   In the first place, any consideration of
them must throw into relief the importance of external
economies, that is, of the complementarity of different
services provided not only within the same industry
but by different industries.   The village grows large
enough to support a doctor, a baker and a cobbler, and
their advent in turn makes possible the arrival of a news-
agent, and so on; and as the community grows, so an

improved transport service, drainage system, water supply, post office, milk delivery and other simple advantages accrue.

For example, if an island off the west coast of Scotland depends for its health on the services of a doctor, it follows that the island cannot long remain inhabited should those services be withdrawn. If the island is so remote, and transport to it so difficult, that the doctor cannot look to other patients for his emoluments, the island must have a certain minimum size of population for his services to be retained. Should it fall in numbers below that minimum size, those services are withdrawn, and the population will leave or fail to survive (if left in complete isolation) on the presumption that live births must fall and the death-rate increase.

There are not only economic limitations of this kind to the economic viability of an isolated population, but also biological limitations. The age-distribution (and birth-rates) must be such that a sufficiency of the population is passing through the child-bearing ages (and having children) to replace those who die. These biological limits are of great interest in studying the survival possibilities of small, relatively homogeneous, racial groups, but in an economic study they need not be analysed in any detail.

Once the minimum has been exceeded a whole new host of possibilities open up. Thus economic advantages may be gained not necessarily continuously, but, as it were, in quanta, or by crossing "humps", discontinuous leaps forward. The community can support a policeman, and law and order improve; a school or theatricals, and education progresses. There are more and more humps to cross. Finally, if the village becomes a town or a city, the cross-relationships which permit increased efficiency

10

in satisfying need may be yet more numerous, and indeed very difficult to trace and to identify.

The minimum, like the maximum, population is not absolute but depends upon the degree of organization assumed, and the standard of living that is accepted. Some groups might dispense with a baker; others would not.

Another example is that of the producer skilled in marketing, whose faculties would not be fully exploited until, for one reason or another, demand reached a certain size.[1] Above a certain size of market, the marketer's rôle would be different in kind, and not merely in degree. This argument has sometimes been used in connection with an increase in capital and hence of demand, which might lead to entirely new ways of combining factors of production; in other words, to a discontinuous leap forward on a path of economic progress. The same reasoning can be applied to population growth. Population growth may either take place at the same rate as, or less fast than, the growth of capital, i.e., if the whole economic system has expanded. Either provides the possibility of increasing returns, which may indeed accrue even when population changes faster than capital.

The degree to which increasing returns may be realized is not a mere technical question, but a question of economics, theoretical and applied, that is of a generalized theory of economic growth and of a review of the specific investments to be made. In that light the size of the optimum must be discussed.

§ 3. *The Optimum Population on Static Assumptions.* The term "optimum population" was frequently used in the economic literature between World War I and the Great

---

[1] Robbins, 1934, p. 13.

Depression.[1] Most writers defined the optimum population more or less explicitly as the size of population consistent with maximum economic welfare.[2] It was recognized by some that the term "maximum economic welfare" involved questions of the distribution as well as of the production of real income, and that this difficulty already gave some ambiguity to the concept. The size of the optimum was thought, in general, to be determined by the availability of natural resources per head for varying actual sizes of population, and by the facilities that existed for economic co-operation, both internally to an area and in relation to the inhabitants of other areas.

The detailed history of the idea of the (static) optimum cannot be given here.[3] Cannan first formulated it in this way:[4]

> ". . . At any given time the population which can exist on a given extent of land, consistently with the attainment of the greatest productiveness of industry possible at that time, is definite."

He gave the theory more precision (and a name) in his later work. Carr-Saunders used the idea in his discussions of actual populations.

The notion was often stated in terms of production per head, not of welfare. For example,[5] it would be argued that an area was over-populated when returns per head were less in that area than they would have been if the populations had been a little smaller. This point had, of course, nothing to do with the point at which any visible

---

[1] Keynes began the debate with some remarks in the second chapter in his *Economic Consequences of the Peace*, 1920.

[2] See, for example, Chapter 3 of Cannan, 1928, and Dalton, 1928, p. 28.

[3] A large part of it was summarized excellently by Professor Robbins in his essay on the theory, 1927.

[4] Cannan, 1888, p. 22.

[5] See Robbins, 1927, p. 120.

pressure on the means of actual subsistence had appeared; the optimum was passed once real output per head began to fall.

Reflection on how precisely to define the optimum led to the refinement of the concept, but at the same time to its being criticized as of little value. It was thought to be highly artificial to select "average real income" as the one test of an "optimum"—so many other facets of life were omitted from the concept; it was thought misleading because population movements were dynamic, and because changing numbers were alleged to be more important than size; it was criticized because it abstracted from age-distribution problems (on a first statement); it was derided because, as usually stated, it had abstracted from direct consideration of problems arising from international trade, and from changes in industrial technique. These criticisms effectively debarred the static concept of the optimum from a fashionable rebirth in the discussions that preceded the Population Report of 1949.

All these objections are, however, really one objection: that which is made to the static abstract analysis of population problems. That such an analysis has its limitations is important to remember, but that this should be an absolute deterrent to a cautious use of the technique may be disputed.

Possible objectives for a single political unit might be the maximization of:

(a) power;
(b) income per head for a section, or class, of the community;
(c) expectation of life (over-all average, or the average for a class);
(d) economic security;
(e) output per head.

If each of these objectives is considered in turn it will be found that even this five-fold classification is insufficient. Within each of the five divisions there are further alternatives—different ends to choose from—and there are yet other headings altogether outside the five here listed.

The optimum size of population will be larger very often in a society of exploiters and exploited than in one of equal abilities and equal rights, for reasons that can be worked out quite adequately by the device of a total product curve. The total product curve, which is in effect a quantum index relating national product to number of workers available (some fraction, not necessarily constant, of total population being deemed to comprise the working population), may shift over time, and have to be entirely redrawn.

The new product curve might present a different possible optimum by any of the criteria. Greatest possible output per head might now be attained with a greater or less working population than before. Thus a general rise in productivity can be shown not *necessarily* to lead to the disappearance of all population problems, since after such a rise it may happen that the optimum size of population is smaller than before (although *any* population may now have the capacity to be better off).

At any given moment, in relation to that somewhat abstract idea of "total product", an actual working, and total, population is probably rather too small or too large. It could hardly be expected that population size should remain exactly right for long, except by extraordinary luck, since underlying techniques are so constantly changing.

In war-time, populations usually seem to be too small, partly because of military demands, partly because of the needs of industrial production. In peace-time they seem sometimes to be too large, perhaps because of a sluggish economic demand for the services of labour, or the failure of individuals, or of the state, to provide some rather necessary amenities (e.g., schools, houses or water), or because of sudden fluctuations in external trading conditions.

What should be sought, however, is the optimum that is justified by long-term rather than short-term conditions of demand and supply. But the static optimum for, say, 1980 may be inconsistent with natural increase changes from the static optimum at some other date; and, in discussing possible optima, dates, as well as economic institutions, have to be assumed as part of the essential framework of reference.

§ 4. *Ecological Equilibrium.* The propagation and the nourishment of different organisms are both co-operative and competitive processes. So soon as the relative extent of this co-operation and competition is known it is possible to predict the ecological equilibrium size of any particular population in relation to all the others. The trick is to discover the functional relationships between the size of population A and the size of population B, C, D, etc.; once all these were known, and if it could be assumed that all populations tend to increase in the given environment of the earth, all populations could be predictable. Some of these functional relationships are known and others are being discovered. But man is busy modifying the functions themselves. He is always aiming to disturb the "natural" ecological balance in favour of some favourite objective of his that he has in mind. (He thinks that he is acting in his own interest, but is not always correct in this view.) Any reasoning from ecology as to the future of human populations has to be qualified by remarking that (a) the environment laid down by the original functions is being changed, and (b) human populations may choose not to expand to the limit.

At a given date (or over a short period) the functional relationships may, however, be taken to be constant, and, as a first approximation, some static relationships can be worked out. At a later stage in the exercise we can speculate about the time needed, in principle, for the adjustments towards any equilibrium to be made. At the moment we are concerned only with the sizes of different populations that are consistent with each other, not with their rates of change.

A well-known example of this type of reasoning is the parable of a Juan Fernandez type of island, where grass is supposed to be available to support goats, and the goats support wolves. The goats live on the grass and thrive until the wolves arrive, the number of goats depending upon the amount of grass available. A pair of wolves, left on the island by some careless sea-captain, batten on the goats and drive them to the rocky hills in the centre of the island. If the wolves successfully pursue the goats and exterminate them, they doom themselves to early extinction. If the agility of the goats develops sufficiently for a minimum number of them to survive, then an ecological balance is struck between the maximum number of goats that the wolves can pick off from time to time, and the maximum number of wolves that can survive on this wearisome diet.

This story has sometimes been used to support the Malthusian argument that population is limited by food alone. It can also be used to demonstrate the need for conservation of capital resources.[1] If the goats had a little more power and intelligence they could build a

[1] See Sauvy, 1952.

fence, exclude the wolves, and multiply up to some maximum number.

But the optimum sized population for the goats is also the optimum sized population of goats from the point of view of the wolves—without the ring fence. For the wolves could maintain a larger population if there were a larger population of goats. Further, the wolves, if they were concerned for the future of their race as well as for the present, would eat such a number of goats as equalled the natural rate of increase of the goat population. If they ate up the whole of the goats as quickly as possible, they would be literally consuming their capital. But a similar argument could be applied by the goats, if they were not so silly, to the crops of grass. Some animal populations, it appears, move round an equilibrium point rather than settle at the point itself. This may be because the predators that live on, say, population A are related to the size of population A by a more than proportionately increasing function. The more of A there are the much better chance there is of B being propagated (e.g., if B's eggs are hatched in A's entrails). There will be an increase of A to the point where B propagates on a large scale, which will decimate A, so providing insufficient hosts for B, and the cycle will begin again.

Bacteria and minute organisms of many kinds are predators on the human race. It might happen that the vulnerability of that race was more than proportionately increased by some particular increase in its numbers, but of this there is no certain knowledge; in the present epoch, our predators are being fought back faster than they can increase themselves.

The law of life of the individual organism is inexorable. One organism in relation to all other organisms must be more dependent on them than they are on it.   Hence it must follow the given law of growth and decline to an inevitable death.   By an analogy, which seems applicable in all cases, any finite group of organisms is in the same case, if it is small in relation to the total population of partly rival organisms.   But the analogy cannot be applied to life itself, nor to organisms that are capable of endless adaptations to the changing conditions of the universe; the laws of ecology do not predict a lifeless planet.

The human population is, however, mostly in a double relationship with other populations, because it is co-operative up to a point, and beyond that point competitive.   This might be the relationship between the human population and cows, for example: LRR′ representing the number of humans that could exist for the given number of cows on the Y-axis, and QRR′ showing the corresponding schedule for the cow population (Diagram V). Up to R′ the two populations are co-operative and above the line SRT the two populations will tend to move to stable equilibrium at R′.   Populations of either cows or humans to the left of SRT (which is determined by the assumption of vector pull being equally proportionate to distance from the two curves) cannot exist; the vector lines will lead to the origin.   Thus the minimum populations for cows and people are to the right of SRT, a point of unstable equilibrium occurring at R.

R′ may be the highest point for both curves, which may each complete a rough semi-circle and return to its axis.   In this eventuality R′ is a maximum for both populations.   This, however, implies two possible cow populations for any given human population and *vice versa*.   Let the continuation of the human population curve back to the Y-axis be considered.   From R′

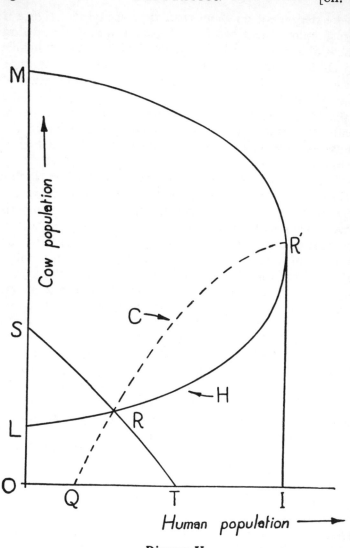

Diagram V

onwards it is negatively inclined for humans, which means that the more cows there are above the critical number measured by IR′ the less humans can survive.   Finally, once OM cows exist humans become extinct.   Beyond IR′ cows are competitive, on balance, rather than co-operative, with humans.

In a period during which the stock of available agricultural land was fixed (or could only be increased at a critically slow rate), some such an interdependence as this might be a realistic restriction on numbers.   If protein is essential for human life, and if protein can only be economically obtained from milk, milk products or meat, then an increase in the number of cattle will be essential, up to some point, determined partly by some other restriction, perhaps the necessity to reserve sufficient land for cereal production without which other essential food-stuffs would be insufficient.   Beyond that point any extra head of cattle would serve to increase the protein available only at the heavy cost of reducing the bread supply, and so restricting the size that the population could attain.   Commodities that are co-operative over one range and competitive over another may be quite common.

Man is an animal, and in a state of nature, if it so happened that his tendency to reproduce were uncontrolled, human populations would be limited in the same way as populations of animals and of plants.   But men have civilized themselves and framed economic systems, which presumably means that they have done certain things which they thought would solve actual problems as they arose.   The economic system, such as it is at any particular date, is in itself a protest against the working of blind ecological laws.   The primitive men who decided to save seed for the next harvest were probably interfering with the laws of nature as then understood by the elders of the tribe.

Interference with the ecological restrictions on population (and on income per head) takes two forms, the organization of production, and the organization of consumption. Production is, in general, breaking through natural limitations to the increase of consumable or useful goods, attained by modifying the form of natural units of raw materials, and consumption is determined not only by what exists, and by what has been produced in the past, but by what is wanted now, and by existing social standards.

Production and demand functions thus constantly change the shape and significance of "natural" ecological relationships. The usual ecological laws depend upon the number of units of a population being functionally dependent on the existing size of that population, so that any given population will grow in favourable conditions; this is no longer true if production decisions can be taken. Similarly, the ecological laws rely on an unchanging need of one set of organisms for the use of others, but needs may change once the possibility of choice is admitted.

§ 5. *The Malthusian and Godwinian Results.* Neo-Malthusian theory concentrates on a relationship between size of population and supply of real income (or "food"), and on a constant demand per head for real income, at a minimum standard. There is, then, a functional dependence of population upon income in the form of subsistence, and diminishing returns are predicted. It follows that population will expand to some point at which the S curve has fallen to equality with the amount of produce indicated by the MSL straight line. (Oy is real income, or "food", OGS the total real product curve,

and MSL, the minimum standard of life, total demand.)
Neo-Malthusian theory equates population with ON_5
when all the forces at work have worked themselves out,
and population is back to its dreary subsistence standard
of life.

The neo-Godwinians assume, on the other hand, that
the rate of increase of population is a *decreasing* function
of an increasing standard of life (they usually think solely

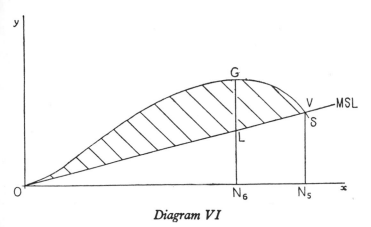

Diagram VI

in terms of natural increase, and of the decline in the
numbers of children per family as income per head
grows); thus, to them the decline in the birth-rate is a
function of the shaded area between the supply curve
and the MSL line.   When this shaded area has reached
some critical level (either for individuals or for the community)—perhaps for the sake of argument when it
reaches the total of OGL—then population becomes
stationary at ON_6.   This determines the future output of
the community.

CHAPTER VI

EQUILIBRIUM AND WORKING POPULATION

§ 1. *The Economic Demand for Labour.* Economic demand may not (or may) be entitled to reverential treatment,[1] but it may, quite neutrally, be recognized to be an important factor in determining the supply of most goods and services. A high demand for hand-painted ties has some effect on the supply of these goods; the mechanism linking supply to demand may be morally justifiable, within such restrictions as the state may rightfully impose, even though the objects produced in response to demand do not, by some æsthetic or moral standard, always seem to merit the price offered for them.

Demand affects the supply of human beings as well as of commodities and services; the connection exists, but its exact nature is not easy to discover.

High rewards for workers in a particular industry, persisting over a sufficient span of years, and not offset by some disadvantages of the work, will attract labour to that industry. But before a worker moves into a new industry he wants to know, of course, not only the ruling rate of wages, but the prospects of obtaining a job. The same principles may be supposed to apply to the longer-run demand for labour. A persistently high demand for labour, that is, the offer of *more* jobs at *higher* wages than before, will very likely increase the economic desirability to parents of having children, for one of two obvious reasons. The first, is that, especially for peasants or

[1] The "sovereignty of the consumer" is regarded as an ethical principle by some.

working-class people, children who earn money are a direct economic asset, and an insurance to their parents against misfortunes; and secondly, those classes of parents who do not look to see a financial return to themselves from their sons and daughters set as their target a standard of living for their potential offspring. The higher that standard the more likely they are to have some children, although evidently if there is an expensive training required, the number of children may be limited.

A "high" demand for labour will mean different things in different economic and social contexts. If children can be put to work at ten years of age they clearly become an economic asset to a working-class family much sooner than if they cannot leave school till they are sixteen. In those parts of Asia where the birth-rate is peculiarly high, children often work at even younger ages, and employment of a kind can always be found owing to the primitive social as well as economic conditions. Hence the high birth-rates there can be explained as partly due to the "high" demand for labour, although the wages and the jobs would not attract European juveniles. The very fact that the expectation of life is low (and that life is "cheap" per unit) means that a larger number of children is economically advantageous to the family.

No one can say how far fluctuations or trends in births are due to changes in parents' response to what they take to be the ruling (and future anticipated) economic demand for children. But that there is a considerable degree of connection can hardly be questioned. One part of the explanation of the falling birth-rate in Britain since 1870 may be found in the decline in the anticipated, and relative, net returns to be gained from children. In the 1860's it was possible for a working-man to expect some return from his children by the time that they were ten, a return that was high relative to his own wage and little reduced from a gross figure by the subtraction of the costs of upbringing and schooling.

The effect of the economic demand is not always easy to trace, because of the division of society into different social classes. The better-off classes, being leaders of social manners, have been handicapped in family-building by their recognition of the value (not all of it economic) of education and training. Setting themselves high ideals on these points, they have tended to restrict their families more drastically than other classes have done. Among their motives, anticipated economic advantage must have been important.

§ 2. *The Supply of Labour.* The supply of working-population comes from two sources, natural "increase" and net immigration (which may take negative values). To some extent, and sometimes by methods, such as infanticide and abortion, that are repugnant, individuals have always attempted to control fertility in most societies that have ever existed. The motives for these attempts have been numerous, but one major motive has undoubtedly been economic, and responsive to the changing labour market.

The control of fertility has been made progressively easier, as improved contraceptive devices have been invented, and knowledge of them made available. For economic reasons contraceptive practices are likely to be improved, and to be even more widely used. There are three ways, however, in which restrictions are likely to be imposed upon their universal adoption.

First, there is the old difficulty of the expense and effectiveness of any contraceptive device, however ingenious. The scientific problem is how to inhibit sperm from fertilizing any ovum, somewhere in the process of the chain of events during which semen makes its way to the uterus. There are weak links in the chain. Many possibilities are still being explored, such as inhibiting ovulation, controlling pituitary hormones, or developing an effective spermicide. (It has often been suggested that the decline in fertility which usually accompanies a rising standard of living is partly due to the more widespread use of soap, since soap is a very potent killer of sperms.)

Current methods of contraception cannot readily be used by men and women with a very low standard of living; there is always, in any society, a "residual group", whose habits are such that the use of *any* contraceptive would be too troublesome. In areas of very high fertility and low levels of living such groups may be significantly large, and substantial social changes will be a prerequisite of the wider use of contraception.[1] There must, after all, be a desire to limit family size, as well as a means of limiting it, and this desire is a function of the standard of living, and of the education and the morale of individuals.

But the difficulties in the way of the "residual" group using contraceptives apply only in slightly lesser degree for hundreds of thousands of peasant villages throughout the over-populated rural areas of India or Egypt, or for that matter Italy and South-East Europe. There has been discussion in the American scientific journals[2] of research work on an anti-fertility drug to be administered orally, which would obviate the disadvantages of existing devices, whether physical or chemical in their action. Even such an orally administered drug would have to be taken at the right time in the right quantity, and, unless some Government chose to subsidize it or distribute it free, its cost might not be negligible. While the perfection

[1] See Stix, 1941, p. 41. [2] E.g., *Science*.

II

of such a method might wipe out many of the present difficulties, there would still be social and economic problems to be solved before it could be used satisfactorily to control the high birth-rates of the world. The individual woman would have to desire family limitation sufficiently to put herself to the trouble and expense of taking the drug. Only in these conditions would it have an effect on birth-rates analogous to the spectacular effects of penicillin and sulpha drugs on the death-rates.

With these qualifications, the possibility of some rapid declines in birth-rates is undoubtedly opened up by the researches still in progress. It is, however, impossible to predict which birth-rates will decline the most; new inventions tend to be exploited much more rapidly in industrialized than in economically backward areas, and any such inventions, once available, might lead to a more rapid fall of birth-rates in Western Europe, which would precede the even steeper fall eventually due in Asiatic and African countries.

The second problem of control of fertility is the attitude of social and religious leaders. Many spokesmen for religions, like Malthus himself, advocate limitation of population only by the method of abstinence, austerity and self-control.

Other schools of moralists take the view that the use of contraceptives is ethically justified if the purpose for which they are employed is a good one. If they are employed to preserve and promote the health and happiness of the family they are justified; if only for the purpose of gratification of "illicit" sexual appetite, they are to be deprecated.[1] Yet other writers, while affecting

[1] This was the point of view expounded by Dr. Sarvepalli Radhakrishnan, Vice-President of India, in his address to a conference on planned parenthood, November 11, 1952 (see *Eugenics Review*, Vol. 45, No. 1, April 1953, p. 15).

neutrality on the moral issues, believe quite simply that "people enjoy sex" and "are entitled to go on doing so".

The values of all societies are, however, changing, nor is the predominant or "official" ethos of any society either accepted, or its precepts followed, by even a majority of its members. As Professor Glass has remarked [1] contraception has been practised increasingly despite state and religious opposition. If it is accepted that increased concern for children by parents is a good thing, and that a high rate of infantile mortality is unavoidable without control of fertility, even believers in some of the religious arguments might accept control of fertility as the lesser of two evils.

The third point which affects control of fertility is the variation in sexual behaviour to be found from one society to another.[2] In man, as against other mammalian species, it appears that sexual behaviour is most easily affected by learning and by social conditioning. Nothing could be more false than the supposition that man's urge to procreate is an unchanging force unaffected by the society in which he lives.

The supply of human beings, economically considered, is a supply of labour. Some economic and social arrangements are conducive to a very rapid increase in population. In an island such as Mauritius, for example, the local demand for hands was exceptionally high in the nineteenth century, and the immigration of Indians to the sugar estates was encouraged. By 1910 government-assisted immigration ceased. Thereafter, a high, and since 1945 an enormous, rate of natural increase has occurred. How can this phenomenon be explained?

No doubt the detailed explanation would require a

[1] Glass, 1953.
[2] See, for example, Ford and Beach, 1952.

separate treatise; but the broad facts seem to be these. The social pressure of the Indians led to a breaking up of estates, which were divided and sold to former labourers in periods of low sugar prices. (The social structure of Mauritius approximated to that of the landholding society imagined by the earlier economists.) With the dividing of some of the estates total sugar production increased. Population over the last thirty years rose enormously, by 32 per cent, and agricultural production by 87 per cent; natural increase, though now at the high rate of 3 per cent per annum, has not outrun the basic output of crops.[1]

Thus, what might seem at first glance to be a case of a high birth-rate swamping any possibility of social advance is in fact a case of population breeding in response to the classic needs of first a plantation and then a peasant society, with a small dominant class of rentiers. The position, it is true, is by no means stable. A slump in sugar prices would cause a temporary disaster, as would hurricanes two years running. But these are hazards of any society, only perhaps more violent. Why has the birth-rate of the Indo-Mauritians not yet been controlled? Surely the answer largely lies in their social and economic state; with only a few children educated to secondary school level, out of a population of nearly 400,000, it is hardly surprising that the high quality small family pattern of living has not yet been adopted. Only when more skilled occupations are open to the Indo-Mauritians is a change in their desire to have large families to be expected.

This is only one example, and the argument does not rest on its validity alone. In every country of the world economic and social factors will be found to operate, and in most the economic will be the more important. In

[1] See *Mauritius, 1951*, H.M.S.O., 1952.

some places, no doubt, a demographic trend persists out of all reference to the current and future economic prospects of the country in which it occurs—just as Vienna could not rapidly re-adjust its population to the new circumstances decreed at the Treaty of Versailles. But in the long run, and despite some exceptions, economic circumstance is likely to be predominant.

Although no exact correspondence between children produced and labour required is likely to be found in any country of the world, and local variations will occur for the reasons suggested, it may be expected that supply will adjust itself to demand more readily as control of fertility is increased.

§ 3. *The Balance of Demand and Supply.* The demand for workers and the supply come towards some kind of balance. Evidently, on Marshallian lines of reasoning, the equilibrium need never be struck, but only be a point to which the economic system would tend if no further changes took place.

In several ways, however, supply and demand for workers are dependent on each other, both through the state of techniques and through the character of the institutional arrangements. This introduces several complications into the analogy of a simple mechanical equilibrium.

For the problem has to be thought of not in terms of finding sufficient food, but of finding the right proportions of all the commodities that need to be produced, and the right techniques of exchange as well as of production. The future of a population depends on these total solutions, not on partial solutions.

As Sir James Steuart wrote:

"We may lay it down as a principle, that a farmer

will not labour to produce a superfluity of grain relatively to his own consumption, unless he finds some want which may be supplied by means of that superfluity; neither will other industrious persons work to supply the wants of the farmer for any other reason than to procure subsistence, which they cannot otherwise so easily obtain. These are the reciprocal wants which the statesman must create, in order to bind society together."[1]

For population to increase there must, on Steuart's principle, be a balanced development of industry as well as of agriculture; a principle that is directly relevant to the world population problem to-day.

Two fears haunt the economist, however, when he reflects on the means of roughly preserving this balance as population grows: first, the fear of diminishing returns, and second, the fear of a failure in demand, giving rise to unemployment whether originating *either* from technological labour-saving improvements *or* from institutional shortcomings.

Fear number one can be summarily disposed of; diminishing returns are not a bogey that ought to frighten anyone capable of discerning the immense ranges of output in all industries, including agriculture, where increasing returns are possible.[2]

For the second fear several anodynes have been applied. The long-term worry is that as technological advance takes place many workers will become redundant. The usual reply is that as wealth increases more needs can be satisfied, and the displaced workers can enter into new,

---

[1] Steuart, 1767, Vol. 1, p. 28.
[2] Cannan and Robbins pointed this out very firmly in the late 1920's. Increasing returns are meant here both in the static and dynamic senses.

or expanded, "secondary" or "tertiary" forms of employment.

Thus, in an advanced economy it would be likely that a relatively quite small proportion of workers would be found to be engaged directly in manufacturing, and a high proportion in the service or "tertiary" sections. One version of this theory has been well argued by Mr. Colin Clark who sought confirmation for it from statistics of distribution of working population in different countries, and certainly the high proportion of employed in "service" industries of all kinds in the U.S., the richest country in the world, seemed, together with some other facts, consistent with his suggested hypothesis that a high ratio of tertiary employment was a criterion of a country's wealth.

But primitive economies, as well as advanced, may have a high proportion of tertiary employment.[1]

Statistics are inconclusive, because in economies emerging from a primitive state nearly all adults and most children are engaged in trade whatever else they may be doing (and classified as doing) for their main occupation. Luxurious demands may promote primary employment (lobsters and furs), and necessitous demands may require manufactures or tertiary employment. There have to be some retailing and transport in all economies, and a high proportion in those progressing from tribal conditions.

One more point may be made on the contrast between the primitive and the advanced economy. Unemployment may be rife in a relatively primitive economy, but go unrecorded. There can be many unemployed under other names (beggars, landless peasants, part-time servants and so on); it is in the advanced economies that servants are difficult to get at the going wage, while in

[1] See Bauer and Yamey, 1951, and the rejoinder by Triantis, 1953.

the under-developed countries service is plentiful, this contrast showing better than statistics where under-employment is severest.

It is not, then, correct to think of economies advancing and "creating" an unemployment problem, which is then more or less adequately solved by a big increase in "tertiary" employment. This is a partial, and not a complete picture.

Let us begin again with definitions. Primary may be defined to include those activities directly concerned with winning results from the human environment, that is, in procuring raw materials or food, by processes directly linked with natural resources. This would include mining, fishing, most agriculture, wood-felling and so on; but not diamond-polishing, fish manure preparation, butter-making or carpentry, which would be in the secondary group. The secondary group covers all manufacturing and preparation of goods up to the stage of a wholesale sale. The tertiary group covers the rest: that is, every kind of service and clerical and administrative work. Thus the classification is inevitably occupational and not industrial, and relates *both* to the stage of production reached, from the raw material to the finished product, *and* to the nature of the activity whereby production is assisted.

A study of the growth of the American economy certainly reveals a high proportion of tertiary types of employment which it has been able to support out of its reserves and surpluses of spending-power. But phenomenal as America's transport, commercial, advertising and beauty parlour types of employment are, its maintenance of primary production at a high level is also significant.

One fallacy that has been committed by some is the

identification [1] of primary types of employment with diminishing, secondary with increasing, and tertiary with constant returns.

The essential point lies in Steuart's phrase that "the statesman must create" reciprocal wants. For an increased population to be supported two conditions are necessary. First, a sufficient economic surplus must be available to meet more than the current needs of the existing adult members of the population. Second, that surplus (and the flow of purchasing-power generally) must be channelled into directions which keep the increased population usefully employed, but there seem to be no good grounds for supposing that a growing economic surplus necessarily results in an increasing percentage of tertiary (or any other particular type of) employment. America is not necessarily the archetype of progressive economies, but an economy which progressed in very special circumstances. In Canada, where somewhat similar circumstances prevail, a similar pattern may be followed. In Britain, on the other hand, there are good reasons for supposing that the danger is that real incomes will be kept down by a failure to shift enough resources into secondary employment, and to keep down the level of tertiary employment, which tends to rise particularly under conditions of an increasing degree of monopoly in industry. In India, and the other heavily populated areas of the world, now embarking on industrialization, a different policy again may be appropriate, but, whatever the conditions, the object of policy is not to increase one or other sector of employment for its own sake, but to provide those types of employment that are most

[1] Professor Sauvy expressly introduced this identification as a hypothesis; but some other writers wrongly assume the identification to be both self-evident and true.

productive in the light of the special economic conditions of the particular country.

As Sauvy has argued, if the seigneurs of a landlord-dominated society take the decision to spend their rents not on employing musicians and grooms but on some goods requiring little labour, some of a previously balanced population becomes wholly redundant. *Mutatis mutandis*, in any society strategic decisions are constantly being taken which may raise or lower the demand for labour. One set of decisions would use increased real incomes to keep labour demand high, and another set might weaken that demand, and would be reflected in a tendency for the rate of emigration to increase.

The statesman may "create" reciprocal wants, in favourable circumstances, by adopting a policy of *laissez-faire*, because he expects that the price mechanism alone will result in the necessary expansion of tertiary employment, and other employment, to take up any slack caused by technological change. But in other circumstances the only ways to keep the population employed may require state planning.

Present knowledge of industrial techniques, and of ways of living, has run so far ahead of average performance that it is difficult to believe that most western countries are too thickly populated. With the necessary guidance on investment and development their working populations could probably in most cases increase, and at the same time enjoy better living.

CHAPTER VII

THE EXPANDING ECONOMY

Two subjects remain to be discussed: whether the conclusions of the last chapters are altered because capital is liable to be too scarce to support population, and, secondly, whether the rates of change of population are liable to be inconsistent with the optimum, or even the possible, rates of expansion of the different parts of the world economy.

§ 1. *Capital per Head of Population.* One way of defining the optimum population would be in terms of capital per head, and another in terms of land per head.

One argument that had a certain plausibility in the period 1946–50 ran as follows: first, in general terms, any country which had more real capital per worker than it had before would *ipso facto* be better off, "real capital" being defined as "stock of machines and industrial equipment". *Ergo*, any industrial country would be better off, so far as the static analysis went, if it had a smaller population than that which it had at present. Secondly, a smaller population than the existing one (whatever it is) would allow more house-room per head of population. *Ergo*, a reduction in population would increase economic welfare.

If these two arguments are accepted, then, apart from any qualifications due to the fact that *changes* in population may be harmful, it must be concluded that every country of the world is over-populated. Furthermore, so far as this static argument is concerned, every country in the world that contains a greater population than one individual is over-populated. That one person, if all the others vanished, would have an enormous volume of capital, and unlimited house-room. (He would not even have to work, as he could live out his life on stored foodstuffs.)

The protagonists of this theory of over-population do not push their argument quite so far as this, since they usually admit that, while a reduction in the size of the population of almost any area must on their theory be beneficial, such a reduction must not be carried to the point where any substantial advantages of large-scale production are lost. But, on their view, losses of this kind are trifling for a considerable range; so they come back to the contention that quite large reductions of population would in most countries be beneficial. The argument proves a great deal too much, as has been shown by the *reductio ad absurdum*. Why is it necessarily fallacious?

The criterion of "capital per head" in determining the optimum requires very much closer examination. It is true that workers in manufacturing in Europe as compared with the United States have less capital equipment per head, and that this often seems to be the reason for a sustained overall relatively low level of labour productivity which depresses the standard of life. But there are many steps to take before it can be argued that an increased capital per head would have the result (even on static assumptions) of raising real net incomes; such factors as the size of the markets secured, and the cost of the capital to be introduced, are two well-known additional considerations.

If the argument in favour of a reduced population assumes that the type of capital remains unchanged, then of course it falls to the ground immediately. A reduction in the number of workers would in that case most probably result in redundancy of machines. The argument must then assume that the stock of capital equipment is adjusted to the new smaller size of working population.

A high amount of capital goods per worker is not in itself advantageous. On the contrary, if there is a given stock of capital in a country (its form being assumed flexible) then, up to some critical point, the greater the population the better; in other words, the *less*, overall, the capital per worker the better off each of them will be per head. Supposing the capital invested in a new town amounts to £100 millions, to cover all buildings, services and equipment. Up to some critical point, at which substantial disadvantages accrue, the more the people using that equipment the lower the cost per head. But this applies if the equipment cost £10 only and not £100 millions. It is an advantage that accrues from spreading an initial capital cost, and has little to do with what is usually thought of under the heading "advantages of large-scale production".

At any given time, the capital equipment of a country is limited, and has had a definite economic cost; the greater the use that can be made of that equipment before it wears out, the lower the cost per head. It is true that if the country suddenly and instantaneously lost some population there would be more capital per head left to use, and as that capital would have already been produced it would be temporarily treated as cost-less, a windfall to the new (smaller) population. But from this arid proposition nothing can be deduced as to whether the country is, or is not, over-populated.

A more fruitful way of looking at population in relation

to capital equipment is to allow first for the cost of that equipment, secondly for the nature of the equipment, and thirdly for the employment opportunities in the community as a whole. If all these have certain assumed values, then it is possible to consider what size of population is "optimum" (say, in terms of greatest possible *net* output per head) for a given quantity of capital. A reduction in the size of population below that optimum figure, whatever it is, would be harmful on this criterion, and not beneficial just because it was a reduction in numbers.

This approach has a special application to the understanding of the phenomenon of increasing urbanization. Much more social and other capital is to be found in cities than in rural districts; the agriculturist, moreover, usually appears in this country to be working in conjunction with a rather low quantity of working capital and building investment. It might thus be supposed that towns were places of relatively high capital per head, and the country a place of low capital per head. But this is sometimes an illusion. For the greater capital of the towns is in constant use by a far denser population. The population density of the city, especially in the day-time, may be several thousand times the density of an extensive rural district. The latter has its roads and railways, but these, even if inferior, are used by far fewer people than the city streets and metropolitan railways. If all the facts were available it might well work out that in some cases the country districts were served by more capital per head than the towns and cities; the overall productivity of the country would be lower, relating value of output to cost, just because of this unavoidable over-capitalization.

The trend towards urbanization can thus be seen as a

method of taking advantage of capital equipment.   Over time and with technical change, this means securing more capital per head; but, at a given time, and with a limited quantity of equipment, the whole point of urbanization is to secure less capital per head.   A static analysis does not therefore permit of the fallacious conclusion that any population may always become individually richer by reducing its numbers.

Some special kinds of "capital goods" are of particular importance; the rise of industrial civilization has taken place *pari passu* with an increased use of motive power; real incomes have increased as horse-power used per head has increased.   The expansion of power use per head depends on the consumption of fuels.   This raises the special "bottleneck" problem of the possible rate of expansion of fuel supplies (oil, coal, water-power and atomic energy), but as will be seen in a later chapter, this problem does not seem likely to be incapable of solution over the next half-century.

§ 2. *Economic Growth.*   The   neo-classical   (Marshallian) answer to the problem of population [1] was that organization as well as invention would result in a "law of increasing return" that would offset any tendency for "diminishing returns" to set in.   Thus Marshall wrote that "an increase of labour and capital leads generally to improved organization, which increases the efficiency of labour and capital", and this is, indeed, his "law of increasing returns", as distinct from any consequence of new techniques and inventions.   Such improved organization was the result of a greater scale of activity (or could only be achieved *with* a greater scale of activity).   "In a

[1] At first posed by Malthus, and then changed into a different form by Ricardo and Mill.

larger scale of production, which is the main feature of higher organization, the layout may, by mere concentration, require less than twice the material of machinery and building, as well as of fuels in order to double the output of the establishment. This is not technique, or new powers of machinery, but simply economy of size." [1]

Such economies of size may spread from one establishment to another, or occur as the result of the simultaneous growth of different industries. In this case they are called by the neo-classicists "external" economies. All this sounds as though the changes might be gradual, "at a more regular pace", as Professor McGregor puts it, than the introduction of inventions and discoveries. But such changes of scale *may* have results as sudden, discontinuous and spectacular as that of a new product like the internal combustion motor engine. A dynamic, and by no means necessarily gradual, increase in output per head may be the direct consequence of an improved organization made available when economies of scale are realized. Ever since Marshall's time this important principle has been known, but its effective application to the analysis of dynamic situations has not been made.

Dynamic economics must take account not only of steady change but of the consequence of shocks due to innovations, and to developments in organization, which affect the structure of economic life. [2]

One of the clearest and most widely discussed state-

[1] McGregor, 1949, p. 20.
[2] Professor Samuelson has pointed out an important danger in dynamic process analysis: "The number of conceivable models is literally infinite and a life-time may be spent in exploring possibilities" (see *A Survey of Contemporary Economics*, ed. H. S. Ellis, 1948, p. 375). The only safeguard is to confine attention to those (possible) sequences of development which, by an act of possibly unscientific judgment, are deemed the most interesting or likely.

ments of a stagnationist theory has been that put forward by Professor Hansen in 1939. He was writing of the long-period, that is, of the change of population over decades. America, he thought, faced an ultimate contraction in numbers, and an immediate decline in its rate of growth.[1] Hansen regarded it as "an indisputable fact" that the prevailing economic system of capitalism had never been able to reach reasonably full employment, or the attainment of its currently realizable maximum real income, without very large investment expenditures. He harked back to Wicksell's view that the operative factor[2] was the prospective rate of profit on new investment. Now this rate of profit had in the past been geared largely to the rate of population growth.

Hansen estimated that of the approximate 3 per cent per annum growth of physical output in Western Europe (4 per cent in the U.S.A.) over a long period, rather less than half might have been attributed to population growth in Western Europe, and a little over half to the same cause in the U.S.A. Thus, very roughly, 40 per cent of capital formation in Western Europe and 60 per cent in the U.S.A. was ascribed by Hansen to population growth.

Since this source of demand for capital, and of labour supply to provide capital goods, was drying up, Hansen predicted that to maintain full employment more and more reliance would have to be placed upon technological developments, and the consequent demand for new investment.

The stagnationists' case originally rested partly on the assertion that there has been a widening of capital and no

---

[1] From an increase of 16 millions in the 1920's to 8 millions in the 1930's, and perhaps 5½ millions in the 1940's according to the forecasts then acceptable (actual increase in the 1940's was 16 millions).
[2] "Active, dominant and controlling factor" was Hansen's phrase.

(net) deepening;[1] but if economies of scale can be proved to have resulted from increased population, then a slower rate of growth will reduce the rate at which such advantages can be realized. It is, unfortunately, difficult to give any quantitative measure of economies of scale, but this does not mean that they are unimportant. If they are important, a cessation of population growth could result in symptoms of stagnation, whatever the trend in the relative proportions of "widened" and "deepened" capital formation.

For example, the cost of retailing, the cost of house-building, the cost of long-distance passenger transport and the cost of entertainment are all substantially less for the urban dweller in Great Britain than for the dweller in a small town or a remote country district. One reason for the persistent trend towards city-building the world over is that closely packed mass-markets are the only markets than can be relatively cheaply provided with shops, dwellings, railway services and amusements. Public services such as drainage, water and electricity and gas can also be laid on economically only for certain minimum concentrations of population, though these services (like the others) may rise sharply in cost if the demand is excessive.

Much smaller though it has been, the recovery in the output of Britain from 1946 to 1950, and of Germany from 1949 to 1952, shows the extraordinary reserves of modern industrial civilization and its powers of adaptation and change.

---

[1] Hansen went so far as to assert in 1939 that "our system of production is little more capitalistic than fifty or seventy-five years ago. It requires, in other words, a period of employment of our productive resources no longer than formerly to reproduce the total capital stock. . . ." He thought that ". . . now with the rapid cessation of population growth, even the widening process may slow down."

The stagnationists' analysis of the rôle played by population in the economic growth of the community was perhaps too much over-simplified.   They emphasized just *one* functional relationship, the alleged dependence of a high proportion of real annual investment upon the rate of growth of the population of a country.   Thus they overlooked, or deliberately ignored, the many possible variants of this relationship, or the cross-relationships that might exist (for example, that population might be itself stimulated to growth if, as the result of some external stimulus, the real national income increased rapidly).   The stagnationists, of whom Keynes himself was perhaps the least dogmatic, emphasized the Keynesian danger of insufficient investment, and wrote this into the long-term as well as the short-term prognostication of our economic ills.

The late Professor Schumpeter, on the other hand, once remarked that :

> "By 'growth' we mean changes in economic data which occur continuously in the sense that increment or decrement per unit of time can be currently absorbed by the system without perceptible disturbance.   Increase of population, resulting in an increase of the supply of labour of at most a few per cent per year (historically an increase of three per cent is already high), is the outstanding example." [1]

Schumpeter explicitly brought out a hidden assumption of many theorists, namely, that the influence of population was numerically so small as to be capable of being "currently absorbed" by a progressive economic system without much evidence of a shock effect.   He himself

[1] "Analysis of Economic Change", *Review of Economic Statistics*, Vol. XVII, No. 4, May 1935, reprinted in *Readings*, etc., 1950.

proceeded to emphasize the much greater importance of major technical "innovations".

Most studies of economic growth have so far been concentrated upon problems of disturbance, that is, upon cyclical questions. This approach has no doubt been due to, and partly justified by, the fact that, apart from major political events like war, the trade cycle has been the major economic event of the last thirty years.

Many models of an expanding economy owe their origin, as Mrs. Robinson has pointed out,[1] "to a simple piece of arithmetic". What they attempt to establish is the existence of a "growth rate" which fulfils certain conditions. For example, if one condition is that the stock of capital in a country has a fixed relation to income (capital is n times income), and another condition is that r per cent of income is saved and used in net investment (net additions to capital stock), then "the piece of arithmetic" tells us that there is a growth rate of r/n per cent which, if followed, would enable these conditions to be fulfilled indefinitely. For n = capital ÷ income, and r = investment in the year ÷ income (× 100), so clearly $r ÷ n$ = investment as a percentage of capital stock; i.e., the growth rate of capital stock. But income is a fixed fraction of capital stock by condition one, and investment is a fixed fraction of income. So income, too, must expand at this growth rate. So must investment, and so, incidentally, must consumption.

This, indeed, is always the basic point of the model, dressed up though it may be to give emphasis to quite different applications. On the assumptions of the model, the economy must continually expand at a pre-determined rate and so must both investment and consumption. Granted the conditions, then, attention is focused on any

[1] Robinson, J., 1952.

difficulties that may arise in the way of maintaining the necessary rate of advance.

Some authors, considering the long-term problems, have worried themselves about the possibility of finding sufficient investment opportunities, others have concerned themselves with the difficulty of expanding consumption, and still others with the possibility of maintaining the required supply of capital goods. Some have used the model to prove that the economy *could* expand, others to show that it was almost certain not to be able to keep up the pace. Very few have related the problem in any specific way to the problems of an expanding (or declining) population.

But the main fear of the model-makers has been of population as a *limiting factor of supply* (a "ceiling") rather than as a limiting factor of demand (as in the literature of the 1930's). Perhaps this concern with a possible shortage of man-power to support an expanding economy is a sign of the times, and illustrates the tacit recognition of the great potential wealth per head in the world believed to be available to an increasing working population in a still growing industrial economy.

No economist can prove by *a priori* reasoning either the stagnationists' thesis or the theory that a limited man-power ceiling is the typical cause of cyclical fluctuations, nor has an empirical approach yet succeeded in yielding definitive results. It can be said, empirically, that population increase and industrial development have, in the last two hundred years, usually gone together. A society can be imagined in which strategic decisions were taken such that all increases in the economic surplus were devoted to raising the standard of living of the existing number of inhabitants, and an increase in numbers was kept rigidly at zero. But experience shows that the momentum of industrial development has more usually hitherto brought increases in numbers far above even the present natural rate of increase. A few countries, like France, have advanced industrially without much increase in population, but their rate of advance has been noticeably slower than that of their more rapidly industrializing neighbours. The same forces are likely to prevail in the future. Britain's economic survival in a competitive world surely implies some continued rise in population, so far as the present arguments provide any guide.

CHAPTER VIII

INTERNATIONAL MIGRATION

§ 1. *Types of Migration.*   Migration is of two kinds: international, and that which takes place within the boundaries of a country or political unit.   It will be convenient to adhere to this conventional dichotomy, although the distinction becomes difficult to maintain as meaningful in periods of fluctuating political boundaries.   Ever since the eighteenth century boundaries have frequently been changed in all the continents.   In the nineteenth century the United States of America extended its boundaries to include territories which are now inhabited by some 92 million persons; and in the period from 1939 to 1946 the U.S.S.R. extended its boundaries to include territories inhabited in 1939 by 18 million persons.[1]   The United Kingdom reduced its boundaries after World War I, when it ceded independence to Southern Ireland.

Thus, what might have been an "internal" movement at one date is regarded as an "international" movement at another.   It is evident, too, that the shifting of boundaries, itself a political event, sometimes follows and sometimes precedes a significant shifting of population from place to place.

So far as Britain is concerned "international" migration is usually identified with trans-oceanic migration, of a permanent or semi-permanent kind, for obvious geographical and historical reasons; while "internal" migration has traditionally been sometimes permanent and

[1] *Economic Bulletin for Europe*, Vol. I, No. 1, July 1949, U.N., Geneva, p. 11.

sometimes temporary or seasonal. Even the "internal" migration has given rise, however, to distinctly "nationalistic" problems, since the net flow has been so marked from Ireland, Wales and Scotland into the English (and Scottish) growing conurbations.[1] Internal migration has been both long-term, following certain trends, short-term, especially in times of war, and cyclical, such as the exodus from the depressed areas; and, although movements of males have been important, the characteristic of internal migration, especially in the nineteenth century, has been the predominance of females among migrants.[2]

The present chapter is confined to problems of international migration. As has already been seen, forecasts of population change made in the last twenty years have paid little attention to the possibility of extensive net migration from country to country. This omission has been defended on the grounds that the scale and direction of migration are *especially* difficult to predict. It must be conceded that guesses as to the future trend of events must, in this, as in other social and economic matters, be subject to a very high degree of uncertainty. But the special degree of uncertainty in regard to migration appears, on examination, to consist merely of the fact that a single change of policy (say a government's decision freely to admit Japanese or Italian migrants within its borders) may have rather large-scale consequences. This may affect the detailed timing of future migratory flows, but the broad picture of the future is perhaps no more uncertain than that which can be formed of other economic developments, and its accuracy will partly depend on how closely past trends can be analysed, and in particular

[1] The "gross" flow was offset by considerable counter-movements in the opposite direction.
[2] See Ravenstein, 1885.

upon how far the interconnections between demographic, economic and political forces can be discerned.

§ 2. *Long-term, Permanent International Migration.* There are three further reasons why the importance of migration for the future of the British and American (not to mention other) populations has often been played down; one is the widely held view that the nineteenth century was the age *par excellence* of mass trans-oceanic movement of population; second is the belief that high birth-rates, producing a demographic "surplus population" are necessary as a push to Europeans to go overseas; and third is the belief that unpredictable political barriers will always prevent mass movements.

First, the simple fact is that migration has been proportionately, and lately even absolutely, as important for Britain and America in the twentieth century as it was in the nineteenth. For example, the gross shifts of population, both in Europe and in the sub-continent of India, from 1939 to 1949 exceeded in scale any mass movements that have ever taken place before in ten years of recorded human history. Excluding the movements of slave labour in the war years, it seems that at least 10 million persons moved permanently from country to country in the years 1946 and 1947 in Eastern Europe, following the readjustments of frontiers. There were enormous movements of population into and out of France. The United Kingdom received an inflow of 500,000 persons from 1939 to 1945, followed by an outflow in the years 1946 and 1947 of some 400,000.[1]

There is a tendency to discount the importance of these movements as being partly forced or political in origin, and as partly cancelling each other out (so far as they affect

---

[1] *Economic Bulletin*, cited above, July 1949, p. 17

total numbers). This last point is valid,[1] and war-time shifts of population are exceptional. But their net final effect is not negligible; nor have politically determined movements ceased to operate in the 1950's. It is as well to recall that nineteenth-century movements of population were also, if in less degree, partly forced and partly political in origin and not wholly spontaneous movements.

Looked back on from a distance, nineteenth-century international migration may seem part of a fairly rational process (with population flowing from less promising economies to those where more opportunity lay), not induced by inexorable political pressures nor giving rise to inhumane consequences. As many historians have pointed out, this was not how the movement always appeared to contemporary observers of, or participants in, it; very few migrants at any period can have suffered the upheaval of moving home, and of finding new ties, without some hardships before their departure, during their transit or after their arrival. Descriptions of the shiploads of Irish immigrants arriving at Quebec or Montreal in the 1850's do not make pleasant reading. The great bulges in the immigration curves represent periods of intense human misery.

The great migratory peoples of the world in the last two hundred years have been the Europeans, the Indians, the Chinese and Japanese and the Africans. The last group was moved to America under obvious duress, but some degree of compulsion has affected other parts of the great migratory flows. Economic push or pull seem, how-

[1] *Net* population shifts resulted, for example, in a gain to Germany, Austria and Italy of nearly 3 million persons from 1939–45, a gross inflow of 7·8 millions being offset by an outflow of 4·8 millions; in the years 1946–7 these countries gained by population shift another 7 million persons.

ever, to have been the main causes of the great majority of individual "free" movements.

The main outlines of the outward European movement are so well known that they need to be only briefly recapitulated. The biggest proportion of it consisted of emigration to the United States of America; total gross immigration to that country was put at 38 millions for the 110 years from 1820 to 1930,[1] of whom 26 millions are estimated to have stayed, and so added (in their lifetimes) to the population.

The gross number of passengers leaving the British Isles for extra-European destinations over the same period was some 20 millions, which can be taken as roughly equivalent to gross emigration. Net emigration was much less than this, owing to the steady backflow of earlier emigrants, and the influx of persons from other countries to live in Britain or to stay there preparatory to a further journey westwards. A great deal of British emigration (and of foreigners *via* Britain) was destined for various parts of the British Commonwealth. A very high proportion of Canada's army in World War I had been born in Britain.

According to a table published in 1924[2] of the 36 million "immigrants" to (passengers arriving in) the United States from 1820 to 1924, 24 per cent ($8\frac{1}{2}$ millions) came from the United Kingdom, 16 per cent from Germany, and 9 per cent from other parts of northern and western Europe; 13 per cent were from Italy, 12 per cent from Austria-Hungary, and 24 per cent from other parts of eastern and southern Europe. British North America and South America provided nearly 10 per cent, the remainder coming from China, India and Japan and other specified or unspecified countries of origin.

---

[1] Willcox, 1931, Vol. II, p. 89.
[2] In the *Monthly Labor Review*, Washington, January 1924.

The countries of origin of American immigrants changed considerably between the periods 1870–90 and 1900–13. In the first period roughly 75 per cent of immigrants were coming from the so-called "old" elements (i.e., from Britain, Scandinavia and Germany in the main), whereas from 1900 to 1913 nearly 75 per cent of the immigrants were "new" (i.e., from Turkey in Asia and southern Europe, especially Italy). America's peak year for "passengers entering" ended June 30, 1907, and in that year 1,285,000 such passengers were recorded; and in another high year ending June 30, 1914, there was an almost equally large number of entrants.

These high figures of inflow into America corresponded with an urgent pressure on population to leave Europe. This pressure had notably shifted from country to country.

Thus, in the 1850's, "British" (i.e., mainly Irish) emigrants had predominated, soon followed by German and Scandinavian. In 1891–95 emigrants from the British Isles still accounted for 20 per cent of the immigration into the United States, while Italy, Austria-Hungary and Russia each accounted for some 12 or 13 per cent. By 1906–10 Austria-Hungary accounted for 24 per cent of the immigrants, Italy for 22 per cent, and Russia for 20 per cent.[1]

In the light of these past events the break in the trends of trans-Atlantic migration that followed World War I assume a special meaning and importance. Three major changes took place: the introduction of the quota system by American legislation, the economic depression of the 1920's in Commonwealth countries, followed by the Great Depression of 1929–32, and the ban on Russian emigration that was enforced by the Soviet revolutionary government.

[1] Ferenczi, 1929, Vol. I, p. 179.

The "natural" or "normal" tendency of migratory flow seemed, up to the period 1920–32, when all these trends were reversed or interrupted by policy, to have followed a regular and intelligible development. Just as in the days of British free trade (which also ended in 1932) Great Britain was the "market of last resort", the market where goods could always be offered for sale by citizens of any country that was short of gold or liquid reserves, so, up to that same turning-point, the United States had been the country of last resort for the family forced to consider the grim prospects of unemployment, or near-starvation, or both, at home. Inevitably the Irish turned to America when in their crisis, as did the surplus workers from England, or the redundant Italians and Austrians; so, too, did the Russians as their economy in turn began to undergo some noticeable modernization. But these huge inflows of immigrants to America had caused immense social and political problems there, and the consequence was a momentous decision to cut down the inflow rather than to tackle the problems themselves.

What were the fundamental causes of the break in the mass trans-oceanic migration of the nineteenth century (actually of the early twentieth century as well, since it persisted at least until 1914)? Were they political, economic or demographic?

Political, certainly; for the American immigration restrictions were imposed as the result of a political agitation in America, brought to a head by the short-term economic problems of demobilization and of an agriculture excessively expanded for war needs. Restrictions on emigration were also political in origin. The Empire Settlement Act of 1922, under which by 1937 400,000 British nationals had been assisted to emigrate to Australia, Canada and New Zealand, was a politically

conditioned measure. But movements on a much larger
scale were intended when the Act was passed. Economic
forces began to operate that put an effective end to the
scheme.

Economic forces became clearly paramount, indeed,
with the onset of the Great Depression. A net return
movement to Europe, and especially to Britain, set in
from 1931. This was a short-term effect. A more long-
term economic force was the decline of the "open spaces"
available for raising food by extensive agriculture overseas.

Demographic changes also played their part. There
were the checks to population caused by the casualties,
and fall of births, of World War I; and the perhaps more
serious check to population growth in Western Europe
caused by the decline in the average size of family. It
has thus been argued that "from the merely demographic
point of view there was certainly no surplus population
available in most countries of north-western and central
Europe" to provide for large-scale emigration in the
period between the two world wars.[1]

The three types of forces must not be regarded as acting
in isolation each from the other, nor must exaggerated
importance be ascribed to any one of them. Political
barriers, important though they are, can rarely be effective
if put across the path of some really powerful economic
drive. Permanent migration need not be trans-oceanic,
which is relatively easy to control (although now by-
passed sometimes by air traffic), but across land frontiers.
In decades when the economic need for immigrants is
great, short-term influxes of labour can rarely be wholly
checked (witness the movements into the U.S. across the
Canadian and Mexican frontiers, or into France from Italy

[1] Isaac, 1951, p. 190.

and Spain), and these eventually may lead to permanent settlement.

Economic forces are, in this connection, sometimes treated in an over-simplified way. It is argued that the main cause of the success of earlier permanent migration was that agriculture was being expanded overseas, providing cheap food for the manufacturing nations of Europe. The economic development was, then, complementary up to 1914, and thereafter the same opportunities no longer existed.

There is a recognizable truth in this well-known interpretation of events; but certain comments on it are required. First of all, it is a telescoping of events to imagine that a major part of the inflow into the United States in the fifty years before 1914 went into an expanding agriculture. The great bulk of the mass immigration went to build up a great new urban civilization, which to this day is for the greater part concentrated in the Eastern and Middle Western sections of the country.

Secondly, the long-term economic factors favourable to inward migration seem to have had less to do with the question of the agricultural/non-agricultural balance than with such structural questions as in which decades the railroads were due to be built, or the road system of the country reorganized; or with the possibility of changing techniques in which capital equipment could be used more and more by unskilled labour; or with opportunities for exploiting the economies of the division of labour (*either* within large *or* between multitudes of small plants).

Thirdly, there is the question of the organization of the capital markets at home and abroad. A certain structure of market at home might have acted as a deterrent to employment, since capital equipment at home could not be provided fast enough to keep all the available labour employed at a reasonable level of productivity. More persons, therefore, may have emigrated than otherwise would have done, and than were strictly necessary to increase agricultural output overseas.

Large-scale permanent international migration from Europe was resumed after World War II. Nearly 3 million persons emigrated from Europe to countries overseas in the five years after the end of the war, a figure to be compared with the $3\frac{1}{2}$ million moving overseas in the years 1920–24 inclusive.[1] This was nearly $4\frac{1}{2}$ times as many as left Europe in the five years preceding World War II.

Many of the factors favourable to migration could be classed as "short-term political", although some were economic. There were separated families and war brides (125,000 of them), political uncertainty at home, displaced persons from Germany with no homes left to return to, the millions of "expellees" of German ethnic origin, returning prisoners of war of various nationalities, Jews seeking their new national home, all these being politically determined. Emigration from Italy and the Netherlands was officially encouraged on economic grounds, that is, because these economies could not be adjusted to employ their fairly rapidly growing populations.

In the receiving countries economic conditions mainly determined the "pull" factors. The exceptionally full employment conditions ruling in the United States, for example, enabled that country to receive 216,000 displaced persons and 96,000 alien wives and fiancées of members of their armed forces by 1951, in addition to normal intake of immigrants under the Quota Act. Australia planned at first to receive 200,000 immigrants a

[1] *Ibid.*, 1952, p. 191. The U.S. Quota Act was passed in 1924.

year by 1950, which proved impossible, and by 1952 the
target had been reduced to 80,000.[1]

Several difficulties had to be overcome in the realization
of this huge programme of emigration, the greater part
of which was carried out by a body called the International Refugee Organization.[2]   There were the physical
obstacles, such as shortage of shipping-space, and the
arrears of house-building in the receiving countries, and
social obstacles, such as the problem of reconciling Yorkshire miners to working side by side with Italians.
Despite all the difficulties, some of which could not be
solved, there was an exceptional tide of overseas migration, the International Labour Office estimate of 1951
being that some 5 million persons in Europe would be
"available for migration" over the next five years, at
least $4\frac{1}{2}$ millions of them consisting of Italians and Germans.   Whether this estimate was accurate or not, on
any reckoning the figure of persons so available must
have been high.

How is the post-World War II wave of "permanent"
migration from Europe to be regarded?   Was it solely
a short-term politically determined phenomenon?   Or
was it the resuming of an economically, and demographically, determined long-term trend?

From one point of view the movement was simply the
aftermath of the war, an unravelling of the knots into
which the Nazi regime had tied Europe.   But why had
these knots been tied?   Simply because the Nazis had
implemented on a colossal scale a manpower plan for
European industry as a whole.   The consequence of that
plan was forced international migration of a hitherto
unprecedented magnitude.

1 *Ibid.*, 1952, p. 194.
2 See Isaac, 1952, and *Economic Bulletin for Europe*, Vol. I, No. 1, 1949.

13

A production plan for Europe as a whole, or for the N.A.T.O. powers as a whole, indeed for any international organization, necessarily involves a corresponding plan for manpower. A manpower plan is likely to need, at some stage, transfers of population from one country to another. If the next fifty years are to see increasing international economic planning in Western Europe, or in Europe and the Atlantic Powers together with the British Commonwealth, then it is likely that some attention will be given by the planning body to the problem of moving population to the places where it is economically most urgently needed. To discuss the future of population movements from Western Europe is to discuss the future of international economic planning, without which such movements are not likely to be very large.

In the 1920's and 1930's large-scale immigration of Indians and Chinese into the Malayan Straits Settlements took place, of the order of 300,000–400,000 persons a year. But in more recent years the Indian and Chinese population there has tended to grow by natural increase rather than by immigration. The late nineteenth- and early twentieth-century immigration of Indians into Ceylon had almost ceased by 1939, and there has been a noticeable back-flow of Indian immigrants to India, and an even more marked back-flow from Burma.[1] The era of large-scale international movements lasted longer in the East than in the West, but increasing barriers have now slowed down the movements there, at least temporarily; internal migration in Eastern countries is now proceeding at a very high rate. The rate of urbanization (i.e., population gains of cities from rural areas) in Japan exceeded

[1] See "International migrations in the Far East during recent times —The countries of immigration", *Population Bulletin*, No. 2, October 1952, p. 27

the increase in its population from 1920 to 1940, and the rate of gain of Indian cities (some 1 million a year) is impressive.[1]

There are often thought to be three obstacles to large-scale mass emigration of the old style in modern conditions. The first two obstacles are real; the third partly illusory. The first is the actual physical difficulty of transfer, now that the shocking hygienic conditions of old-time migration are no longer tolerated. Ships have to be found, and passages paid for. (This is not, of course, a difficulty in the way of migration across land frontiers.) The second is the question of providing capital in the receiving country to house the immigrant and put him to work. The capital required per worker varies from country to country, and according to the occupation to be followed by the immigrant, but the sum needed is nowadays usually large, equal to the whole value of the new worker's output for a number of years. "Adequate" housing (i.e., of a standard that he will accept) can only be provided for the immigrant with great difficulty, if, as is often the case, housing is short for the existing inhabitants of the country.

In the nineteenth century land was "plentiful" in the U.S. and Canada, and scarce in the U.K.; and *both* labour *and* industrial capacity (and social capital) were relatively scarce to land in the U.S. and Canada.

The mass of immigrants could in the long run build capital equipment as well as raise food; and the problem of marketing food was largely a problem of adequate transport facilities which required much labour to provide. Secondly, with the change in social standards mass migration demands special measures to be taken at the receiving end. Some publicists have proposed that "new

[1] *Ibid.*, pp. 54–55.

towns" should be built in Australia, for example; 20,000 immigrants at a time could be housed and employed, but neither the economic organization nor the economic surplus exists to provide for immigrants on such a lavish scale in that country.[1]   Housing is a serious problem for Australians as for others; and the policy of "houses first, immigrants later" is unrealistic if advocated simultaneously with a plan for greatly increased mass immigration.

Asiatic migrations on a huge scale are open to similar objections.   They are, in addition, susceptible to two other weaknesses.   First, most possible Asiatic or African "reception areas" are themselves well populated in relation to their economic resources, and the level of their productive techniques.   Mass immigration would mean great capital outlays per head of immigrants.   Secondly, in these economically and socially "backward" areas emigration would have little or no effect on the population problem, or the economic problem, of the country from which the emigrants come.   (Selective emigration is another matter altogether, as it may have educational and cultural advantages that can be turned to economic benefit, e.g., if Indians settle in the U.S. and provide an educational training centre for Indian students there.)

While the ratio of land to the other factors may have been brought into less striking disharmony in some instances, there still remain very substantial differences, not so much perhaps between land and labour as between capital of an appropriate kind and labour.   Theoretically, therefore, economic gain may accrue from a movement of workers in a direction which tends to equalize more nearly

---

[1] See Barker, 1948, for a statement of this case, and Plant, 1951, for the counter-arguments.   A plan for mass emigration to African territories was put forward by Leone in 1951.

the capital per head of the countries between which the flow takes place, or, more accurately, to optimize the ratio between capital goods (some of them specific) and population.

Economic gain *may* accrue from a movement of persons to countries where output per head is relatively high, and the evidence (for instance, the mere fact of the more or less successful large-scale emigration of the post-war years) seems to confirm that in certain instances it *does* accrue.

There are, moreover, some powerful political (in which are here included social) obstacles to movement. The country of origin is losing its citizens who may be leaving to acquire a new social outlook and way of life. Its cultural survival is threatened.

The economic loss to the country of origin may not be negligible, since it has incurred the whole cost of educating and rearing the young person who now proceeds to spend his or her active life elsewhere. This loss has become far more serious in modern times than ever before, because of the extension of the period of upbringing and education, and because of the increasing expenses of medical care and social benefits. In the same way, other expenses arising for social security make emigration economically unattractive to countries of origin. They are liable to be left with an unduly high proportion of old age pensioners, permanently sick people, and children to support, with a low proportion of active persons on whom taxes to meet these various expenses can be imposed. Some advocates of mass migration have, indeed, discussed the possibility of charges such as these being shared in some way between "losing" and "gaining" countries.[1]

Plans for mass migration may be regarded as unproved

[1] See Sauvy, 1948.

remedies for the economically maldistributed population of the world, as a general rule, although no doubt from time to time mass movements will be advocated. Apart from economic arguments there are several political arguments used in their favour: first, the arguments in favour of the dispersion of such specially placed populations as that of Great Britain[1]; secondly, the need to secure homogeneous populations and to avoid continual strife has prompted such new countries as Pakistan and India to encourage mass exchanges of population; and thirdly, the policy of allowing asylum to the ideologically dissatisfied, or to the genuinely oppressed, has led to the large refugee problem, which up to 1953 has flowed in Europe from east to west on balance, with a trickle the other way.

These political mass migrations, whether contemplated or already taking place, cause rather than spring from economic problems. They will affect in a fairly unpredictable way the population trends of the countries where they occur. It seems safe to say, however, that a mass dispersal (of, say, 20–30 millions in a decade) of Western European citizens to destinations overseas will not take place, for the same objections raised to such mass migrations, when advocated on economic grounds, apply to this proposal equally effectively. The initial economic costs of such movements are prohibitive. But very large mass movements of the scale of 3–4 millions in five years are still economically feasible.[2]

The political factors affecting migration are not so wholly unpredictable as might be supposed, for they are

[1] Here, the mass migration of 20 of Britain's 50 millions is a figure that has been much discussed in recent years.

[2] There are likely to be cyclical fluctuations in the movements, so it is not safe to assume that ten times these numbers will be likely to move in fifty years.

closely linked to economic trends. It has been seen
that each of the two power blocks of the world includes
large and rapidly growing populations among its power-
assets, but there is one important difference. The two
largest Communist powers have a geographically internal
"frontier" territory to develop, the Russians in their
eastern and south-eastern possessions, the Chinese in their
north and west. If the stagnationists are, after all, right,
this existence of a virtual "frontier" gives a considerable
stimulus to the economic growth of the Russian and
Chinese economies.

The two largest Communist powers have themselves no
shortage of population in an absolute sense, and within
the Russian orbit are satellites with a fairly high rate of
increase. Thus, even if Russia has some temporary manpower problems, these can be solved without recourse to
manpower from, say, Italy or Germany. With the
advantages of both an extensive frontier to develop and
adequate numbers for growth, the Communist powers can
look forward to a natural increase in their strength.

The Americans' position must not be over-contrasted
with that of their rivals. Every country has, as it were,
an intensive as well as an extensive frontier, and the
Americans have hitherto been especially skilful at their
development of an internal market, and at intensive
capital formation. But their extensive frontiers lie outside their own territory. The new lands which they can
most naturally develop on an extensive basis are in
Canada, South America and Africa. This means that
the United States must either conquer, dominate, or
co-operate with a number of its allies.

So far as political "trends" are concerned, the flow of
migration must be towards the frontier territories wherever
they are found, and towards the cities and towns. No

other main kinds of flow would be compatible with the maintenance or growth of political power.

If, then, the 1953 division of the world into power blocks continues, sooner or later the "Western" leaders may want to re-open the question of German, Italian and Japanese settlement overseas, for these are the nationalities whose rural populations are numerous enough to provide a surplus suitable for transfer. At the same time other countries of the non-Soviet or Chinese bloc category will want to see that migration takes place on a sufficient scale to relieve population pressure, or to maintain political links.

But the economic changes which are contemplated in various parts of the world may create a migration problem far more acute than any political upheaval has done to date.

There are three reasons why economic development may be hostile to large populations in backward countries. First, these countries are moving from "feudalism", or some system of local oppression, to more advanced forms of economic organization. This kind of move is liable to provoke an acute short-term shortage of food and necessities, for reasons that were touched on in the discussion of "optimum" populations. The old oppressive class may perforce have to withdraw its support from the "tertiary" employees whom it kept occupied, and the new, perhaps more egalitarian, regime will not spend the surplus which it has appropriated in such a way as to offer substitute employment. Or the old oppressive class will "reform" itself, and adopt new methods of agriculture, as England did during the enclosure movement, or as the landlords did in Ireland during the period of the evictions. These sudden improvements in agricultural technique may throw millions of people off the land;

this might happen in a country like Egypt if, for some reason, a much less labour-heavy technique of cultivation suddenly became profitable. Secondly, economic development may cause straightforward technological unemployment if, for instance, machines are introduced which wipe out the demand for labour, total demand not rising fast enough to maintain employment. Finally, the growth of both manufactures and agriculture, though rapid in the developing countries, may not be rapid enough to avoid "frictional" setbacks, which may in some instances imply huge temporary unemployment or even famine. In the short run economic development of a "backward" country may bring disaster.

It is to be hoped that this possibility is widely enough feared to make avoidance of it reasonably probable. But the sudden collapse of a single export industry, or the too sudden adoption of some new techniques of agriculture, would provoke in any one backward country an immense pressure to emigrate. An acute problem of finding a suitable reception area would then face the United Nations.

Thus, although there has been a downward trend in the relative importance of migration since the nineteenth century, the conclusion must be drawn that this trend may be reversed. With economic development new streams of emigrants may appear.

§ 3. *Short-term International Migration.* So far the discussion has been confined to long-term or "permanent" international migration, that is to the movement of "settlers" from country to country. Many people, however, cross frontiers without the intention of living the rest of their lives outside their country of origin. They are of four classes: seafarers or railwaymen, tourists, seasonal workers, and semi-permanent migrants usually to particular industries abroad; some of all these, particularly of the last two categories, may become permanent migrants, just as, conversely, some of the would-be permanent migrants eventually return home.[1]

Seafarers and tourists can be omitted from any lengthy consideration, although even these categories play some part in the prospecting of new ways of living, and in the growth of cities and towns. Seaports all over the world attract settlers of different nationalities; seas, it is said, like rivers, naturally unite and do not divide, the divisions often being political or social in origin, rather than economic or individual.

It is incorrect to think of world population as entirely static, of people as being rooted to their homes until a sudden change occurs. They are perpetually oscillating, like the electrons in a gas, darting here or there, mostly of course on short journeys, but to a considerable extent across frontiers, until for some reason or other the pull becomes strong enough to fix them in a new habitat; and the individual then, perhaps, pursues a new and shorter daily oscillatory path (to and from his work, to holiday places and so on). There can be little doubt that the consequence of seasonal and semi-permanent migration is that permanent migration becomes more practicable. For the seasonal worker, like the agricultural workers moving into France from Spain at harvest time, may make friends and establish social contacts that eventually lead him to live in a French village; or the male workers brought into the mines from Poland or Italy may decide to stay in England or France, or wherever the mines are,

[1] According to a calculation of Willcox 35–39 per cent of migrants entering the U.S. in the twenty-three years to 1914 returned home within the same period; the backflow was 15 per cent from 1923–30, and over 100 per cent during the Depression.

and to send for their families.   Short-term migration is a useful method of solving some of the economic problems of the geographical uneven distribution of labour without grave commitments being entered upon.

Unfortunately it is nearly always the receiving country that secures these benefits, the idea often being that if there is any unemployment the immigrants are to be the first to be thrown out of work, and if necessary deported. From an international point of view this is a reprehensible practice, but it does not directly concern us as a population matter.

The main point about the seasonal and semi-permanent migration of workers is that it satisfies in practice the need which theory foresaw for some safety-valve.   Short of complete migration, which is hampered by various important economic and social frictions, there are these intermediate stages in the movement of population. These short-term movements deserve, therefore, very careful study, since they are pointers to the relative economic and demographic structures of the economies between which they take place on any scale.

§ 4. *Migration and Trade Cycles.*   For many years economists have speculated upon the relation between migration and fluctuations in general economic activity.   In relation to population change, migration is mainly important for its long-term effects.   Short-term fluctuations are significant only so far as they affect the trend.

Whether there are very long cycles in economic affairs still remains an undecided question.   Kondratieff concluded, in his well-known article of 1926,[1] from the

---

[1] Of which a translation appeared in the *Review of Economic Statistics*, Vol. XVII, No. 6, November 1935, p. 105, which was reprinted in *Readings in Business Cycle Theory*, 1950, p. 20.

statistical evidence then available, that "the existence of long waves of cyclical character is very probable." The course of economic development proceeded, he thought, through a series of long as well as of short waves. His first "wave" lasted for about sixty years from 1780, the second for forty-seven years, and the third had not concluded at the time that his contribution was made.

If there are long cycles, lasting half-centuries—or perhaps others persisting for a hundred or two hundred years —can they be identified and measured, and can useful predictions be based upon them? Professor Hicks, in the famous footnote with which he concluded his well-known theoretical work,[1] threw out the startling suggestion that the industrial revolution lasting two hundred years was perhaps a very long secular boom, and that, if so, it might have been largely due to the unparalleled increase in population. He somewhat cryptically remarked that this would help to explain why, "as the wisest hold, it has been such a disappointing episode in human history". But why should a boom lasting for two hundred years be such a disappointing event? In itself, such a result would seem to be a matter for rejoicing. Professor Hicks's point must be not that the boom as such was bad, but that because it was *only* a boom it was bound to come to an end—how and when it would end, the context shows, Professor Hicks was too cautious to forecast, since this would depend on the virtually unpredictable trend of innovations in techniques.

The central issue of the problem of the long-term cycle, if there is one, is indeed this issue of what direction the trend of innovation is likely to follow, and what character the innovations are to have. For most economists would agree (with varying degrees of emphasis) that great stress

[1] Hicks, 1946, p. 302.

must be laid on the supply of investment opportunities which is provided by invention and innovation; therefore they would accept the view that it is important that there should be a sufficient amount of innovation to keep the factors of production more or less fully employed.

There would be less agreement on the importance of the character of the innovations. The subject has been in dispute ever since Ricardo re-wrote his chapter on machinery. The extreme *laissez-faire* view would be that in the very long run the character of the innovations was of no importance. What matters, on this view, is that the cheapest method of production should always be followed. In the long run this will result in output per head, and hence real income, being as great as it is possible for it to be. In the short run, of course, the innovation may be extremely labour-saving, and so cause unemployment and starvation among displaced workers, but, on this view, such short-term evils need short-term remedies.

The more historically-minded schools of economists attach some importance to the character of the innovations. They think that it may matter very much, even in the long run, whether an innovation is labour-saving or labour-complementary. The technological unemployment caused by the first type of innovation may have, they argue, long-run repercussions; and if this is not accepted, they fall back on Keynes's aphorism on long runs.

The relevance of this debate to the present problem is that migration is, economically, the adjustment in space of the low-paid worker to the (relatively) high-paid job opportunity. The adjustment does not take place easily, and there are many frictions to slow down or divert movement, but as a long-run phenomenon migration should roughly tend to correspond to that ideal adjustment that the *laissez-faire* theorist depicts. Or, alternatively, it should flow in the directions which, on a historical view, are most likely to be beneficial, having regard to stability of employment and to such other additional criteria as the historicist wishes to introduce.

For the interpretation of the mass migrations of the last two hundred years the *laissez-faire* theory is perhaps useful to this extent: that it emphasizes the increase in output per head resulting from the movements that took place. On the other hand, the social and economic frictions to movement must not be overlooked; just as, even under free trade, purchasing power parity of different currencies is rarely complete, so real output per head, and real wages, vary from country to country, not only in the short but in the long run. The migration of workers which could bring them into equality fails to take place because of cost of movement, the inertia of existing arrangements, and social factors, such as the desire for propinquity to friends, and for the sharing of a common language.

What tends to be left out of either extreme economic or extreme historical determinism is the importance of acts of choice, when strategic decisions are taken. This process goes on continuously. There are strategic decisions taken by investors, and those who decide what types of capital equipment are to be made; and other strategic decisions are taken by consumers, not only the "seigneurs" of Professor Sauvy's illustrative examples but by consumers as a whole, whenever they have a surplus to spend above that necessary to purchase conventional necessities. If Mr. Jones decides, permanently, to give up smoking and to visit the theatre weekly, the total, as well as the partial, demand for labour is thereby affected. The importance of this type of decision is hardly likely to be recognized when it is relegated to the dull category labelled "change of taste".

In the nineteenth century these matters were very fully debated, and strategic decisions were taken to develop a type of civilization which was particularly well suited *both* to a very rapid increase in population *and* to a high long-term rate of migration. The detailed history of these decisions cannot be set out here, but the broad points can be fairly clearly recognized. First, there was the decision to "improve agriculture", which involved enclosure Acts. The social consequences of this were seen first in England, and later, even more acutely, in Ireland; in the mid-nineteenth century the agrarian revolution affected Germany as well. Many people had to leave the land as the decades went by (some precipitately, when a harvest failed). Secondly, there were the innovations in transport, which involved a steady high demand for labour, and also meant that much larger urban concentrations were now becoming economically possible. Thirdly, there were the legislative changes, which abolished paternalistic regulation of economic affairs (the Speenhamland system, and the control of prices and usury), so exposing the increasing masses of people deliberately to economic pressure. Fourthly, it was decided, on balance, that the manufacturing interests of a nation were paramount, since the greatest increases in real wealth seemed to lie chiefly in their capacity; the textile, iron and steel, and coal industries received an especial fillip, and both old and new markets for their products were captured or developed. Fifthly, with the new surpluses of real incomes accruing (over and above minimum needs) to certain social groups "tertiary" occupations of many kinds became economically more attractive. Clerking, advertising, domestic service and holiday resorts flourished.

All five of these points are characteristics of nineteenth-century England, which increased apparently its real wage-rates per head, as did Germany, Belgium and other countries, with extraordinary rapidity between 1860 and 1890, although in the period from 1890 to 1913 a kind of plateau was reached, due to what Professor Phelps-Brown has labelled a "climacteric".[1] This check to progress was not, according to some distinguished contemporary observers, inevitable. It resulted perhaps from a strategic decision by managers and trade unionists to take life more easily, to buy leisure and relaxation rather than progress with their efforts. But another important reason, both for the rapidity of the nineteenth-century advance and for the slowing down of the 1890's, was the stage then reached by technological development. As Professor Phelps-Brown has pointed out, the really large-scale *application* of the inventions associated with steam and steel had been made by the 1890's; thereafter the vast processes of re-equipping must have been complete, and all that remained to do was replacement. The *new* techniques coming along, in electricity, internal combustion engines and chemicals, did not reach the stage of large-scale application for some decades.

Rapid and unprecedented as the mid-nineteenth-century advance was in Great Britain, it did not suffice to give full employment to the population that was still growing, as natural increase remained high. The great developments partly depended upon, as well as inspired, an increase in population, indeed, a very large increase in population; but they were not sufficient to keep the whole British and Irish population within these islands. For exactly the same reasons as they were wanted at home, people were also wanted abroad. The age of steam and

[1] Phelps-Brown with Handfield-Jones, 1952.

steel came to the United States only a little later than to this country; corresponding developments also began in what is now the Commonwealth.

Migration of a long-term kind has not necessarily come to an end. But it will not cease merely because there are now no longer any geographically undiscovered corners of the earth worth talking about. In the first place, many parts of the earth *are* still unprospected, in the economic sense. New techniques are available for prospecting them much more rapidly than in the past. The search for raw materials may create new townships and cities, in quite remote and even unexpected places. Secondly, the massive application of new techniques may yet require labour in large quantities. Thirdly, even with our knowledge limited to existing techniques, any density map of the world suggests that there must yet remain strong economic tendencies for a substantial movement of peoples.

On a long-term view fairly large-scale international migration appears, indeed, to be unavoidable. Just how it is to take place, and how the worst frictions that it implies are to be avoided, is a problem that will occupy several generations of statesmen.

Migration has fluctuated with trade cycles since 1913, although, according to the data analysed by Professor Brinley Thomas,[1] the tendency before that date was for the building cycle, which is believed to be longer than the usual trade cycle, to have the greater effect. Consequently, in the earlier period, when Britain was having a constructional slump the U.S. was having a constructional boom, and emigration actually tended to be relatively high.

Professor Thomas, like Professor Brown, detects an

[1] Thomas, 1951, p. 215.

14

important structural change in the British, indeed in the Atlantic, economy occurring in the 1890's.[1] This, he believes, accounts for the failure of British economic development in the period 1897–1913 to fit into the Kondratieff pattern—a failure discussed at length by Schumpeter.

Short-term fluctuations in migration are presumably inevitable so long as short-term cycles occur, whether they are "building cycles" or "trade cycles", or simply cycles generated by speculation or recurrent political crises. A severe recent fluctuation has occurred in Australian immigration policy. Migration, being in a sense marginal to an economy, is always liable to suffer more than any other kind of human activity. (One of the distressing features of short-term migration has been the tendency of the receiving country to regard immigrants as a cushion, to be used, by deportation, in case of a slump.)

If men were all "economic men", in a rather strictly abstract sense, desiring only the fruits of "output per head" in general and not particular satisfactions, most countries would allow and encourage far more immigration than in fact they do. For the cost of rearing a child, and educating him or her, is heavy, and economic gain would accrue to a country which took full advantage of any surpluses of labour overseas, and cut down its birthrate to a minimum. A mature, civilized state is, indeed, somewhat liable to pursue this policy, especially when its civilization is highly cerebral, and it places high economic value upon education and not much upon the pleasures of domesticity. Thus it pursues, by choice, a policy which would inevitably be pursued by a state in which all men coldly aimed at an "economic maximum". The

[1] *Ibid.*, p. 250. Like Professor Brown he associates the change with the era of electricity, internal combustion and chemicals.

final logical step to take is to import slaves, or persons with no civic rights, or a minimum of rights, so that labour supply is bought like a commodity. Why should any adults have children of their own, from an economic point of view? In agrarian societies there are clear reasons, or in societies where people have reason to fear their old age if they have no issue; but in modern industrial societies, with some social security and no possibility of economic reward from children the motives disappear.

These propositions offer a *reductio ad absurdum* to the argument that population matters, and especially questions affecting migration, can be considered as economic questions, in total isolation from assumptions about "ends", or from assumptions about "tastes"—such as the "taste" for having a family of one's own.

There are fairly strong economic arguments in favour not only of large-scale migration on a permanent basis, but for greater freedom of short-term movements. Studies in the United States have shown how important a part large-scale internal migration plays in that country—on a continental scale. The economic benefits of such movements, if they could be free elsewhere, are probably very great. But the social and political objections to a greatly increased flow of persons, though sometimes ill-founded, cannot all be brushed aside; many of them could be overcome if international agencies handling the detailed arrangements were well staffed, and provided with adequate funds. Civilization may be enriched, not threatened, by migration, so long as the flow does not lead to worsened or new forms of racial or nationalistic rivalry.

PART III

FUTURE PROSPECTS

CHAPTER IX

GREAT BRITAIN

How many people there will be in Great Britain fifty years hence can be estimated only if some complex of demographic, economic and political events can be predicted; modern population theory affords no safe basis of prediction, unlike a theory which ascribes to human reproductiveness an unchanging value. Moreover, no modern theory can fail to take some account of both internal and international migration.

How many people there ought to be in Britain at that date is an even more widely debatable question, answerable according to the values and objectives that are held to be paramount. Clear simple answers to our problems must almost necessarily be unsound, so great and numerous are our present uncertainties.

Fortunately, however, this does not mean that Britain's population problem cannot be rationally debated. Results in some ranges are more likely than results outside those ranges, and some sizes of population are likely, in the event, to be "better", by acceptable criteria, than others.

§ 1. *Demographic, Economic, Political and Social Objectives and Factors.* To avoid repetition, this chapter will be divided into two, rather than three, main sections; in the first section demographic and economic considerations will be reviewed together, and in the second there will be a brief discussion of political and social factors.

The thesis advanced here is that the economic factors

outweigh the others.   For there are facts from which it can be argued that the key factors, in the case of Britain, determining its population size, are likely to be economic more preponderantly than demographic or political, important though these two classes of influence may also be.   In this respect Britain, in the mid-twentieth century, is not necessarily typical; other countries at the same date, or Britain at different dates, may have been influenced less by economic than by demographic or social forces and developments.   Britain by the mid-twentieth century was at a point in its historical development when its demographic structure was comparatively stable and controlled.   Its political future, though uncertain, seemed fairly likely to lie within a range of possibilities none of which would affect the population that it could support quite so seriously as would its economic strength, although of course some unforeseen political cataclysm could easily upset this balance of different forces.

Past trends have been used by some writers to show first, that Britain's population *will* be, and secondly that it *ought* to be, either smaller than, or equal to, its 1950 size.

Britain's demographic position is not strong, however, in that it has an aging population and a rather sharply falling number of persons in the more fecund age-groups. Its population pyramid does not suggest expansion in the near future, unless family size habits were to be suddenly and substantially changed, and it suggests that even to maintain the present size of population by natural increase will require a change in the broad downward trend in the habit of reproducing children.   For reasons of this kind those who argue on the basis of demographic projections alone generally estimate that the British population will in 1975 be of about the same size as it was in 1950,[1] and rather less (though perhaps not much less) by the year 2000. Demographically speaking, a continued population of 50 millions in Britain for another half-century is to be regarded as a fairly high achievement, and a somewhat lower figure is usually thought to be more probable.

There is no doubt that demographic factors are of great importance. If there are no fertile wives of sufficient strength or will-power to bear children (or an insufficiency of these with a given pattern of family size), or if there is an insufficiency of virile husbands, clearly the population must in the long run decline accordingly. Demography, in this somewhat platitudinous sense, is the paramount factor. Even so, other factors may still have their effects (for instance, if the fecundity and strength of the mothers is a function of the food supply, and this in turn a function of economic organization). But in the second half of the twentieth century Britain's population is not, even in this limited sense, likely to be mainly determined by demographic forces. The demographic forces are themselves much more likely to be both outweighed, and operated upon, by economic conditions, and the range of demographic possibilities is too wide for these forces alone to be at all a safe basis for prediction.

Statistics are, by their very nature, incapable of "proving" this point, but they run in a way not inconsistent with its likelihood. For example, there can be little doubt that, to the extent that other things are equal, the birth-rate has risen in the twentieth century in

[1] See, for example, not only the Royal Commission's projections (already quoted above) but also the estimates of the Materials Policy Commission, 1952, Vol. II, p. 131. M. Bourgeois-Pichat estimated a 2 per cent growth in the population of England and Wales between 1950 and 1980 (quoted in the *Economic Survey of Europe Since the War*, 1953, p. 160), his estimate being based on prospective natural increase alone, exclusive of migration.

Britain with prosperous economic conditions, and fallen in less prosperous conditions. The *extent* of this rise and fall cannot be definitively measured because of the effects of long-term trends, which certainly exist but cannot be eliminated except by an ultimately arbitrary estimate, and the changing internal structure of the population in respect of occupation, place of residence, social status and other vital non-"demographic" factors, which again can be only imperfectly measured. But the fact of the rise and fall is well established, and makes some apparent "demographic" movements more correctly describable as g in our notation, that is cyclical economic effects.

When economic conditions fluctuated slowly and in long waves the longer- and medium-term demographic factors (a and b) may well have been better worth selecting as of paramount importance. But in the twentieth century two world wars and one world slump have affected Britain (excluding Ireland of course) far more profoundly in a few years than any single economic or political event of the nineteenth century ever did. The short- and medium-term political and economic factors have become paramount.

Left to themselves the long-term demographic factors seem to imply a diminishing population in Britain within the half-century, or at most a very slight growth. But the history of the first half of the twentieth century suggests that these factors will not remain undisturbed; demography is like the spring of a mantelshelf clock, the strength of which is known. But we do not know whether the master of the house (or some interfering guest) may not rewind the clock, alter its speed, or even manipulate the hands. We cannot therefore predict, on the basis of the spring alone, what time its dial will record at a given interval from 1950; we have to arrive at some guess how serious the outside disturbances will be.

There are, however, reasons for supposing that the demographic structure of the country is less unstable than at some earlier periods, and also better controlled. By "stable" is here meant resistant to herd-like changes in mass behaviour, or to the effects of other great changes, which implies that greater "control", or choice, is exercised by individual parents in their decisions on the sizes of their families. In the nineteenth century a fall in the death-rate almost inevitably meant a large rise in population, the main reason for this being that the rate at which potential parents had children was liable to continue at its previous high level. A similar situation prevails in many backward countries to-day. But in Britain a fall in the death-rate would not provide a similarly firm basis for predicting a rapid increase in population, not merely because specific death-rates are already low for the child-bearing age-groups of women, but also because of the rapidity with which an educated and culturally advanced community can adjust its births to its mortality situation. Whether, in any particular circumstance, the power of control *will* be exercised is a particular question; that it *can* be exercised (it sometimes has been) in Britain is now beyond dispute.

§ 2. *Economic Arguments for a Stable or Falling Population.*
Many powerful economic arguments can be brought to support the demographers' view that Britain's population will never much exceed 50 millions, and that it will probably fall (and certainly *ought* to fall) below that figure. These economic arguments for a smaller population are fourfold, relating to land, labour, capital and overseas trade.

First, with regard to land, that term has several different economic meanings. In its simplest possible sense it denotes a sector of the earth's surface. So far, but only so far, as agriculture is extensive this is a relevant sense. The density of population to land in the United Kingdom is 0·342 per hectare (or of land to population 2·92 hectares per head); for England and Wales alone the figure is 0·477 per hectare (that is only 2·1 hectares per head).[1] If countries are ranked by density, England and Wales come out rather high in the list.[2] The figures tend to sound more frightening when expressed as "persons per square mile"; 2·1 hectares per head (i.e., about 5 acres) does not sound so bad, until it is recalled that the figure includes *all* land, and not only land used for, or available for, agriculture.

The density figure in itself proves neither that population is too dense, nor that the country could economically become even more thickly populated. Economists who fear a shortage of Britain's land in this connection are (or should be) thinking less of the overall density figure than of the amount of cultivable land available, and of the cost of maintaining it cultivated. Land, as a unit of extension, is the subject of many competing demands. The naturally best land agriculturally for miles around often tends to be near the towns; indeed its existence there may have been one reason for the siting, and growth, of the town in that position. The competing demands of the town for land may thus not only take land away from agriculture but some of the naturally "best", and more or less irreplace-

[1] For England alone, without Wales, 0·522 or 1·9 hectares a head. This can be converted into acres per head by multiplying by 2½.

[2] In population per square kilometre England and Wales had a figure of 291, just below the Netherlands, 312, and above Belgium, 283, but well below the 500 of the Egyptian Nile Valley or the 360 of some Indonesian islands (see *Preliminary Report on the World Social Situation*, U.N. Dept. of Social Affairs, New York, 1952).

able-land. Well-known examples are the land of the Lea Valley near London, and the market-garden land to the west of Hammersmith, and the fertile strip that lies between Birmingham and Coventry.

Cultivable land in Britain is limited, and is evidently scarcer than in many other countries. This will not be a factor of importance in restricting the growth of British population *unless* this land has to be used at a cost so extravagantly uneconomic (that is, so dear) that population would be better served by emigration on a mass scale, or that families can no longer be supported at a tolerable standard of living, or that actual starvation must set in. Those who regard the limited quantity of land as a major factor, now, and in the near future, limiting population growth, fear one or other of these dangers.

It will be argued below that these fears, in respect of British agriculture, though by no means groundless, are less overwhelming than they may appear at first sight. There are reasons for supposing that the dangers envisaged may be staved off in the future as in the past, although not necessarily by following the same policies as heretofore.

§ 3. *The Supply of Raw Materials.* Many raw materials were "plentiful" per head of population in the early days of Britain's industrial revolution : iron ore and lead, as well as coal, copper and tin, were exported in the first half of the nineteenth century, whereas now Britain is deficient, in relation to its own and to the world's demands, of every raw material except coal, which itself is surplus to domestic demand only in exceptional years—and will be deficient permanently from about 1960, according to current estimates. There are far fewer counter-arguments available than to the allegation that Britain's agricultural potential is too low. The raw material position is undoubtedly very serious. Britain cannot live as an industrial nation without an assured flow of imports of raw materials. Those who forecast an interruption to that flow, for whatever reason, rightly draw attention to the corollary that Britain's population, in those circumstances, would be too great.

If a cross-classification is made, those raw materials which are the sources of power may be regarded as having special importance for an industrial country. Until very recently the main fuel materials were coal, oil, natural gas and water-power. Coal and lignite provided [1] 47 per cent of the world's energy supplies, and liquid fuels 20 per cent, the rest being supplied by natural gas (7 per cent) and hydro-electricity (6 per cent), or being provided in unrecorded ways by non-commercial sources (19 per cent). In units of "coal equivalent" the use in mid-century varied from less than half a ton per head per annum used in Asia, to over 7 tons a head used in North America. If the countries using over $1\frac{1}{2}$ tons a head are classed as "developed", this will include North America, Northern Europe, Oceania, the Union of South Africa and the U.S.S.R., and exclude the rest of the world. Europe and North America produced and consumed 72 per cent of the world's solid fuels in 1949. The "developed areas" as a whole produced and consumed some 88 per cent, and also provided 30 million tons of coal for under-developed countries or ships' bunkers. Europe as a whole was much more dependent for its energy upon solid fuels, however, than was North America.

The position with regard to liquid fuel sources was very

---

[1] Based on figures for 1949 (U.N. Statistical Papers, Series J, No. 1, *World Energy Supplies in Selected Years, 1929–1950*, New York, September 1952).

different. Europe produced less than 2 per cent of the world's crude oil, but consumed 11 per cent of the world total.

Europe's share of world production of solid fuels declined between 1929 and 1950 (from 48 per cent to 41 per cent), and Britain's share declined even more steeply than this.[1] This trend seems likely to continue, as new sources of solid fuel are opened up in less developed parts of the world.

In 1929 Britain's consumption of commercial fuel per head (in tons of "coal equivalent") was greater than that of any other European country except Belgium, at 4·11 tons against Belgium's 4·53; by 1950 Britain's average had risen to 4·42 against Belgium's 3·50. Norway and Sweden also had high figures of use of energy resources.

Britain's fuel position over the next fifty years can hardly be discussed seriously except in relation to that of Western Europe as a whole, and to the world political situation. For evidently any substantial rise in its fuel usage per head to, say, the level reached by the U.S. in 1937 (5·89 tons a head), or 1950 (7·51 tons a head), would imply a linking of Britain's electricity industry with continental hydro-electric sources, or heavy coal imports, or much heavier liquid fuel imports from a peaceful Middle East. It is also, of course, vital that Britain should succeed in expanding its own coal output, but the most optimistic planners could hardly suppose that all the energy needed could be derived from this source of fuel. It seems, indeed, more likely that for economic as well as technological reasons British coal will become in an increasing proportion a raw material, and that other sources of energy will be sought and developed, such as atomic power.

[1] From 19 to 14 per cent.

Evidently Britain's industrial growth, and therefore the population that it can support, depends upon, among other factors, the solution it finds to the problem of fuel Atomic energy may have become commercial by the end of the period.

The point for population growth is, however, this: whatever solution is found in detail it will demand, so far as can now be seen, a very heavy capital investment. If *no* solution is found, then the economy must tend to contract, and so must the population; if *any* solution is found, in any of the directions that now seem even remotely feasible, an investment must be incurred so great as to demand at least as large a working population as the present, and possibly a larger one, in order to gain economic results from a huge indivisible expenditure.

Those who argue that fuel supplies will dictate a smaller population must rest their case, therefore, on the belief that the fuel problem will be only partially solved, and that, if increased energy per head is required, it will be obtained not by tapping new sources of energy, but by reducing the number of "heads ' and making full use of the limited resources available within our boundaries, or purchasable at a reasonable price on the world markets.

§ 4. *The Balance of Payments Argument.*   Britain's balance of payments problems are short-term, medium-term and long-term.   The effective case against a growing population in Britain over the next fifty years must rest on a long-term analysis.

Three propositions are usually advanced.   The first is that, however much world production expands over the next fifty years, world trade is unlikely to expand so much, and may hardly expand at all.   The second is that Britain will be competing, in this narrow world market for exports, with a few powerful rivals, as well as with smaller but rising competitors, and that both these classes will be strategically well placed to secure together an increasing share of the limited world trade at Britain's expense (the best to be hoped for Britain being a stationary share). Finally, the third proposition is that the volume of imports required by Britain will be geared to the size of its population. Each of these propositions is defensible in the light of past experience, and together they add up to a formidable argument in favour of a static or reduced British population.

The first proposition depends on the extrapolation of a trend that was very marked between 1913 and 1939. Between those dates, world manufacturing production approximately doubled, but the volume of world trade in manufactures failed to rise.[1] Some observers [2] think that the long-term downward trend of foreign trade in manufactures as a proportion of industrial output must persist, at least until 1960; but few have prognosticated a reversal of the trend at a later date. If so, by 1960 world trade in manufactures may not be more than 40–50 per cent above the 1937 level. Britain's share of this trade rose to 23 per cent in 1950, as against 19 per cent in 1937, but thereafter fell, concomitantly with the industrial re-emergence of Germany and Japan on world markets. On Professor Robinson's calculations of Britain's chances to earn currencies by exports (visible and invisible), not more than 80 per cent of the volume of 1938 imports can readily be financed in 1960. He suggests that the moral is that the economic system will have to be adjusted to be viable with a long-term lower level of imports. Some would

[1] MacDougall, 1947, p. 85, and see *Industrialization and Foreign Trade* (League of Nations, 1945), p. 157, and Diagram VII, p. 226, where an index for mining and manufacturing is shown.

[2] E.g., Robinson, A., 1953, p. 3.

15

evidently proceed from his argument to the corollary that British population is too great.

The second proposition is based on the judgment that Britain's foreign competitors are going to be strategically better placed to develop foreign sales than Britain will be.   In 1952 about 75 per cent of world exports in manufactures was in the hands of seven leading countries—the U.S.A., the U.K., West Germany, France, Canada, Belgium and Switzerland.   An eighth country, Japan, seemed likely soon to rise to about the fifth place.   The U.S.A. and the U.K. had by far the largest individual shares.[1]   It has been shown that even in 1950 the U.K.'s share of trade in general had declined as compared with 1937, and in 1937 there had already been a heavy fall in the percentage of world trade accruing to the U.K. and to France, while the shares of the U.S.A., Japan and Canada had risen very substantially, and those of Sweden, Belgium and Germany quite noticeably, since 1913.   Thus Britain has a twofold problem: of selling against the keen rivalry of a few of the most industrialized countries in the world, which have, moreover, several sources of economic strength as exporters that are not available to Britain, and secondly, of meeting the competition of less powerful but rising industrial nations springing up all over the world.

The first part of this problem is, in effect, that Britain is in an especially vulnerable position in relation to the wider world issues of chronic dollar shortage and industrialization of under-developed areas.   The second part is due to the compound interest effect of any economic advantage, one kind of relative economic strength paving the way to a more than proportionate acquisition of another.

[1] *Ibid.*, 1953, p. 3.

Britain's trade relations with Brazil in recent years, for example, aptly illustrate both these difficulties. At a time when Brazil was flourishing in boom conditions and attracting more and more American capital, and with that capital developing a two-way trade with the U.S., Britain had to curtail its trade with Brazil owing to bad debts and currency difficulties; it would seem that the economic power of the U.S. suffices to override bad debts and Brazil's own dollar shortage, both of which are nearly fatal to the development of a healthy non-dollar trade. Britain would not be able to play a large part in the industrialization of under-developed areas, nor to compete effectively in the world market for industrial products, if its financial liquidity remained low.

The third proposition is based upon a judgment as to the future of British agriculture, on the character of Britain's social and economic development, and on the likely future terms of trade for agricultural products, raw materials and other imports deemed necessary to this country.

§ 5. *Counter-Arguments (Demographic and Economic) in Favour of a Stable or Increasing Population.* Arguments on demography, where they proceed from factual statements to normative assertions, unavoidably are based upon social views or social prejudices. Demography as a science provides techniques of analysis, not results or conclusions. In the particular case of Great Britain there are no demographic facts that suffice to support the view that the British population *must* fall, or *must* stay stable, over the next fifty years. Family size has declined, but not in such a way, or for so long a period, as makes it impossible to imagine that population might not again rise by natural increase.

The birth-rate of Great Britain is the result, so it is contended here, mainly of the social and economic environmental conditions, rather than of some underlying trend in family-building behaviour, determined by internal or external forces of a non-economic character. That British populations are still capable of high rates of natural increase is sufficiently proved by the birth-rates that prevail among the European settlers of Northern Rhodesia, for example, and by the high proportion at home of unmarried females aged 18 to 24.

What are the main economic factors that are likely to affect the possibility, and desirability, of Britain supporting a larger population over the next fifty years? Those at present known to be likely are the opening up of new sources of raw materials, the development of new forms of power, the increasing application of scientific knowledge to the supply of food (both in agricultural techniques and in the development of synthetic processes), the bringing of the simpler kinds of capital equipment into co-operation with the reserves of under-employed labour of the world, the mass application of scientific and technical development to ways of building, distribution and domestic work, and a widening of the capital already invested into means of large-scale transport. All these processes have begun; it is not idle speculation to assume that these visible trends will persist.

On such an assumption, it is far from clear that Britain will, or should, have a smaller population in the year 2000 than it had in the year 1950. It will be noted that this is not the same thing as supposing that Britain will regain its economic supremacy, nor even that there will not be grave economic crises for this country to overcome. But Britain is well placed, both geographically and culturally, in relation to the world's population densities. Peaceful world development along the lines just mentioned almost unavoidably implies British economic development.

Several of the economic features of the next fifty years seem likely to work in the direction of preserving the importance of the urban industrial civilization, which runs in a great north-west–south-east belt, from Glasgow and Manchester to Prague. Air transport brings remote places near, and so "puts them on the map", but, at the same time, the easier transport becomes, the greater the advantages of concentration. Thus, when steam navigation opened up the Great Lakes and the China coast, this enhanced, and did not detract from, the growth of Liverpool, Rotterdam and Hamburg. When London Transport extended the possibility of suburban living deep into the home counties, this did not take activity away from the vicinity of Piccadilly Circus, but extended the great wheel of which that Circus is the hub. So, too, the industrial and agricultural growth of India, China, Africa and South America may well bring increased trade and activity to the skilled industrialists of Western Europe as well to those of Eastern America.

That is not, of course, a certain outcome of the trend of economic events, but only a possibility. It depends upon, among other factors, the form that the economic development of overseas areas takes. Long-distance transport is, even to-day, the smaller part of total transport; local transport is always denser than long-distance hauls. But if the sketch that has been given is even approximately correct there seems to be no economic-geographical reason why Britain, granted a favourable form of rapid world economic development, should not support an even larger population in A.D. 2000 than in 1950.

What then of the economic objections, of the "burden" argument, or the balance of payments problem?

The first of these arguments cannot be precisely refuted, because the shapes of all the dynamic functions involved are not known. But it seems likely that a large, and rather wide, capital base will still be essential to the British economy. Britain's survival as an industrial nation demands the adaptation of its industries to extensive changes in the world situation; it starts off on this task with an alarmingly large legacy of obsolescent or even obsolete industrial and domestic buildings and equipment, and social capital. To replace that stock, to increase it, and to make full use of the new replacements may require a larger rather than a smaller working population.

For example, the existence of a building industry of one million operatives is an asset so long as an extensive policy of replacement can be afforded, and is required by demand. Or again, a modernized iron and steel industry, consisting of larger units of production than were common in Britain in the 1930's, needs a large home market if economies arising from high consumption are to be secured.

Those who argue against a rising population on the grounds that it imposes a "burden" on the economy sometimes seem to fear that the country will have too little capital per head, and at others that the labour force will be insufficient to sustain the burden. A situation can indeed be imagined where both factors would be insufficient for any added burden. But the two factors cannot be scarce relatively to each other at the same time. If the "burden" argument, as applied to Britain, is a manpower argument, then it can indeed be seen, from British experience in World War II, that the manpower problem rapidly becomes acute for this country when a great economic burden is imposed, additional to the normal necessity to produce enough for current consumption, and for "normal" capital formation. This provides, however, an argument for an increased, not for a reduced, population in the long run. If the "burden" is the short-run burden of raising children, then immigration ought to be encouraged rather than child-raising. But there are obvious social reasons for not pressing this point to its logical conclusion.

The introduction of highly labour-saving capital appliances might weaken the argument in favour of a higher population, and strengthen the case for a form of economic development that could be attained with a smaller working population. But let us imagine what would be the result if the present factory employed population of Britain [1] attained an output per head double that which it now attains. If it were distributed as at present, surpluses of unsold goods would soon arise; but if it could be suitably re-distributed, some persons perhaps leaving industry altogether for service occupations that cannot be now manned, and some (or all) taking part of their increased real income in the form of increased leisure, the final result could hardly fail to be that the total employed population (factory and non-factory) would rise rather than decline. For there are innumerable unsatisfied needs that could then be satisfied within these islands or abroad.

The true problem then arising would not be so much that of employment as of raw materials and of imports generally. This brings us once more to consider the

[1] The M.O.L. gives a figure of 8,483,000 persons employed in all manufacturing industries (excluding building and contracting, gas, water and electricity, transport, distributive trades and miscellaneous services)—*M.O.L. Gazette*, February 1953.

crucial difficulty; how far the problem of procuring imports is insoluble, and whether it is, as some suppose, the inexorable law of diminishing returns at last restraining the British population from further advance, after, for two centuries, successive exploits of ingenuity have succeeded in resisting that law.

As already noted, this formidable problem is to be thought of as long- rather than as short-term in its effects on population. Sometimes the two kinds of effects have tended to become confused with each other. In the difficult years from 1946 to 1950, the British export drive coincided with a painful recuperation in world agriculture, and, in the same years, Britain had to meet the difficulties created by its violent losses in capital assets at home, at sea and abroad. Calculations to the effect that if population were to be increased by 1 per cent, this would involve a rise of 2½ per cent in *exports*, to pay for the extra imports involved, were made at that time. But the numerical results (they varied between one authority and another) were based on assumptions as to the marginal propensity to import, and the terms of trade, which took no account of any long-term dynamic changes that might be favourable to this country, and the current economic conditions of that period, with its succession of crises, seemed to justify a pessimistic outlook.

A long-term self-denying policy should enable Great Britain to live comfortably with imports limited to only 80 per cent of the quantity imported in 1938. Western German agricultural production, inefficient though it is in output per man compared with British, provides 55 per cent of German bread grain needs, and 95 per cent of its meat requirements (the German diet is of lower high-quality protein value than the British). Even in value terms Western German agricultural production exceeds that of the U.K., although the arable area is not much greater in Western Germany than here.[1] Again, Western Germany's consumption of motor spirit and diesel oil was about half that of the United Kingdom. Britain imported three times as great a value of manufactured goods as Western Germany. The U.K.'s imports are still on the scale that might be expected of a country that had for decades followed a policy of free trade, while Western Germany had the advantages (and, of course, the disadvantages) of an autarchic system built up over a long period, which kept down its standard of living but insulated it from adversities of fluctuating foreign currency balances.

This is not an argument in favour of the U.K. copying the industrial and commercial pattern of autarchic Germany. But the contrast illustrates the point that Britain could, if pressed, or if the political choice were made, hope to manage on a far lower level of imports than it now deems indispensable.

Furthermore, there are some grounds for hoping that Britain's export prospects are not so dim as is feared. Mr. Tyszynski has indeed shown [2] that, excluding German and Japanese trade, even in 1950 the U.K.'s share of trade had declined in general from 1937, and in 1937 there had already been a heavy fall. But while he pointed out the seriousness of this trend, he also analysed the main industries in which Britain gained a share from 1937 to 1950, notably agricultural machinery, electrical goods, vehicles and non-ferrous metals, and he, like Professor Phelps-Brown,[3] produced evidence to suggest that Britain's export prices rose less than the world average

1 See *Economic Survey of Europe Since the War*, E.C.E., 1953.
2 Tyszynski, 1951, p. 6.
3 Phelps-Brown, 1949.

in 1950 (from pre-war), and that the failure to gain a greater export trade was at least not primarily due to higher relative costs.

The pessimism that suggests that Britain's long-term trading problem is insoluble (that is, that it can never balance its overseas accounts, and must eschew population growth for fear of exacerbating this difficulty) is largely founded on the belief, much publicized for political reasons, that the failure to sell abroad was due solely or mainly to British real wages (or real wages inclusive of social benefits) being out of line with world costs generally. There are two schools of thought on this issue. The extremists of the pessimistic school treat the problem as in effect self-evident.[1] If more exports are not sold prices are too high; wages should therefore be reduced, or the pound devalued as a means to securing the same end. The more moderate of these "classical" thinkers take their stand on the law of comparative costs, as of long-term significance.[2]

The opposing school rests its case upon two factors, the elasticities of demand and supply, and the importance of the income factor rather than the price factor in determining the volume of international trade. They argue that it would be unavailing for Britain to devalue its currency at frequent intervals, and that the solution to the balance of payments problem is an appropriate change in the structure of the British economy. This presumably implies a policy of deliberate reduction in Britain's propensity to import, and an increase in its capacity to export.

The merits of these opposing views cannot be finally resolved. The future population of Great Britain is seen,

[1] See Kent, 1951, and Robbins, 1953.
[2] See Viner, 1953.

however, clearly to depend upon which type of industrial and commercial policy is pursued, and upon how far it is successful. If Britain is to support a larger population, it must succeed in overcoming the obstacles to its exports, both visible and invisible, and in restraining by a cautious policy the volume of the imports it requires.

This is, however, only an incomplete part of the economic problem that faces Britain. The wider problem is none other than that of the development of the backward areas, which means in a practical sense, the development of the whole world. The future population of Britain, like many other results, will depend upon the pattern of investment in many other countries. Mere restrictionism, necessary in some directions, will not solve Britain's balance of payments difficulties. Only if the countries which need investment, either in the direct form of capital goods, or in the indirect form of consumption goods to provide a "wages" fund during a period of build-up, want to obtain these goods from Britain, can this country continue to fulfil a function analogous to that which it has long performed. The size of the future population that Britain can support will be decided not within these islands but on the larger world stage.

§ 6. *Political and Social Pros and Cons.* The relationship of population size to political power is possibly as complex as most other strategic relationships; evidently it would be foolish and naïve to suppose that the most populated countries were the most powerful, yet, on the other hand, there may well be considerable substance in the view that, other things being equal (particularly real incomes per head), the larger political entity exceeds in strength the smaller. The main reason why population alone does not spell power is that the economic link between a potential labour force and an effective production of military material varies in its leverage from one country to another; those with a much higher productivity per head gaining a military potential out of proportion to their size.

French writers have traditionally been aware of the importance of population size for military strength. But they have, perhaps, tended to overlook the importance of what was contained in the "other things equal" qualification to this doctrine. British writers have tended to avoid explicit discussion of the theme. Yet in everyday controversy there is general recognition of the power factor implied by population.

According to the dogmas of a small clique of economists, discussion of these matters is inconsistent with the scientific calling of disciples of the art of which Adam Smith was one of the founders; yet Smith himself emphasized that the first duty of the sovereign was defence, and did not hesitate to discuss the fiscal and economic consequences of this institutional duty and necessity.

In the eighteenth century Gibbon remarked that no state was thought, by the ablest politicians, to be capable of maintaining above 1 per cent of its members "in arms and idleness", which presumably meant that about 2 per cent of the national income was then, in peace-time and at a pinch, available for defence purposes. In the French Wars, Pitt no doubt exceeded this maximum. At the beginning of the twentieth century a figure of 3 per cent was thought to be high, and in 1913 4 per cent represented an unheard-of arms race. The Fascist powers (Germany and Italy) reached 12–14 per cent in the years leading up to World War II. At present the U.S. seems to be spending about 15 per cent of its national income on arms. Evidently the military resources of a nation will depend largely (and for material reasons only, ignoring moral factors) upon the size of its national income, and the degree to which it can tax its resources for such purposes.

Crude population numbers nevertheless still play some part. However severely the strategic rôle of infantry has declined, it remains the arm of final tactical assault, and essential for police purposes and the occupation of hostile territory. A country like Britain, which can raise four and a half millions in the armed forces,[1] carries more weight in the world to-day (just for that reason) than a country like Sweden, with a fighting force perhaps no less efficient man for man, but smaller.

In this section we are concerned with Britain's political power only. Another factor in that power must be how it can be mobilized, and the relation of the mobilized force to the civilian industrial (and, of course, commercial and professional) echelons that support it. Economies of scale become very important in this context, as well as degrees of organization. It seems doubtful whether an island power with much less than 50 millions could have fought a war so effectively as Britain fought World War II; even so, and even with a far more successful mobilization of total manpower than Germany, Britain was outnumbered and outgunned heavily as a European power.

It was observed on theoretical grounds that militarists tended to regard the "optimum" population as some size larger than the economic optimum. This rule seems to apply to Britain, even on the most realistic assumptions. Let it be assumed that Britain has no plan to become a first-class power again, but only to maintain its

[1] In addition to which there were 1·5 millions under arms in the Home Guard.

second-class status, with a potential military strength great enough to secure its alliances, and reasonable treatment from its allies. Even on this basis, Britain is short of manpower. In previous wars it had imperial armies on which it could rely to fill this gap. If the assumption is made that these will no longer be available, then it seems fairly clear that Britain itself would be far stronger militarily if it could maintain a population not of 50 but of 70 or 80 millions. It might well become dangerously weak militarily if its population fell to 40 or 45 millions. composed predominantly of elderly and middle-aged people.

Should this power diagnosis have any merit (some further arguments in its favour arise from a review of the world situation), it would appear that British population policy, on political grounds, should be directed, if economically possible, to favouring natural increase, *and* at the same time a steady stream of European immigration. On this view, the British economy, and military plan, should be based on a closer link with Europe. As a nation of 50 millions our strength is not high; as part of a group of 240 millions (the N.A.T.O. size) or 290 millions (N.A.T.O. plus the sitters on the fence) British–Western European prospects of survival are very high indeed. What, then, of integrating Britain more closely with Western Europe?

Such a policy implies the freer immigration of Europeans into Britain. But it does not imply either a failure to develop east-west trade or a weakening of links with the empire. Such links must be maintained for economic no less than sentimental reasons; and may ultimately strengthen, not weaken, Britain's demographic position as some high-quality dominion citizens return to Britain for their education and even their careers. A dispassionate review of statistics of exports and of their places of destination readily illustrates the force of this contention.[1]

[1] The following percentages relate to the value of U.K. trade with the Commonwealth in imports, exports and re-exports:

	1913 %	1929 %	1937 %	1949 %
Imports . . .	25	29	39	48
Exports . . .	37	44	48	55
Re-exports . .	13	21	16	—

CHAPTER X

WORLD POPULATION

FOR some other countries, in addition to the U.K., economic factors are likely to predominate in determining their population growth, but to the world as a whole a different argument is perhaps applicable. A large proportion of the world's total population lives under circumstances which have given fuller rein to what are best called demographic impulses.

World population growth, as a whole, has apparently accelerated markedly in recent decades. The consequence is that the world is facing a process which may surpass in importance the "demographic revolution" of the western countries in the last hundred years.[1] The large group of countries with high fertility and considerably lower mortality, a mortality which may decline even more spectacularly in the future than in the past, may quadruple in numbers within fifty years, if there is no emigration. The countries with high mortality as well as high fertility (which include most of the larger countries of Asia and Africa, outside the U.S.S.R.) have yet to feel the impact of medical and sanitary reforms that have reduced death-rates elsewhere. Birth-rates are liable to rise rather than fall in those countries in which a reduced death-rate has resulted in a population with a lower average age than before. While it is admittedly impossible to predict how long the acceleration in the growth of world population will continue, already its accelerated

[1] See *Preliminary Report on the World Social Situation*, U.N., Dept. of Social Affairs, New York, 1952, p. 18.

growth presents large problems, and no end to that growth can yet be seen.

The consequences of this demographic surge will be felt throughout the fifty-year period now under discussion. The half-century to A.D. 2000 can hardly fail to be one in which the numbers on the globe increase at a rate that may outrun the economic organization to support them.

It would be inaccurate to describe this situation as population outrunning the means of subsistence, or to pretend that the current situation necessarily illustrates one instance of an inexorable "tendency" of population to multiply too fast. It would be nearer the truth to suggest that the special demographic circumstances of the world have posed an economic problem which will be extremely difficult to solve, but which is not in principle insoluble.

Since 1913 world population has increased perhaps a little more rapidly than the production of foodstuffs by world agriculture. Such would seem to be the conclusion derivable from the accompanying graph,[1] which is based upon the best statistics available at the moment (those compiled by the League of Nations and the United Nations); but it must be remembered that index numbers of production over such a long period are open to a wide margin of error, and subject to several difficulties of interpretation. An index number for "mining and manufacturing" output, shown on the same graph, rose out of all proportion to the recorded increase in population.

If these index numbers can be taken to represent, very roughly and tentatively, changes of real significance, some very interesting conclusions can be drawn. First, it is obvious that, as might be expected from the perishable

1 See Diagram VII.

nature of foodstuffs, and from the fact that world population as a whole lives above the absolute minimum apart
from local famines, the output of food and the increase
of population have, on the long view, advanced at something like the same rate.   But the output of food has been

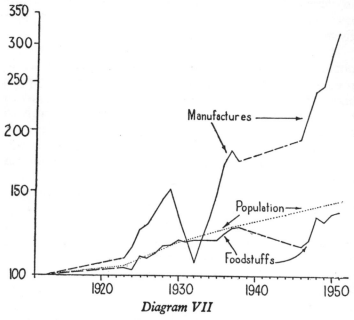

Diagram VII

World trends in Population, Foodstuffs and Manufacturers,
1913–1950 (1913=100)

apparently rather erratic.   It cannot be definitely concluded that it is *more* erratic than changes in population,
since censuses are not taken every year, but it seems very
likely that in peace-time this is so.   There were violent
shifts in population numbers in the war years; but in
those years food production also fluctuated violently.   It
cannot be argued from the trend that population tends

to increase faster than food output.   In the late 1920's the curves illustrate the well-known phenomenon of the period of agricultural surpluses.   Food output was then tending to rise faster than population.   In the world, as then organized politically and economically, the result was a serious crisis, but this was not due to everyone having too much to eat.   It was the period of "poverty in the midst of plenty".   In World War II there was a staggering reduction in world agricultural output, far greater as a percentage than the temporary drop in population—if it fell at all for the world as a whole.   The post-war crisis of balances of payments and continued rationing were largely the consequence of this set-back to world food production.

The overall rate of increase in population being of the order of 1 per cent per annum, it would seem that the world needs to expand its production generally, and its food supply also by a rate of about 1 per cent.   This would by no means be a technically insuperable task. The problem is not that of population increasing faster than food supply in this literal sense.

But the food problem of the world is nowadays seen as a problem of nutrition ; so that the population problem is a problem not merely of food but of economic and social organization.

§ 1. *The Food Problem.*   The nutritional needs of individuals vary, and it cannot be assumed that scientific knowledge of the requirements, even on average, of a consumer is definitive or complete.   Vitamin deficiencies are known to exist on an extensive scale in many parts of the world, and, according to current dietetic theory, animal proteins and other essential ingredients of a "protective" diet are especially scarce.   Starting from a calculation of needs, the United Nations' experts arrived at much the same conclusion [1] as the F.A.O. reached in 1946. [They conclude that to bring the diets of people living in the Far East, the Near East and Africa up, even in a moderate degree, towards an adequate level, would need twice as great a quantity of cereals as are now produced, and much more than twice as much in the way of pulses, meat, milk, eggs and fish.] In Latin America and Europe the percentage increase (except for pulses) could be smaller; but even in Oceania and North America, some increase is necessary. But in the Far and Near East, the increase in cereal production since the last world war has only been half that of population, and even in Europe the agricultural recovery has been disappointing.

Thus, the food problem is not in itself a population problem; it is a problem of remedying some of the hopeless malnutrition so long endemic in many parts of the world, and mainly the result of bad organization and of poverty. The remedies which the United Nations' experts suggest (such as the big increase in meat and milk consumption) are not necessarily the most economical, or the most effective, ways of meeting the undoubted dietary deficiencies. The experts' remedies seem indeed to have been thought out more fully from the nutritionist's than from the economist's point of view.

Even in Europe, where birth-rates are falling, and populations beginning to age (although not yet to decline, in general), population increase has outrun food production. The position is unusual. Since 1913 the total population of Europe (excluding the U.S.S.R.) has risen by 21 per cent, but grain production has declined by 5 per cent. Potato production has risen slightly, and sugar-beet production considerably (41 per cent). Total livestock (ex-

[1] *Ibid.*, p. 44.

cluding horses) has risen by 10 per cent, and the horse population has declined by 17 per cent. European agriculture thus seems, as a whole, to have stagnated; although the story for various separate regions and countries of Europe gives a different account of the matter than the European average. What seems to have happened in Europe as a whole is that the increased population has been supported partly by increased imports and partly by the foodstuffs released by the gradual abolition of the horse and other draught animals.

Great political disturbances have ravished European agriculture since 1913, and large shifts in agricultural populations have not improved the ease of management, or the continuity of cultivation. Agricultural land in Europe has been lost, for other purposes, on quite a substantial scale (4·3 million hectares from 1911 to 1938, and a further amount, 2·4 million hectares, from 1938 to 1950). The decline in land use affected grain production most of all, and fallow land; the acreages of permanent grass, industrial crops and potatoes and vegetables all increased over the last fifty years. In 1938 the U.S.S.R. had 102 million hectares sown to grains, about 15 per cent greater than the area of the whole of the rest of Europe put together. Russia before 1914 was, of course, a heavy exporter of grain to Western Europe, supplying about half the needs of that part of the world.

Eastern and Mediterranean Europe have had a rather different production history from that of Western Europe. Territorial changes after both world wars had the effect of progressively shifting surplus grain-producing areas from Western to Eastern Europe. Other particularly adverse factors have affected the twentieth-century development of European agriculture, such as the disturbing effects of two world wars (both of which decreased population to some extent, but food production to an even greater extent); of the agricultural depression of the 1930's; and of the sweeping changes of land tenure in the U.S.S.R. with its initially upsetting consequences. In a more suitable political and economic atmosphere European agriculture seems to be technically capable of a much more rapid advance than can yet be recorded. A large-scale flow of agricultural products from the East to the West is a technical possibility, for example, and there are many other ways in which the land resources of Europe as a whole could be far better exploited with existing technical knowledge.

Agricultural statistics make it very noticeable that some of the best agricultural practices, in terms of output per unit of input, the latter measured in units of various factors of production, seem to be obtained in the more industrialized, and more densely populated, countries of Europe. Thus the yields per cow (expressed in thousands of litres) are highest in the Netherlands, Denmark, Belgium, Switzerland and the United Kingdom. Professor Dudley Stamp has emphasized the same point by means of an index of agricultural production, which shows yield per acre highest on average for industrialized European countries.

On the world scale, a similar law seems to prevail; the more industrialized a country, the higher the productivity of its agriculture. In Japan, for example, rice yield per hectare is more than three times as high as that of India. Diminishing returns in agriculture in the strict technical sense seem to occur here and there, but are the exception rather than the rule. To increase the use of fertilizer in the world as a whole would more than proportionately increase the yield in tons of food, assuming that all other factors of production were to be held constant; where agriculture has been "industrialized" yields seem often to have increased more than proportionately to the additional capital invested.

But are there not diminishing returns to labour? The answer to that point is not so certain, for while there seems to be disguised unemployment, and an over-supply of labour in some agricultural areas, in others additional labour could be employed with a more than proportionate increase in the tons of food produced (for example, in areas of not fully exploited land hitherto very lightly and extensively cultivated, or in labour-intensive market gardening not yet pushed to its limits). The net effect of these two opposite forces cannot easily be assessed, but at least it can be said that even strict, non-temporal, diminishing returns apply only to a part of the agricultural industry.

As for diminishing returns in the looser sense, operating over time, and representing returns to changes in the scale of agricultural operations, there seems to be very little reason indeed for supposing that they need come into force for the next few decades, and still less over a fifty-year period. [Technological advance is by no means exhausted, or confined to manufacture, nor have existing discoveries all been fully exploited.]

But this amounts to a review of the technical rather than of the economic possibilities. There is an additional semi-technical point which bedevils any discussion of the economic forces that affect the chances of realizing that potential increase of food supply that a growing world population will need to keep alive and well. The additional point is that the *distribution*, between countries, of reserve supplies of agricultural land is uneven, and will lead to an unbalance in the balances of payments that the separate countries maintain.

For, as Professor Dudley Stamp has pointed out,[1] the surprising idea has to be accepted that agriculturally speaking the United States is one of the principal under-developed countries of the world.[2] Despite the high yield per man-hour of its agriculture, its yield per acre is low for a temperate climate, and its conservation, though improving, still inadequate. Together with the United States, Argentina, Canada and the U.S.S.R. are the countries from which really large increases of food supply could most readily be achieved. Compared with their immediate potential, the untapped potential of the tropical parts of Africa or other continents is remote and ineffective—so far as present technical knowledge affords any answer. At best, the tropical areas would require extensive and risky investment, while the extensively farmed areas in temperate climates may well yield increasing returns to quite moderate investment in fertilizer and machinery.

There is very little doubt that sufficient food *can* be produced to meet not only the population growth of another fifty years, but to increase the amount and quality of the food eaten by the larger proportion of the world's inhabitants. The relevant question arises, however, what economic conditions are necessary for this result to occur? What stimulus will produce that increase in food supply which nutritionists declare to be desirable?

Two kinds of farming situation reveal high " efficiency "; first, the kinds that prevail in north-western Europe, especially in Denmark and the United Kingdom. Yield per hectare is high in these countries, where farming is

---

[1] L. Dudley Stamp, *Land for Tomorrow*, 1952, pp. 114–15.

[2] The U.S.A. is certainly an under-developed area, in a more general sense, if the use of that term preferred by Professor Viner is accepted (see p. 238, below).

mechanized, and the farmers live in close contact with a highly industrialized, and densely populated, urban civilization.   Secondly, there is the situation that prevails in the more favoured agricultural regions of China and Japan, where farming is highly efficient in the sense that nothing is allowed to be wasted, and intensive production of small plots of land provides a high level in food raised per hectare, by methods akin to those used in Western market gardening.   In both instances there is an economic reason for the kind of agricultural economy that flourishes, the north-western European having to supply food in a region where land is dear, and labour cost rising, but capital goods are relatively cheap, and consumption goods in adequate supply.   In these circumstances managerial skill and organization will be well rewarded, for the real incomes of farmers will be kept reasonably high so long as they maintain their output by increasingly capitalistic methods.   In China, on the other hand, the pressing need for subsistence, and the absence of cash-crop markets, or a full supply of consumer goods, encourages a system of very small, largely self-sufficient, intensively cultivated family land holdings.

It must not be thought that extensive farming, such as is practised in the U.S.A. or Canada, is necessarily inefficient (except where it is accompanied by bad farming methods leading to soil erosion), for extensive farming, too, largely originates from the economic situation of the prairie farmers, with plentiful land, dear labour and distant markets to serve.   But it is wasteful in its use of land, and therefore it is wasteful of an important scarce resource, so far as world population presses upon land resources (or nutritional need results in such pressure).

Nutritional need is not the same thing as economic demand.   From a population point of view the raising of

nutritional standards is essential.   For population growth
to slow down, and cease to be determined largely by blind
urges, it is necessary that standards of living should rise;
and if these rise, it follows that nutritional needs will
become better satisfied.   For those needs are among the
most urgent demands that men with money to spend will
make upon the economic system.   The prospects of
raising the economic living standards of the world are
directly relevant therefore to the question whether or not
population pressures will be alleviated.

§ 2. *Economic Prospects.*   It cannot be said that, apart
from the neo-Malthusians and the neo-Godwinians mentioned in an earlier chapter, there are many economists
willing to risk their reputations upon a sketch of the
future course of world economic development and hence
of world population; a subject to which, however, it is
now most relevant to address ourselves.

Food supplies have already been discussed; we now
have to consider what type of economic development is
necessary to secure that food.   Is the distribution of
economic activity, and of incomes, throughout the world
going to be consistent with the bringing to market of the
necessary supplies?   Are other kinds of shortage going
to restrain the growth of population by imposing unpleasant forms of check to the increasing means of subsistence?   Will the world's population be halted by
shortages of clothing or shelter, or drugs, or raw materials,
or by diseases particular to overcrowding?

The economic prospects of the world are determined
not merely by the amount of its wealth, and the size of
its real income, but by the distribution of these quantities.
For it is by the offer of a distribution of wealth or income
that men àre induced, for the most part, to work and

produce more wealth or more income, though in some important instances, it is true, they work for quite different motives.

Incomes are distributed throughout the world in a very uneven manner, and a tendency has been at work to even out some of the international differences of income, just as there has been a movement within countries to alleviate the discrepancies between the purchasing power of different individuals or classes. This "tendency" or "movement", vaguely or deliberately towards more egalitarian income distribution, has been counteracted by powerful and impersonal (as well as personal) economic forces with a quite opposite or reactionary tendency. Greater economic power has accumulated in the hands of a few powerful people, and been used further to increase the differences of income.

The net result has been, so far, some increase in equality. But, even within a single country, this increase does not necessarily please all classes, or indeed even any particular class. For, supposing there are, say, three classes in a community, A, B and C, with average incomes of $£x$, $£y$ and $£z$ respectively, it would be an egalitarian measure to increase the number of people in class B by diminishing the number in class C. But if this were done on a large scale the average *income* of class B might be less than $£y$ after the change, so that even though greater equality of income was achieved, and greater average income for the community as a whole, the average income of *each class* might quite conceivably fall. But, though many, perhaps a majority, would have higher incomes, some would necessarily have lower incomes, and each class might have, on average, a lower income. People tend to identify status with income, and even though thousands more may become doctors and professional men, skilled artisans instead of unskilled workers, and so on, they may judge themselves ill-used after the change because they can no longer expect so high an income as someone in their (new) class could have expected before the change.

Greater equality is practically impossible to attain unless the average incomes of each class can be reduced. So it is an unspoken, and politically unpopular, objective of any egalitarian policy to *reduce* the average income of nearly every class in the community, so as to *raise* the average income of the community as a whole.[1] The two objectives of greater equality, and of increased overall average real income per head, are almost inevitably accompanied by reduced average class income per head, the reason being that the first two objectives are attained most easily by raising people from the lower to the higher classes.

If this reasoning is applied to international affairs, it will be seen how difficult it will be for the nutritionists' ideals to be realized without conflict and friction.   Voices are already being raised to protest against the consequences of increased egalitarianism.

Some writers seem to think [2] that there has *not* been any progress towards a rise in real *per capita* income in the world since 1913, because only a small, and shrinking, proportion of world population has had a rapid increase in its standard of living, and the rest of the world has had only a slight increase, or remained stationary.   Nevertheless, the median world income has almost certainly declined, and this is wrongly supposed to imply that there

---

[1] This is a secondary but important objective of some egalitarian policies, the idea being to increase productivity by offering individuals better chances of rising from class C to class B; and also to take advantage of technological opportunities at a more rapid rate than would be tolerated if this alleviation were not offered to those who originally composed class C.

[2] See Singer, 1949, p. 1.

has not been a rise in income, and that there has not been an increase in equality.

A fall in median income is not inconsistent with either of these results; in fact, it has been already conceded that real incomes have everywhere risen or stayed stationary.

It is important to realize that the slow rise to greater real incomes of the enormous hordes of poor people in the world would possibly reduce some of the real incomes of those now much more fortunate, and would almost certainly reduce the *average* of each social or economic group's real income, into which groups some of the backward peoples of the world succeeded in penetrating. If they become textile workers in their thousands, textile wages may fall; if they become coal-miners, coal prices may decline. Organized labour in the more advanced countries has long been frightened by this possibility, and has sought, in capitalist countries, to protect its members' interests by restrictions on migration and the support of monopolistic enterprise.

Furthermore, those living in countries usually classified as under-developed have also been living in economies mainly supported by the production of primary raw materials or agricultural products (cash crops for food or industrial use) ; these classes of product have usually been produced under much more competitive conditions than some of the principal products of the more advanced countries. For this, and other reasons, the quantum of manufactured products obtainable for a given quantum of primary goods declined steeply from 1913 to 1939, as Dr. Singer points out,[1] by something like 40 per cent. This shift in the terms of trade against the interests of the primary producers has led their leaders to look very sceptically at plans to keep them primary.

[1] *Ibid.*, p. 5.

From their point of view, increases in efficiency in the production of primary products have mainly been passed on to the customer.   Increasing returns are of no avail to them, for they produce competitively for a market with an inelastic demand and lose when production is high. Their trading terms deteriorate, and their customers gain all, or more than all, the advantage of new methods. Their main objective is, therefore, to secure by hook or by crook a more rapid industrial development, and both to import and to make more capital goods.

What is an under-developed country, and what types of country are classified, in United Nations documents for example, as under-developed?   Varying definitions are given, but this seems to be because the line between "developed" and "under-developed" countries has to be drawn arbitrarily for any particular purpose, rather than because of uncertainty as to the general meaning of the term.   Under-developed means, in general usage, poor countries, those with relatively low real *per capita* income, and the term is no doubt a euphemism, like the term under-privileged.[1]   One major economic problem of the world is precisely the fact, moreover, that the under-developed (poor) countries are not necessarily so profitable to develop, or so "ripe for development" whatever the system of profits in force, as are some of the already industrialized countries.

The economic conditions necessary to secure food and

[1] Professor Viner, in a full discussion of the word, has pointed out the difficulty of equating "under-developed" with low ratio of population to area, or countries with high interest rates, or ratio of capital to other factors, or ratio of industrial output to total output, or "young" *versus* "old"; but having knocked down these Aunt Sallies to his satisfaction he suggests that countries with good prospects of using more factors of production are to be called under-developed.   This makes the term useless for ordinary speech, as the principal under-developed countries in the world would then probably be the U.S.A. and Canada. (See Viner, 1953, pp. 94–8.)

other requirements of the increasing population of the world are, therefore, to be defined in terms of deliberate policies, rather than of natural forces. This is not a veiled way of hinting that all major economic activities should be regimented or planned in detail; it is instead a conclusion that seems to follow from the facts of to-day, and it amounts to stating that some degree of international economic planning is necessary, unless population increase is to lead to international disaster. The "natural forces" of ordinary greed and selfishness would lead to increased investment in advanced countries, extended monopolistic and perhaps military power exercised by citizens of a few leading countries over the rest of the inhabitants of the world, and gross economic exploitation of the peoples of the backward areas, as a source of cheap labour. This policy would in the long run be likely to fail for economic as well as for political reasons, but might succeed for a fairly long "short run".

International economic planning may be assumed over the next few decades to be at a minimum; this seems a more likely assumption than the more optimistic assumptions often made when the United Nations Charter was drafted, and in the immediately succeeding years. Experience has shown that the international lending of dollars on a large scale is unlikely, but that, from time to time, the United States is prepared politically to make gifts to other nations. Policies for the next fifty years must take account of a continuing dollar gap tending to recur, since America's propensity to export is so much stronger than its propensity to import, and a flow of lending, or gold, to balance the accounts will not be available.

In this situation, the under-developed countries will undoubtedly be found trying to finance their own capital development, by squeezing a surplus for investment out of their own inhabitants. Britain industrialized itself from its own capital resources, and the newly industrializing countries will most likely aim at following along the same hard path. By this means they will aim at creating the flow of capital and consumers' goods locally, which will form the real offer that they can make to their agriculturalists to induce them to increase their supplies; and similarly to their suppliers of buildings, clothing and other necessities. To a large extent they will pull themselves up by their own bootstraps, though welcoming any economic help from abroad that is offered on politically acceptable terms.

The future offers *either* a period of more intensive imperialist exploitation *or* a system of joint investment by the under-developed countries themselves and the advanced countries, the share of the former in their own development becoming larger than is often anticipated. There are many serious political difficulties in the way of the second of these two possibilities, arising not only from the world struggle for power but from the internal social structure of most of the under-developed countries, which is often ill-adapted for encouraging substantial economic development.

Supposing that all these internal political difficulties can be overcome (an uncertain hypothesis), there will still remain the problem of deciding what types of investment should be encouraged first in the under-developed countries. If the U.S.A., Canada, Argentina, Eastern Europe and Russia are to supply most of the increase in basic food, investment in less-developed countries than these should partly be directed to supplying other foodstuffs, and all other types of services and of manufactured articles, that can be sold in the food-producing areas; the less-developed countries will also see some economic advantage in producing manufactured goods for their own home markets. (It will be difficult for Professor Viner to convince them that the U.S.A. succeeded industrially *despite* its commercial policies.)

If the less-developed countries follow mildly protectionist policies (they have already gone a long way in this direction), there will arise a danger of the over-development of certain closely competing types of plant, equipment and skills.

A further major problem as to the type of investment to encourage in an under-developed country is directly related to population increase. If capital equipment is installed in, say, India, which needs labour during its process of construction, this may take into employment thousands of workers who would otherwise be raising food, more or less effectively, on the land.[1] If they are taken off the land long enough, others, owing to the high birth-rate, will replace them, and, should the construction eventually come to an end, the constructional workers will become as redundant as the Irish navvies became when railway building in Britain ceased.

Something depends upon how far the workers drawn into constructional or, later, industrial employment react to their new environment. If they acquire a higher standard of life and at the same time adopt methods of family limitation, there may be some net benefit to a country faced with a serious demographic problem. But if they are employed at real wages not much higher than they would make on the land, their habits may not change, and the situation will grow worse again unless constantly increasing injections of capital can be made to the

[1] This is a reasonable assumption in view of the high percentage at present engaged in agriculture.

17

economy. The only alleviating influence will be the increased real income for the country as a whole, which will presumably result from the use of the capital goods when completed.

If, however, some highly mechanized form of equipment is installed (say, earth-moving machinery that will do the work of hundreds of manual workers), this will provide the service of the capital goods perhaps not more cheaply, but more expeditiously, and with less social disturbance. For instead of two hundred workers being taken from the land, and used in unskilled work, only three or four men may now be required, to receive training and act as crew to the machine. There will be no large secondary increase in population, and the national income of the country will rise more rapidly than any induced population change.

If this argument is correct, there is something to be said for the apparent paradox, that it is better to install, in certain instances, labour-saving capital into under-developed and heavily populated countries, despite the cheapness of the labour on the spot. Britain's nineteenth-century industrial revolution began, after all, with a small population, and took the form of the creation of numerous small workshops, as well as of a few large enterprises. That revolution was also accompanied by, or to some extent preceded by, a revolution in agriculture. The growing towns provided more and more opportunities for work, and larger markets, together with what are now, and were then, thought to have been miserable social conditions.

Countries like India start from a different position in that they already have very large populations. They, too, will need numerous small workshops, employing a rather low amount of capital per head, to employ their large, and demographically growing, population. Such workshops, and primitive small factories, are springing up in their thousands all over the world; and if small machine-tools are supplied to these workers, the world will soon see a prodigious increase in the goods supplied to the world markets. The suggestion made here is not that this kind of development is wrong—it is, indeed, inevitable—but that it should be supplemented, where possible, by the provision of large heavy equipment, at strategic points in the backward economies, regardless of whether or not such equipment is labour-saving.

For example, fertilizer plant, irrigation, power lines and transport facilities are all types of investment that spring to mind as needing to be done mainly on a large scale, although even these kinds of investment can sometimes be partly carried out on more primitive lines. Heavy items of "indivisible" expenditure are often not suitable for piecemeal construction, even where labour is plentiful; their economy of scale is gained in use rather than in being made. This is especially true of transport facilities, which, more than any other kind of social capital, played a major rôle in the economic development of Britain,[1] and will no doubt play a similar rôle in China, India, Africa and South America.

Design of the heavy capital equipment to be installed should, however, take account of the population situation, and of the high degree of disguised unemployment prevailing in the backward countries. A form of transport equipment that would "permanently" (i.e., until wholly replaced or renewed) need a large labour force to maintain it might be appropriate in an under-developed country even though too costly in maintenance to install in an advanced country with high real wages. Any such

[1] Marshall, 1899, pp. 331–2.

choice of labour-using designs must be exercised with care, as labour costs may rise in the under-developed areas quite rapidly as capital, of various types, becomes available to the working population.

The choice of policy for the under-developed countries is not between industrialization and more intensive agricultural development.   So long as the world is organized into separate, more or less sovereign, political entities, no country will accept the rôle of being a mere agricultural provider, although as Denmark has shown, that rôle can be both technically advanced and profitable.   But even Denmark has had to encourage officially industry as well as agriculture, owing to the fact that its agriculture is exposed to world competition, and reliance on that activity alone is thus dangerous.

The true choice is between one kind or another of industrialization; for the rest, the development of agriculture is dependent upon the development of industry "at home",[1] as well as upon the country's attractiveness as a depository for foreign investment.   Agriculturists need markets near at hand, for the most part, as the long haul of food across the oceans must be regarded as exceptional, and the development of towns and cities in backward areas is a necessary complement to the rise in agricultural output needed.

The Indian peasant who produces very little surplus under current conditions, fails to manure his land, or even to work all the hours that he could, is not merely backward; he is responding to an economic environment of poverty.   If he produced a surplus over his own and his immediate neighbours' needs, that surplus could probably not be sold.   The millions who starve in famines lack

[1] I.e., in whichever under-developed country the argument is applied.

often any purchasing power, and cannot earn anything in current conditions.   The problem of poverty has to be met, as it had in nineteenth-century Britain, partly by industrialization; what that cannot cure will form a remaining social problem to be dealt with as such.   A discussion of this aspect of the problem would take us too far afield; it may at least be said that social services to relieve unavoidable poverty are already necessary, and have already been partly inaugurated.

§ 3. *Social Changes.*   Extensive social changes, as well as economic, may be required before the world population problem assumes a more manageable size.   Rapid population growth in countries like India, often exposed to famine, is unfortunately a serious handicap to the social changes, and to the economic development, from which together an economic advance is to be expected.[1]   This is the consequence of a vicious circle led by a demographic upsurge, leading back through an economic difficulty to yet a further demographic increase.

To believe this is not to believe in the inevitability of the sequence perpetuating itself, or still less in the view that India, or any other part of the world, is in some absolute sense over-populated.   The vicious circle can be summed up in the general statement that, with few exceptions, the countries in which a high proportion of people are engaged in agriculture are also countries where real incomes are relatively low, where nutrition is poor, and where there exist serious cultural as well as economic barriers to agricultural expansion.[2]   The danger of this vicious circle is that as labour becomes very cheap in relation to other means of production the circle will never be broken.

[1] See Hajnal, 1952, p. 304.   [2] See Taeuber, C., 1950, pp. 75–6.

But investment of two distinct types, labour-replacing and labour-cooperative, if judiciously selected, may serve to break the circle.

At what pace industrial development will proceed, and at what pace it will have any effect upon the high birth-rates of different social classes, is not known, nor is arm-chair speculation on these points of much value. The basic research has not been done whereby even the past influences of changed economic conditions upon birth-rates could be established, so that there is little upon which to base views as to the future.

In every part of the world research workers are seeking to discover more precisely the factors of all types that affect demographic change, and administrators and technicians are seeking to initiate or sponsor those medical and industrial changes that are favourable to a better life for the poor, in continents where poverty has never been uncommon. It is not known how soon, or even whether for certain, an increased standard of living will result in a more controlled birth-rate, but it is known that without such an increase the birth-rate will remain uncontrolled.

The work of the devoted international civil servants, of the technicians whose salaries are financed by various international bodies, and of the civil servants and indus-trialists of the under-developed countries themselves, is probably inadequate in scale, and ought to be increased in scope. It represents the most serious attempt yet made to meet the problem of world economic develop-ment in an orderly, humane and rational way. Perhaps this work will secure greater and more popular support from the countries with some economic surplus over their needs, as the severity of the population crisis of the half-century ahead forces itself more and more to be recog-nized; for, although there seems to be no insuperable economic difficulty to prevent the world from weathering this great demographic storm, to get through it will demand a large part of the energies of peoples and governments the world over. For this reason, as well as for others not within our scope, the current preoccupation of statesmen with the problem of power in its crudest sense seems to be especially unfortunate; population pressure will almost certainly become so important, within a few decades, as to form the main preoccupation of whoever find themselves in the rôle of the ultimate peacemakers of this century.

BIBLIOGRAPHY

ABRAMS, MARK, *The Population of Great Britain*, Allen & Unwin, London, 1945.

ADAMS, WILLIAM FORBES, *Ireland and Irish Emigration to the New World from 1815 to the Famine*, Yale University Press, 1932.

BARKER, DUDLEY, *People for the Commonwealth; the Case for Mass Migration*, T. W. Laurie, London, 1948.

BAUER, P. T., and YAMEY, B. S., "Economic Progress and Occupational Distribution", *Economic Journal*, Vol. XLI, 1951.

BERTRAM, J. C. L., "Population Trends and the World Biological Resources" in *New Compass of the World*, 1949.

BEVERIDGE, Sir W., "Population and Unemployment", *Economic Journal*, December, 1923.

BLACK, JOHN D., "*Coming Re-adjustments in Agriculture . . .*", *Journal of Farm Economics*, 31 (1, Part 1), 1–15, February, 1949.

—— and Kiefer, Maxine E., *Future Food and Agriculture Policy; a Program for the Next Ten Years*, McGraw Hill Book Co., New York, 1948.

BOIARSKI, A., "Certain Aspects of the Population Problem", [*Soviet*] *News*, December, 1951.

BOURGEOIS-PICHAT, M., in *Economic Survey of Europe since the War*, E.C.E., Geneva, 1953.

BOWEN, I., "Note on the Report of the Economics Committee", *Yorkshire Bulletin of Economic and Social Research*, Vol. 2, No. 2, July, 1950.

BOWLEY, A. L., "Births and Population in Great Britain", *Economic Journal*, Vol. XXXIV, 1924.

BROWN, A. J., *Applied Economics*, Allen & Unwin Ltd., 1947.

BUER, MABEL C., *The Historical Setting of the Malthusian Controversy*, London Essays in Economics in Honour of Edwin Cannan, Routledge & Sons, 1927.

CANNAN, EDWIN, *Elementary Political Economy*, 1888.

——, *A History of the Theories of Production and Distribution in English Political Economy from 1776 to 1848*, 3rd Edition, P. S. King & Son, Ltd., Westminster, 1924.

——, *Wealth*, 3rd Edition, 1928.

——, "The Changed Outlook in regard to Population 1831–1931", *Economic Journal*, Vol. XLI, p. 519, December, 1931.

CANTILLON, RICHARD, *Essai sur la nature du commerce en général*, Londres, Fletcher Gyles dans Holborn, 1755 (reprinted London, Macmillan, 1931).

CARROTHERS, W. A., *Emigration from the British Isles*, P. S. King & Sons, 1929.

CARR-SAUNDERS, A. M., *Population*, Oxford University Press, 1925.

Census 1951, England and Wales, Preliminary Report, H.M.S.O., 1951.

Census 1951, Great Britain, One Per Cent Sample Tables.

Census of Scotland, 1951, H.M.S.O., Edinburgh.

CHANG, PEI-KANG, *Agriculture and Industrialization*, Harvard University Press, Cambridge, Mass., 1949.

CLARK, COLIN, *Conditions of Economic Progress*, 1st Edition, 1940; 2nd Edition, 1951.

CLARK, F. LE GROS, and PIRIE, N. W. (Ed.), *Four Thousand Million Mouths*, Oxford University Press, London, 1951.

CONNELL, K. H., *The Population of Ireland, 1750–1845*, Clarendon Press, Oxford, 1950.

COOK, R. C., *Human Fertility*, Gollancz, London, 1951.

COX, PETER R., "Estimating the Future Population", *Applied Statistics*, Vol. I, No. 2, June, 1952.

DALTON, H., "The Theory of Population", *Economica*, Vol. VIII, 1928.

DARWIN, CHARLES GALTON, *The Next Million Years*, Rupert Hart-Davies, London, 1952.

DAVIS, J. S., "Our Changed Population Outlook", *American Economic Review*, Vol. XLII, No. 3, June, 1952.

DE CASTRO, JOSUE, *Geography of Hunger*, Gollancz, London, 1952.

DODD, N. E., *The Listener*, Vol. XLVII, No. 1212, May 22, 1952.

EISNER, R., "Under-Employment Equilibrium Rates of Growth", *American Economic Review*, March, 1952.

ELLIS, HOWARD S., *Survey of Contemporary Economics*, Blakiston, 1948.

——, *Readings in Business Cycle Theory*, Allen & Unwin, London, Vol. II of Blakiston Series of republished articles on Economics; Chairman for Vol. II, Gottfried Haberler. First published in Great Britain, 1950.

FELLNER, WILLIAM, *Monetary Policies and Full Employment*, University of California Press, Berkeley, Los Angeles, 1946.

FERENCZI, IMRE, *The Synthetic Optimum of Population*, International Institute of Intellectual Co-operation, League of Nations, Paris, 1938.

——, "Migrations (Modern)", *Encyclopædia of Social Sciences*, Vol. 10, 1933.

—— and WILLCOX, W. F., *International Migration*, Vol. I, *Statistics*, International Labour Office, Bureau of Economic Research, 1929.

FIELD, J. A., *Essays on Population and Other Papers*, University of Chicago Press, 1931.

FOOD AND AGRICULTURAL ORGANIZATION, UNITED NATIONS, Yearbooks.

——, *The State of Food and Agriculture*, 1948 and later years.

FORD, C. S., and BEACH, F. A., *Patterns of Sexual Behaviour*, Eyre and Spottiswoode, 1952.

FORSYTH, WILLIAM D., *The Myth of the Open Spaces*, Melbourne University Press, Melbourne, 1942.

GLASS, D. V., *The Struggle for Population*, Clarendon Press, Oxford, 1936.

——, (Ed.), *An Introduction to Malthus*, Watts, London, 1953.

——, "Population and Family Limitation", *The Listener*, Vol. L, No. 1274, July 30, 1953.

GODWIN, WILLIAM, *Of Population. An Enquiry concerning the Power of Increase in the Numbers of Mankind, being an answer to Mr. Malthus's essay on that subject*, Longman, Hurst, Rees, Orme & Brown, Paternoster Row, London, 1820.

HAJNAL, J., Review of M. Pierre George's "Introduction", 1951, in *Milbank Memorial Fund Quarterly*, Vol. XXX, No. 3, July, 1952.

HANSEN, A. H., "Economic Progress and Declining Population Growth", *American Economic Review*, 1939.

——, *Business Cycles and National Income*, W. W. Norton & Co., Inc., New York, 1951.

HANSEN, MARCUS LEE, *The Atlantic Migration, 1607–1860*, Harvard University Press, Cambridge, Mass., 1940.

HARROD, ROY F., Memorandum submitted in 1944 to the Royal Commission on Population (*q.v.*), reprinted as "The Population Problem" in *Economic Essays*, Macmillan & Co., Ltd., London, 1952.

——, *Towards a Dynamic Economics*, Macmillan & Co., Ltd., London, 1948.

HICKS, J. R., *Value and Capital*, Clarendon Press, Oxford (2nd Edition), 1946.

HIGGINS, BENJAMIN, "Concepts and Criteria of Secular Stagnation", from *Essays in Honour of Alvin Hansen*, New York, 1948.

——, "The Doctrine of Economic Maturity", *American Economic Review*, March, 1946.

—— "The Theory of Increasing Under-Employment", *Economic Journal*, June, 1950.

HILL, A. V., "The Ethical Dilemma of Science", Address to the British Association in the *Advancement of Science*, Vol. IX, No. 34, 1952.

H.M.S.O., Colonial Report: *Mauritius, 1951*, pub. 1952.

HUBBACK, EVA M., *The Population of Great Britain*, Penguin Books, 1947.

ISAAC, JULIUS, "International Migration and European Population Trends", *International Labour Review*, Vol. XLVI, No. 3, September, 1952.

JEFFERSON, MARK, "Distribution of the World's City Folks", *Geographical Review*, Vol. 21, 1931.

KENT, T. W., "1947 Comes Again", *Lloyds Bank Review*, October, 1951.

KEYNES, J. M., *The Economic Consequences of the Peace*, Macmillan, London, 1920.

——, "A Reply to Sir W. Beveridge", *Economic Journal*, December, 1923.

——, "Some Economic Consequences of a Declining Population", *Eugenics Review*, Vol. XXXIX, April, 1937.

KONDRATIEFF, N. D., *Review of Economic Statistics*, Vol. XVII, No. 6, p. 105, November, 1935, and reprinted in *Readings in Business Cycle Theory*, H. S. Ellis, Allen & Unwin, 1950.

LEAGUE OF NATIONS, *Industrialization and Foreign Trade*, U.S.A., 1945.

LEONE, ENRICO DE, "The Distribution of People on the Earth and the Euro-African Problem", *Idea*, Rome, June, 1951.

LORWIN, L. L., and BLAIR, J. M., *Technology in Our Economy*, Monograph No. 22, Temporary National Economic Committee, 1941.

MACDOUGALL, G. D. A., "Britain's Foreign Trade Problem", *Economic Journal*, March, 1947.

MCCLEARY, G. F., *The Malthusian Population Theory*, London, 1953.

MCGREGOR, D. H., *Economic Thought and Policy*, Oxford University Press, 1949.

MALTHUS, T. R., *First Essay on Population*, London, 1798; 2nd ed. 1803.

——, *Principles of Political Economy*, London, 1820.

——, Article on "Population", Supplement to the fourth, fifth and sixth editions *Encyclopædia Britannica*, 1824.

MARSHALL, ALFRED, *Economics of Industry*, 3rd Edition, 1899.

——, *Principles*, 8th Edition, 1938.

MATERIALS POLICY COMMISSION, *Resources for Freedom*, Vols. I–V, Report to the President, United States Government Printing Office, Washington, June, 1952.

MEEK, R. L., *Marx and Engels on Malthus*, Lawrence and Wishart, London, 1953.

MILLS, F. C., "Economic Growth in the United States", *American Economic Review*, 1951.

Ministry of Labour Gazette—Numbers Employed in Great Britain: Industrial Analysis, February, 1953.

MOULTON, H. G., *Controlling Factors in Economic Development*, Brookings Institute, Washington, 1949.

MUMFORD, LEWIS, *Technics and Civilisation*, London, 1946.

NOTESTEIN, F. W., *Population—The Long View*, The Harris Memorial Foundation Lectures, Chicago, 1945.

——, Review of Report of Royal Commission on Population (British) in *Population Studies*, Vol. 3, No. 3, December, 1949.

—— and others, *The Future Population of Europe and the Soviet Union*, League of Nations, Geneva, 1944.

OSBORN, FREDERICK, "Possible Effects of Differential Fertility on Genetic Endowment", Address to the American Eugenics Society, reported in *Population Index*, Vol. 18, No. 3, July, 1952.

PAN CHIA-LIN, Article with I. B. TAEUBER, "The Expansion of the Chinese North and West", *Population Index*, Vol. 18, No. 2, April, 1952, Office of Population Research, Princeton University.

PEARL, R., *The Biology of Population Growth*, Johns Hopkins University Press, Baltimore, 1925.

PENROSE, L. S., *The Biology of Mental Defect*, London, 1949.

PHELPS BROWN, E. H., "Wage Levels after Two Wars", *Westminster Bank Review*, November, 1949.

——, and HANDFIELD-JONES, S. J., "The Climacteric of the 1890's: A Study in the Expanding Economy", *Oxford Economic Papers*, New Series, Vol. 4, No. 3, October, 1952.

PLANT, G. F. (C.B.E.), *Oversea Settlement*, Oxford University Press, London, 1951.

POLITICAL AND ECONOMIC PLANNING, *Population Policy in Great Britain*, London, April, 1948.

Quantitative Inheritance, Papers read at a Colloquium held at the Institute of Animal Genetics, Edinburgh University, under the auspices of the Agricultural Research Council, April 4–6, 1950, H.M.S.O., London, 1952.

RADHAKRISHNAN, Dr. S., "Planned Parenthood", an Address to a conference on planned parenthood, printed in *Eugenics Review*, Vol. 45, No. 1, April, 1953.

RAVENSTEIN, E. G., "The Laws of Migration", *Journal of the Royal Statistical Society*, Vol. XLVIII, 1885.

REDDAWAY, W. B., *The Economics of a Declining Population*, Allen & Unwin, London, 1939.

Registrar-General's Statistical Review, 1950.

REINHARD, M. R., *Histoire de la Population Mondiale, de 1700 à 1948*, Editions Domat-Montchrestien, [1949].

ROBBINS, LIONEL, *The Optimum Theory of Population*, London Essays in Economics in Honour of Edwin Cannan, Routledge & Sons, 1927.

——, "Notes on Some Probable Consequences of the Advent of a Stationary Population in Great Britain", *Economica*, Vol. IX, 1929.

——, "Certain Aspects of the Theory of Costs", *Economic Journal*, March, 1934.

——, *The Economic Basis of Class Conflict*, Macmillan, London, 1939.

——, *The Theory of Economic Policy in English Classical Political Economy*, Macmillan, London, 1952.

——, "The International Economic Problem", *Lloyds Bank Review*, January, 1953.

ROBINSON, AUSTIN, "The Future of British Imports", *The Three Banks Review*, No. 17, March, 1953.

ROBINSON, JOAN, "The Model of the Expanding Economy", *Economic Journal*, Vol. LXII, No. 245, March, 1952.

ROBERTS, MICHAEL, *The Estate of Man*, Faber & Faber, 1951.

RODWAY, A. E. (Ed.), *Godwin and the Age of Transition*, Harrap & Son, 1952.

ROYAL COMMISSION ON POPULATION, Selected Papers, 1949–50.

——, Report, Cmd. 7695, H.M.S.O., 1949.

SALTER, ROBERT M., "World Soil and Fertilizer Resources in Relation to Food Needs", *Science* (published by the American Association for the Advancement of Science), Vol. 105, January–June, 1947.

SAMUELSON, P. A., *Economics: An Introductory Analysis*, McGraw Hill Book Co., Inc., New York, 1948.

SAUVY, ALFRED, "Some Aspects of the International Migration Problem", *International Labour Review*, Vol. LVIII, No. 1, July, 1948.

——, *Théorie Générale de la Population*, Vol. 1, *Economie et Population*, Presses Universitaires de France, 1952.

——, "Productivité, Production, Population optimum, Application à l'Europe occidentale", *Population—Revue Trimestrielle*, janv.–mars, 1952, Institut National d'Etudes Demographiques, Paris.

SCHUMPETER, JOSEPH A., "Analysis of Economic Change", *Review of Economic Statistics*, Vol. XVII, No. 4, May, 1935.

——, *Capitalism, Socialism and Democracy*, London, 1943.

SCHMOOKLER, JACOB, "The Changing Efficiency of the American Economy, 1869–1938", *Review of Economics and Statistics*, Vol. XXXIV, No. 3, August, 1952.

SCOTT COMMITTEE, *Land Utilisation in Rural Areas*, Cmd. 6378, August, 1942.

SINGER, H. W., "Economic Progress in Under-developed Countries", *Social Research*, Vol. 16, 1949.

SMITH, J. RUSSELL, "Science, New Machinery and the Population of Asia", *New Compass of the World*, by Weigert, Stefansson and Harrison, London, 1949.

SMITH, KENNETH, *The Malthusian Controversy*, London, 1951.

SNYDER, CARL, "Capital Supply and National Well-being", *American Economic Review*, June, 1936.

SPENGLER, JOSEPH J., *French Predecessors of Malthus*, Duke University Press, Durham, North Carolina, 1942.

——, "The World's Hunger—Malthus 1948", *Proceedings of the Academy of Political Science*, 23 (2): 53–71, January, 1949.

SRAFFA, P. (Ed.), *The Works and Correspondence of David Ricardo* C.U.P., 1951.

STAMP, D. L., *Land of Britain*, London, 1948.

——, *Land for Tomorrow, the Under-Developed World*, American Geographical Society, Indiana University Press, 1952 (published in Britain by Faber & Faber as *Our Undeveloped World*, 1953).

STEUART, Sir JAMES, *An Inquiry into the Principles of Political Œconomy—being an essay on the Science of Domestic Policy in Free Nations*, Vols. I and II, London, 1767.

STEWART, JOHN Q., "Empirical Mathematical Rules Concerning the Distribution and Equilibrium of Population", *Geographical Review*, Vol. 37, 1947.

STIGLER, GEORGE J., "The Ricardian Theory of Value and Distribution", *Journal of Political Economy*, Vol. LX, No. 3, June, 1952.

STIX, R. K., "Contraceptive Service in Three Areas", *Milbank Memorial Fund Quarterly*, Vol. XIX, Nos. 2 and 3, April and July, 1941.

STONE, R., "The Fortune Teller", *Economica*, February, 1943.

SWAROOP, S., *Growth of Population in the World*, World Health Organisation, Epidemiological and Vital Statistics Report, Vol. 4, April, 1951.

SWEEZY, PAUL, "Declining Investment Opportunity", Ch. 32 of *The New Economics*, ed. by S. E. Harris, London, 1948.

——, "On Secular Stagnation" from *Post-War Economic Problems*, ed. S. E. Harris, 1943.

TAEUBER, CONRAD, "Utilisation of Human Resources in Agriculture", *Milbank Memorial Fund Quarterly*, Vol. XXXVII, No. 1, January, 1950.

TAEUBER, IRENE B., "Ceylon as a Demographic Laboratory; Preface to Analysis", *Population Index*, October, 1949.

TERBORGH, GEORGE, *The Bogey of Economic Maturity*, Chicago, 1945.

THOMAS, BRINLEY, "Migration and the Rhythm of Economic Growth, 1830–1913", *Manchester School of Economic and Social Studies*, Vol. XIX, 1951.

TIZARD, Sir HENRY, Address to British Association, 1948, *Advancement of Science*, Vol. V, No. 19.

TRIANTIS, S. G., "Economic Progress, Occupational Redistribution and International Terms of Trade", *Economic Journal*, September, 1953.

TYSZYNSKI, H., "World Trade in Manufactured Commodities 1899–1950", *Manchester School, etc.*, Vol. XIX, 1951.

UNITED NATIONS, *World Population Trends 1920–1947*, Population Studies No. 3, December, 1949.

——, *Economic Bulletin for Europe*, Vol. 1, No. 1, 1949.

——, *Demographic Yearbooks* 1949–50 and 1950–51.

——, Department of Social Affairs, *Population Bulletins*, No. 1, December, 1951; No. 2, 1952; also *Preliminary Report on World Social Situation*, New York, 1952.

——, *Measures for Economic Development of Underdeveloped Countries*, May, 1951.

——, *World Energy Supplies in Selected Years 1929–1950*, New York, September, 1952.

——, *Economic Survey of Europe since the War*, E.C.E., 1953.

VINER, J., *International Trade and Economic Development*, Oxford, Clarendon Press, 1953.

WALLACE, R., *A Dissertation on the Numbers of Mankind in Ancient and Modern Times*, Edinburgh, 1809 (1st Edition, 1753).

——, *Various Prospects of Mankind, Nature and Providence*, London, 1761

WIENER, NORBERT, *Cybernetics, or Control and Communication in the Animal and the Machine*, Cambridge, 1949.

——, *The Human Use of Human Beings*, London, 1950.

WILLCOX, WALTER F. (Ed.), *International Migration*, Vol. 1, *Statistics*, 1929; Vol. 2, *Interpretations*, 1931, International Labour Office, Bureau of Economic Research.

WOOLF, BARNET, "Environmental Effects in Quantitative Inheritance", p. 81 of *Quantitative Inheritance*, H.M.S.O., 1952, *q.v.*

WRIGHT, H., *Population*, Cambridge Economic Handbooks, V, 1923.

YEARBOOK OF THE WEST INDIES AND COUNTRIES OF THE CARIBBEAN, Skinner & Co., Ltd., London, 1951.

YULE, G. U. (C.B.E.), "The Growth of Population and the Factors which Control it", *Journal of the Royal Statistical Society*, Vol. LXXXVIII, 1925.